Ebrard on the Epistle to the Hebrews.

BIBLICAL COMMENTARY

ON THE

EPISTLE TO THE HEBREWS,

IN CONTINUATION OF THE WORK OF OLSHAUSEN.

DR JOHN H. A. EBRARD,

PROFESSOR OF THEOLOGY IN THE UNIVERSITY OF ERLANGEN.

TRANSLATED FROM THE GERMAN

BY THE

REV. JOHN FULTON, A.M.,

GARVALD.

WIPF & STOCK · Eugene, Oregon

Wipf and Stock Publishers
199 W 8th Ave, Suite 3
Eugene, OR 97401

Biblical Commentary on the Epistle to the Hebrews
in Continuation of the Work of Olshausen
By John H. A. Ebrard
Copyright©1853 Public Domain
ISBN 13: 978-1-55635-791-6
Publication date 1/9/2008

CONTENTS.

	Page.
INTRODUCTION,	1
THE EXORDIUM,	9

PART FIRST.

The Son and the Angels,	29

SECTION FIRST.

The Son is in himself superior to the Angels,	32
A practical intermediate Part,	63

SECTION SECOND.

In the Son Man is raised above the Angels,	70

PART SECOND.

The Son and Moses,	113

SECTION FIRST.

The New Testament Messiah is in himself, as Son, superior to Moses,	115
Intermediate Passage of a hortatory kind,	130

SECTION SECOND.

In the Son Israel has entered into its true rest,	139

PART THIRD.

Christ and the High Priest,	173

SECTION FIRST.

Christ and Aaron,	175
Intermediate Part of a hortatory kind,	188

CONTENTS.

SECTION SECOND.

The Messiah, as a High Priest after the order of Melchisedec, is a superior High Priest to Aaron, . . . 210

PART FOURTH.

The Mosaic Tabernacle and the Heavenly Sanctuary, . . 242

SECTION FIRST.
The two Tabernacles correspond to the two Covenants, . 243

SECTION SECOND.
The construction of the Mosaic Tabernacle, . . . 257

SECTION THIRD.
The Service of the Tabernacle. The Blood of the Bullocks and the Blood of Christ, ... 279

PART FIFTH.

The laying hold on the New Testament Salvation, . . 312

SECTION FIRST.
Theme of the Exhortation, ... 313

SECTION SECOND.
First Motive. Danger and consequences of falling away, . 320

SECTION THIRD.
Second Motive. Calling to mind their former Faith, . 323

SECTION FOURTH.
Third Motive. The historically demonstrated power of Faith, 329

SECTION FIFTH.
Fourth Motive. The blessing of Chastisement, . . 352

SECTION SIXTH.
Fifth Motive. The choice between Grace and Law; a choice between Salvation and Judgment, . . . 362

SECTION SEVENTH.
Concluding Exhortations, ... 367

APPENDIX.

ON THE DATE, DESTINATION, AND AUTHOR OF THE EPISTLE TO THE HEBREWS.

CHAPTER FIRST.

	Page.
The Circle of Readers,	379

CHAPTER SECOND.

Time of Composition,	383

CHAPTER THIRD.

Whether written originally in Greek,	389

CHAPTER FOURTH.

The Writer. A) External Testimonies,	394

CHAPTER FIFTH.

Continuation. B) Internal Reasons,	407
A) Particular Intimations,	408
B) The Doctrinal Import,	409
C) Words and Phrases,	415
D) The Style,	417

CHAPTER SIXTH.

Conclusion. The particular Hypothesis,	420
Literature,	430

INTRODUCTION.

THE Lord Jesus Christ has said: *Search the Scriptures, for they are they which testify of me.* The Holy Scriptures of the old covenant testify of Christ, and that not merely because particular prophecies pointing to Christ are to be found here and there in them: The entire history of the revelation of God in the old covenant is one great preintimation of the future Messiah; and this *fact*-revelation and *fact*-prophecy formed the condition and the basis of the particular *word*-prophecies which God gave in a supernatural manner by his special instruments. It is wrong to overlook this unity of basis; but it is equally so to attempt to derive these particular word-revelations as developments from that basis, and to overlook their properly supernatural character. In the garden of Eden immediately after the fall, God directs the hope of the human race to a son of the woman, who is to break the power of the serpent; Eve exults in her first joy as a mother—she has born a man child, and with him she has received Jehovah back again; she regards her child as the promised one who is to win back for men the favour, nearness, and possession of Jehovah. She is mistaken. The human race must first go deep downwards in order to be able to rise upwards —yes, it must pursue an ever downward course, all human greatness must be brought low, until humanity is so humbled as to be capable of placing itself in a purely receptive relation towards the salvation provided; then, and not till then, will the woman's seed be *given* to it; for it cannot *produce* that seed.— This is the fundamental law of all revelation and all prophecy in the Old Testament.

INTRODUCTION.

After that judicial visitation by which the degenerate race of man was buried and baptized (immersed, sunk) in the flood, Noah, who came forth from this baptism as the father of a new humanity, the second Adam of the old covenant, lays on Shem's head the blessing that the Lord shall be his God; Canaan shall serve Shem, Japhet shall live with Shem in peace and friendship.[1] And when the families of men, five generations after Noah, are *separated* from each other, the promise is made to the Shemite Abraham on account of his faith, that his posterity shall form the central point of a future *reunion* of mankind in the blessing. But *not until after three generations of affliction* will God put the seed of Abraham in possession of the inheritance promised to him (Gen. xv.)

Here begins the operation of that wonderful *principle of delay*, according to which the last part of a promised epoch is extended anew to a period embracing several epochs, and the last of these is again distributed into several epochs, and so forth. The third generation after Abraham, that of Joseph, with which the affliction properly speaking first begins, lengthens itself out again to three generations. On the expiration of these comes the promised redemption of the seed of Abraham from affliction (Gen. xv.), but in such a manner as that the redemption then first begins, and this too only typically and preliminarily. Israel is redeemed from the Egyptian bondage; as in Noah the human race, so under Moses the seed of Abraham passed through a baptism, and came forth from a baptism in the Red Sea; Israel was emancipated through Moses, but came not through Moses into its rest, into the possession of the promised land. Joshua conducted it into the land, but the land was not yet entirely possessed, Israel continued to be harassed and oppressed by the heathen, and the last forty years previous to the battle at Ebenezer were truly again years of bondage. Being again delivered by Samuel, the people obtained in Saul a king, but not after God's heart, full of carnal timidity and carnal courage, insolent and faint-hearted. The king after God's heart, David, must again himself reproduce the destinies of the whole seed of

---

[1] To dwell in the tents of any one = to be hospitably received by any one.

Abraham in his own individual life, and, through much tribulation, enter into glory. But yet his reign was one of war and conflict, not of peace, and the triumphing prince of peace, Solomon, was after him.

Doubtless there was given in David a fulfilment of the old promises of salvation, but one that was merely human, therefore lying under the curse of everything human, and liable to pass away. Hence there was opened up to David by means of the prophet Nathan (2 Sam. vii.) a second perspective view of the promised salvation, in the fulfilment of which, however, the same law of delay obtains as in the first. *Not David, but his seed after him shall build a house to the Lord;* for him the Lord will build a house, and will be his father, and he shall reign with God for ever. David immediately perceives, and rightly (2 Sam. vii. 19; comp. chap. xxiii. 1), that this wonderful prophecy "points to the distant future," and represents the form of " a man who is God." And, in like manner, Solomon, when he consecrates the temple of stone (1 Kings viii. 26—27) acknowledges that that prophecy of Nathan's is not yet fulfilled by this act. Therefore, when Solomon sought, by intercourse with the nations, by marriage and philosophy, to break through the limits of the Mosaic law, he wrongly anticipated a freedom which was to become possible only through the new covenant, plunged himself and his people into idolatry, and brought about a deep national decline; and so his proverbs and his song of songs are placed as monuments, not merely of his wisdom, but at the sametime also of his folly, among the Chethubim of the Old Testament canon.

Solomon's temple of stone then, was only a first, a provisional fulfilment of Nathan's prophecy. Under him, and after him, the kingdom, power, and glory of Israel fell more and more into decay, and as ungodliness increased, the prophets, and Elias among the number, looked around for the judgments of God. But to him it was revealed that the Lord is not in storm and fire, but in the still small voice; and Joel, too, uttered the same truth. The people deserve indeed even now judgment and destruction; but with the judgment the Lord will grant forgiveness; He will first pour out His Spirit, and then come to judgment. Redeeming grace is to go before judicial severity. The eye of hope was now turned to redeeming grace; the promised descendant of David was more and more clearly revealed to the prophets. He is not to be born in palaces; as the first, so the second David must be sought by the daughters of Zion in times of sore travail, of heavy afflictions, by the sheepfolds of Bethlehem (Mic. v. 5.) The daughter of the house of David, so haughty under Ahaz, must, by unheard of sufferings, be brought to conduct herself in a purely receptive manner as a maid (עלמה) in order to bring forth the son, and she will then, no longer trusting in her own strength, call him "GOD WITH US." Israel, appointed as the servant of God to convert the heathen, but altogether unfit for this work (Is. xlviii.), and himself an idolater (Is. xliv.), is to be again brought into bondage by a force coming from the Euphrates (Assyrian, later, from Is. xxxviii. onwards, Babylonian); in the time of his subjugation the true servant of God will come, will first work out by his atoning sacrificial death the inward redemption, the forgiveness of sins (chap. liii.), then convert the heathen (chap. liv.), and finally convert and deliver the still hardened Israel (chap. lxiv.—lxvi., comp. Rom. xi.) But here again comes in a delay. Not 70 years, as Jeremiah has prophesied, is the subjugation of Israel under the heathen to last; but as Daniel has revealed, 7. × 70 years, nay, as is immediately added by way of correction, still longer (inasmuch as from the building of Jerusalem under Nehemiah 7 × 62 years were to elapse.) After 70 years indeed, Israel is to return to their land; but the subjugation under the heathen is to continue over five centuries.—Accordingly, the rebuilding of the temple under Zerubbabel was again but a type of the building of the temple already promised by Nathan, which God himself was to undertake. And so Malachi, the last of the prophets, directed the eye of the people to the *messenger of the Lord*, who was soon to come to his temple, to visit and to sift Israel, and to separate the wheat from the empty chaff (comp. Matth. iii. 12.)

This signification and course of prophecy must of itself have appeared to any one who gave attentive heed to the Old Testament, and who in heart and mind belonged to that covenant; not, however, to the impenitent, not to the mass of the people of Israel. Now the two books of the New Testament in which is represented the insight of the spiritually-minded Israelites into the Old Testament revelation after it was brought to full maturity by the Holy Spirit, are, the Gospel of Matthew and the Epistle to the Hebrews, to which, however, the address of Stephen (Acts vii.) is to be added as a very important passage having the same character. Stephen adduces from the collective history of the Old Testament (in which he points throughout with special emphasis to the principle of delay already noticed[1]) rather the negative proof—that the law and the temple, although divine, are not the highest and last form of the revelation and dwelling-place of God. Matthew adduces rather the positive proof—that Jesus is the promised son (seed) of Abraham and David, that in him, therefore, the first prospect disclosed to Abraham (Gen. xv.), as well as the second opened up to David through Nathan (2 Sam. vii.) have found their termination. Matthew, too, refers to the same law of delay, when, in chap. i. 2 ff., he shews, that in place of the three תורדות, Gen. xv., there came three great periods, that of typical elevation until the time of David, that of decline until Jeremiah, and that during which the house of David was in a condition of poverty and lowliness until Mary. In conducting this proof, however, the Evangelist does not of course take as the frame-work of his particular reasonings an exposition of the Old Testament prophecy, but a record of the New Testament fulfilment. The Old Testament prophecy is by Matthew taken for granted as already known. The Epistle to the Hebrews, on the contrary, goes out from the Old Testament, formally developes the component parts of that dispensation in a treatise systematically arranged, and shows how, in all its parts, it points to Jesus. The history of Jesus is here taken for granted as known. This method is more remote, more indirect, and more philosophical than the other.—Stephen's *practical aim* was to defend himself from the charge of speaking blasphemy again the law and the temple; that of Matthew was to furnish t Jewish Christians with a written substitute for the oral preachi of the twelve. What practical necessity occasioned the writi of the Epistle to the Hebrews?

No book of the New Testament, and, in general, of the H(Scriptures, owes its origin to a mere subjective literary choice,

[1] Comp. my Crit. of the Gospel History, 2 ed. p. 689.

a mere love of writing on the part of the author. The Epistle to the Hebrews, accordingly, however systematic and almost scientific its contents are, was occasioned by a practical necessity. The investigations concerning its author we must refer from the introduction (to which they do not belong, and where they are not as yet even possible) to the close of the commentary; but, for the better understanding of the epistle itself, some preliminary observations respecting the occasion of it must needs be made.

It is evident from Acts ii. 5, and Acts xv., and Gal. ii., that the Jewish Christians, though not resting their justification before God on the Mosaic law, yet *observed that law* (Acts ii. 38, iii. 19, 12.) And this too was quite natural. For that law was not only given by God, and not yet abrogated by him, nay, observed even by Christ himself (Gal. iv. 4 s.), but besides this, being national as well as religious, it had become so entirely a part of the Israelitish customs and manner of life, it was so wrought into the texture of the whole conduct and life of that people, that so long as they were a people, and so long as Jewish Christians were members of the Israelitish state, a renunciation of those national customs was purely inconceivable. It may, indeed, be doubted whether the Israelites who had become Christians, continued to fulfil those legal observances which bore a more optional character. It can scarcely be supposed, for example, that every one who fell into a sin would bring the guilt or the sin-offering into the temple. On the other hand, the manner of preparing meats, the observance of the Sabbath, &c., remained the same.

Indeed, until the destruction of Jerusalem, when God, by the overthrow of the Israelitish state, put an end to Israelitish nationality and customs, the hope of seeing Israel converted as a whole, although it had been ever lessening, was not entirely given up; and this of itself was a reason for the Jewish Christians not separating themselves from the Israelitish community. Thus the Jewish Christians, or to speak more correctly, the Israelites who believed on the Messiah, were in the habit of frequenting the temple for daily prayer. But the hatred of the unbelieving Jews towards them grew more and more intense. Towards the end of the fiftieth year they no longer suffer the presence of the apostle Paul in the temple (Acts xxi. ss.), although they dare not yet openly cast him out as a Jewish Christian, but avail themselves of the pretext that he has taken a Gentile Christian into the temple along with him. But that the time came when Christians as such, Jewish Christians also, were no longer suffered to appear in the temple, may be inferred from the Epistle to the Hebrews. The persecution of the Christians under Nero may have emboldened the Jews; their courage rose when they saw the Christians sacrificed also by the Romans. This period of affliction for the church in Jerusalem may have begun in the sixtieth year. There were, however, weak ones in whose minds conscientious scruples might be awakened by this exclusion from the Theocracy of the old covenant. They were not yet able to walk without crutches. They were afraid lest with the privilege of access to the temple and of fellowship with the commonwealth of Israel, they should lose at the same time their claim to the common salvation of God. Such weak ones are not to be sought among the older members of the church who had already grown grey in Christianity, but rather among the neophytes and such as were on the point of conversion. Conversion to Christianity threatened to come to a stand. And yet it was the last hour; and whoever was to be saved from the judgments impending over Israel must be saved now. In these circumstances the Epistle to the Hebrews was written, designed for a certain circle of neophytes and catechumens then existing; useful for all in future times who should occupy an analogous position. The aim of this epistle is to prove from the nature and principal elements of the old covenant itself, that the revelation and redemption through the Messiah promised in the old covenant, is represented even in the old covenant as an absolute revelation, as sufficient in itself, by which the Old Testament types become superfluous.

THE EXORDIUM.

(Chap. i. 1—3.)

WHILE all the rest of the New Testament epistles begin by mentioning the name and office of their authors, as also the churches for which they are intended, this form of introduction which was usual in ancient times is wanting in the Epistle to the Hebrews. Some have sought to account for this circumstance by saying that the author intended to compensate for the effect of a formal superscription by the solemn and highly oratorical style of the introduction. This supposition, however, will not suffice fully to explain the case. The *impression* that would have been made on the readers and hearers by the name of an apostle or some other authoritative person, might indeed be compensated by the impression which the lofty utterance of the heart and mind of such a person could not fail to produce; they could, so to speak, hear the *man* from the force of the *words*, and forthwith believe that they saw him before them. But the want of the *superscription* itself was not thereby compensated. We can scarcely conceive that any one would have addressed a letter to a church without mentioning his name at all. It only remains therefore to be supposed, that this writing which we hold under the name of the Epistle to the Hebrews was originally accompanied by a shorter epistle properly so called, and therefore that the epistle itself was not one in the proper sense of the term. And this supposition is confirmed by a number of considerations drawn from the substance of the epistle, to which our attention will be directed at the proper time, and of which we will here specify some of the most striking. The hortatory passages are not, as in the most of the other epistles, closely engrafted on the didactic, so that the doctrinal parts pass naturally into the practical; but the former are wound up in a strictly scientific manner without any hortatory and practical side-glances, and the latter are abruptly placed between the doctrinal sections (chap. ii. 1—3, iii. 1—19, v. 11 —6, 12, &c.) The practical parts too, show a systematic form the result of reflexion,—an intended transition to a new doctrinal section is introduced in the form of a short hortatory or personal remark (iii. 1, viii. 1.) The particular sections of the doctrinal parts are, however, marked by a peculiar species of *formal superscriptions*, of which we shall soon have to speak, and the nature of which can be seen from the translation which we have annexed to the commentary. Moreover, the course of the investigation and the reasoning in the doctrinal parts is often so intricate, so many ideas are often compressed into few words, that we can hardly suppose the object of the epistle was fulfilled by a single reading before the assembled church (as we must suppose was the case even with the most didactic of Paul's epistles, that to the Romans, which however might easily be understood on a first reading); but it rather appears, that this Epistle to the Hebrews was designed, after having been read, to serve as a groundwork for a formal course of instruction, very probably of instruction for catechumens. This opinion is confirmed also by the passages chap. v. 11 ss.; vi. 1 ss., where the writer makes some systematic remarks on the *method* of instruction to be pursued in the Christian Church; with which may be compared also the passage viii. 1, where again in a systematic form a recapitulation is given of what has been said on to that place, as the foundation of what is farther to be brought forward.

After all, then, we shall not be chargeable with undue boldness if we maintain, that the Epistle to the Hebrews was, in respect of its *form*, not an *epistle* in the proper sense, but a *treatise*. That this assertion implies no denial of its having been written with a practical aim is evident from what has been said in the introduction; all that we think and say is, that in respect of its *form*, it goes beyond the nature of an epistle, of a direct effusion in which the writer transfers himself in spirit to his readers, and speaks to them although not without a plan (comp. the Epistle to the Romans), yet always without the consciousness of system and from the immediate impulse of the heart, and that it therefore thoroughly bears the character of a *systematic treatise*. Hence also we account for the absence of the address which is indispensable to every epistle. A mere verbal salutation by the person who conveyed the writing could not supply the place of this address, not even on the supposition of its being a treatise. It would be too strange to suppose, that the author who had written so much should not write a few additional lines with his own name. These accompanying lines, however, in the case before us, would be addressed not to the church, but rather to some individual *teacher* in it, and we can easily see from this how they might come to be lost.

That the writing was intended for a certain limited circle of readers, not for a circle of churches, not even for one entire church, is very evident from chap. iii. 6, v. 12. The persons there addressed form quite a definite circle of persons represented as undergoing a course of instruction. This, of course, does not imply that the writing was not used for a similar object in all analogous cases beyond this circle, and that, in this way, at a very early period, it may not have obtained a circulation suited to its high importance.

The three first verses, inasmuch as they develope the ground-idea of the epistle, form a sort of introduction to the principal parts which follow from ver. 4 onwards. The structure of the period in these verses has justly been noticed by all commentators as remarkable for its beauty. The period is as perspicuous and clear as it is long, rich, and complicated; a fine succession of thought expressed in a form finished even to the minutest detail, gives it a claim to rank among the finest periods of the Greek authors. The first verse gives forth in a majestic style the ground-theme of the whole treatise. *The revelation of God in his Son is opposed to the revelations of God by the prophets* as the higher, as the one, undivided, absolute revelation. To confirm this the *person* and *work* of the Son are developed in ver. 2—3.

Ver. 1. The *subject* with the clauses in apposition to it forms a series of parallel antitheses to the verbal-predicate with its qualifying clauses. " God who has spoken to the fathers by the prophets." Λαλεῖν is used in the sense of דָּבַר to denote the *revealing* utterance of God, in which sense it frequently occurs in the Epistle to the Hebrews (ii. 2, ix. 19, &c.), and elsewhere in the New Testament (Acts iii. 24; James v. 10; 2 Pet. i. 21.) By the πατέρες here are meant, of course, not merely the patriarchs, but all those former generations of Israel that have preceded the ἡμεῖς, those at present living; in a word: the forefathers. The idea implied in προφῆται is to be understood in a similarly wide sense; even in the Old Testament נביא does not always denote merely the prophet with reference to his special office, but sometimes quite generally, every organ of divine revelation. It is so used here. Προφῆται here, according to the context, comprehends all Old Testament organs of revelation, in so far as they were *mere* organs of God, in opposition to the Son, who, according to ver. 3, was more than a mere organ. It is doubtful, however, in what sense the preposition ἐν is to be understood. The interpretation given by those who take προφῆται to denote the *writings* of the prophets, and refer the ἐν to these writings, is, on account of the parallel member ἐν υἱῷ, altogether untenable. Much more may be said in favour of that explanation which we find already given by Thomas Aquinas, and afterwards adopted by Beza, Carpzov, Alberti, Bleek, and others, that ἐν is to be taken in the strictest and most proper sense in which it is used in Greek. According to this, ἐν cannot be referred immediately to λαλεῖν (for the author surely does not intend to say that God has spoken in the prophets—within them,—he rather says that God has spoken to the fathers by the prophets), but ὤν must be supplied. God was in the prophets and spoke to the fathers; he was in the Son and spoke to us. But although, in itself considered, it might be proper enough to speak of God being in the prophets (*i.e.* relatively through his Spirit), and in like manner of God being in Christ (by the absolute hypostatic presence of the Logos in him), still it is in the highest degree improbable, that an author whose purpose it was from the outset to mark with the strongest emphasis the *difference* between the Son and the prophets, and the superiority of the former over the latter, should have placed those two entirely different modes of the indwelling of God parallel to each other by means of the same expression. I decidedly agree therefore with the interpretation of Chrysostom, Oecumenius, Luther, Calvin, Grotius, and

Tholuck, that the ἐν here in both places has an *instrumental* signification, and is to be understood in the sense of the Heb. בְּ, "by." Granted that this use of the word cannot be shown in the genuine Greek profane literature, there is nothing to prevent our regarding it as a Hebraism. Bleek, indeed, thinks the language of the Epistle to the Hebrews bears a so purely Greek character, that we must hesitate to admit the supposition of a Hebraism; but how easily might such an unconscious Hebraism slip from the pen of a native Israelite, who naturally *thought* in Hebrew what he *wrote* in Greek, however careful he was to construct his periods in genuine Greek! And is not the use of οἱ αἰῶνες in ver. 2 likewise a Hebraism? But are not *unconscious* Hebraisms in the use of prepositions much more easily accounted for in an author who in other respects writes good Greek, than *conscious* Hebraisms in the use of nouns for which (as for οἱ αἰῶνες) genuine Greek expressions (ὁ κόσμος, τὰ πάντα) were quite at hand?

The adverbs πολυμερῶς and πολυτρόπως, according to Tholuck and others, have no specific intelligible meaning, because no ἁπλῶς or ἐφάπαξ stands opposed to them, but are used merely for the sake of amplification. But ἁπλῶς and ἐφάπαξ, as we shall immediately see, would not even have formed a right antithesis. That a writing of which the tot verba tot pondera holds so true, begins with an amplification, is a supposition to which recourse will then only be had when every possibility of another interpretation has been cut off. Already several among the Fathers, and then Calvin, Limborch, Capellus, J. Gerhard, Calov, and Bleek, explain πολυμερῶς as pointing to the different *times* and *periods*, πολυτρόπως to the different *ways* and *forms* of the divine revelation in the Old Testament dispensation. This interpretation, however, does not precisely bring out the idea of the writer. Πολυμερῶς does not contain precisely a chronological reference; the antithesis is not that God has spoken *often* by the prophets but only *once* by his Son (according to which less would be attributed to Christ than to them), but the opposition is, between the *distribution* of the Old Testament revelation among the prophets, and the *undivided fulness* of the New Testament revelation by Christ. Πολυμερῶς means not "many times," but "manifoldly," "in many parts." In like manner, the Old

Testament revelation is said to be one of *many forms*, in opposition to that τρόπος which was not one among the many, but the one which outweighed the many, the absolute, which fully corresponded with the οὐσία. Thus we see how a ἅπαξ or ἁπλῶς could not follow in the opposite member of the sentence. The real antithesis to πολυμερῶς and πολυτρόπως lies in ver. 2, 3.

The time denoted by πάλαι is commonly explained of the time before Malachi, with whom the succession of the prophets ceased. But surely the writer does not mean to say specifically, that God has spoken in times of old, but no more since these times. Πάλαι is rather explained simply from the antithesis ἐπ' ἐσχάτου, &c., without supposing that a remote and heterogeneous allusion is made to the interval between Malachi and the Baptist.

But the expression ἐπ' ἐσχάτου τῶν ἡμερῶν τούτων (that the reading ἐσχάτων is false may now be considered as fully established) with which we pass to the second member of the sentence —the predicate,—stands in need of being interpreted itself. Here also, the supposition of a Hebraism is indispensable, not one that can be said to be either involuntary or voluntary, but one that was quite as intended as it was necessary, inasmuch as it relates to a dogmatical conception specifically Jewish. Formally explained according to the Greek grammar, the words would signify "at the end of these days." But what days are to be understood by these? The aetas of the writer? But the incarnation of Christ took place at the beginning not at the end of the period. Or are we to understand the days of the prophets? But these did not reach down to the time of Christ; and πάλαι too would then form no antithesis. With reason, therefore, have Bleek and others explained ἐπ' ἐσχάτου, &c., as equivalent to the Hebrew בְּאַחֲרִית הַיָּמִים. Conformably to the Old Testament prophecy, the Israelites distinguished the period of the world which then was as the עוֹלָם הַזֶּה from the period of glorification which was to begin with the resurrection the עוֹלָם הַבָּא; the advent and work of the Messiah was to form the transition from the one to the other, and this was therefore wont to be viewed and denoted partly as the *end of this time*, partly also as the beginning of the future. That the Messianic or "last" time would again divide itself into two periods—that of the life of Jesus in his humiliation, and that of his coming again in glory—was as yet not at all known to the Jews, and the Christians of the apostolic age had as yet no intuition at least of the *length* of the intervening period, nay could not have such an intuition, hence they included the whole period from the birth of Christ on to his promised coming again in the ἔσχαται ἡμέραι (Acts ii. 17; 1 John ii. 18.) In opposition to it then, πάλαι denotes the whole antecedent period, the *time of the promise of the Messianic prophecy* which preceded the time of the fulfilment.

In the time of the fulfilment has God spoken to us by his Son. The idea expressed in υἱός needs limitation on two sides. Firstly, υἱός is not simply synonymous with λόγος (John i.), it is nowhere in the Holy Scriptures used to denote the only begotten *qua* eternally pre-existent. And therefore, formally at least, the ecclesiastical terminology goes beyond the biblical usage, when it transfers the name Son to denote also the relation which that person holds in the Trinity; this transference, however, is indeed perfectly justifiable, because he who with respect to his incarnation is called υἱός in Scripture, is the same who before his incarnation existed from eternity with the Father. Indeed, the doctrine of Scripture (John i. 14) is not that the eternal Logos *was united* to a son of Mary, to a human nature in the concrete sense; but that the eternal hypostatical Logos *became man*, assumed human nature in the abstract sense, concentrated itself by a free act of self-limitation prompted by love, into an embryo human life a slumbering child-soul, as such formed for itself unconsciously and yet with creative energy a body in the womb of the Virgin, and hence he who in the Scripture is called υἱός *qua* incarnate is one and the same subject with that which with respect to its relation of oneness with the Father is called ὁ λόγος or ὁ μονογενής. Nay, even *qua* incarnate he can *only therefore* be called the Son of God because in him the eternal μονογενής became man. And hence, in the second place, we must guard against explaining the idea involved in the υἱός from the relation of the incarnate *as man* to the Father, as if he were called "Son" in the sense in which other pious men are called "children" of God. For it is evident even from the antithesis to the προφῆται, chiefly, however, from the second and third verses, that υἱός is the designation of the man Jesus *qua* the incarnate eternal λόγος.

This is apparent chiefly from the absence of the article. Exactly rendered, we must translate the words thus—" God spake to us by one who was Son," who stood not in the relation of prophet but in the relation of Son to him. If it were ἐν τῷ υἱῷ, then Christ would be placed as this individual in opposition to the individuals of the prophets; but as the article is wanting it is the species that is placed in opposition to the species (although of course Christ is the single individual of his species.)

Ver. 2. The description of the person of the υἱός begins in the second verse, from which it evidently appears how God hath revealed himself by Christ not πολυμερῶς καὶ πολυτρόπως, but absolutely and perfectly. Christ was more than a human *instrument*, he was *himself God*.

The principal question in the interpretation of this verse is whether the clause ὃν ἔθηκεν, &c., denotes an act which preceded that described in the clause δι' οὗ, &c., or one which followed it. The meaning of the second clause is clear; from it therefore we must set out in our investigation.

Οἱ αἰῶνες (as in xi. 3) is used in the sense of the Hebrew עוֹלָם עוֹלָמִים to denote the *worlds*, while in Greek it signifies only the *times*. By the Son has God made the worlds; we find the same in John i. 1 ss.; Col. i. 15—22. The eternal self-revelation of God in himself, through the eternal utterance of his fulness in the eternal personal *word* which God speaks *to himself* (John i. 1) and in the breath of the eternal *spirit*, forms the ground and therewith the eternal (not temporal) *prius* of the revelation of himself proceeding from the will of the Triune in a sphere which is not eternal, but one of time and space, which is not God but creature. And as the will which called creation into being is the will of the one Triune God, the Son and the Spirit were therefore partakers in the work; the world was made by the Father through the Son.

Now, in what relation to this act does the act denoted by the words ὃν ἔθηκε κληρόνομον πάντων stand? Were we to regard it as *an act preceding* the creation of the world, we might then be tempted to explain it of the eternal generation of the Son himself. But how in this case can an *all things* be spoken of which the Son receives as an inheritance? How can it be said: *whom* (the Son) *he made heir*, how can the Son be presupposed as *already existing*, if it be his generation that is intimated in these words? The only sense then that can be affixed to the words on this hypothesis is something to the effect, that God already before the creation of the world destined the Son, who was generated from all eternity, to be its future possessor. But what practical aim could such an idea have in the context,—not to say that a *before* and *after* can have no place in eternity? We are, therefore, compelled to turn to the other view, that of Tholuck, according to which ἔθηκε, &c., is to be understood of an act of God performed in time towards the incarnate Son of God, namely, that *crowning* of the incarnate one following upon his sufferings, which is afterwards more particularly described in chap. ii. ver. 9, and of which the Apostle Paul speaks in Phil. ii. 9—11. The Son of God having, out of eternal compassionating love, laid aside the *glory* which he possessed in eternity (John xvii. 5), and having in his incarnation come under the category of time, and here again having glorified his inner being under the form of a human free will, and under the form of obedience manifested his eternal love (Matth. xxvi. 39; Heb. v. 8, x. 7), forthwith received back again that *glory and honour* (John xvii. 5), received the dominion over heaven and earth from the Father's hand as his crown and his just reward, and received this as the incarnate, who still continues to be man, not divesting himself of the nature which he once assumed (Heb. vii. 26, comp. with ix. 12, 24.) And thus it is shown at length in Heb. ii. 5, that in him as their head and king mankind are exalted above the angels.[1]

---

[1] We must here guard ourselves against a representation of this subject which sprang up in the scholastic period, and passed also into the period of the Reformation, chiefly into the Lutheran theology—a representation which unconsciously leads back to Nestorianism, and from which, if one would escape its consequences without giving up itself, there is no other outlet but Eutychianism. It is this—that the divine and the human nature in Christ were two parts, or portions, or concreta, which were united in the one person of Christ "as fire and iron are united so as to make redhot iron," and that the one part, the divine, always remained in possession of the δόξα, while the other part, the

In this then lies the great difference between Christ and the prophets. The prophets were heralds of the promised future *inheritance;* Christ is the *heir* himself, the Lord and King in the Kingdom of God. The inheritance, as it appeared to the prophets, was still more or less limited to the people of Israel; at least the participation of the Gentiles in it appeared as yet under the form of a reception of the Gentiles into the community of Israel; the inheritance as it has appeared in the fulfilment, is that kingdom of Christ which embraces the whole human race (Ephes. ii. 19), nay heaven and earth (Ephes. i. 20 ss.)

human, was only raised to a participation in the δόξα at the exaltation of Christ. When Eutyches taught (Mansi, tom. vi. p. 744): ἐκ δύο φύσεων γεγεννῆσθαι τὸν κύριον ἡμῶν πρὸ τῆς ἐνώσεως, μετὰ δὲ τὴν ἕνωσιν μίαν φύσιν (εἶναι), the acute Leo justly observed at the conclusion of the ep. Flav. that the first clause (Nestorian), was quite as wrong as the second (Monophysite.) Tam impie duarum naturarum ante incarnationem unigenitus Filius Dei dicitur, quam nefarie, postquam verbum caro factum est, natura in eo singularis asseritur. The two natures, the Divine and the human, the filius Dei and the filius Mariae, were not first separately existent, so that their union constituted the entire Christ; but the Logos, retaining his *natura* divina, his Divine *nature*, and laying aside the μορφὴ θεοῦ, assumed in place of this the μορφὴ δούλου, i.e., he assumed the *nature of men* (an assemblage of *properties*, not an *existens*), and thus both natures, the Divine and the human, must now be predicated of him. As, if a king's son, in order to free his brother imprisoned in an enemy's country, were to go unknown into that country, and hire himself as servant to the prison-keeper, he would be both a real king's son and a real servant; the nature of a king's son belongs to him (only not the μορφή but also the δόξα and τιμή of such), for he would still be the son of a king; but the nature of a servant also belongs to him, for he really performs a servant's work and endures a servant's sufferings. But such a person could never have arisen through the *union* of a king's son with a servant. Never could it be said of him as is said of Christ in the formula of concord (epit. ep. 8), the unio personalis is not a mere combinatio, quia potius hic summa communio est, quam Deus cum assumpto *homine* vere habet, or affirm. 6: Quomodo *homo, Mariae filius,* Deus aut filius Dei vere appellari posset, aut esset, si ipsius humanitas (this is evidently understood as an existens concretum) cum *filio Dei* non esset personaliter unita. If we regard the two natures as two subsistences or parts, constituting together the one person, there remains then no way of escape from the extremest Nestorianism except that to which Eutyches had recourse, namely, that the one part participated in the properties of the other. Nestorianism is therefore by no means the opposite of Eutychianism, but merely what it presupposes. He who has no part in the former needs not the latter to help him out. In "Philippism" lies the saving of our theology from such errors.

Upon this, then, follows that second clause *by whom also*, &c., simply by way of confirming and at the same also of explaining the preceding. Christ was appointed heir of the universe, nay, this universe has received its being through him. How proper and natural is it, that he through whom the universe was made, after having humbled himself and accomplished the gracious will of the Father, should as his reward be also invested with the dominion over the universe as with a *permanent inheritance.*— The principal idea in κληρονομία is not that of a possession which any one receives through the death of another, but a possession which he on his part can transfer as an inheritance to his posterity, consequently, a permanent possession over which he has full authority. (The passage chap. ix. 16 ss. would agree with this interpretation if we were at liberty to translate διαθήκη there by "testament." There too it would be the κληρόνομος himself who had heired the inheritance, not through the death of another, but who by his own death had acquired the right to transfer the inheritance to others. Still when we come to that passage we shall find that there is no reason for departing from the usual *biblical* signification of the word διαθήκη.)

Ver. 3. The twofold idea which lies in the second verse is in ver. 3 farther explained. These two things were said: that Christ has been appointed *in time* (after the completion of the redemption-work) to the theocratical inheritance of the *Kingdom of God*, and that Christ is the *eternal* ground of the entire universe. The second of these things is here repeated in the apposition which belongs to the *subject* of the third verse: ὤν ἀπαύγασμα τῆς δόξης καὶ χαρακτὴρ τῆς ὑποστάσεως αὐτοῦ, φέρων τε τὰ πάντα τῷ ῥήματι τῆς δυνάμεως αὐτοῦ ; the first in the verb ἐκάθισεν, &c., which contains the predicate and the apposition belonging to the predicate-idea ποιησάμενος, &c., consequently, in the words καθαρισμὸν ποιησάμενος τῶν ἁμαρτιῶν, ἐκάθισεν ἐν δεξιᾷ τῆς μεγαλωσύνης ἐν ὑψηλοῖς. (For that ποιησάμενος is in apposition not to the subject ὅς but to the predicate-idea contained in the verb, appears not only logically, from the idea itself, but also grammatically, from the want of a καὶ before καθαρισμόν.)

With regard to the reading, we may consider it as fully made out after Bleek's searching investigation, that the words " δι᾽

ἑαυτοῦ" before καθαρισμὸν and ἡμῶν after ἁμαρτιῶι are to be cancelled.

We proceed now to the *first member of the sentence*—the subject with its appositions. Chiefly the expressions ἀπαύγασμα τῆς δόξης and χαρακτήρ τῆς ὑποστάσεως require here a thorough investigation. Erasmus, Calvin, Beza, Grotius, Limborch, and others have understood ἀπαύγασμα of *the passive light, i.e. reflection* or *reflected image* which a lucid or illuminated body throws on a (smooth reflecting) surface. According to this, Christ would be represented here as an image or reflection of the Father's glory, consequently, his hypostatical separate existence from the Father is considered as *presupposed*, and emphasis laid on his qualitative sameness with the Father. Others again, as Capellus, Gomarus, Gerhard, Calov, Bleek, have understood ἀπαύγασμα rather as denoting the *active light* or the *rays* which continually emanate from a shining body. According to this, the son would be represented rather as a *perpetual life-act of the Father*. But the first signification, as Bleek has shown, is, although etymologically defensible, still against the grammatical usage; the second, on the contrary, appears to me to be not justifiable on etymological grounds, or at least to rest on unprecise expressions, and even the first, I would hesitate to defend on etymological grounds.—Ἀπολάμπω, with reference to any body, signifies to throw out a light from itself, ἀπαστράπτω to dart forth flashes of lightning from itself, ἀπαυγάζω to throw out a lustre *from itself* (not to produce a reflection on another body.) The nouns ending in μα, however, denote, not the *act* as continuing, but the *result* of the act as finished. Thus κήρυγμα is not the act of announcing, but the announced message; in like manner Philo calls his Logos an ἀπόσπασμα ἢ ἀπαύγασμα τῆς μακαρίας φύσεως (ed. Mang. tom. i. p. 35), where ἀπόσπασμα must denote the separated part, and ἀπαύγασμα, consequently, the secondary light radiated from the original light. In the same sense do we take the expression here. It denotes, not the brightness received from another body and thrown back as a reflection or a mirrored image, nor the light continually proceeding from a shining body as a light streaming out and losing itself in space, but it denotes a light, or a bright ray which is radiated from another light *in so far as it is viewed as now become an independent light*.

The expression ray-image (Germ. Strahlbild) best answers to the original; as a ray-image, it is a living image composed of rays not merely one received and reflected, but it is conceived of as independent and permanent, it is more than a mere ray, more than a mere image; a sun produced from the original light. We fully agree therefore with Bleek when following Chrysostom and Theophylact, he finds the best interpretation of ἀπαύγασμα in the expression of the Nicene creed φῶς ἐκ φωτὸς, but we differ from him when he thinks that this interpretation is sufficiently rendered by the German word " Strahl"—" ray."

The original light from which the manifested ray-image has proceeded, is denoted by the word δόξα (scil. αὐτοῦ, θεοῦ). Many commentators, as Tholuck, wrongly interpret this of the Schekinah, that cloud of light under the Old Testament dispensation in which God revealed His presence and glory in a manner perceptible to the outward sense to Moses, then to the High Priest in the holy of holies, and last of all to the shepherds, Luke ii. 9. This would be impossible if for no other reason than this, that, as the original light was then a light perceptible to the sense, much more must the ἀπαύγασμα proceeding from it be a brightness apparent to the bodily eye. But, moreover, according to this explanation, the Son, the absolute, adequate, personal revelation of the Father would be degraded beneath the Old Testament imperfect, typical, form of the Divine manifestation, seeing that he would be represented as an ἀπαύγασμα of the latter, which was not even itself an ἀπαύγασμα, but was a mere reflection. Without doubt, therefore, those are right who understand the expression δόξα in the supersensible meaning in which it was used by John, and explain it of the eternal essential glory of the Father, that *light inaccessible* of which Paul speaks in 1 Tim. vi. 16, and which God himself is (1 John i. 5.) God's own eternal unsearchable essence is light throughout, not a βύθος, not a dark original basis which must needs first develope itself into brightness, but light clear to itself, and self conscious, and comprehending in itself the fulness of all possible things, an original monad—which bears in itself, and calls forth from itself the possibility and reality of all monads,—full of wisdom and love. This is the original glory of the Father's essence, and this original glory was manifested to itself in eternity, and to the creature in time, inasmuch as it allows to proceed from itself the Son, a living independent ray-image, in whom all that glory finds itself again, and reproduces itself in an absolute form, and in whose existence and manifestation the love, as in his nature and qualities, the wisdom of the Father represents itself.

This interpretation of the ἀπαύγασμα τῆς δόξης is confirmed by the expression which follows in the second member—χαρακτὴρ τῆς ὑποστάσεως. Substantially the same thing is denoted by ὑπόστασις as by δόξα, only regarded from another point of view. Δόξα signifies the essence of the Father with reference to his glory in which he represents himself before the eyes of the suppliant creature; ὑπόστασις denotes this essence *as* essence and without regard to its outward manifestation. Originally ὑπόστασις signifies *solidity*, then *reality, being, existence*. It is well known, that the term in its philosophical use acquired an ambiguity of meaning which led to mistakes in the Arian controversy. The Alexandrines taking the word in the sense of "subsistence" described to the Son a proper ὑπόστασις (an independent existence) along with the Father, which gave great offence to the Western Christians, inasmuch as they took the word in the older sense to mean "essence," and therefore of course could ascribe no other essence to the Son than to the Father. In the passage before us ὑπόστασις is evidently used in the *older* sense. True, Calvin, Beza, Salmeron, Gerhard, Calov, Suicer, and others found a difficulty in the Son's being represented as a mere reflection of the Father's essence, seeing that he himself participates in this essence, and were therefore induced to understand ὑπόστασις rather in the later sense, so that the person of the Son was designated as an exact image of the person of the Father; this, however, on the one hand, would involve the anachronism of transferring a later speculative theological terminology to the apostolical times, to which the designation of the Father, Son, and Spirit as three ὑποστάσεις was as yet so unknown that the author could not possibly have used the word in the sense of "person" without being unintelligible to his readers; on the other hand the whole difficulty which has given rise to this false meaning rests on an unsound interpretation of the word χαρακτήρ.

Χαρακτήρ does not any more than ἀπαύγασμα denote a mere

reflection, a copy. Derived from χαράσσω it denotes not, as Wahl and Bretschneider assert, " an instrument for engraving," a style or chisel, but the mark made by a stamp, the *features carved* on the stone, or the gem, or the seal-ring. It thus comes to signify metaphorically, the features of a countenance, the features of character,—and, thirdly and finally, in a weakened signification, it is also used for a " characteristic mark," a token by which anything is known (like τύπος) (thus we speak of the *character* of a species of plants.) But χαρακτήρ never denotes the *copy* of one body left by a seal or signet on another, it never signifies the *image* or the *copy* of the features of a countenance; Lucien speaks rather of εἴκονες τῶν ἀντιμόρφων χαρακτήρων (de Amor. p. 1061). The third of the above significations is evidently not suitable here; the Son can in no intelligible sense be called a distinguishing mark or sign of the nature of God; not less unsuitable is the second, viz., *stamp* in the sense of expression, characteristic quality, which, besides being a figurative and abstract signification, is inadmissible partly, because the Son cannot possibly be merely a quality of the Father, and partly because the parallelism with ἀπαύγασμα requires a concrete term. We must therefore take χαρακτήρ as meaning *stamp* in the sense of a form cut out or engraven. As it belongs to the δόξα to concentrate and reproduce itself in a form composed of rays, a sun, so it is proper to the οὐσία or ὑπόστασις to stamp itself out (or according to the ancient mode of viewing it: to engrave) in a manifest form or figure. This form or figure is not, however, to be viewed as a *copy* (as if the ὑπόστασις itself had already a form which was now copied in a second form) but as an immediate and substantial rendering visible and corporeal, of the ὑπόστασις. The idea is therefore substantially the same as that which is expressed in the words ἀπαύγασμα τῆς δόξης.

If it be asked, who is the ὅς to whom these appositions belong, whether the Logos *qua* eternally pre-existent, or the Logos *qua* incarnate in time, it follows from what has been already remarked on the relation of the third verse to the second, that in general they belong more properly to the former. By means of the ὤν is represented the *permanent nature* not the *temporal acting* of the *Son*. This, however, must not be so regarded, as if that *eternal relation of the Son to the Father* had been *altered* by his coming into the sphere of time. Even when he walked in lowliness on the earth, as Zuingle has already remarked, he could speak of himself as "the Son who is in heaven" (John iii. 13).[1] Even when he had exchanged the form of the world-governing world-embracing eternity, for the form of life *in* the world, and *under* earthly historical relations, he was in the kernel of his being still ever one with the Father, still the brightness of his glory and the stamp of his nature, only that he now revealed this nature more in historically human relations, so to speak, as *practical* love and holiness and wisdom. Thus also the second apposition explains itself: φέρων τε τὰ πάντα τῷ ῥήματι τῆς δυνάμεως αὐτοῦ. First of all, it is evident, that by ῥῆμα cannot be meant, as the Socinians explain it, the preaching of the gospel, but only the creative Omnipotent word which lies at the foundation of the world's existence; then, that φέρων, in like manner as ἀπαύγασμα and χαρακτήρ is to be rendered not abstractly, but concretely (sustinere, comp. Num. xi. 4; Is. ix. 6); finally that αὐτοῦ applies in a reflexive sense to the Son, and not to the Father.[2] The meaning then is, that the Son sustains the universe by the

[1] This, of course, again is not so to be viewed, as if the Son of God had remained in heaven as a *part* or *portion* of Christ, and taken part in the *world-governing* omniscience and omnipotence, while the human nature as another *part* upon earth was without omnipotence and omniscience. This would land us in a more than Nestorian separation of the person of Christ into two persons. But the eternal Son of God, entering into the category of time and the creature, emptied himself, during the period of his humiliation, of the μορφὴ θεοῦ, *i.e.* the participation in the *government of the world* and the world-governing omnipotence, omniscience and omnipresence, and manifested his divine attributes and powers in *temporal human form*, in the form of *particular miracles*. But his oneness of *being* with the Father, although assuming another *form*, remained unaltered.

[2] As the older manuscripts have no spiritus, αὐτοῦ also might be written, without thereby changing the reading as Calov thought "with godless temerity." But Bleek has shown, that in the hellenistic literature αὑτοῦ only stands where in the first person ἐμαυτοῦ would stand, *i.e.* where an emphasis lies on the "self;" on the other hand, that αὐτοῦ stands where in the first person ἐμοῦ would stand. Τῷ ῥήματι τῆς δυνάμεως αὑτοῦ would have to be translated "with the word of his *own* power." There is no occasion for this emphasis here. And just as little occasion is there for departing from the reflexive signification of αὐτοῦ, here the only natural one.

omnipotent word of his power. Here too, it is the eternal relation of the son qua *eternal* to the universe that is spoken of, that relation, the ground of which was given in the words of verse 2 δι' οὗ καὶ ἐποίησε τοὺς αἰῶνας. Only it must not be forgotten here also, that this eternal relation of the Son to the universe was not in the least altered by this,—that the Son becoming man was the sustainer of the world in another sense, namely, the centre of the world's *history*, and the redeemer of humanity and reconciler of heaven and earth.

The subject of the sentence denoted by ὅς (υἱός) is therefore neither the Logos qua eternal *exclusive* of his incarnation, much less is it the incarnate as such; but the subject is Jesus Christ the *incarnate, in so far as he is the eternal* Son of God, who, as the Logos, has an eternal being with the Father, and whose doings in time could *therefore* form the centre-point and the angle of all that is done in time.

This action in time of him who is the eternal ray-image and exact stamp of the Divine nature, is now described in the *predicate* of the sentence, in the words καθαρισμὸν ποιησάμενος τῶν ἁμαρτιῶν, ἐκάθισεν ἐν δεξιᾷ τῆς μεγαλωσύνης ἐν ὑψηλοῖς. The genitive τῶν ἁμαρτιῶν which we cannot well translate otherwise than "purification *from* sins" is explained by this, that in the Greek it can also be said αἱ ἁμαρτίαι καθαρίζονται. Καθαρίζειν corresponds to the Hebrew טִהַר, and finds an intelligible explanation in the significance which belonged to the Levitical purification in the Old Testament cultus. Those, therefore, would greatly err, who should understand καθαρίζειν of moral improvement, and so interpret καθαρισμὸν ποιεῖν as if the author meant to represent Christ here as a teacher of virtue, who sought by word and example the improvement of men. And even those might be said to be in error who explain καθαρισμός of the taking away of guilt by atonement, but do this only on account of passages which occur further on in the epistle,—as if the idea of the biblical καθαρισμός were not already sufficient to confirm this the only true explanation. The entire law of purification, as it was given by God to Moses, rested on the presupposition that man, as sinful and laden with guilt, was not capable of entering into immediate contact with the holy God. The mediation between man and God, who was *present* in the holiest of all, and in the holiest of all *separated* from the people, appeared in three things; 1, in the sacrifices; 2, in the priesthood; and 3, in the Levitical laws of purification. The sacrifices were, (typical) acts, or means of atoning for guilt; the priests were the instruments for accomplishing these acts, but were by no means reckoned as more pure than the rest. Hence they had to bring an offering for their own sin before they offered for the sins of the people. The being Levitically clean, finally, was the *state* which was reached positively, by sacrifices and ordinances, negatively, by avoiding Levitical uncleanness, the state in which the people were rendered qualified for entering into converse with God (through the priests) "without death" (comp. Deut. v. 26); the result, therefore, of observances performed, and the presupposed condition of faith and worship. The *sacrifices* were what purified; the purification was the taking away of *guilt*. This is most clearly set forth in the law respecting the great festival of atonement (Lev. xvi.) There we find these three principal elements in the closest reciprocal relation. Firstly, the sacrifice must be prepared (ver. 1—10), then the high priest must offer for his own sins (ver. 11—14); finally, he must "slay the sin-offering of the people" (ver. 15), and sprinkle the mercy-seat and the whole sanctuary with its blood, and "purify it from the uncleanness of the children of Israel" (ver. 19), and then, lay the sins of the people symbolically on the head of a second beast of sacrifice and drive it laden with the curse into the wilderness (ver. 20—28.) For,—ver. 30—"on that day your *atonement* is made that ye may be *cleansed;* from all your sins before the Lord are ye cleansed." The purification in the biblical sense, consists in the atonement, the gracious covering (כִּפֶּר, ver. 30) of guilt. (In like manner, were those who had become Levitically unclean, for example the lepers Lev. xiv., cleansed by atoning sacrifices.) An Israelitish or Jewish-Christian reader, therefore, would never associate with the expression καθαρισμὸν ποιεῖν what is wont to be called "moral improvement," which, so long as it grows not on the living soil of a heart reconciled to God, is empty self-delusion and a mere outward avoiding of glaring faults; but the καθαρισμός which Christ has provided, could in the mind of the author and his readers be understood only of that gracious atonement for the whole guilt of the whole human race, which Christ, our Lord and Saviour, has accomplished through his sinless sufferings and death, and from which flows all power of reciprocal love, all love to him our heavenly pattern, and all hatred towards sin on account of which he had to die. It is easy to repeat these words of the scriptural author with the mouth; but he alone can say yea and amen to them with the heart, who with the eye of true self-knowledge has looked down into the darkest depths of his natural, and by numberless actual sins aggravated, corruption, and who despairing of all help in himself, stretches forth his hand to receive the offer of salvation from heaven.

For his faithful obedience unto death on the cross the incarnate was crowned, inasmuch as, without his having to give up the form of existence which he then had,—the human nature, therefore as man and continuing to be man—he was exalted to a participation in the divine government of the world. This participation is expressed by the words *sitting at the right hand of God*. Never, and nowhere, does the Holy Scripture apply this expression to denote that form of world-government which the Logos exercised as eternally pre-existent; the sitting at the right hand of God rather denotes everywhere, only that participation in the divine majesty, dominion, and glory, to which the Messiah was exalted after his work was finished, therefore *in time*, and which is consequently exercised by him as the glorified Son of Man *under the category of time*. Already in Psalm cx. 1, where the expression for the first time occurs, it applies to the future, the *second David*, at a future time to be exalted.

The expression finds its explanation in the old oriental practice, according to which the king's son, *who was himself clothed with royal authority*, had the liberty of sitting on the king's throne, at his right hand. This signification lies at the foundation of the figure already in Psalm cx.; that Jehovah is there represented as contending in behalf of the Son, while the Son rests himself, has nothing to do with the figure as such, and is not inherent in the expression " to sit at the right hand of God" as such, (although of course that feature in Psalm cx. also finds its counterpart in the exalted Christ.)

That explanation which arose amid the tumult of confessional controversy rests on an entire misapprehension of the figurative expression, namely, that as God is everywhere, the right hand of God is also everywhere; to sit at the right hand of God means therefore to be everywhere present. This interpretation is quite as mistaken as if one were to understand by δεξιὰ θεοῦ, a particular place where God sits on a throne (a mistake which Luther falsely attributed to Oecolompadius.) In the expression ἐκάθισε ἐν δεξιᾷ τῆς μεγαλωσύνης there lies solely the *idea of participation* in the divine dominion, and majesty (μεγαλωσύνη, majestas denotes here God himself), without any local reference whatever.

On the contrary, the expression ἐν ὑψηλοῖς that is added, contains a distinct determination of locality; whether we connect it with the verb ἐκάθισεν, or (which is better, as, otherwise, ἐν ὑψ. would have to stand before ἐν δεξιᾷ) with the noun μεγαλωσύνη. Ἐν ὑψηλοῖς is the Hebrew בַּמְּרוֹם, equivalent to בַּשָּׁמַיִם. But the "heaven" never in the holy Scriptures denotes the absence of space or omnipresence (see on this my scientific crit. of the ev. history, 2 ed. p. 601 s.),—it always denotes either the firmament, or that sphere of the created world in time and space where the union of God with the personal creature is not disturbed by sin, where no death reigns, where the glorification of the body does not need to be looked forward to as something future. Into that sphere has the first-fruits of risen and glorified humanity entered, as into a place, with a visible glorified body to come again from thence in a visible manner.

Thus is described the *inheritance* (ver. 2) which the incarnate Son has received, and the author, after these introductory words in which he lays the foundation, now passes to the first principal inference which follows from them; namely, that that Son, the organ of the New Testament revelation, is superior to the angels, the organs of the Old Testament revelation. The carrying out of this inference forms the first part of the Epistle to the Hebrews, chap. i. 4—ii. 18.

PART FIRST.

(Chap. i. 4—ii. 18.)

THE SON AND THE ANGELS.

WE encounter here the first instance of a phenomenon peculiar to the Epistle to the Hebrews, namely, that the announcement of a new theme is closely interwoven with the end of the last period of a foregoing part. The author passes forthwith from that which he has brought to a conclusion, to a new idea flowing from it, with which an entirely new perspective opens itself out. It follows prima facie and in general from the *inheritance* of the Son described in ver. 3, that the Son must be higher than the angels. This then opens up a new theme, which is, to show that it is and must be so, and that this superiority of the Son to the angels will admit of being demonstrated in particulars. But this theme at which the author has arrived is a *principal* one, and one to which he has purposely come. It possesses in his view not merely the importance of a collateral idea, but of one with which, from regard to the practical aim of his epistle, he has especially to concern himself.

It is only from a complete misapprehension of the phenomenon to which we have referred, and which recurs in chap. ii. 5, iii. 2, iv. 3—4 and 14, &c., that we can explain why Bleek should deny, in opposition to De Wette, that a new section begins at ver. 4, and why Tholuck should understand ver. 4 as a "collateral idea," which, however, the author would specially impress upon his readers. Even in relation to ver. 3, ver. 4 is not a "collateral idea," but rather a conclusion to which the author has directed his course in ver. 1—3. But *why* was it of so much importance to him to carry out the comparison of the Son with the angels? Tholuck is certainly right when he says, that his object could not be to combat a party like that at Colosse who occupied themselves with the worship of angels, for the author, who usually draws his practical applications very closely, and, in order to do so, breaks without hesitation the connection of the theoretical reasoning, gives no admonition whatever against the worship of angels. The only practical inference which he draws is in chap. ii. 2— that the word spoken by the Son is still more holy than the law which was given by angels.—Bleek is therefore of opinion, that the belief of the Israelites in the co-operation of the angels in the giving of the Sinaitic law, led the author to speak of angels; but thus outwardly apprehended, this serves as little for explanation as the strange remark that the thought of God's throne reminded the author of the angels who are around his throne.

The true motive of the author lies deeper. *The entire Old Testament is related to the New as the angels are related to the Son;* this is his (first) principal idea, an idea of wondrous depth, which throws a surprising light on the whole doctrine of angels. In the old covenant, mankind, and as part thereof also Israel, is represented as far separated from the holy God by sin, and the angels stand as mediators between them. The mediation in the Old Testament is a double one, a chain consisting of two members, of *Moses*, and the *angel of the Lord. There* stands a man who, by his vocation, by his position, by his commission, is raised above other men with whom he stands on the same level as a sinner, and brought nearer to God, yet without being nearer to the divine nature or partaking in it. *Here* stands the form of an angel, in which God reveals himself to his people, brings himself nearer to the people's capacity of apprehension, becomes *like* to men yet without *becoming* man. God and man certainly approach nearer to each other; a *man* is commissioned and qualified to hear the words of God; *God* appears in a form in which men can see him, but there is as yet no real union of God with man. But in *the Son,* God and man have become personally one, they have not merely approached outwardly near to each other. God has here not merely accommodated himself to man's capacity of apprehension in an angelophany, a theophany, but he has personally revealed the fulness of his being in the man Jesus, inasmuch as that ἀπαύγασμα of his glory was man. And in the person of this incarnate one, not merely a member of humanity has come near to God, but as he who was born of a virgin is himself eternal God, in him as first-fruits of the new humanity has mankind been exalted to the *inheritance of all things.*

It was necessary that the author should show how the two mediators of the Old Testament, the angel of the covenant and Moses, find their higher unity in Christ. To show this of the angel of the covenant is the problem of the first part, to show it of Moses, that of the second part (comp. chap. iii.—iv. chiefly chap. iii. ver. 3 : *for this man was thought worthy of more glory than Moses.*)

The question may still be asked, however, why the author speaks of the *angels* in the plural, why he does not place the individual *angel of the Lord* side by side with the individual Moses ? The answer is very simple; because the *angel of the Lord* was not a particular individual from among the angels. He was not a person distinct from God, not one of the number of created angels whom God used only as an instrument; but the *angel of the Lord* (מלאך י״י) was God himself as he appeared in the *form* of an angel.[1] (Comp. chiefly Jud. xiii. ver. 21 with ver. 22.) The author speaks of angels, therefore, because it was not a certain individual angel who was to be placed by the side of Moses as the second member in the chain of mediation, but because, when God would manifest himself to Moses and to the high priests, he borrowed the form and figure of his appearance from the sphere of the angels, of those angels whom he also usually employed when it was necessary under the old dispensation to make Divine revelations manifest to the eyes of men.

The comparison of the Son with the angels, divides itself again

---

[1] The theocratical מלאך י״י the Jehovah who was enthroned above the tabernacle and the ark of the covenant, is not to be confounded with the *angel* Michael (Dan. x. 13), who, after the temple and ark of the covenant had ceased to exist, and the nation of Israel was scattered among other nations, was chosen of God to be the guardian angel of this people. This angel was certainly distinguished from God and his Son (according to Rev. xii. 7); was a creature, one of the created angels.

into two sections, which are also outwardly separated from each other by a practical part inserted between them. In the first of these sections the author shows, that the Son is superior to the angels already in virtue of *his eternal existence* as the Son of God (chap. i. 4—14, upon which is engrafted in chap. ii. 1—4 the practical suggestion, that the New Testament revelation is still holier than that of the Old Testament); in the second he shows, that in the Son *man* also has been exalted above the angels (chap. ii. 5—18.)

SECTION FIRST.

(Chap. i. 4—14.)

THE SON IS IN HIMSELF SUPERIOR TO THE ANGELS.

Ver. 4. In the words κρείττων γενόμενος τῶν ἀγγέλων lies, as has been already observed, the theme of the whole part, while in the words ὅσῳ διαφορώτερον, &c., the special theme of the first section is expressed. The participle κρείττων γενόμενος stands in apposition with the *subject* of ver. 3 ὅς *i.e.* υἱός. The subject of whom it is affirmed that he is superior to the angels, is therefore not the Logos as pre-existent but still *the incarnate Son of God as the organ of the New Testament revelation;* this appears partly, from the context and the train of thought, inasmuch as it was the business of the author to demonstrate the pre-eminence of the new dispensation over the old, partly, from the γενόμενος "become" (by no means = ὤν), partly, from the κεκληρονόμηκεν.

The argument for the superior dignity of the organ of the New Testament revelation is derived from this—that God already under the old dispensation assigned to the future Messiah whom he there promised, a *name* which plainly enough declared, that this promised future Messiah should be at the same time the eternal Son of the same nature with the Father. In this light, and from this point of view, then, are to be understood also the particular proofs adduced from the Old Testament ver. 5—14, and so understood they present no difficulty. They can only then appear difficult and obscure when it is supposed that the author meant them to prove, that a dignity superior to the angels was ascribed in the Old Testament either to the Logos *as such*, or to the historical individual Jesus *as such*. Nothing of this; however, is said even in the remotest degree. The author lays down the thesis that the *Son* in his quality as *organ of the New Testament revelation* is exalted above the angels, and in proof of this he appeals to the fact, that the Old Testament ascribes to the Messiah this dignity, namely his being the Son of God in a manner which is not affirmed of the angels. As a middle member between that thesis and this proof, nothing farther needs to be supplied than the *presupposition* that the υἱός ver. 1—3 *is identical with the Messiah promised in the Old Testament*. But that the readers of the Epistle did presuppose this, that by the υἱός ver. 1—3 in whom God has revealed himself " at the end of this time " (consequently in the " Messianic time ;" see above) they understood Jesus Christ, and again that they held Christ to be the Messiah, will surely not require to be proven here.

Κρείττων—the author uses the same expression, in itself quite relative and indefinite, also in the analogous comparisons chap. vii. 19 and 22, viii. 6 and ix. 23, x. 34, &c. The Son is superior to the angels, because (in as far as) " he has obtained as an inheritance a more distinguished name than they." On the idea of the inheritance see the remarks on ver. 2. The act of the κληρονομεῖν is one performed *in time;* nothing is said of the Logos as eternally pre-existent. But neither is it anything that took place in the time of Jesus that is spoken of; the author does not refer to those events recorded in Matth. iii. 17, xvii. 5, in which the voice of the Father from heaven to Jesus said : This is my beloved Son. The author *could not* in consistency with his plan refer to these events ; for his object was to prove his particular theses and doctrines from the records of the Old Testament itself, for the sake of his readers, who were afraid of doing what might involve a separation from the writings and the ordinances of the old holy covenant of God with the people of Israel. Accordingly, his object here is to show, that already in the Messianic prophecies the Messiah was represented not as a mere man, but received a name such as was given to no angel, a name which indicates an altogether exclusive and essential relation of oneness with God. The perfect κεκληρονόμηκεν points to the time of the Old Testament prophecy.

"Ὅσῳ διαφορώτερον παρ' αὐτοὺς κεκλερόνομηκεν ὄνομα. It is evident that ὄνομα here, where the author treats (ver. 5 ss.) precisely of the name υἱός, is not (with Beza, Calov, and others) to be translated by "dignity."—Παρά c. Acc. instead of the genitive, is no Hebraism, but a genuine Greek construction, formed to avoid unsuitable applications of the genitive (such as would occur here.) Διαφορώτερον, not more excellent, higher, but *more distinguished, more singular*. Critics in their wisdom have indeed doubted the accuracy of the fact here stated, affirming that the name "sons of God" is given not merely to men— Ps. lxxxix. 27; 2 Sam. vii. 14—but also precisely to angels—Job i. 6, ii. 1; xxxviii. 6; Dan. iii. 25.[1] Those make shortest work of it, who deny to the author of the Epistle to the Hebrews a thorough acquaintance with the Bible; Bleek deals more modestly, when he supposes that the author was not versed at least in the Hebrew original, and explains his overlooking those passages by the circumstance, that the LXX., which he made use of exclusively in his citations, and the knowledge and use of which he presupposes in his readers, who were acquainted with Aramaic, but not with Hebrew—has in those passages ἄγγελοι θεοῦ in place of בְּנֵי אֱלֹהִים. This would indeed ward off the moral charge of carelessness and inconsiderateness from the author's person, but not that of falseness and groundlessness from his reasoning. On a more thorough and impartial investigation, however, it will appear here again, how much the foolishness of the Scriptures, and of their writers enlightened by the holy spirit, is superior to the pretended wisdom of the children of men. If, in these days, a preacher were to say in a sermon, or in a book designed for edification, that Christ receives in the

---

[1] The passages Gen. vi. 2, where it is the descendants of Seth that are spoken of and alone *can* be spoken of (comp. my "Weltanschauung der Bibel und Naturwissenschaft" in the "Zukunft der Kirche," 1847, p. 369 s.) and Ps. xxix. and lxxxix. where בְּנֵי אֵלִים are spoken of, have no connection at all with this subject.

New Testament a name which is applied exclusively to him, for to whom of all that are born of woman has the Father said: This is my *Son?*—would any one have a right to object to such a preacher, that he must be unacquainted with those passages of the New Testament in which Christians are called *sons of God*, and besides that he must be ignorant of the passage Heb. ii. 10, where the author speaks of "many sons of God?" Is it not then quite a different thing to apply a common name in the *plural* to a *class*, from what it is to apply the same as an individual name in the *singular* to an individual. Even where the New Testament speaks of υἱοῖς θεοῦ instead of τέκνοις θεοῦ, as in that very passage Heb. ii. 10, even there this difference still obtains, as no one assuredly will deny. And in like manner our author, in reference to the Old Testament, would be quite right, even if there were no other difference (which is not the case) than that between the plural as applied to the class, and the singular as applied to the individual. He himself, indeed, in ver. 5, makes the distinction between the *name* of Christ and that of the angels to consist in this—that God has said to no individual among the angels: "Thou art my Son; I have begotten thee." It makes already even an *essential* difference, whether the idea of son comes to its full manifestation in an individual, or in a class. —As, however, in the New Testament, the difference between the predicates "Son of God" and "children of God," is not merely one of number, but as, in addition to this, there is a *qualitative* difference in the *kind* of designation, so is it also in the Old Testament. When JEHOVAH in Ps. ii. 2 and 7, declares his anointed to be his son whom he has *begotten*, this is something different from what is said, when the angels as a class are called sons of the ELOHIM, who has *created* them. Nay, this difference is, in respect of the expression, even greater and more marked than that in the New Testament between υἱός and τέκνον. The angels are called sons of God in so far as God is the Elohim, the all-governing Creator of all things, and they have come forth from his creating hand, and have lost by no fall this their primitive relation to God as his children;[1] the Mes-

---

[1] In Job ii. 2 Satan is not reckoned among the "children of God;" but *distinguished* from them. That he should come בְּתֹכָם (locally) is something extraordinary.

siah, on the other hand, is called the Son of God, in so far as God is JEHOVAH the free, self-sufficient one, proceeding from himself, and independent of all creatures.[1] In reality then, the Son has received a διαφορώτερον ὄνομα παρὰ τοὺς ἀγγέλους, and the form of ver. 5, *for to whom*, &c., shows plainly enough, that the author was clearly conscious of that difference. Bleek's view is correct, however, so far, that the author would feel less concern in omitting all *express* reference to the passages in Job and Daniel, as the readers in their Septuagint could not be misled by those passages.

At ver. 5 then, begins the proof that the Old Testament already assigns to the future Messiah a name, such as is never given to an angel. We shall without prejudice explain these particular passages in their original connection, from which it will appear, whether our author has invested them with a meaning which they do not bear.

Τίνι γὰρ εἶπέ ποτε τῶν ἀγγέλων—at εἶπε is to be supplied from ver. 1 θεός as the subject. Ποτέ does not serve to strengthen the τίνι (Kuinoel, Bretschneider, Wahl) but is independent, signifying "at any time," and thus forms a marked antithesis with πάλιν. This καὶ πάλιν is to be extended in the following way (Bleek and others): καὶ τίνι τῶν ἀγγέλων πάλιν εἶπε; "to which of the angels has he *at any time* said: Thou art my Son? and to which has he *again* said: I will be to him a Father."[2] This contains clearly the two ideas: God has used such expressions to an angel *not even a single time;* but to the Son *not merely once* but *again and again.*

The words cited are to be found in Ps. ii. 7. Not much that is really of importance depends on the usual question, whether this Psalm contains a direct prophecy of the Messiah, or an indirect one, or none at all. Let us enquire chiefly, who was its author, when it was written, and what occasioned it. Assuredly, this sublime lyrical effusion had a *historical occasion,* which

---

[1] See this correct interpretation of the אֶהְיֶה אֲשֶׁר אֶהְיֶה in Drechsler: Einheit und Aechtheit der Genesis p. 10, with which is to be compared my treatise ueber das Alter des Jehovahnamens in Niedner's Zeitschr. für hist. Theol. 1849 p. 506.

[2] It would be much harsher to extend the phrase thus: καὶ πάλιν ἐρωτῶ· τίνι τῶν ἀγγέλων εἶπε.

affords the explanation of it in its subjective human aspect. For, let it be ever so prophetic, it is still essentially not a מַשָּׂא, not a נְאֻם יְהוָה, it does not begin with כֹּה אָמַר יְהוָה, but is a *psalm* an *hymn*, an effusion of religious poetry, which has beneath it a נְאֻם יְהוָה as the basis on which it moves, and to which pointed reference is made in the 6th verse חֹק־יְהוָה. We are therefore justified in seeking a humano-historical occasion for the psalm. It cannot then have been written before the time of David, since the hill of Zion is spoken of as the royal seat; least of all in the time of Solomon (as Bleek would have it), since, according to 1 Kings v.; 1 Chron. xxii, Solomon reigned in peace, and in his time there is not the slightest trace of such a violent insurrection of rebellious nations as is described Ps. ii. 1 ss. After the division of the kingdom, there was under Uzziah a subjugation of the neighbouring heathen nations, but only in a very partial degree, and the revolt of these heathen had become something so common, that it would scarcely have so powerfully moved the soul of a poet,—besides, in this case, we should have expected to find among the hoped-for blessings of the future some mention of the re-union with the northern kingdom. There remains, therefore, no other time in which the Psalm can well have been written, but that of David. Against this ver. 6 has been adduced, as not properly applicable to the anointing of David, seeing that David was anointed as a boy at Bethlehem. But supposing that ver. 6 applies to the person of David (which would first require to be investigated), the object of the words עַל־צִיּוֹן הַר־קָדְשִׁי would certainly not be to give a dry, outward, prosaic determination of locality—of the place of the anointing. The poet would rather denote the whole wondrous series of divine acts by which the shepherd was exalted from his anointing by Samuel onwards, guarded amid the many dangers to which his life was exposed, until at length he came to be acknowledged by all the twelve tribes, and was brought to the summit of his dominion in the residence which he took by conquest, and which he founded —I say the poet would comprehend this whole series of divine acts in a poetical unity; and as we would denote the same thing by the one symbolical expression : God has exalted him to the throne of Zion, so the poet denotes it by the symbolical expression entirely similar : " God has anointed him to be King in Zion."

It is not said that Samuel anointed him, but that God anointed him. This interpretation would be all the more unobjectionable, that there is nothing to hinder our translating עַל by "over," and taking the words עַל־צִיּוֹן to denote the term. ad quem: God has anointed him (to be King) over Zion. Still, as already observed, we can by no means regard it as decided that ver. 6 speaks of the person of David. And thus every motive for placing the psalm in another time than that of David falls to the ground.

Precisely in David's life-time we find a state of things which remarkably corresponds with that described in the psalm. We read in 2 Sam. viii. that Hadadezer the King of Zobah rebelled against David, who subdued him, and that the Syrians of Damascus hastened to his assistance with a mighty host, of which David alone took 21,700 prisoners. Shortly before this, David had also put down rebellions on the part of the Philistines, Moabites, Ammonites, Edomites, and Amalekites, and so there was then a time when almost the whole heathen world known to the Israelites had risen up in hostility against Israel and Israel's King (and consequently, according to the views of the ancient heathen, against Israel's God—for it was believed that with the people their gods were vanquished.) After David's victory, Thoi, King of Hamath, sent to him presents in token of homage, so that there is not wanting an occasion also for what is said in vers. 10—12.—But in vers. 7 and 12 we find a statement which more than anything else confirms us in the view that the second psalm was written at that time (certainly after the victory was completed), and, moreover, that no one but David himself sung this hymn of thanksgiving and hope. The poet rests his firm hope upon this —that God has said to him: "thou art my son." A word to this effect had been spoken to David in the charge which he received from God by Nathan the prophet, shortly before the Syrian war. When he wished to build God a temple, Nathan disclosed to him that *he* should not build God a temple, but *his posterity* (זֶרַע as a collective); yea, God will build it an house, and *establish its throne for ever; God will be its Father, and it will be his Son.* Now we know certainly (from 1 Kings viii. 17 ss.), that Solomon applied that prophecy to himself in such a way that he undertook the building of the temple, and we must even say that in this he did perfectly right; for if the "posterity of David" was to build a temple for God, there was no reason why the first member of that posterity should not immediately put his hand to the work. Only, it must not be forgotten, that Solomon himself by no means thought that the prophecy of Nathan as yet found its complete fulfilment in his erection of the temple. He says this most distinctly in 1 Kings viii. 26—27. He considers it as a benefit still to be prayed for, that those words of Nathan to David should be verified, for *his* temple is as yet not a house in which God may truly dwell. Not less clearly was David conscious of this, that Nathan's word would first obtain its full accomplishment "in the distant future" (לְמֵרָחוֹק), "in a man who is the Lord, Jehovah himself" (2 Sam. vii. 19)[1], or, as it is explained in Chron. xvii. 17, "in a man who is exalted up to Jehovah." On this promise so well understood, David builds the hope which he expresses in Ps. ii. We know now the time, the occasion, and the author of the second psalm. And it is only now that we have the necessary preparation for enquiring into its contents. One might feel tempted to refer the contents of the psalm (as Bleek does) to the earthly historical king (to David according to our view, to Solomon according to Bleek's.) Thus David would compose the psalm sometime during the insurrection of the Syrians,—in ver. 1—3 he describes the raging of the heathen against Jehovah, and against himself, the anointed of Jehovah,—then, in ver. 4, he expresses the certain hope that God will laugh at his enemies and utterly destroy them, and in ver. 6 he confirms this hope, by calling to mind the covenant-faithfulness of God, who has helped him hitherto, and has raised him to be King over Zion. But in ver. 7 there comes an obstacle by which this interpretation is entirely overturned. David appeals in ver. 7 to this—that God has said *to him :* "Thou art my son"—has said *to him :* he will give him the ends of the earth for a possession. When had ever such a promise been given *to David ?* It is expressly said in 2 Sam. vii. 12, that David shall not build an house to the Lord, but shall sleep with his fathers; *not to him, but to his seed after him,* will God establish the king-

---

[1] If אֲדֹנָי ׳י were not in apposition to תּוֹרַת־אָדָם, but vocative, the latter expression could have no possible meaning.

dom for ever and be their Father. It is quite clear then, that David in the second psalm speaks in the name of his seed after him, that he adoringly looks forward to the fulfilment of that glorious hope in *the distant future*, 2 Sam. vii. 19 : it is clear that the insurrection of the Syrians forms *merely the occasion, but not the object and import* of the second psalm.

The second psalm presents to us not an historical but an ideal picture. After the general insurrection of the southern and northern nations bordering on Israel had been quelled, and David had begun to reflect on this event, and to compare it with Nathan's prophecy, there opened up before him a grand prospect stretching into the future; what had befallen him appears as a type, as a typical instance of a great ideal law which would again and again repeat itself, until it found its perfect manifestation in the time of the "seed after him," his view of which seed had already in the prayer 2 Sam. vii. 19 concentrated itself into the concrete form of " a man who is to be exalted up to Jehovah." For, apart from the fundamental law of all poetical intuition, according to which what is general (as in the case before us "the posterity") individualizes itself in the eye of the poet, it could not remain hid even from that *reflection* which is divested of all poetry, that the fulness of the prophecies given in 2 Sam. 7 must find their *final* accomplishment in a *concrete descendant*. If, in opposition to David, "who was to sleep with his fathers," the royal dominion was to be established for ever in the house of David or the seed of David (2 Sam. vii. 16), this certainly could not be accomplished thus—that his descendants, one after the other, for ever should also " sleep with their fathers;" but the one part of the fulfilment must consist in this, that God should show a fatherly forbearance towards the sins of the particular descendants (2 Sam. vii. 14), the other part certainly in this, that at length an individual would come, in whom the endlessness of the dominion, and the absoluteness of the relation of son, should find adequate manifestation. Now, *we know*, as has been already observed, from 2 Sam. vii. 19, and 1 Chron. xvii. 17 (the passage comes of course from the royal annals which form the basis of both books) that David really understood that prophecy in this and in no other sense, and Ps. ii. 7 compels us to refer the psalm to an *individual* who was the seed κατ᾽ ἐξοχήν promised to David.

As the heathen had assembled against him to throw off his yoke, so, transferring himself in spirit to future times, he sees how the nations of the earth (the representation is here purposely general, and nothing is said of the Syrians) would also rise up against the future perfect King, and that out of hatred to the living holy God who has anointed him. But, in like manner, he sees also already, how the living God will deride the folly of the children of men. God himself speaks in majestic calmness the simple word: "I have anointed my King upon Zion." (It is quite evident that this is not spoken of David, but of that *seed after him*.) Now David hears that future King himself speak words of holy confidence; he hears him say, that he will often confess and freely proclaim that the Lord has declared him to be his son, that the Lord has anointed him. (His real being he derives not by his carnal descent from David, but by the word of the promise of Nathan to David—he is begotten by the *word of God*. In the phrase "this day," it is evident that the royal singer sees in ideal vision *his own time* when he received the promise, blended with the *future time,* that of the perfect *seed,* and thus the "this day" forms a direct antithesis with the times in which David was begetting, or had begotton corporeal descendants.)—Further, David hears in verse 8 the *seed* reminding God of his promises (2 Sam. vii.), in verse 9 he hears God answering in accordance with these promises; and finally, in verse 10—12, David concludes in his own name with an admonition to the kings of the nations to be in subjection to that promised "son;" soon the time shall come when he shall execute judgment on the heathen.

In the prophecy of Nathan, the prayer of David connected with it, and the second psalm, there lies before us *the germ of the whole Messianic prophecy.* In the second psalm, it appears still in the form of lyrical elevation, and it is more than probable, that the meaning of that first grand presentment remained a mystery undisclosed to the majority of David's contemporaries, and the generations immediately following, just as, at a later period, the prophecies of the divinity of the Messiah (Mic. v. 1, and Is. ix. 6) were locked up from the great mass of the Jewish people.) Still, the consciousness of the importance of Nathan's prophecy never vanished (1 Kings xv. 4; 2 Kings viii. 19, &c.)

But when, after the separation of the kingdoms, outward and inward decay increased more and more, and God by his prophets (first of all by Amos and Hosea) gave intimation of the coming exile, he then also again put into the mouth of the prophets the promise, that after the exile there should come a צמח דוד born in a low estate, brought like the first David from the sheep-folds of Bethlehem, not from kings' palaces (Mic. iv.—v.), a branch springing from the roots of the hewn stock of the house of David (Is. xi.), an Immanuel born of the lowly maid of the house of David (Is. 7);—and of the substantial identity of this *branch* with the "son," Ps. ii. and the "seed," 2 Sam. vii. on the one hand, and the Messiah on the other, there can no reasonable doubt be entertained.

Our author—who, in connecting the passage 2 Sam. vii. 14 with the second psalm, makes it sufficiently evident that he had interpreted and understood the psalm in connection with the prophecy of Nathan—simply calls to mind the fact, that in the very first commencement of the Messianic prophecy[1] there is ascribed to the Messiah a relation of Sonship to God, such as is never applied, even approximately, to any one of the angels. A relation of such a kind, that the Messiah *derives his real being not from David but from God.*

For this was, as we saw, the import of the words *to-day I have begotten thee.* We shall therefore not have to inquire long in what sense the author of our epistle understood the σήμερον. In no other than the only natural sense. It denotes neither the eternal present, nor the time of the incarnation of Jesus, nor that of his resurrection, ascension, &c., but the time of that promise which was given by Nathan, in opposition to the (later) time when David begat Solomon (2 Sam. xii. 24.) It all hinges upon this—that the υἱός does not derive his real being from David.

The second citation 2 Sam. vii. 14 has received its explanation in what has been said above.

---

[1] The idea of the Messianic prophecy we understand here, of course, in the narrower sense, as the prediction of a definite, royal, descendant of David. In the wider sense, Gen. iii. 15; and Deut. xviii. 15 are also Messianic prophecies.

Ver. 6. The proofs of the assertion that the Son has received a higher *name* than the angels are, in truth, closed with the two citations in ver. 5. In ver. 6 ss. there follow certain other arguments, in which also the *superiority* of the Son over the angels appears, although not precisely that which consists in the *name*. The sixth verse is unquestionably one of the most difficult in the whole epistle. With regard to the construction, πάλιν seems, according to the position of the words, to belong to εἰσαγάγῃ; still, there is no difficulty in deciding, and by the consent of the best interpreters (Peschito, Erasm., Luth., Cal. Beza, Capellus, Grot., Limb., Hammond, Bengel, Wolf, Carpz., Kuin., Bleek, and others), it has been substantially determined, that according to the sense it can belong only to λέγει, parallel to the πάλιν (εἶπε) ver. 5; consequently, that we have here an easily explicable hyperbaton. It cannot be "a second bringing in of the first-born into the world" that is here spoken of, as Olshausen rightly observes, seeing that nothing has been said of a first. And thus, from the outset, we are spared the fruitless trouble of deciding whether the "two bringings in" are to be understood of the eternal generation and the incarnation, or of the incarnation and the resurrection, or finally of the resurrection and the second coming.

What, however, is meant generally by the εἰσάγειν εἰς τ. οἰκ. can only be determined by looking more particularly at the citation itself and the meaning of it.

The words καὶ προσκυνησάτωσαν αὐτῷ πάντες ἄγγελοι θεοῦ are to be found verbatim in the LXX. cod. Vat. Deut. xxxii. 43. The cod. Alex. has πάντες υἱοὶ τοῦ θεοῦ, and for this in a subsequent place ἄγγελοι where the cod. Vat. has υἱοί; but the Vatican reading is here, as it almost always is, the older and the more genuine, and is confirmed by the citation before us.

It has indeed been maintained (Pattr., Kuinoel, &c.) that this citation cannot be taken from Deut. xxxii., but is derived from Ps. xcvii. 7, where we find the words προσκυνήσατε αὐτῷ πάντες οἱ ἄγγελοι θεοῦ. But those who have adopted this view have been driven to it by the circumstance, that in Deut. xxxii. the words in question are not to be found in the Masor. text of the Hebrew original. How could the author, it was thought, appeal to a passage which was a mere spurious addition by the

Alexandrine translators? But as it is evident, notwithstanding, that he follows, in respect of form, the passage in the LXX. Deut. xxxii., and deviates from Ps. xcvii., it was found necessary to have recourse to the subsidiary hypotheses, *a*, that the author has had both passages in his memory, *b*, that he was conscious of the spuriousness of the passage in Deut. xxxii., *c*, that he therefore intended to cite the other passage, *d*, but, notwithstanding, intentionally or unintentionally borrowed the *form* of the words from Deut. xxxii.

The artificial nature of the operation here presupposed, almost bordering upon the ludicrous, would of itself suffice for the refutation of this view. In addition to this, however, it enables us to escape from Scylla only to fall into Charybdis. For, if the words in Deut. owe their existence to a spurious addition, the words in Ps. xcvii. owe theirs to a manifestly false translation.

The Hebrew original runs thus—אלהים השתחוו־לו כל, and in the context, it is not the angels that are spoken of, but the false gods of the heathen, who will yet be constrained to bow before Jehovah. Nor is anything said there of a "bringing in of the first-born into the world;" the subject is simply and solely the sovereignty of Jehovah, before which the idols shall be destroyed. And, even in the (spurious) superscription which the psalm bears in the LXX.: Τῷ Δαυὶδ, ὅτε ἡ γῆ αὐτοῦ καθίσταται, not a word is to be found either about the οἰκουμένη or the bringing in of a son into it.

While it is thus impossible to find in the verse before us a citation from Ps. xcvii. 7, all becomes right when we consider the citation as taken from Deut. xxxii. 43. For, with respect, first of all, to the absence of the words in the Masoretic text we must with all our deference to this text as resting on ancient and strong tradition, never forget that we have in the LXX., particularly in the Pentateuch, an *equally ancient* recension of the Hebrew text. That the Seventy did not fabricate these words but found them in their original, is also Bleek's view. We have here, therefore, not a genuine text opposed to a spurious addition, but a reading opposed to a reading. And, moreover, in the 6th verse, according to the proper sense of the words cited, all mainly depended upon this, that in accordance with the general religious consciousness and understood phraseology, the angels should be represented as having merely the position of worshipping spectators, when the setting up of the Messiah's kingdom is spoken of. We will farther explain and justify this assertion. The determination of the time here referred to ὅταν δὲ, &c., one might be tempted to explain from the circumstance, that when Moses sang that song, Israel who, in Hos. xi. 1, is called the first-born of God, was just about to enter as a people among the nations of the earth. This explanation would at least be incomparably better than that according to which it is the entrance of the Logos from eternity into time that is mentioned. There is no mention here of the κόσμος, but of the οἰκουμένη, the sphere of the earth as inhabited by the nations.

But as αὐτῷ must plainly be referred to the same person that is called πρωτότοκος, while αὐτῷ again refers in the passage cited, not to the then Mosaic nor to the post Mosaico-Messianic Israel, nor to the ideal Israel, but to *Jehovah who will help his people*, it follows, that the author also, in the word πρωτότοκος, cannot have had in his mind either the real or ideal Israel, or the Messiah as such, and we shall therefore have to look out for another explanation of the εἰσάγειν.

We must first however ascertain more particularly the meaning of the passage Deut. xxxii. 43. Moses in vers. 15—18 rebukes the sins of Israel at that period, those numerous manifestations of the obduracy of their hearts which the people gave, in spite of the mighty acts of God which they had witnessed. In vers. 19—35 he threatens them with terrible punitive judgments in the future, should they persist in these sins, in this obduracy. The punishment threatened is concentrated in this, that if the people should continue to be ungrateful for their redemption from the Egyptian bondage, God would at length take back from them the freedom which he had given them, and leave them to fall anew into a still more terrible bondage among a heathen people. We know that this was fulfilled, and how. We know how, from the time of Joshua to that of David, God conducted the people to the pinnacle of prosperity; how, from David to Zedekiah, he let them fall into all the depths of hapless degeneracy; how, in spite of prosperity and adversity, the people of Israel sank deeper and deeper into corruption, until, at length, God caused to be fulfilled the threatening first uttered by Moses, and afterwards repeated by Amos, Hosea, Micah, &c., and let the people fall into bondage to the heathen nations, the Babylonians, Persians, Macedonians, Syrians, Egyptians, and Romans. But Amos, Hosea, Micah, Isaiah, &c., were not the first who predicted a re-deliverance from this affliction, for Moses had already foretold, Deut. xxxii. 36—42, that God would have compassion on those who were humbled and converted by those chastisements; then should it be known that it is he alone who can help and save. *Moses prophesies, then, in* vers. 36—42 *of the same re-deliverance which has been more specially described by the later prophets, as the deliverance through the Messiah, consequently, as the Messianic salvation.* Now here, in ver. 42, it is said (according to the reading maintained in the LXX.): the angels shall worship the Lord, *i.e. Jehovah the Saviour.* This Jehovah, the Saviour, appears indeed in the mouth of Moses to be quite identical with Jehovah generally, with God, but the Christian readers of the Epistle to the Hebrews knew already and acknowledged, that the Jehovah who should arise and come forth in the Messianic time for the salvation of his people is *God the Son, the Incarnate.* Two things must not be forgotten if we would rightly apprehend the meaning and the argument of the verse before us—first, that the author simply testifies to the Godhead of Christ, ver. 2, 3, as a thing already known to his readers through the apostolic preaching, and acknowledged by them, without deeming it necessary to adduce proofs for this doctrine; secondly, that for this very reason (as well as on account of the whole train of thought, ver. 4, ss.) the aim of ver. 6 is not to prove that the Messiah is the Son of God, but that the Messiah, who is known to be identical with the Son of God, is, even in the Old Testament dispensation, placed higher than the angels. For, it was on this point that the readers needed to be instructed. They had no doubts about the Messiahship of Jesus and the divinity of the Messiah, but this whole Messianic revelation was still in their eyes but an *appendix* to the Mosaic revelation, given only on account of Moses and Israel, only a blossoming branch of the religion of Israel. They had yet to be brought to know, that the divinity of him who was the organ of the New Testament revelation necessarily involves his infinite elevation above the organs of the Old Testament, that the old dispensation was ended on account of the new, and that this new dispensation was on account of all mankind, not on account of the old. This they had yet to be taught, and this is precisely what is designed to be proved on these verses, the proof being drawn from the divinity of Christ, already acknowledged by the readers.

In ver. 5 the author has shown that the Messiah *even when he is prophesied of as David's Son*, is said to be the Son of God in a sense in which it is said of no angel. In ver. 6 he shows, that a place above the angels is assigned to the Messiah *moreover, when he is represented as Jehovah the Saviour himself*. When the Messianic salvation is described, the angels receive only the place of *worshipping spectators; organs* of this salvation they are not.

The εἰσάγειν τὸν πρωτότοκον, &c., will now explain itself. The writer evidently means to express the idea, that these words are connected with a passage which speaks of *the entrance of Jehovah the Saviour into the world*, hence, of the entrance of the *Son* into the world. He says, designedly, not υἱός, which would denote the incarnate, but πρωτότοκος, which, like the μονογενής of John, denotes the eternal Son of the Father, the πρωτότοκος πάσης κτίσεως (Col. i. 15). The ὅταν serves now, of course, to determine not the time *in* which, but the time *of* which Moses spake in Deut. xxxii. 43. The idea with all its modifications would have to be expressed thus: "But again he says *of the time* when he shall introduce the first born into the sphere of the earth," &c. He calls it the *sphere of the earth*, not the *world*, because the Redeemer appears in Deut. xxxii. 42 specially as the finisher of the exile, as he who should offer to his people a *national restitution* among the nations of the οἰκουμένη. He has in reality also offered this to his people; his disciples after him too did the same (Acts iii. 20, καιροὶ ἀναψύξεως breathing times from the yoke); but as Israel remained obdurate, they lost the offered deliverance, and remain deprived of it until they shall turn to the Lord after the fulness of the Gentiles is come into the church (Rom. xi. 23, ss.)

In vers. 7—9 a third argument follows. A statement concerning the angels is here opposed to one concerning the Son. The following is what is implied generally in the opposition. The angels, the mediators of the old covenant, stood in a very outward relation to the salvation that was to be wrought out; they had not to work out that salvation, but only to bear witness of it; they stood in the closest relation to nature, and the appearances of nature, chiefly those of a terrible kind. These appearances of nature had only a preparatory and pedagogical aim; the Son, on the contrary, stands in the closest relation to the inner moral life. God employed angels to impress with fear a rude unsusceptible people by means of miracles; the Son has founded a kingdom of righteousness consisting of those who become partakers of his nature in free and joyous love.—The author, accordingly, devotes himself more and more to a comparison of the *inner nature* of the old and the new covenant.

The seventh verse presents again a peculiar difficulty. So much indeed is evident, that the πρός is to be rendered not " to" but "respecting," in " reference to;" for the words here cited, Ps. civ. 4, do not in themselves form an *address* directed to the angels. It is doubtful whether the Sept., which is here cited word for word, has correctly rendered the sense of the original Hebrew. In the 104th Psalm the greatness of God in nature is described. In ver. 2 it is said: God makes use of the light as a garment, of the heaven as a tent, ver. 3, of the clouds as a chariot, &c. In the words which immediately follow עֹשֶׂה מַלְאָכָיו רוּחוֹת the *subject* must be רוּחוֹת and the predicate מַלְאָכָיו, *he makes the winds his messengers, flames of fire his servants*, he employs the winds and the flames as his servants, just as he makes use of the clouds as his chariot.—But does the Greek translation give the same sense? This is impossible, even grammatically, for then the words would have to run thus: ὁ ποιῶν ἀγγέλους αὐτοῦ τὰ πνεύματα, &c. But the article is at ἀγγέλους and not at πνεύματα. In spite of the rules of the language Calvin, Beza, Bucer, Grotius, Limborch, Michaelis, Knapp, and others have so rendered the Greek words as to make them correspond with the Hebrew.[1] But then these words themselves would not be suitable to our context. For, in the statement that God employs the winds as his messengers, nothing is

---

[1] The strange interpretation given by Bengel and Meyer—God makes his angels out of wind, out of a fine but still material substance, while the Son is immaterial and uncreated – needs no refutation.

expressed respecting the nature and rank of the *angels*, but only respecting the use of the *winds*. But, as we have already observed, the rules of the language render every doubt here superfluous. The Greek words can be rendered in no other way than this: "*who maketh his angels winds and his ministers a flame of fire.*"

Here, then, is another instance in which the writer appeals to a statement in the Sept. which owes its existence to an incorrect and inaccurate rendering. (So also Olshausen.) The attempt of Calvin, Beza, and others, to make the Greek words correspond with the Hebrew original in spite of the rules of grammar, is, as we have seen, vain and inadmissible; but equally so is, on the other hand, the attempt of Luther, Calov, Storr, Tholuck, and others, who would interpret the Hebrew original, in spite of the context of the psalm, according to the rendering of the Sept. Wherefore have recourse to such arts? Would any one in the present day take it amiss if a preacher were to give an excellent sermon on the verse, " The heart of man is a perverse and fearful thing ?"[1] And yet this verse will in vain be sought in the original text; the Hebrew words have quite another meaning. But though the idea is not to be found in that particular *place* of the original text of the Bible, it is still not the less *biblical;* and the same holds good of the idea in the citation before us. Throughout the New Testament (for example Rom. viii. 38; 1 Pet. iii. 22), the angels, at least a class of them, are regarded as δυνάμεις of God, *i.e.* as personal creatures furnished with peculiar powers, through whom God works wonders in the kingdom of nature, and whom he accordingly " makes to be storm-winds and flames of fire," in as far as he lets them, so to speak, incorporate themselves with these elements and operations of nature. It is a truth declared in the Holy Scriptures of great speculative importance, that the miracles of nature, for example the lightnings and trumpet sounds on Sinai, are not *wrought* immediately and directly by God the Governor of the world, but are *called forth* at his will by exalted creatures specially qualified for this work. This position the angels hold; they are there to work terrible wonders in the sphere of nature before the eyes of a yet uncultivated people. The writer found this idea expressed

---

[1] [The above is a translation of Luther's version of Jer. xvii. 9.]

shortly and tersely in that passage of the Sept., and he was quite as entitled to appeal to it in addressing his readers who made use of the Sept. as we are, in presence of a congregation using Luther's translation of the Bible, to appeal to that expression about the perverseness and fearfulness of the heart of man.

In the eighth verse πρός is, of course, to be taken in the same sense as in ver. 7, not as marking an address but as signifying "in reference to." It can therefore not be inferred at least from the preposition πρός, that the author regarded the passage in Ps. xlv. 7, 8 as a direct address to the Son of God. The words are spoken *in reference to the Son of God*. In how far they are so will be ascertained from a consideration of the passage in its original connection.

The 45th Psalm is a carmen epithalamium on the marriage of a king with the daughter of a foreign king, as appears from verses 10—12, and, according to ver. 2, the song is presented to the king by one of his subjects. There is not the slightest occasion for considering the psalm as a direct prophecy of Christ. And as the superscription plainly designates the psalm a song of songs, שִׁיר־יְדִידֹת, it is in all probability one of an ancient origin, and not belonging to the period after the exile, when already men had begun to discover more in the psalms than such human relations. The superscription ascribes the psalm to Korah, the contemporary of David and of Solomon. But, apart even from this superscription, the psalm suits no other king so well as Solomon. That hope which we found expressed by David (2 Sam. vii. and Ps. ii.) of an everlasting confirmation of his throne, recurs here, ver. 7; the king who is the subject of this song, is described as very rich; he has, according to ver. 9, ivory palaces, as Solomon had, 2 Kings vii.; he has gold of Ophir (ver. 10) as Solomon (1 Kings ix. 28); the daughter of Tyre, *i.e.*—according to the analogy of *daughter of Zion*,—the city of Tyre[1] congratulates him (ver. 13), and Solomon stood in close alliance with Tyre (1 Kings vii.;) the choice, too, of a foreign king's daughter not only occurred in the case of Solomon (comp. the song of songs)—this might be the case also with later kings— but in Solomon such a choice might as yet be justified, while, at

---

[1] Hitzig indeed understands the princess Jezebel as meant by the daughter of Tyre; she, however, was from Sidon.

a later period, a song celebrating a marriage so contrary to the law would scarcely have received a place among the collection of sacred songs. Already was the voice of prophecy lifted in all its majesty against Jezebel; and a powerful tribunate was formed in the cause of the theocracy against Amaziah (1 Kings xiv. 19, ss.) and later kings.—Some indeed find in ver. 17 a feature which does not answer to Solomon. The words " instead of thy fathers shall be thy sons" (*i.e.* these shall richly compensate for thy departed ancestors) are said not to be applicable to Solomon, as he had only a single ancestor who bore the crown. We might therefore be tempted to explain ver. 17, " thy sons shall compensate the *want* of ancestors;" but it is not probable that the poet should have referred to this want. Indeed there is no need of having recourse to any such shifts. Solomon had in reality no want of ancestors; and although only the last of these had borne a crown, this involved, according to the ideas then entertained, no defect of honour; nay, we find already from the book of Ruth, which was written with a view to exalt the house of David, how readily the real ancestors of David and Solomon were acknowledged as such, although they lived in a humble station. The poet could therefore with all propriety express the idea, that the glory of the ancestors of Solomon would be equalled and even surpassed by that of his posterity.

How now are the Hebrew words Ps. xlv. 7, s. to be translated? From ver. 3 to ver. 10 Solomon is addressed throughout, from ver. 11 onwards his bride is addressed. There is then in the outset no occasion for viewing the words, *thy throne, O God, is for ever and ever*, as an interposed ejaculatory prayer to God. How unsuitable would it have been, if the poet had placed the everlasting throne of God in opposition to the throne of David as not everlasting! Further, it is also evident, that we are not at liberty with Gesenius and Olshausen to translate the words by " thy divine throne." Even if the words were כִּסֵּא אֱלֹהֶיךָ (according to the anaolgy of הַר־קָדְשִׁי), that rendering would still be unnatural, and the other, " the throne of thy God," would be more proper. The words כִּסְאֲךָ אלהים, however, cannot signify, even grammatically considered, " thy divine throne" (this would require כסא אלהים כסאך), but only " thy throne, O God." An instance, indeed, seems to occur in Lev. xxvi. 42 (according to Gesenius' explanation), where the *genitive* is immediately joined to the *noun with the suffix* (אֶת־בְּרִיתִי יַעֲקוֹב my covenant of Jacob); but there יַעֲקוֹב is evidently not the *genitive of quality*, but the *adverbial accusative of relation*, and the relation of a covenant made by God with Jacob is evidently a different one from that of a throne *of divine majesty belonging* to a king; so that that passage does not afford the least analogy for the one before us. But granting that there were such an anlaogy in a grammatical point of view, it is still contrary to the sense and spirit of the Hebrew language to use אֱלֹהִים as a genitive of quality, and to flatten and degrade the idea of God or of divinity in a heathenish style to the idea of creature-majesty. Modern pantheism, indeed, speaks of a divine locality, or of a " divine" opera; heathenish insipidities of this kind were foreign to the purity of the Israelitish monotheism.

On the other hand, it was not foreign to the Israelitish mode of conception and expression, to denote persons who stood as the agents and representatives of God by the word אֱלֹהִים (sing.) or הָאֱלֹהִים (plur.)—not, however, by הָאֱלֹהִים sing.—compare Psalm lxxxix. 27, lxxiii. 15, &c. They were thus denoted, not because they were regarded as creatures equal with God, but because, in their relation to those who were subject to them, they were clothed with Divine authority. This might, with perfect propriety, be said of the " seed of David"—Solomon—especially at the time when reference is made to that prophecy of Nathan, that the throne of David should be established for ever and ever.

The Psalmist after those words thus goes on : " A sceptre of righteousness ($\epsilon\dot{v}\theta\dot{v}\tau\eta\varsigma$ = מִישׁוֹר in the Sept. frequently) is the sceptre of thy dominion; thou hast loved righteousness and hated iniquity. *Therefore* has thy God, O God, anointed thee with oil of joy more than thine associates." By the " associates" cannot be meant those holding office about the king's court; for, that the king is exalted in prosperity and glory above the officers of his court is true, and has ever been true not merely of righteous, but of all kings, the unrighteous as well, and could not therefore with any reason be represented as a special blessing consequent on the righteousness of Solomon. Least of all can the $\mu\epsilon\tau\acute{o}\chi o\iota\varsigma$

be explained, with Olshausen and others, of the angels; to these neither the Psalmist nor our author can have referred in this word; we shall soon see that the point of comparison between the Messiah and the angels lies in quite another part of the citation. The associates are evidently his associates in royal dignity—other kings; and the Psalmist says, that on account of his righteousness Solomon has received more joy, prosperity, and glory, than any other king of the earth. The anointing with oil of joy is not to be understood of the anointing to the office of king or prophet, or even of the anointing with the Holy Ghost in general, but the figurative expression is derived from the well-known custom of anointing the head at festivals (Deut. xxviii. 40; Psalm xxiii. 5, xcii. 11; Matth. vi. 17), and " to be anointed with oil of joy" is equivalent to being blessed with joy and prosperity.—That אלהים in the eighth verse is again vocative follows, not merely from the analogy of the seventh verse, but is evident of itself, and serves rather for the further confirmation of the correct rendering of ver. 7. It is impossible that אלהיך can be in apposition with אלהים; even in a vocative address such a construction would be foreign to the spirit of the Hebrew diction; besides, here in the nominative or subject such a redundance would be all the more intolerable, as the emphasis which it involves is altogether without occasion or aim. The LXX. have therefore rightly understood אלהים as the vocative and אלהיך as the subject. That אלהים has no article is explained by this, that it is not an address to God, the one, definite, well-known, but an address to a man.

The repeated address אלהים applied to Solomon close beside the designation of Jehovah as אלהים is certainly highly significant. The poet addresses him thus not out of flattery, but under the influence of the theocratic feeling that the dominion of God over Israel finds its manifestation in the dominion of the anointed of God over Israel. This involves the idea that the theocratic king is the *fulfiller of the will of God in Israel*.

How then does our author apply this passage? He does not say that these words of the psalm are in the sense of their author an *address* to Christ (comp. the remark on πρός), but that they are spoken *of Christ*, are applicable to him. That exalted dignity and rank was ascribed to Solomon *because, and in so far as* his sceptre was a sceptre of righteousness, *because, and in so far as* he loved righteousness and made the will of God his will. The Psalmist contemplates Solomon then as the *ideal* of a theocratic king, such as was conceived in 2 Sam. vii. and farther delineated in hope, Psalm ii. In as far as Solomon in reality made the will of God his will, in so far might he be accounted the *seed* promised to David, in so far might the predicate אלהים be assigned to him. It is quite possible and comprehensible, that in the first years of his reign it was believed that the prophecy of Nathan, 2 Sam. vii., and the hope of David, Psalm ii., 2 Sam. vii., found their fulfilment in Solomon, while the words of David were forgotten that the Lord spake " of the distant future." (It was thought, too, in the time of Constantine, that the reign of the thousand years had commenced!) But it soon appeared how mistaken this belief was, how far Solomon departed from a faithful fulfilment of the will of God. Although, however, that psalm—as a hymn on Solomon—was shown to have proceeded from human error, it did not, therefore, and in the same degree, *cease* to be prophetical, but it then first *became* a prophecy. It became apparent that the ideals delineated in that psalm under the guidance of the Holy Spirit would first be realized in the *future*. The ideal of the righteous king who absolutely fulfils the will of God, and to whom, therefore, the predicate אלהים truly belongs, and whose dominion is to have an everlasting continuance, is only very imperfectly fulfilled in Solomon, is first perfectly fulfilled in Christ. Thus those words cited from the psalm are spoken *respecting the Son*. In the sense of their human author they are neither a direct nor an indirect prophecy of Christ, but the object of which they treat, Solomon, was a real, a living prophecy of Christ, a type and prefiguration, and, in as far as those words represent Solomon in his typico-ideal not in his human-imperfect character, they are certainly in the sense of the Holy Spirit a prophecy pointing to our Saviour.

Inquire we now finally, how far we have in that declaration of the Psalmist *a proof of the superiority of the Messiah over the angels*. Three things are declared of the ideal of a theocratic king—consequently of the Messiah ; *a*, he is אלהים; his authority is the authority of God himself; *b*, his dominion is endless; *c*, both are true because he perfectly fulfils the will of God. The perfect theocratical king—therefore Christ (which required no proofs for the readers of the Epistle to the Hebrews)—stands in this threefold relation above the angels. *He is the absolute revelation of God and therefore himself God; the angels are only servants. He is King of an imperishable kingdom; the angels execute only periodical, commands; he rules in a moral way as founder of a kingdom of righteousness, and his whole dignity as Messiah is founded directly on his moral and spiritual relation to man; the angels are only mediators of outward appearances of nature, by which a rude, unsusceptible people are to be trained for higher things.*

Ver. 10—12. As ver. 8 s. is connected with ver. 7 by the words πρὸς τὸν υἱὸν, so is ver. 10 still more closely connected with ver. 8 s. by a mere καὶ, and indeed we shall soon see, that the two members ver. 8—9 and ver. 10—12 taken together, form the antithetical member to ver. 7.

Here also we will first consider the passage quoted (Ps. cii. 26—28) in its original meaning and connexion. The words in themselves have no difficulty; the Sept. has rightly rendered them, and the author follows the Sept.; the meaning of the words too is clear. But the question again recurs, how far these words, evidently spoken of *God*, can afford any proof of the superiority of the *Son* over the angels. The supposition that the author of the Epistle to the Hebrews by mistake, *i.e.* from complete ignorance of the context from which he took the passage, considered those words as an address directed to *Christ*, is too awkward to find any acceptance with us. The author of the Epistle to the Hebrews can scarcely be conceived of as so senseless, that, without any occasion, he should use words which apply to God as if they applied to the incarnate Son of God. So coarse a mistake would certainly not have escaped detection; for it is not to be forgotten that his *readers* were also in a certain sense his *opponents*, and would scarcely have allowed themselves to be drawn away from their deep-rooted prejudice in favour of the old covenant and the Old Testament Israel, by *bad* and *untenable* arguments. That supposition is all the more improbable when it is considered, that the author has evidently quoted all these

passages not from memory, but has carefully copied them from
the LXX., so that he could not possibly be ignorant of their
original context. In general, however, it is a very superficial
and shallow view that would lead us all at once to consider the
use of Old Testament passages in the New Testament as parallel
with the exegetico-dogmatic method of argumentation pursued
by the Rabbins. The apostles and apostolical men have,
indeed, exhibited in their epistles such a freedom from the spirit
of Jewish tradition, such an originality and youthful vigour of
new life, such a fineness and depth of psychological and historical
intuition, and the whole system of Christianity in its freshness
and originality stands in such contrast to the old insipid anti-
Messianic Judaism, and appears so thoroughly a new structure
from the foundation resting on the depths of Old Testament
revelation, and not a mere enlargement of the Pharisaico-Rabbi-
nical pseudo-Judaism, that it were indeed wonderful, if the same
apostolical men had in their interpretation of Old Testament
passages held themselves dependent on the Jewish exegesis and
hermeneutical method. In reality, however, the apostolical
exegesis of the Old Testament stands in directest opposition to
the Jewish-Rabbinical, so that one can scarcely imagine a more
complete and diametrical difference. In the Rabbinical interpretation it is always *single words*—studiously *separated* from the
context—from which inferences, arbitrary, of course, are drawn.
The Rabbins affirm, for example, that when a man lies three
days in the grave, his entrails are torn from his body and cast in
the face of the dead; *for* it is written in Mal. ii. 3, "I will also
cast the filth of your festivals in your face." (Sepher joreh
chattaim, num. 66.) Nay, the later Rabbinism, as a direct
result of this arbitrary procedure, went the length of drawing
inferences even from single letters. They taught, for example,
the transmigration of the soul, and that the souls of men ever
continue to live in men; thus the life of Cain passed into Jethro,
his spirit into Korah, his soul into the Egyptians (Ex. ii. 12 ss.),
for it is written Gen. iv. 24 יקם קין, and ק, י, and מ are
the first letters of Jethro, Korah and מצרי. (Jalkut rubeni,
num. 9.) The genuine pharisaical principle which forms the
basis of all this, is, *that the letter as such* is what is most significant.
The New Testament writers, on the contrary—as we have seen

in reference to Heb. i. 6—9, and as we shall see more and more as we proceed with the epistle—drew all their arguments from *the spirit* of the passages *considered in their connection*. Nothing at all is inferred from the mere letters of the passages quoted. In Ps. xlv. there is not a syllable about *angels*. When the author, notwithstanding, has adduced that passage as a proof that the Messiah is superior to the angels, he has, as we have seen, necessarily reckoned on a *rational consideration of the passage on the part of his readers*, and a *reflective logical comparison* of the passage with that in Ps. civ. 4, and the force of the argument proceeds only from such a judicious interpretation and attentive examination of the ideas and references objectively contained in both passages.

The procedure which he uniformly follows is not that of collecting passages in which the *words* " Son" and " angel" occur, and arbitrarily interpreting them—thus the Rabbins would have done—but of adducing the weightiest passages in which the Messianic salvation is prophesied of (substantially, although not at all under the name " Messianic"), and from these developing the *idea of this salvation*. Thus in vers. 7—12 the simple and fundamental idea which he wants to show is, that while the angels are employed by God as *ministering in temporary appearances of nature*, the Messianic salvation, on the contrary, is ever represented, *a*, as the lifting up of the man, the theocratical king, immediately to *God*; *b*, as the immediate saving act of God himself; *i.e.* in one word ; *c*, as an immediate relation of God to men without the intervention of mediation by angels. He finds this *idea* of the Messianic salvation in those expressions of the Psalms, but not dry outward statements respecting the *person* of Christ.

In ver. 8—9 the important truth was stated, that the true theocratical king, when his dignity is described, receives not the predicate " angel," but the predicate אלהים. He enters without the mediation of an angel, a מלאך י״י, into *immediate* unity with God himself. Have we then in ver. 8—10 a description of the saving work of a man who is one with God, we are therefore entitled to expect that in ver. 10—12 a passage will be adduced as a counterpart, in which the Messianic salvation is described as an *immediate* act *of God* to man, without the interposition of angels. For this is the difference between the Mosaic economy of the law and the Messianic economy of the gospel: *a*, in the economy of the law the man, Moses, is God's *servant*, and enters as yet into no immediate contact with God himself, but only with a form of the divine manifestation in the מלאך י"י; in the Messianic economy, on the contrary, the theocratic king is himself אלהים in an immediate relation of oneness with God, while nothing is said of the mediation of angels; *b*, in the Mosaic economy, God works upon men through angels; in the Messianic, God works immediately and directly on men without the need of angels. This latter idea, as has been already said, we must expect to find proved by a quotation in vers. 10—12.

Let us look now at the psalm. It is a song of complaint תְּפִלָּה, לְעָנִי and according to ver. 4 written during the exile; and it is evident from ver. 14 (thou shalt arise and have mercy upon Zion), that the author bewails not the sorrows of an *individual* but the misfortune of *his people*, although he represents this in an individualized lyrical form as his own affliction. After having pourtrayed in vers. 2—12 his own wretched condition, *i.e.* the condition of the Israelite and the Israelites, he appeals in ver. 13 to the immutability and eternity of God. It is self-evident that it is not the eternity as a metaphysical attribute of God, nor his unchangeableness as the immaterial Spirit that is spoken of, but the unchangeableness of Jehovah in his acts, in his relation to Israel, in a word the divine *covenant-faithfulness*. Upon this he grounds the inference ver. 14, that God shall again have mercy upon Zion, then will the heathen and their kings fear him (ver. 15), and men will speak of the saving work of God to coming generations (ver. 19), that God, namely, has looked down from heaven and heard the cry of the prisoners (vers. 2—21.) It is, then, *the deliverance from the captivity* that is here spoken of, consequently *the Messianic time*. The prophets before the exile had represented the Messiah as the *deliverer from the exile*. Not till towards the end of the exile was it revealed to Daniel, that the Messiah should come not immediately after the seventy years of the exile foretold by Jeremiah *in the strict sense*, but after seventy years of weeks; *i.e.* just that the state of being under the yoke of the heathen, which is substantially a state of exile, would, even after the local return to Canaan, stretch over a period of seventy years of weeks. The 102d Psalm does not yet discover the difference between a state of exile in the stricter, and in the wider sense; the Psalmist simply prays for the speedy arrival of the promised time of the redemption and the salvation, that salvation which, when it actually appeared, Luke i. 68, was denoted literally in the same way in which it had been denoted in Ps. cii. 20 as "as God's looking down upon his people."

At the conclusion of the psalm the prayer is again concisely expressed in the words, "Take me not away in the midst of my days (ere I have witnessed the deliverance of the people), *thy years* are to all generations." Here too the prayer for deliverance is enforced by the thought of God's unchangeableness, which implies here, besides the idea of the covenant-faithfulness of God, also that of his greatness. Upon this follow the words: "Thou hast in the beginning (לְפָנִים, κατ' ἀρχάς) laid the foundations of the earth, the heaven also is the work of thy hands. They shall perish, thou shalt remain," &c. The fundamental idea there then is, that *the hope of the promised Messianic deliverance rests upon God alone, and not on any kind of creature-help.* Emphasis is expressly laid on the fact that the heavens also and celestial beings are subject to time and to change, and that upon them the hope of the Messianic salvation cannot rest.

Thus do we find here, in reality, the precise idea expressed which we were led to expect. Ver. 8 s.: the Messianic salvation, in so far as it appears as the act of *a man*, an anointed one, "the seed of David," is already according to the prophecies of the Old Testament far superior to angel-revelations, is immediately divine, eternal, everlasting. Vers. 10—12 : the Messianic salvation, in so far as it appears as the act of *God*, is already according to the expectation of the Old Testament an immediate act of *God alone*, of which no creature, no celestial creature even, is capable.

Thus the Son, as in vers. 8—9, so in like manner in vers. 10—12, appears in a threefold opposition to the angels, ver. 7. *a, The Messianic redemption is an act of the everlasting faithfulness of God himself, not of a creature. b, It is everlasting, not mutable.*

c, It is founded on a moral relation of God to men, on the faithfulness of God, not on a relation to nature.

In conclusion then we see, that vers. 8—9 and vers. 10—12 are the two members parallel to each other, which taken together form the complete antithesis to ver. 7.

Ver. 13 forms the key-stone of the whole argument. Let us look back for a moment on the course of the reasoning. The New Testament revelation of God in the Son was opposed to that of the Old Testament as the absolute to the relative, ver. 4, and the absoluteness of the former derived, 1, from the name *Son* which is assigned in the Old Testament to the promised Messiah, but to none among the angels, ver. 5; 2, from this, that where the (Messianic) saving work of God, *i.e.* of the πρωτότοκος is prophesied of, merely the place of worshipping spectators belongs to the angels, ver. 6; 3, ver. 7—12, from the *immediateness* of the union of God with men in the Messianic salvation, from its *everlasting duration* and its *spiritual nature,* inasmuch as it rests on the reciprocal relation of human righteousness, vers. 8—9, and divine faithfulness, vers. 10—12.—It had been shown in ver. 8—9, as well as in ver. 10—12, that an immediate elevation of man to God, and an immediate act of grace on the part of God towards man, without the interposition of angels, were already laid down in the Old Testament as the fundamental characteristics of the Messianic salvation. This *immediateness* is now in ver. 13 still farther confirmed by a crowning passage from the Old Testament in which it is most clearly expressed. The Messias, it is said, shall sit upon God's throne, and take part in the divine dominion. Nowhere is this represented as belonging to an angel.

The quotation is from Ps. cx. 1. Bleek cannot allow this psalm to be taken as prophetical of the Messiah, because the hope of a personal Messiah was foreign to the time of David. This objection needs no refutation after what has been said at ver. 5. Tholuck also (Hebraerbr. Beilage i. p. 10) has rightly directed attention to 2 Sam. xxiii. 1 ss.—that saying of David in which he expresses so definite a hope of a definite posterity who should fulfil Nathan's prophecy, 2 Sam. vii. That we have, in Ps. cx., also an expression of that hope grounded on 2 Sam. vii.

should no longer be doubted. We by no means need to appeal to the declaration of Christ, Matth. xxii. 42 ss.; even if we were able, without doing violence to a sound understanding, to agree with those who regard that declaration not as Christ's real opinion, but as intended by him half in jest merely to lead the Pharisees into an inextricable difficulty—even if we were at liberty to adopt such a view, the composition of the 110th Psalm by David, and its Messianic signification, would still stand fast of itself. The remarkable representation of a sacerdotal king like to Melchisedek, which we find in this psalm, will not at all suit a time subsequent to that of David. The later kings stood partly in hostile relation to the priesthood, cultus, theocracy, and worship of Jehovah, partly, even when they stood in a peaceful and friendly relation to these as in the case of Hezekiah and Josiah, they showed this precisely by *not* invading the rights and offices of the priests; the attempt of the otherwise pious Uzziah to combine the priestly functions with the kingly was punished by God himself with the infliction of the disease of leprosy. In such a period, such a psalm, with the representation which it gives of a priest-king, could not have been composed. To unite the priestly with the kingly dignity was at that time as little to the *praise* of a king, as it is now to the praise of the emperor Henry IV. as an emperor, that he invested bishops and popes. As this, on the contrary, was a commendation under Charles the Great, and even under Henry III., so also was *that* a ground of praise in the time of David, of David the protector of the high priesthood against Saul, the man after God's heart, in opposition to whom the priests had no occasion for watching over and defending their rights, because they had no reason to dread any malicious invasion of these from the despotism of the king. We must therefore seek for the *date* of the psalm in the time of David.—With respect to its *contents*, modern critics have held the psalm to be a hymn upon David sung by one of his subjects. The first words correspond with this explanation: the Lord (God) said unto my lord (the king.) But the words immediately following, in which God is represented as having spoken, will not apply to David. It is easy to comprehend how Solomon should receive the predicate אלהים as the theocratic ruler, especially when he is contemplated as the ideal *seed of David*, and fulfiller of the will of God. But it cannot be comprehended how an Israelite should have spoken of David's sitting upon *God's throne*; for the throne of God was, as we learn from Ps. xi. 4, xxxiii. 14, &c., in the heaven;[1] a sitting upon God's throne was not applicable to David even by the boldest hyperbole, still less would ver. 4 be suitable to David, in which Jehovah is represented as having sworn to the king—the same who is spoken of in ver. 1—that he shall be a priest and king at the same time, and that *for ever* לְעוֹלָם. When had ever such a thing been promised to David? Bleek thinks there is no trace of the psalm's referring to the *future;* but do not ver. 1 (*the Lord said*) and ver. 4 (*the Lord hath sworn and will not repent*), refer plainly enough to a *prophecy* that had been given and was still *unfulfilled* (וְלֹא יִנָּחֵם fut.)? It is possible, indeed, that a prophecy referring to David's own future destinies *might* be meant; but it will be difficult to find any prophecy of such an import in reference to David. Nowhere else must we look for the נְאֻם י״י mentioned in Ps. cx. than in that very prophecy of Nathan, 2 Sam. vii. with which we are now so familiar, and there it is said, twice in succession, not of David, but in express contradistinction to him, of his seed: וַהֲכִינוֹתִי אֶת־מַמְלַכְתּוֹ ver. 12, and עַד־עוֹלָם, וְכוֹנַנְתִּי אֶת־כִּסֵּא מַמְלַכְתּוֹ, David shall indeed die, but his seed shall reign for ever. There, too, we find the words עַד־עוֹלָם of Ps. cx. 4. And we have already seen at ver. 5 of our chapter, that although Nathan had spoken of the *seed* collectively, David might yet expect, and did expect, the fulfilment of this promise in no other way than in a definite individual of his posterity. (With this the objection of Bleek falls of itself to the ground— that the idea of a personal Messiah was unknown in the time of David). What remains of Ps. cx. 4 finds its explanation also in 2 Sam. 7. Nathan had revealed to David that he was not appointed to build the Lord an house; he was appointed merely to reign; but his seed after him was to build an house to the Lord, and the Lord would build an house for it. If now the

---

[1] The mercy-*lid* over the ark of the covenant which shut out the accusing testimony (the ten commandments) from the view of God, is indeed in Luther's translation, but now here in the original, designated as a seat or throne of God.

seed of David was to do in a higher and more excellent degree that which in a less degree the builders of the tabernacle had done, this might properly be considered as a uniting of priestly-ecclesiastical with civil functions, and might be represented in the language of lyrical poetry as a government " after the order of Melchesedec." But if the seed of David is to have an house built for him by the Lord himself, and is to reign for ever and ever, he is thereby exalted to God's own throne ; God has built for him his house and his throne, he has built God's house ; the dominion of both is thus endless and unlimited, and becomes accordingly one and the same.

But while it is impossible that David can be the object of the psalm, he can be, and is, its author. For, from what other individual of the time of David are we at liberty to expect such an unfolding of the Messianic hope, than from that king who gave utterance to the prayer with which we are already familiar in 2 Sam. vii. 18—29 and chap. xxiii. 1 ss.?

This passage from the Psalms, then, is cited by our author. No angel, but a man, is chosen to an immediate unity of *dominion* with God, to absolute rule over all enemies, over the whole world. The angels, on the contrary, as the author says in ver. 14, by way of recapitulation, and looking back to ver. 7, are *ministering* spirits λειτουργικὰ πνεύματα ; they exist only on account of those who are appointed to be " heirs of salvation." *It is not the angels that are called into a relation of oneness with God, but man.* In this antithesis, the whole train of thought finds its conclusion.

A PRACTICAL INTERMEDIATE PART.

Chap. ii. 1—4.

In ch. ii. 1—4 the author immediately adds a practical application of the foregoing. All the more carefully must we hold fast the *New Testament* doctrine. Περίσσως is a familar expression, especially with the apostle Paul. Why the comparative is used here appears from the train of thought, which is as follows (as is plain also from ver. 2 and 3.) Apparently, the authority of the Mosaic law is higher than that of the gospel ;

for there God revealed himself by angels, here by a man. But it follows from what has been said, that the New Testament revelation, far from having less authority on that account, possesses rather *an authority by so much the greater*, that it was not given through the mediation of angels, but is immediate, consequently, that greater heed must be given, not to esteem it lightly.

Μήποτε παραῤῥυῶμεν, A.D. and other manuscripts read παραρυῶμεν, which, however, is not a different reading, nor an error in the writing (Tholuck), nor a poetical form, but, as Sturz (de dial. Maced. et Alex.) already perceived, and Thiersch (de Pent. vers. Alex. p. 85) has since further proven, nothing more than an Alexandrian orthography. The form παραῤῥυῶμεν cannot be the conj. pres. act. of παραῤῥυέω, as this verb nowhere occurs, but is supplied by the grammarians for the explanation of certain forms. We have here simply the conj. aor. sec. pass. of παραῤῥέω to flow by,—lest we *unconsciously slide past* (comp. Sept. Prov. iii. 21). Some supply τὰ ἀκουσθέντα, in which case it would signify—" that we forget not the things we have heard," but this gives an almost tautological idea. When others supply τὴν σωτηρίαν in the sense of "everlasting happiness," something heterogeneous is thereby introduced into the words. The best way certainly is to supply τῶν ἀκουσθέντων; "that we may not even yet entirely fall away from the doctrine we have heard." For this was the specific danger that threatened them. Whoever of those Jewish Christians should once treat what specifically belonged to the New Testament as a *secondary thing*, to which he needed not to give such anxious heed as to its connexion with the Mosaic ordinances and law, might come *unconsciously and imperceptibly* to lose entirely his Christian knowledge and love for the Gospel. (Similarly De Wette, Bleek, Tholuck.)

Ver. 2—3. The idea already implied in the first verse,—that the gospel *because* given to men by Jesus possesses all the higher and holier claims, is now further unfolded as the ground of what is said in ver. 1. Εἰ introduces an argument e concessis; that the law is βέβαιος (*i.e.* has a fully attested divine authority) was undisputed on the part of the readers. This authority, however, rested substantially on the fact, that the law *was promulgated by angels*. The question presents itself, whence arose this view of the co-operation of angels in the giving of the law from Mount

Sinai. Among the more recent theologians the opinion is pretty prevalent, that this was a belief entertained by the Jews in the time of Christ, a rabbinical notion, of which Stephen (Acts vii. 53), Paul (Gal. iii. 19), and the author of this epistle availed themselves for their respective objects. If it should be granted that it was nothing more than a notion belonging to that time, it would not therefore follow that it was superstitious; on the contrary, there lay beneath it a profound truth. Moses did not make the law but received it; the voice which spake the ten words, Ex. xx., the finger which wrote them, could not, however, be immediately ascribed to God; it was rightly conjectured that those appearances were brought about by the agency of exalted creatures, and that forms of revelation so external do not correspond with the eternal and invisible nature of God. And that is precisely what our author means to urge, namely, that the revelation of God in the *person* of Jesus Christ is one which is absolutely adequate; that, however, which consists in the mere *utterance of a law* is not adequate. The whole reasoning, therefore, would rest on a profound truth, even if that view respecting the co-operation of angels on Mount Sinai were a mere rabbinical theologumenon.

But it is not a mere theologumenon; it has a *real* foundation in the statements of God's word, of the old Testament. We will not, indeed, and are not warranted to refer here to the מלאך יי; for although it is always of importance to bear in mind that God, in the time of Moses, chose for the form in which he appeared that of the angelic species, still, the *angel of the Lord* was no individual created angel; least of all would this explain the use of the plural in the passage before us—δι' ἀγγέλων. We would rather refer—in as far as regards, in general, the origin of the doctrine of angels before the exile—to the passage in Joel iv. 11 (at the final judgment the Gentiles shall assemble together; "there God lets his mighty ones come down") compared with 2 Kings xix. 35 ("the angel of the Lord came down and smote the camp of the Assyrians.") With reference, however, to the special co-agency of angels on Sinai, we would appeal, with Olshausen, to the two passages Deut. xxxiii. 2 s.: Psalm lxviii. 18. In the first passage, in the song of Moses, it is said: God shined forth from Mount Paran, he came with ten thousand of holy ones. The form רִבְבוֹת is stat. constr. plur. of רְבָבָה myrias; רִבְבוֹת־קֹדֶשׁ, therefore, means multitudes or hosts of holy ones. It is then said in ver. 3: Yea he loveth the tribes; *all his holy ones are at thy hand; they sit at thy feet; he receives thy words.* Those who sit are evidently the Israelites who sit at the foot of the mount, as it were at God's feet; the subject to *receives* can be no other than Moses. There is thus an antithesis between the "they" and the "he." But this antithesis cannot be that which results from placing emphasis on the וְהֵם, for then וְהוּא must have stood before יִשָּׂא. But, as this is not the case, וְהֵם can only be used in opposition to the foregoing קְדֹשִׁים, *so that these holy ones are plainly distinguished from the Israelites as different persons.* It may also be supposed on other and independent grounds, that the Israelites are not meant by these "holy ones." In the first place, the former are never by Moses either described as holy ones or designated by that epithet; in the chapter immediately preceding (chap. xxxii.), he speaks much of their unholiness and obduracy. But in the second place, if by these holy ones the Israelites are to be understood as meant, then must we give to בְיָדְךָ the signification "in thy *protecting* hand," "in thy protection," a signification which this expression had not yet obtained in the time of Moses. Finally, the idea as a whole—that God protects the Israelites, and bears them, as it were, in his hands—would be altogether out of place in this description of the giving of the law from Sinai. Four distinct and independent reasons, then, compel us to render the words: "all his holy ones stand at thy hand (at this side, near thee), and to explain this of the hosts of angels standing near to God. In the same way must we explain the "multitudes of saints" spoken of in ver. 2. The Alexandrian translator must also have perceived that angels were spoken of here; he has, in true Alexandrian fashion, put into the text the correct interpretation of רִבְבֹת קֹדֶשׁ, by substituting the words ἐκ δεξιῶν αὐτοῦ ἄγγελοι μετ' αὐτοῦ in place of a translation of the to him obscure words אֵשׁ דָּת לָמוֹ ver. 2.

The other passage to which we would refer, and which serves to confirm our explanation of the foregoing, is Ps. lxvii. 18. The 68th Psalm belongs to the time of Solomon; not to an earlier period, since in ver. 30 mention is made of the temple in Jerusalem; nor to a later, as in ver. 28 the princes of Naphtali and Zebulon appear with presents before the 'King, which could not possibly have taken place after the separation of the two kingdoms; chiefly is ver. 32 applicable to Solomon, where mention is made of the Egyptian and Ethiopian ambassadors bringing gifts, and also ver. 17, where it is said that God from this time forth for ever has made his dwelling place "on the hill."—In this psalm we read ver. 18: "the chariots of God are twenty thousand, many thousands; the Lord is with them on Sinai in the holy place."—The author of our epistle, therefore, was fully justified by what he read in the Old Testament in calling the law *a word spoken by angels.*

This word was $\beta\acute{\epsilon}\beta a\iota os$ (see above), and every $\pi a\rho\acute{a}\beta a\sigma\iota s$ (positive transgression), nay, even every $\pi a\rho a\kappa o\acute{\eta}$ (negative omission) received its just recompense. To designate the recompense, the author, who evidently aims at elegance of style, uses the more select, more rare, and sonorous word $\mu\iota\sigma\theta a\pi o\delta o\sigma\acute{\iota}a$.— If this held good already of the law,—how shall we escape (namely, the just recompense) "if we neglect so great $\sigma\omega\tau\eta\rho\acute{\iota}a$, which is confirmed to us by those who heard it as one which, at the first, was spoken by the Lord ?" A twofold antithesis to the law is here specified. First, the law was a mere word ($\lambda\acute{o}\gamma os$) which, indeed, laid commands upon men, but imparted no strength or inclination for their fulfilment, the gospel, on the contrary, is a *salvation,* a *redemption,* an act. (Some would, most unhappily, and without any occasion given in the text, but rather destroying the beauty of the idea, explain $\sigma\omega\tau\eta\rho\acute{\iota}a$ by $\lambda\acute{o}\gamma os$ $\tau\hat{\eta}s$ $\sigma\omega\tau\eta\rho\acute{\iota}as$ with an arbitrary reference to Acts xiii. 26.) Secondly, the *salvation* has been revealed and preached to men, directly and *from first hand,* by the Lord *himself,* not from second hand by the angels. This is implied in the words $\dot{a}\rho\chi\grave{\eta}\nu$ $\lambda a\beta o\hat{\upsilon}\sigma a$, &c. ($'A\rho\chi\grave{\eta}\nu$ $\lambda a\mu\beta\acute{a}\nu\epsilon\iota\nu$ used by later Greek writers instead of the classical $\check{a}\rho\chi\epsilon\sigma\theta a\iota$.) The *beginning* cannot, of course, be understood here as forming an antithesis to the *continuance*; as if the two acts $\dot{a}\rho\chi\grave{\eta}\nu$ $\lambda a\beta o\hat{\upsilon}\sigma a$ $\lambda a\lambda\epsilon\hat{\iota}\sigma\theta a\iota$ and $\dot{\epsilon}\beta\epsilon\beta a\iota\acute{\omega}\theta\eta$ were co-ordinated, and the sentence to be resolved thus $\dot{a}\rho\chi\grave{\eta}\nu$ $\check{\epsilon}\lambda a\beta\epsilon$ $\lambda a\lambda\epsilon\hat{\iota}\sigma\theta a\iota$ $\kappa a\grave{\iota}$ $\dot{\epsilon}\beta\epsilon\beta a\iota\acute{\omega}\theta\eta$, in which case the idea would be—that the salvation was at first spoken by the Lord himself, but afterwards had been delivered to us as sure by those who heard it. Where then would be the difference between the *salvation* and the law? The law, too, was *at first* given by God, and then brought by angels to men. The author of our epistle, however, lays no emphasis on the fact, that the salvation was given from God ὑπὸ τοῦ θεοῦ, but that it was brought to men *from the very first by* (διά) *the Lord*, consequently, not first by intermediate persons. Ἐβεβαιώθη, is therefore, of course, not co-ordinate with ἀρχὴν λαβοῦσα λαλεῖσθαι, but λαβοῦσα depends on ἐβεβαιώθη. *That* the *salvation* was revealed directly by the *Lord* is what has been delivered to us by the ἀκούσαντες the ear (and eye) witnesses as a certainty, and consequently, as a divine authentication of the σωτηρία.

Some have found in vers. 1—3 a proof, that the epistle to the Hebrews could in no case have been written by the apostle Paul. (Euthal., Luth., Calv., &c.) For Paul, far from excluding himself from the number of eye-witnesses, rather lays all weight on the fact, that he had seen the (risen) Lord himself, 1 Cor. xv.; Gal. i. This argument is, however, without force; other grounds there may be against the Pauline origin of the epistle, but in these verses there is none. It is one thing to have once seen the risen Lord, it is another thing to be an ear-witness of the *salvation* spoken by Christ, *i.e.* of the entire revelation of God in Christ. (Comp. Acts i. 21.) The same Paul, who in writing to the Corinthians who doubted of the resurrection, or to the Galatians who disputed his apostolic mission, appeals to the former fact, must yet have acknowledged that he was not an eye-witness of the *salvation* in the latter sense. Moreover, the 1 plur. in ver 1 is not *communicative*, but merely *insinuatory*.

Ver. 4. It is quite consistent with the practical aim which our author never loses sight of, that he attaches only a subordinate value to the confirmation of the Gospel by miracles. He says —συνεπιμαρτυροῦντος. Μαρτυρεῖν means to bear witness of a thing which is still under question, doubtful,—ἐπιμαρτυρεῖν to testify of a thing already established,—συνεπιμαρτυρεῖν to give an additional testimony to a thing in itself certain, and confirmed by proofs from other sources. This implies that the *salvation* in Christ does not properly stand in need of confirmation by miracles, but bears already in itself the testimony of its truth. And, indeed, it will never happen, that a heart which is *inwardly* far from the truth of the Gospel, which is wanting in repentance and self-knowledge, the spiritual hunger and thirst, will be, so to speak, forced into an acknowledgment of the truth of this Gospel by an appeal to the miracles which accompany it. On the contrary, to such hearts the miracles are rather προσκόμματα, "that with seeing eyes they see not, and with hearing ears they hear not." Only the heart which has first experienced in itself the miracle of regeneration, of creative renewal, is capable of the *humility* which *believes*, even where it does not *comprehend*. For this very reason, however, the miracles are not something *non-essential*; but, as in the time of Christ, so still, they serve the end of being boundary stones between faith and unbelief, *signs* of God for the believing spirit, intimating that he is a living God, who stands above, not beneath his works, chiefly as the distributor of life and the Saviour, above that nature which is fallen by sin, and is subject to death, (in which view the resurrection of Christ, the first-fruits forms the centre point of all miracles),—and *signs* of faith which, in miracles, learns and exercises humility.—It is, moreover, worthy of observation, that this very passage which ascribes to miracles the humble function implied in the word συνεπιμαρτυρεῖν, furnishes a *principal proof of the historical reality of the miracles*, and, with this, of the supernatural character of Christianity in general. A man who wrote before the year 70, speaks of miracles, even where he does not give them a high place, as of well-known and undisputed facts!

Miracles may be regarded in a fourfold aspect, first, with respect to their *design* as σημεῖα (אוֹת), signs, miraculous testimonies in behalf of any truth; secondly, with respect to their *nature* as τέρατα (מוֹפֵת), *i.e.*, supernatural acts; thirdly, with respect to their *origin* as δυνάμεις, because wrought by higher powers; and finally, in their *specifically Christian* aspect as πνεύματος ἁγίου μερισμοί, as exercised by those who, according to the will and wise distribution of God, are endowed with the particular gifts of miracles (comp. 1 Cor. xii. 11.)

SECTION SECOND.

(Chap. ii. 5—18.)

IN THE SON MAN IS RAISED ABOVE THE ANGELS.

In the first section it was shown, that already the Old Testament points to a future absolute revelation of God to man, a revelation through a Mediator, by whom man should enter into immediate contact with God and God with man, and that this predicted revelation of God is, even in the Old Testament, placed higher than that which was given through the mediation of angels. It was therefore the dignity of the Son as such, his person and office, that was first spoken of.

In the second section, on which we now enter, the one idea already implicitly contained in the first section (i. 8—9), namely, that in the Son, *man* is immediately exalted to a union with God such as belongs not to the angels, is taken up and independently carried out. Here again, the 5th verse, which contains the new theme, is connected by means of the conjunction γάρ with the concluding words of the foregoing section. The new idea—that the divine dominion over the future kingdom is ascribed not to the angels but to the son of man, follows quite naturally upon the exhortation in ver. 1—4 as a new proof, but at the same time comes into co-ordination with the whole of the first section, chap. i. 5—14; the first section was the one foundation upon which the exhortation, chap. ii. 1—4, is made to rest; chap. ii. 5, together with its further development in ver. 6—18, forms the other foundation.—Thus the author, with great beauty of style, bridges over the space between the concluding words of the first section and the announcement of the new theme, just as we observed before in chap. i. 4.

Before, however, proceeding to follow out exegetically this new theme, it may not be without advantage to view somewhat more closely the ground-idea of the new section in itself, and to make ourselves familiar with it. That not merely the Son as the eternal only begotten of the Father or the first-born (πρωτότοκος) of every creature is higher than the angels, but that *man also as such* is called (of course in Christ) to a much more immediate union with God than belongs to angels, and that therefore man, as regards his proper destination, is higher than the angels, —this is a statement which at first sight will appear surprising, as we are generally wont to regard the angels as *superior* beings. And, indeed, it is not without reason that we do so. For, according to the statements of the Holy Scripture, the angels are endowed with higher and less limited gifts and powers, and although as creatures they cannot be conceived of as unlimited by space, and consequently, as incorporeal, still they have an unspeakably freer and less circumscribed relation to space and to matter than men have in their present state. They clothe themselves with visible matter and put off this garment again; they transfer themselves to wheresoever they please, they are not bound to a body of clay, and as they are without sexual distinction, (Matt. xxii. 30) there exists among them neither any development of the individual from childhood through the various steps of age, nor of the race, through successive generations. The entire species has come from the creative hand of God *complete* in all its individuals, complete as the diamond which sparkles with perpetual and unchanging lustre.—How now, shall we reconcile it with this, that our author should place above the angels poor weak *man*, hemmed in by space and a gross body, developing himself upon the basis of animal sexuality? Just in the same way as we can reconcile it with the weakness and meanness of the rose-bush, that there is in it, notwithstanding, a more excellent life than in the diamond. The enamel of the rose when it has reached its bloom is something far superior to the glitter of the diamond. So also will man, when he reaches the bloom of his *glorified* life, unspeakably excel the angels in glory. Man's superiority lies just in his *capability of development.* When the diamond is once disturbed by the ray of a burning reflector it is irrecoverably gone; so are the angels, once fallen, for ever lost, according to the doctrine of Scripture. The rose can with difficulty be hurt, and even from its root it will still send forth new life; so was man rendered capable even by sin (the possibility of which, though not its actual entrance, was necessary in consequence of his freedom) of entering into full spiritual life-fellowship with God, through the help of the Saviour entering into him, nay, capable of receiving the person of the redeeming Son of God as a member into his race. Hence also, it is the planet-system that has been assigned to man as the habitation and the theatre of that absolute revelation of God in Christ,—the planet-system, in which the antithesis between the fixed-star-like, or angel-like independent *sun* and the animal-like dependent *moon* finds its genuine human reconcilement in the *planets*, and most completely in the *earth*—while the angels, as the "hosts of heaven," have their dwelling place in the fixed stars, where there is no opposition between illuminating and illuminated bodies, where planets do not revolve round suns, but fixed stars around fixed stars.[1]

In ver. 5 the ground-idea is first of all expressed in a negative form. The οἰκουμένη ἡ μέλλουσα, the future terrestrial globe, *i.e.* the future kingdom (comp. Isa. lxvi. 22) הָעוֹלָם הַבָּא is nowhere represented in the Old Testament as ruled over by angels. The positive antithesis to this follows in vers. 6, 7 in the form of a citation which plainly enough implies the statement, that *man* rather is appointed to the dominion over "all things."

Ver. 6, 7. The citation is taken from Ps. viii. 5—7; the passage is quoted according to the Sept., with this exception, that the words καὶ κατέστησας αὐτὸν ἐπὶ τὰ ἔργα τῶν χειρῶν σου, which are not found in the original Hebrew but are added in the LXX., are omitted by our author. The manner in which he introduces the quotation διεμαρτύρατο δέ πού τις λέγων appears at first sight strange, but in nowise implies that the writer (as Koppe, Dindorch, Schulz thought) did not know where the citation was to be found.[2] For we find a similar indefiniteness also in chap. iv. 4, where the words cited ("God rested on the seventh day") are of such a kind that it was impossible the author could be ignorant of where they originally stand. That he knew this, too, in the case before us, is evident from the exactness with which he cites according to the Sept.; while at the same time he omits those words of the Sept. which

---

[1] See this view further developed and vindicated in my essay "Die Weltanschauung der Bibel und die Naturwissenschaft" in the journal "Die Zukunft der Kirche," principally in p. 31 ss. and p. 55 ss.

[2] Still less, of course, does it imply, that he meant to throw doubt on David's being the author of the psalm, and to represent its author as an unknown person;—as Grotius thought.

do not belong to the original. Πού τις is therefore a mere arbitrary mode of expression (which was peculiar also to Philo, comp. Bleek on this passage);.the author forbears to specify the place of the citation, just because he takes it for granted that it was quite well known. In the same way might a writer or speaker in our own time say—"one has said: Here I stand I can do nothing else." With respect to the quotation itself it presents two difficulties; a, the words παρ' ἀγγέλους evidently appear to belong to those words of the citation from which the author draws his inferences, comp. ver. 5. His object is to prove from the passage in the psalms, that man was indeed made lower than the angels, but only for a time, not for ever; rather, that precisely to man, and not to the angels, is the dominion over the οἰκουμένη ἡ μέλλουσα ascribed. But those very words παρ' ἀγγέλους have no foundation in the original Hebrew, the words there are וַתְּחַסְּרֵהוּ מְעַט מֵאֱלֹהִים. b, The words βραχύ τι are evidently understood by the writer, ver. 9, in the sense of *time* as meaning "a short time." "We see Jesus who was for a short time made lower than the angels crowned." To take βραχύ τι there in the sense of *degree* would yield no sense whatever. Consequently the author has also in ver. 7, in this citation, understood βραχύ τι in the sense of *time*. But מְעַט in the Hebrew, and βραχύ τι in the Sept., according to the opinion of its authors, are to be understood in the sense of *degree*; this at least is the most prevalent opinion among more recent critics (also that of Olshausen.) The only thing then that remains for us is here again to give the psalm itself our direct and unprejudiced consideration. Whether or not the psalm was written by David is here a matter of perfect indifference; reasons, however, will appear occasionally and unsought for, to warrant our ascribing its authorship to him. Let us consider, first of all, the psalm itself.

"Jehovah, our Lord, how mighty is thy name upon the whole earth, thou whose honour is praised[1] above the heaven." Here,

---

[1] תְּנָה cannot be imperf. which in a relative clause would be altogether without sense. If we derive it from נתן then it must be the 3 sing. praet. with ה fin. (comp. ver. 7 שַׁתָּה instead of שַׁתָּ) and apocopated ן. In this case אֲשֶׁר must point back to שִׁמְךָ. " Thy name,

already, there is an evident antithesis between earth and heaven. The God, whose majesty is praised above in all heavens, disdains not to acquire for himself also on the poor small earth a glorious mighty name by the acts of his covenant-faithfulness (as the Lord, our Lord.) Ver. 2, " Out of the mouths of babes and sucklings hast thou established a power for thee, because of thine adversaries, to subdue the enemy, the avenger." It is not easy to say what the poet had in his mind here. At first sight we might be tempted to imagine a reference to some special case, in which a hostile warrior had, by the weeping and lisping of a child, been moved to pity towards its parents. But a definite case of this kind which the readers of the psalm might have been able to call to mind without farther description, does not occur in all the Old Testament ; nor is it the enemies of a man but the enemies of God that are spoken of ; and, besides, the subsequent part of the psalm treats solely of the high position which God hath assigned to man as such. We must, therefore, find in ver. 2 a reference of a more universal kind. God has on account of his enemies, for their subjugation, provided a power, and that out of the mouth of weak sucklings ! By the enemies of God we must understand the whole power opposed to God on the earth, the kingdom of darkness, the kingdom of the serpent; by the power which God hath provided we are to understand the whole of those preparations which God hath made or promised to make for overcoming the darkness. What are the preparations of this kind with which we are made acquainted in the Old Testament? Has God, perhaps, promised that he will at one time send hosts of angels who shall trample on the serpent's head ? No ; when his object is to chastise sinful men, he places a cherub with a flaming sword before the closed gate of paradise ; but when the future redemption from the bondage of the serpent, from death, is spoken of, then

which has made thy glory above the heaven." This, however, is a very forced idea. The simplest way is to point the word thus תֻּנָּה (as Pual of תִּנָּה Jud. v. 11, xi. 40, which corresponds well enough with the ἐπήρθη of the LXX.), or, if it be thought preferable, to point תָּנָה in the sense habitare, from which תָּנוֹת "dwellings" is derived. But the latter root did not belong to the Hebrew till after the captivity, while תָּנָה celebrare is a primitive poetical expression.

no mention is made of an angel, but the seed of the woman is to bring the salvation, hence, though erroneously and hastily, she fixes her hope on the boy that first comes from her womb, she has now a man child, and thinks that with the seed of the woman she has at the same time recovered the possession of the God whom she had lost (left behind in paradise.) And from this time forth, all hope of salvation was turned towards the birth of the heirs of the theocratic blessing, and on the preservation and protection of these first-born. The original promise of the seed of the woman separates itself into many branches; when a son is born to Lamech he calls him Noah, for he hopes that he will bring comfort to men in their trouble and labour upon the earth which God has cursed (Gen. v. 29); all the hope of Abraham is turned towards the birth of Isaac and the preservation of his life, Isaac's hope rests upon Jacob; the whole prospect of future salvation always rests on such weak beings; upon the child which slumbers in a basket among the sedges of the Nile, rested the salvation of Israel; and, moreover, David's entire faith rested on the seed, which was to be the Son of God, and was to reign for ever with God. (Comp. Hofmann, Weissag. u. Erfullung. part i. p. 195.) This psalm then certainly suits no author better than David. The same royal singer, who in Psalm ii. and cx. admired the divine majesty of the seed promised to him, is, in Psalm viii., lost in adoring wonder that God has selected a lowly son of man as the instrument of his divine conquests.

Sucklings, weak children, are the threads on which the hope of Israel hangs. (How natural was it for the reflective reader already here to carry out the antithesis; God has not told his people to direct the eye of their hope to the appearances of angels, and to hosts of angels.)

The 4th verse of the 8th Psalm contains nothing that might serve to confirm what is said in ver. 3; that the poet considers the heaven as the work of God, can be no reason or proof that God has chosen children to be the instruments of his power. We are therefore not entitled to give to כי the argumentative signification "for," but must render it as a syntactic particle by "when," so that ver. 4 forms an antecedent clause to ver. 5. "When I look upon thy heavens the work of thy fingers, the moon and the stars which thou hast prepared; what (I must then exclaim) is man that thou are mindful of him, and the son of man that thou visitest him." To translate the words מַה־אֱנוֹשׁ "how excellent is man," as Böhme and Kuinoel do, is forbidden by the sense of אֱנוֹשׁ, which, as is well known, always designates man on the side of his weakness and frailty. The whole passage is evidently rather an exclamation of adoring wonder, that God, this mighty ruler of all heavens, should let himself down to poor weak man, the suckling, and should give him so high a rank. The words מַה־אֱנוֹשׁ then, express the contrast between the weakness of man and his high destination, —not, however, the result of the latter. The antithesis vaguely and generally implied in ver. 2—that He who is enthroned in the heavens disdains not the earth as the scene of his majesty—is thus rendered more definite in ver. 3—5.

But the promised glory is at first only *promised*; it lies still in the future; that it may *soon* be realized is the hope which the Psalmist expresses in the 6th verse of the Psalm: וַתְּחַסְּרֵהוּ מְּעַט מֵאֱלֹהִים, "thou hast made him to want a little of God." חסר signifies "to want," in Piel, "to cause to want," so in Eccles. iv. 8, "I cause my soul to want good." The rendering: "Thou hast made him a little less than God" is therefore, to say the least, arbitrary; nor does it suit the context, in which all emphasis is rather laid upon this, that man, who is not "a little" but infinitely inferior to God, is, notwithstanding, appointed to share with God in the dominion over the world. We are therefore to understand מִן not in the comparative, but (as in Eccles. iv. 8) in the privative sense, and מְעַט not as significant of *degree*, but of *time*. *For a little while* must man be deprived of God—not God qua Jehovah, for it is purposely not מִמֶּיךָ, but God qua Elohim, *i.e.* the contemplation and enjoyment of the visible nearness of God in his glory as the Creator; but the time comes when he shall be crowned with glory and honour, and shall reign over all the creatures of God (ver. 6—9.) Thus does God make his name glorious on the earth (ver. 10.)

The second difficulty in regard to βραχύ τι now disappears of itself. We see that מְעַט is to be taken in the sense *of time*. But the first difficulty, too—namely, that παρ' ἀγγέλους is not found in the original Hebrew, is now easily removed. *If we suppose this* παρ' ἀγγέλους *to be also not in the Greek text, the force of the argument drawn from the citation remains still quite the same.* The psalm contains the idea, that God who rules over all heavens has made the salvation to rest *precisely on weak sons of men*, and has destined *the sons of men to be the future lords of his kingdom.* If also the antithesis be not expressly stated, that it is not angels who are the promised saviours and rulers, it is still clearly enough implied in the train of thought which is pursued. The LXX. have actually put this antithesis into the text, although not in the clearest manner; the writer of our epistle, who always cites from the LXX., could do the same with all the more safety that the whole argumentative force of the passage depends *not at all upon those words which owe their existence to an inaccurate rendering of the original.* Nay, he might do this with all the more reason, seeing that the translation παρ' ἀγγέλους, although inaccurate, is yet by no means without occasion. The LXX. were induced to adopt it because the Hebrew does not say: "Thou (Jehovah) hast caused him to want *Thee* for a short time," but "Thou (Jehovah) hast caused him to want *Elohim.*" They thought that אֱלֹהִים must denote a subject different from Jehovah (or a plurality of such.) And there is something true in this, if we are not justified in at once understanding אֱלֹהִים of the *angels.* Without doubt, however, אֱלֹהִים denotes God in a different point of view from יְהוָה. He is called Jehovah as the personal, living, free-willing, and hence, chiefly, as the faithful covenant-God; Elohim, on the other hand, as the adored, all-governing, Creator and Lord of the worlds, in his creative majesty. The Psalmist, therefore, would not, and could not, say: Jehovah, thou hast caused man to want *Thee;* since God qua Jehovah has never withdrawn himself from men. But he might truly say: Jehovah, thou hast made man to want the godhead—the contemplation of and intercourse with the world-governing godhead in its glory. The idea which the LXX. have substituted for this: "Thou hast made him lower than the angels," evidently agrees with it substantially; for this is substantially wherein the superiority of the inhabitants of heaven consists, that as they serenely fulfil the will of God, so they enjoy the undisturbed vision of God, and intercourse with him. The gist of the argument, however, rests, as we have said, not on παρ' ἀγγέλους; on the contrary, there follows in ver. 8 still another inference such as does not presuppose any express mention of angels at all in vers. 6—7.

Ver. 8. The words and meaning are clear. When the author draws the inference from the fact of *all things* having been (in the way of promise) made subject to man, that *nothing* can be excepted—he, thereby, suggests to every thinking and attentive reader the special application, that the angels also will then be subject to man.

Here this train of thought concludes. With the words νῦν δέ, which must be regarded as belonging to ver. 9, an entirely new train of thought begins, the design of which is to show, in how far man has been already invested with the glory and elevation above the angels ascribed to him in Ps. viii., and in how far he has still to expect this. At present, indeed, man as such, *i.e. humanity*, has not yet attained to that elevation. Still, in *the person of Jesus*, who (although the Son of God, and already in himself higher than the angels, according to chap. i. yet) by his incarnation has been made lower than the angels like to us, a first-fruits of humanity is raised above the angels. But he is raised only to draw *all the rest* after him; for it was necessary that he should suffer, just in order that as a captain he might make many sons partakers of his glory.

How then was it possible, that such a commentator as Bleek should so entirely mistake and misunderstand a train of thought so clear throughout! He acknowledges (in p. 259) that "it seems as if the person whom we are to understand as meant by that man, ver. 6 s., were first designated in ver. 9," and yet denies that the writer of the Epistle to the Hebrews has used the ἄνθρωπος in ver. 6 in the general collective sense! But, in truth, the opportunity was too tempting of fastening upon our author, here again, a grossly Rabbinical misunderstanding of a psalm. True, the writer says not a single word of the Messiah in vers. 6—7, but places in opposition to the species angels to whom the οὐκ. ἡ μέλλ. is not to be made subject, the species *sons of man* to whom (according to Ps. viii. and Heb. ii. 10) it is to be made subject, and "it seems" as if the relation of Jesus to this general prophecy were first spoken of in ver. 9—and yet, the author must have taken the eighth Psalm, which is not Messianic, for a Messianic Psalm! True, the expression מה־אנוש cannot, as Bleek himself acknowledges, be understood with Kuinoel as pointing to the glory, but only as pointing to the weakness and frailty of man, and בן־אדם as parallel with אנוש can only denote the "son of man" in his impotency—and yet, the author of the Epistle to the Hebrews cannot possibly have had understanding enough to find out this simple sense; but although " it seems" that he first speaks of Christ in ver. 9, he must yet necessarily have meant the Messiah by the pregnant term υἱὸς ἀνθρώπου—however different this expression is from ὁ υἱὸς τοῦ ἀνθρώπου. True, what is said in ver. 8—10, as we shall afterwards see, is altogether inconsistent with this supposition which has nothing to rest upon, and Bleek is there driven to an extremely forced interpretation of the sense; but yet, the author of the Epistle to the Hebrews must bear the charge of a Rabbinico-Messianic explanation of the Psalms, which owes its existence solely to modern mistrust of the writers of the Bible.

What ground, then, can there be for departing from the simple interpretation of the words *as they stand*? Indeed, had the author said, "*Not to the angels* has he made the future kingdom subject *but to the Son;* for one testifies," &c.—then, Bleek might be right. But the author has in chap. ii. entirely relinquished the comparison of the angels with the *Son as such*, and purposely shows, from ver. 5 to ver. 18, that not merely the *Son,* as firstborn and Messiah, but that in him *humanity as such* is exalted above the angels, and that therefore it was necessary that the Son of God should become a member of *humanity* (vers. 16—18.) —We remain therefore firm and unshaken in the view, that, in vers. 6—8, not merely in the sense of the Psalmist, but also in the sense of our author, it is *man* or *humanity* that is spoken of and by no means the Messiah.

In vers. 9, 10 there follows a new chain of thought consisting of three links. *a, Man as a whole* is at present not yet exalted above the angels. *b, The man Jesus* is, however, already exalted, and he is exalted, *c,* as *leader of the rest of humanity*, for which he has secured by his sufferings the possibility of a like exaltation.

The first of these points needs no farther explanation either grammatically or otherwise. The second, on the contrary, already with respect to the construction, requires a more particular consideration. Three constructions are possible. The first and most natural is to take Ἰησοῦν as object, ἠλαττωμένον as adjectival attribute of Ἰησοῦν, and ἐστεφανωμένον as predicate to the object. *Man* is not yet exalted; but we see *Jesus* who, indeed (although as *first-born* already higher than the angels, yet through his incarnation) was for a time made lower than the angels, already, on account of his sufferings unto death, crowned with glory and honour. By the being *crowned* is meant, of course, nothing else than the having *all things subject to him*; he who is crowned is thereby set up as ruler. And the glory and honour with which Jesus has been crowned is just that in virtue of which, since his ascension, he now, not merely as the Son of God, but rather also as the exalted son of man, excels the angels, and is the object of their adoration. In Phil. ii. 5—10 we have the best commentary on the passage before us. Before him who once humbled himself to the death of the cross every knee now bows, those who are *in heaven* and on earth, and he bears a name which is above *all* names.

The adjectival attribute, however, ἠλαττωμένον βραχύ τι, was evidently necessary, because the author would make it plain that he speaks here not of that *glory and honour* which Christ enjoyed *before* his incarnation, as the *first-born* (chap. i.), but of the honour which the *incarnate*, after having been humbled to the condition of men, made subject to misery and death, has *received* as the reward of his *suffering unto death*. Hence he designates Jesus expressly, as him who *like* us was for a time made lower than the angels.

The words διὰ τὸ πάθημα (as Olshausen also rightly observes) cannot with Beza and Jac. Capellus be made grammatically dependent on ἠλαττωμένον, but only on ἐστεφανωμένον. The question, however, why ἐστεφανωμένον does not stand as antithetical to ἠλαττ. before διὰ τὸ πάθημα finds its answer in the simple remark, that the *emphasis* here does not rest on the antithesis between the humiliation and the exaltation, but on that between the not yet exalted man and the already exalted Jesus. Ἐστεφανωμ. is therefore antithetical with οὔπω . . . .

ὑποτεταγμένα, and must like ὑποτεταγμένα be placed at the end.

Bleek, who construes the sentence in the same way, finds himself now in vers. 9, 10 involved in an evident perplexity, owing to his erroneous interpretation of vers. 6, 7. He must admit that mention is first made of the *person of Jesus Christ* in ver. 9, and yet, according to his opinion, mention was already made in vers. 6—8 of ὁ υἱὸς τοῦ ἀνθρώπου. There remains for him, then, no other way of escaping from this difficulty, but that of explaining vers. 6—8 of the *Messiah as promised,* vers. 9, 10 of *Jesus* as the fulfiller of that prophecy. The following is the meaning which he assigns to the verses before us : According to the promise, *all things* are to be made subject to the Messiah ; all things are, however, not yet made subject to the Messiah actually come, to Jesus, (he has still enemies and unbelievers on the earth.) This seeming objection to the Messiahship of Jesus the author now seeks to remove by saying, that Jesus, although not yet *exalted* over all, is still in the meanwhile *crowned*.—Here, in the first place, the respected theologian contradicts himself when he finds the historical person Jesus mentioned in the sentence νῦν δέ, and not first in the sentence τὸν δὲ ἠλαττ. (see his own interpretation p. 260), and when he finds an antithesis between the αὐτῷ in the sentence νῦν δέ and the foregoing αὐτῷ, which can only be found between the νῦν δὲ .... αὐτῷ and the τὸν δὲ Ἰησοῦν. In the second place, he completely loses sight of the author's train of thought, which has nothing to do with the question whether or not upon earth, among men, all have already subjected themselves to Christ, but is solely occupied with the question, whether the ἄνθρωπος (whoever this may be) is still lower than the *angels* or has *already* been exalted above the *angels*. In the third place, he takes for granted that there is an antithesis between the ὑποτάσσειν αὐτῷ τὰ πάντα and the στεφανοῦν τὸν Ἰησοῦν, of which there is not the slightest indication in the words.[1] In the fourth place, we must expect to find as the conclusion, the assurance that to Jesus who is already

---

[1] The idea which Bleek finds in this passage must have been expressed in Greek thus :—Καὶ τῷ μὲν Ἰησοῦ οὔπω ὁρῶμεν τὰ πάντα ὑποτεταγμένα. Βλέπομεν δὲ αὐτὸν ἐστεφανωμένον γοῦν δόξῃ καὶ τιμῇ, καὶ οἴδαμεν ὅτι ἃ ἤρξατο ὁ θεὸς ταῦτα καὶ τελειώσει.

crowned, all things shall at some future time be also actually *made subject*. Instead of this, we find the conclusion, that in Jesus and through him, many also of the *rest of men* shall attain to a participation in that glory and honour; proving most clearly that the author in vers. 6—8 had in view *not the Messiah*, but *man as such*.

Other commentators differ from our explanation even in the construction. Some take τὸν δὲ ἠλαττ. as object and Ἰησοῦν in apposition to it. "But we see him who was for a little made lower than the angels, namely Jesus, crowned," &c. Every one must see how forced this is as a construction. But besides this, the meaning which it yields would only be suitable, if by the ἄνθρωπος in vers. 6—8 might be understood the Messiah. But, even in this case, a contradiction would arise, namely, with ver. 8, in which the αὐτῷ must also be understood of the Messiah. Thus something would be affirmed of the Messiah in ver. 9 which is denied of him in ver. 8. A third construction (Tholuck and others) makes ἠλαττ. the object, Ἰησοῦν the predicate, and ἐστεφ. apposition to the predicate. "We see man made for a little while lower than the angels *in Jesus* who has been crowned."[1] The whole passage would, according to this, be an answer to the question where and in whose person are we to find that humanity which is spoken of in vers. 6—8. But this interpretation is impossible even in a grammatical point of view; the words in order to have this meaning must run thus: Ἰησοῦν τὸν διὰ, &c. In general, however, the Greek would not express by a mere placing together of two accusatives such a formally declared judgment, in which by the predicate is expressed not the contents, but the compass of the idea contained in the subject, in which an answer is given not to the question what? but to the question who? We should rather have expected the following: τὸν δὲ . . . ἠλαττωμένον βλέπομεν ὅτι Ἰησοῦς ἐστι ὁ διὰ &c. or τὸν δὲ . . . ἠλαττ. βλέπομεν Ἰησοῦν εἶναι. But also, with respect to the sense thus obtained, the justest doubts may be entertained. The proposi-

---

[1] Similarly Olshausen: "We acknowledge Jesus who is crowned with honour and glory to be that one who was made a little lower than the angels." This must have been expressed thus: Ἰησοῦν τὸν διὰ κλ. ἐστεφανωμένον.

tion in ver. 8, that man has not yet entered on the glory promised to him, would thus in ver. 9 be not *limited* but *reversed*. For, if by that *man who was made for a little lower than the angels* spoken of from ver. 6 to ver. 8, we are, according to Tholuck's explanation of ver. 9, to understand none other than Jesus, and according to ver. 9 Jesus is already exalted, then it cannot be said in ver. 8 that *man* has *not yet* been exalted.

Thus the simple explanation given above is confirmed on all sides.—

The author passes to the third *link in the chain of thought* in the words: ὅπως χωρὶς θεοῦ ὑπὲρ παντὸς γεύσηται θανάτου. There are two points to be determined here, the one pertaining to *the reading*, the other to the *connexion* of ὅπως with what goes before.—The *reading* wavers between χάριτι θεοῦ and χωρὶς θεοῦ. Theodoret, Theodorus of Mopsuestia, and the Nestorians read χωρίς. And Marius Mercator, Theophylact, and Œcumeneus put forth the charge that this reading owed its existence entirely at first to the invention of the Nestorians. Occasion was doubtless given for this charge, by the manner in which the Nestorians availed themselves of this reading in their doctrinal controversies with the Catholics. They understood χωρὶς θεοῦ as more exactly determining the subject contained in γεύσηται, and thus obtained the rather strange sense: Jesus has tasted of death without his Godhead, *i.e.* the divine part in him remained unaffected by his death. But, however *convenient* this reading might be to those excellent critics, it by no means owes its *origin* to the Nestorians. First, because the words χωρὶς θεοῦ ὑπὲρ παντός explained without prejudice and without artifice, can yield no sense favourable to the Nestorians; secondly, because two hundred years before Nestorius, the reading χωρὶς θεοῦ was known to the ancient Church Father Origines. And not merely known! For he mentions the reading which stands opposed to it as one to be found "in several manuscripts" (ἔν τισιν ἀντιγράφοις.) *In his time* then, the *majority* of the manuscripts had the reading χωρίς. When, therefore, at a later period, Jerome says, vice versa, of the reading absque Deo, that it occurs only in quibusdam exemplaribus, very little weight is to be attached to this, partly, because the most eminent *Latin* Fathers, Ambrose, Fulgentius, Vigilius and others, adopted the reading absque, partly, because it is not difficult to understand how the more flat and easy reading χάριτι should have come gradually to be preferred to the more difficult, and, on doctrinal grounds, suspected χωρίς. This satisfactorily explains how it should happen, that on to the 6th century to which our oldest MSS. extend, the ancient reading χωρίς was almost entirely suppressed; hence it has been preserved only in the single cod. num. 53, in a scholium to cod. 67, in a cod. of the Peschito, and in the Patristic citations before referred to.

The same course was pursued in regard to the reading χωρίς as has recently been pursued by Bleek; it was rejected on internal grounds, and because it yielded no proper sense. But this very circumstance is a guarantee for its genuineness. The reading χάριτι is certainly clear as water, most easily understood, and—most futile, nay unsuitable. Christ has, by the grace of God, tasted death for all. That not merely the giving up to death together with its results, but that even the tasting of death should be traced to the grace of God, has something startling in it. Still, it might be said, that χάριτι θεοῦ refers only strictly to the words ὑπὲρ παντός. And this is certainly worthy of being listened to. But still, the meaning thus attained remains *futile*, inasmuch as there was no necessity or occasion whatever to mention in this context, in which the subject treated of is the exaltation of man above the angels, that Christ was given up through the grace of God; at least χάριτι θεοῦ might be thrown out of the text without producing any perceptible defect in the train of thought. The reading, certainly, is *easy*, especially in comparison with the other, from which even Bleek could extract no suitable sense;[1] nay, it lay quite at the hand of every copier who thought for a moment of how the offensive χωρίς might be suitably recast.

The reading χωρὶς θεοῦ is the more difficult, more significant, more suitable. Certainly, if with Paulus in Heidelberg we explain χωρὶς θεοῦ "forsaken of God," an idea arises which is out of place here. But is it not evident, that χωρὶς θεοῦ is rather to be taken along with ὑπὲρ παντός? True, Bleek thinks

[1] Olshausen also thinks that if the reading χωρίς be adopted, nothing remains but to render the words "in his state of being forsaken by God."

that πᾶς denotes here merely the human race, and that the author consequently cannot have intended to say that Christ has tasted death for *every* being in heaven and on earth with the single exception of God; but he intends merely to say, that Christ has tasted death for men. But if the author intended to make this latter statement, why then did he not write ὑπὲρ πάντων or ὑπὲρ πάντων τῶν ἀνθρώπων? Why did he rather choose the *enumerative* singular "for every one?". (It is self-evident that παντός is not neuter, and cannot be translated by *universe*.)— We find the best commentary on this passage in ver. 8 and in 1 Cor. xv. 27. In the latter passage we meet quite a similar thought, quite a similar limitation to that which lies here in χωρὶς θεοῦ. At the resurrection, writes the apostle Paul in that passage, *all things* shall be put under the feet of Jesus, πάντα γὰρ ὑπέταξεν ὑπὸ τοὺς πόδας αὐτοῦ (a reference to Ps. viii., just as in the 8th verse of our epistle.) Ὅταν δὲ εἴπῃ, he continues, ὅτι πάντα ὑποτέτακται, δῆλον ὅτι ἐκτὸς τοῦ ὑποτάξαντος αὐτῷ τὰ πάντα. There was occasion for the same restriction in our passage. In ver. 8 the writer had laid emphasis on that very πάντα in Ps. viii., and thence proven, that *absolutely all things, the angels as well*, should be made subject to man. In a way quite analogous to this, he will now in ver. 9 show, that Christ by his death has reconciled *absolutely all things, heaven and earth*. The same is said in Eph. i. 10,—*i.e.* that side by side with this capital and central fact in the human sphere, no other analogous acts of God in the sphere of the angels can be placed; that, rather, *all creatures, the angels likewise*, participated in the blessed fruits of the death of Jesus. And this he expresses *first*, by again saying ὑπὲρ παντός, and *then*, inasmuch as he limits this παντός merely in reference to *God*, shows, that the παντός refers to *everything except God*, consequently also to the angels. Christ has tasted death for *every one*, God himself alone excepted.

It is quite evident, then, that the preposition ὑπέρ in *this* context does not denote the vicarious satisfaction; for Christ has made this only for sinners, for men and not for angels. Ὑπέρ is here therefore to be rendered not " in the place of, instead of," but "for, in behalf of." The angels also, although they need no atonement, have yet likewise enjoyed in *their* way the blessed fruits of the death of Jesus. If, in general, their happiness consists in the adoring contemplation of the majesty and love of God, then the contemplation of this most wonderful act of self-sacrificing love must form the consummation of their bliss (comp. 1 Pet. i. 12.) And if there is joy among the angels over every sinner that repents, then the death of Jesus, by which the way to repentance and conversion has been opened up for all sinners, must have been the fountain of a sea of joy to the angels.

The second question to which we now pass is *how the particle ὅπως is to be explained and construed.* First of all, it is most natural to take ὅπως as dependent on ἐστεφανωμένον; but this seems to give an idea which has no proper meaning. The crowning and exaltation of Christ took place in order that he might suffer death for all. How is this possible, seeing that his death preceded his exaltation? The critics have therefore blindly sought in their own way to escape the difficulty. Some have assigned to ὅπως a new signification; Erasmus, Kuinoel, and others, the signification of ὥστε, Schleusner that of postquam, which, in a grammatical point of view, is absurd. Others have had recourse to artificial constructions. Bengel and Böhme, in a truly reckless manner, are for making ὅπως dependent on ἠλαττ.! Grotius, Carpzov, Storr, and Bleek, on a short clause to be supplied from the noun πάθημα : ὃ ἔπαθεν. But all these artifices are unnecessary. Ὅπως depends actually on ἐστεφανωμένον, can depend on nothing else, and needs to depend on nothing else; for a meaning perfectly good results when only (with Wetstein) the proper emphasis is given to the χωρὶς θεοῦ ὑπὲρ παντός. Christ was exalted that he may have suffered death *for all with the single exception of God.* This is certainly not spoken with logical precision; thus spoken it would be: that the death which he has tasted, might be for the benefit of all. This brevity, however, this condensation of two small clauses into one, is *extremely natural.* So, for example, might a teacher say to a youth who was going out for the first time into the world : "See that you remember my words and admonitions also when you are away, that I may not have taken pains with you in vain," *i.e.* that the pains which I have taken with you may not be in vain. (Olshausen also substantially makes ὅπως dependent on ἐστεφανωμένον : " that he might be one who had tasted death *for all.*")

Jesus, then, must be exalted, in order that his death may be for the benefit of all, of men and angels. So long as he was only the crucified man Jesus, so long his death was indeed an objective vicarious death of atonement for guilt not his own, but it yielded no real fruit either to men or angels. Not till the incarnate one was exalted and glorified, and crowned King in heaven, did it become possible for him to send the Holy Spirit, and thus to effect the *appropriation* on the part of man of the salvation which had been objectively wrought out, and therewith to bring *joy* to the angels over the conversion of men.

In ver. 10 we have the third link in the chain of thought to which the clause ὅπως, &c., has formed the transition, nay, which was already implicitly contained in that clause. This part can therefore be connected with the clause beginning with ὅπως by means of an explicative γάρ, "namely." Had this transition-clause been wanting, then we must have expected δέ instead of γάρ. (*Man* has not yet attained to the dominion; *Jesus*, however, is already crowned; but, through him, the *rest of mankind also* are to be led to glory.) The author, however, is not so fond of sharply distinguishing his thoughts from each other, as rather of making rhetorical transitions from the one to the other.

With respect, now, to the construction of the tenth verse, it is self-evident, *a*, that ἔπρεπε γὰρ αὐτῷ is the governing clause; *b*, that the relative clause δι' ὃν depends on αὐτῷ; *c*, that the subject to ἔπρεπε is formed through the infinitive τελειῶσαι; and *d*, that τὸν ἀρχηγὸν depends on τελειῶσαι as its object. The only doubtful point is, whether the accusative ἀγαγόντα, with what belongs to it, is *accusative of the subject* to τελειῶσαι (consequently, together with τελειῶσαι, forms an acc. c. inf.), or, whether ἀγαγόντα is in *apposition* to the *accusative of the object* ἀρχηγὸν. In the latter case, the word in apposition would be placed before its principal word, in order that the latter may receive all the greater emphasis (just as in ver. 9, the attribute ἠλαττωμένον was placed first, and Ἰησοῦν followed for the sake of the emphasis.)

That the αὐτὸς δι' ὃν, as subject of the verb τελειῶσαι, is different from the ἀρχηγός as the object of this τελειῶσαι, as also, that the ἀρχηγός is Christ, is self-evident; the αὐτὸς δι' ὃν is, therefore, God the Father. If now, following the former construction, we render the words thus (with Olshausen) : " it became him for whom and through whom are all things, in bringing many to glory to make the leader of their salvation perfect through suffering," then God the Father is here the one to whom the action expressed by the ἄγειν belongs, and this whole clause πολλοὺς υἱοὺς εἰς δόξαν ἀγαγόντα receives the place of a mere *accessary* limitation, to some extent a conditional limitation. If God (thus we might explain the idea), if God would bring many sons to glory, then must he make him whom he has chosen as their captain, perfect *through suffering*. The emphasis rests here on the words διὰ παθημάτων. That the *suffering* was necessary is the kernel of the thought, all the rest serves only for preparation.—If again, following the other construction, we render the passage thus: " For it became him for whom and through whom are all things to make the *captain* of their salvation perfect through suffering, as one who should bring *many* sons to glory," then, the emphasis here rests evidently on πολλοὺς υἱοὺς ἀγαγόντα and ἀρχηγόν. It is, however, precisely one of the peculiarities of our author's style to place such principal clauses as it were in the *periphery* of his sentences, and this of itself would suffice to give the preference to this second construction. In addition to this, there is the beautiful parellelism resulting from this construction between the Ἰησοῦν placed after, and the ἀρχηγόν, in like manner, placed after. Moreover, the two ideas are thus placed antithetically to each other: at present, *Jesus* alone is exalted; but he is exalted as a *leader of others*. The train of thought, then, absolutely requires that the emphasis in ver. 10 should rest upon this—that through Jesus *the rest of mankind also* attain to glory, consequently, on the *end* and *result* of the suffering of Jesus—but not on the means, the suffering itself. And how strong the emphasis which the author lays upon that *result* he shows by giving a twofold expression to the idea that through Jesus many attain to glory, first, in the words πολλοὺς υἱοὺς ἀγαγόντα, and then, in the word ἀρχηγός. We are not, therefore, at liberty to sink the clause πολλοὺς υἱοὺς ἀγαγόντα into a mere accessary limitation, which, according to the former construction, would be unavoidable, but must necessarily give the preference to the second construction. Ver. 10 is connected with ver. 9 as an explanation of it; there, as we saw, all the stress lay on ὑπὲρ παντός; in ver. 10, too, it must therefore be shown how *others also* attain to glory through Jesus. And the same idea is followed out also in ver. 11. It is shown in ver. 11 how the glory of *Christ* is participated in by *man*, but not why it was necessary that Christ should *suffer* in order to procure this glory.

We render the passage accordingly: "It became him for whom and through whom all things subsist, to make perfect, through suffering the *captain* of their salvation, as one who should bring *many sons* unto glory." The idea that Christ could not be a first fruits of others without suffering, finds its explanation in the passages John xvi. 7; xiv. 2, 3. Πρέπειν, as also ὀφείλειν, ver. 17, seems to denote not a fatalistic necessity, but a necessity lying in the nature of the thing, and therefore in God's own wise, world-governing will. That the Father is here designated by δι' οὗ τὰ πάντα, which is usually a term of designation for the Son (Rom. xi. 36; 1 Cor. viii. 6; ἐξ οὗ is generally said of the Father) is explained partly, by the paronomasia with δι' ὅν, partly by this,—that the Father is here regarded not as the creator, but as the governor of the world, through, and under, whose guidance the work of salvation is accomplished.

In vers. 11—13, there follows a further train of thought which, however, does not stand along with the rest of the members in vers. 5—8, vers. 9—10, vers. 14, 18, as co-ordinate with them, but as subordinate to the member in vers. 9, 10 containing, namely, a *mere explanation of the idea* in ver. 10 (that through the one *Son*, others also should become *sons*.) It is shown in vers. 11—13, that *already in the Old Testament it is said, the Messiah shall receive his subjects into his own relation of sonship with God*. First of all, in ver. 11, the proposition is thetically laid down that the ἁγιάζων and the ἁγιαζόμενοι stand in the relation of brethren coming from one head of a family. With respect now, firstly, to the meaning of the expression ἁγιάζειν, it denotes here not sanctification in the special sense, as an effect of faith in the atonement, and as such different from justification; but, just as little does it denote justification as such, as was thought by many of the old Protestant commentators. The expression ἁγιάζειν denotes here, rather, the total change in their relation to God which takes place in the members of the new covenant, in opposition to the relation of the natural man to God. This wide signification is explained by the sense and usage of the word ἅγιος. Ἅγιος is, in the first place, used in a dogmatico-metaphysical sense of God. God is holy, because he is in himself the perfect one, and the fountain of all good,—also of all that is morally good as corresponding to his own nature. God is further holy, in relation to personal creatures, *i.e.*, he is righteous; here ἅγιος denotes the consistency of the divine dealings towards us with his nature. In the second place, however, ἅγιος is used in a historical sense of the creature, and forms in this sense the antithesis to all that which by sin has become estranged from God, separated from God, and morally *bad* or essentially *profane*. Those things are holy, which are withdrawn from the profane natural life, and devoted to the service of God. Those persons are holy, who are withdrawn from the sinfully-natural life, *and are placed in a relation of grace and redemption to God*. Hence in the Old Testament the Israelites, and in all the apostolical epistles the Christians, are called οἱ ἅγιοι, although they are by no means already sinless. Only, in the third place, does ἅγιος come to denote (and in this case ὅσιος is rather used) the state of a personal creature who is absolutely free from sin, or who has become free (1 Pet. i. 16.)—The ἁγιάζειν in the passage under consideration is an instance of the second of these usages, and denotes the total act by which Christ withdraws his own people from the natural life of death, and places them in the sphere of a new life which rests upon his atoning death, has its source in his resurrection, consists in the appropriation of salvation through repentance, faith, and renewal of life, and will at one time be perfected in sinlessness and glorification.—The other and stricter signification of ἁγιάζειν, in which it denotes the special renewal of life proceeding from faith (John xvii. 17; comp. Heb. xii. 14) belongs to the third usage of ἅγιος.

Who, now, is the εἷς, the common parent, in relation to whom the ἁγιάζων, Christ, and the ἁγιαζόμενοι, the subjects of the Messiah's kingdom, are called brethren,—*i.e.*, who is he whose *sons* Christians become through the *sanctifier?* Hunnius and Carpzov thought it was Adam; Bengel, Schmid, and Michaelis that it was Abraham. All these (as also Olshausen) found, accordingly, in ver. 11 the idea expressed that the Son of God, as *incarnate*, has entered into a relation of brother to men. Then is ver. 11 an answer to the question,—*by what means* has Christ made *many* to be *sons*? Ver. 10 : Christ, as *leader*, draws many sons after him, ver. 11 : for he has become man, and therefore comes from the same common ancestor with *those who are sanctified*.—This interpretation is, meanwhile, decidedly wrong. Not until ver. 14 does the author pass on to show, that Christ, in order to raise us to a participation in his sonship with *God*, must needs take part in our sonship with *Adam*. The citations also in ver. 12 prove, as we shall see, not that it was necessary for the Messiah to become man, but simply that the Messiah should stand in the *spiritual* relation of a *brother* to the subjects of his kingdom, that he should lift them up to his relation of oneness with God. Finally, the designation of Christ here as the *sanctifier*, and the *sons* as the *sanctified*, also shows, that it is not the *physical relationship* which we, the sons of Adam, have from our birth onwards with Christ as the son of Mary, of David, of Abraham, of Adam, that is here spoken of, but the *spiritual* relationship into which we enter with him through our being *sanctified*. In ver. 11, then, we are not told *by what means* Christ raises us to sonship with God (namely: that for this end it was necessary that he should become a son of man), but, rather, in this verse it is repeated by way of explanation that Christ makes us his brethren, and as the *sanctified* raises us to sonship with God. Thus, with the ancient Greek commentators and Tholuck, we must explain the εἷς[1] *of God*, the *spiritual* father as of Christ so also of those who are descended from Christ. But it is, certainly, *to this descent from Christ*, not to the " common origin from God" (Bleek) that the idea expressed in the ἐξ ἑνός is to be referred, as appears of itself from what has been just said.

It still remains to be observed on these words, viewed grammatically, that πάντες along with τε—καὶ— forms a pleonasm.

For which cause, &c. Because the Messiah is destined to enter into the relation of a brother with the members of his kingdom, not merely into that of a ruler over them—*i.e.* to exalt them to a participation in the sonship—therefore, he is not ashamed already

---

[1] Calvin is for taking ἑνός as the neuter and supplying γένους. This is, grammatically, not possible.

in the Old Testament to call his subjects brethren, *i.e.* therefore does an analogous relation appear also in the anointed one of the Old Testament.—It is in this elegant rhetorical manner that our author connects his proofs from the Old Testament vers. 12, 13 with the thesis ver. 11. From what is said in ver. 11 it *becomes intelligible* how, already in the Old Testament, such passages as Ps. xxii. 23 could occur. There lies therefore, of course, in these Old Testament passages at the same time, vice versa, a *testimony* to the truth of what is said in ver. 11. This is plainly the aim of the author, to prove by these citations that even in statements of the Old Testament this relation of brother to the members of his kingdom, this calling to exalt them to the place of *children*, is attributed to the expected Messiah.

The great majority of commentators have not rightly apprehended the bearing of the 11th verse, and, hence, have not known what rightly to make of the citations, vers. 12, 13. We say nothing of the insipid view of those who, as soon as they come upon an Old Testament citation, ignorantly presuppose that the author's design was to prove that Jesus of Nazareth is the Messiah, and who then imagine they have done something wonderful when they show that the passage cited contains " no direct prophecy pointing to Christ." It is nowhere the aim of the author throughout the entire epistle to prove that Jesus is the Messiah; this he presupposes, chap. i. 1—3, as an acknowledged fact on the part of his readers.—Those again may be said relatively to have best apprehended these citations, who think their design is to prove, that even, according to the statements of the Old Testament, *it was necessary that the Messiah should become man*. We know, indeed, that according to the plain words of the author in ver. 11 this also cannot be right. Not that the Messiah, the Son of God, *must of necessity become man*, not that the *incarnation* was the *means* of exalting the rest of men to the place of *children*, is what would here be proven from the Old Testament,—this *means* is first spoken of at ver. 14,—but that, even in the Old Testament, it was reckoned as *a part* of the calling of the Messiah, *i.e.* the Anointed, the theocratical king, that he should not merely *rule over* his subjects from above, but in *brotherly ministerial love* lift them up to the same close *filial fellowship with God* in which he himself stood as the anointed of God.

On the *erroneous* supposition that ver. 2 is intended to prove the necessity of the incarnation, of the Messiah's becoming a child of Adam, the three citations have been interpreted in the following manner. In Ps. xxii. 23 David the king is not ashamed to remember that his subjects are at the same time his brethren, by virtue of their physical descent from Adam or Abraham. Now, as the first David was a type of the second David, there must also exist in the case of the latter a basis of physical brotherhood with men. (So also Olshausen.) But, in the first place, David wrote that psalm not as the king, but as a fugitive from Saul (see infra); and secondly, from the fact that David *mentions* a physical relation as subsisting between him and his subjects, it cannot be inferred that this relation belonged *essentially* to his character as anointed of the Lord, and must therefore repeat itself in the second David. With equal justice might it be said, that because David in the 51st Psalm laments that he was conceived in sin, the second David must needs also have been conceived in sin.—The second passage is supposed to be taken from Is. viii. 17. Isaiah in his character as a prophet says, that he puts his trust in God, and therefore retains the consciousness that although he is a messenger of God to the people of Israel, he is still at the same time a member of this people, and has to exercise faith in his own prophecy. Consequently, Christ also, the absolute prophet, must be a member of humanity to which he was sent. But it is the manner of all prophets to speak at the same time as men, and one might perceive in this a trace of their relative and imperfect character, and be led to an inference precisely the reverse, namely, that the absolute prophet must needs have been a prophet in the pure sense of the word, and not at the same time one of those to whom he was sent. If, therefore, these citations are to be understood in this sense, the force of argument which they contain appears feeble indeed. (On the third citation which, indeed, has been the best understood, see below.)

We now come to look at these citations from a quite different point of view. If our explantion of ver. 11 is right, then the author intends to prove by the citations in ver. 12 s., not that the Messiah must needs have taken part in our relation of sonship to Adam, but *that it belongs to the calling of the Messiah to raise the subjects of his kingdom to his own Messianic relation of sonship to God,* to that close union and fellowship of grace with God in which he stands as the anointed of God. Let us now see whether the citations in reality prove this.

The first is the passage in Psalm xxii. 23. It is well known that this psalm was ascribed by tradition to David, and was regarded as typical by the early Christian Church. From the place which it occupies in the first book of the Psalms of David it appears, according to Delitzsch's excellent investigations (Symbolae ad Psalmos illustrandos), that this psalm was included in the collection appointed by David himself (comp. 2 Chron. xxiii. 18 with Psalm lxxii. 28.) The situation, too, which is described in Ps. xxii., under the figure of a circle composed of destructive wild beasts and wicked men, applies more fitly to no one than to David when Saul persecuted him, hunted him from cave to cave, and from one hiding place to another, and surrounded on every side the mountain which he frequented. It is, however, not a mere individual trust in God which David expresses in the psalm; he was through Samuel anointed of God to be king, he had the promise of the throne, and on his faith in this promise did that confidence rest. When, now, the apostles find in those sufferings of David and his deliverance out of them, a type of the sufferings and the resurrection of the second David, this is not mere caprice on their part, but a thing for which they have ample warrant. The conflict of Jesus with his enemies was, throughout, and in the closest manner, parallel to David's conflict with Saul. There, as here, we see, on the one hand, the man after God's heart, the anointed of God, who knows that he, although chosen to attain to glory and to establish his kingdom, will, despised, and alone, receive the exaltation from the hand of God; there, as here, stands, on the other hand, the possessor of worldly power, who fears with groundless suspicion lest the anointed of God should seek to cast him down from his power with the weapons of rebellion. But to this was to be added, that this relation was first developed in Jesus in that absolute purity and perfection which it as yet wanted in David. David, although he shrunk from laying his hand on Saul, had yet gathered around him a band of fighting men, Jesus had only humble fishermen and publicans. Thus the conflict which is pourtrayed in Psalm xxii. had reached only a typical, inadequate development in David ; what David sings in that psalm first found its full truth in the second David. And when, moreover, our Lord himself in his anguish on the cross actually acknowledged the opening words of the 22d Psalm as containing the most perfect expression of his situation, how can critics, shutting their eyes against the light of day, still deny that the psalm expresses a relation which in itself was a prophecy in act pointing to Christ ?

The suffering Messiah of the Old Testament, then, in that psalm expresses the resolution in the midst of his affliction that if God should save and exalt him—in other words place him on the promised throne and make him *king*—he will declare to *his brethren* the faithfulness of the Lord, and will also raise them up to such a knowledge of God, and such an assurance of their gracious relation to him, as that they too should praise the Lord with him. He calls his future subjects brethren, not from regard to their being descended from Abraham in common with him, which would be two jejune a meaning, but it *is the feeling of royal love* that teaches him to regard his future subjects as brethren, and plants so deep in his heart the *care* for their salvation, for their growth in the knowledge of God. Herein, evidently, lies the significance of the declaration that David regards his future royal vocation as a *ministerial* one, that he counts it as belonging to his future duties as king, not merely to rule over his subjects outwardly as a caliph, but as one truly anointed of God *to lead them into that relation of nearness to God in which he himself stands, and on account of which* he, the man after God's heart, has been anointed to be the Messiah of Israel. If, now, the first, the imperfect David, held it as an essential part of his Messianic calling to love his subjects as brethren in God, to care for the salvation of their souls, and to lift them up to his own relation of sonship to God—how could the second, the perfect, David be inferior to him in this ? No ! the inference was certainly altogether logical and warranted :—if, already, the anointed of the Old Testament was not ashamed to regard his subjects in such a sense as brethren, so much the more will it be the part of the New Testament Messiah, to raise the subjects of the Messianic kingdom of the New Testament Israel to that relation of sonship with God in which he stands, and to make them *sons*.

The second citation is generally supposed to be taken from Isaiah viii. 17; the third is the passage in Isaiah viii. 18, consequently, the immediate continuation of ver. 17. If, however, the second citation was really from Isaiah viii. 17, it must with reason appear strange, that our author should by a καὶ πάλιν separate from each other these two verses which, although containing two different elements of thought, would still have formed but *one citation* (just as in chap i. 8, 9.). This καὶ πάλιν compels us to look for the second citation in another place than immediately before the third. Indeed the words קִוִּיתִי־לוֹ (LXX. καὶ πεποιθὼς ἔσομαι ἐπ' αὐτῷ) are to be found not merely in Psalm viii. 17 but also in 2 Sam. xxii. 3, and, already the older commentators, and among more recent theologians, Tischendorf, have recently traced our citation to its original source.

And, indeed, it is only in the connection to be found in 2 Sam. xxii. 3 that the words cited involve the proof which, according to the context, we must expect to find in them.— Isaiah, after having, in chap. vii. 1—8, chap. viii., communicated divine revelations concerning the nearer (chap. viii.) and more remote (chap. vii.) destinies of Judah, begins a hortatory address on the 9th verse of the 8th chapter, a sermon as it were on the text given in chap vii. 1—8, viii. "Rage ye people, and be broken in pieces!" he exclaims; he sees in the spirit one kingdom falling down upon another and one after another destroyed; he fears not this, however, Jehovah alone is to be feared, Jehovah alone is to be trusted in. His people dreads other powers and trusts in other helpers; but Isaiah "trusts in the Lord." The first person sing. (on which our author by means of an ἐγώ lays emphasis) stands there merely in opposition to the cotemporaries of Isaiah, who had set their trust on something earthly. How, now, from the fact that Isaiah was more believing than his fellow-countrymen, can the inference be drawn that the Messiah shall exalt his subjects to the relation of brotherhood with himself, and of sonship with God?!

In 2 Sam. 22, on the contrary, we have *a song which David sang when God had preserved him from Saul.* Ver. 1 There David declares that Jehovah had been his shield and had covered him. (How naturally, according to the ordinary association of ideas, must our author have been led from the prayer of petition in Ps. xxii. to the corresponding prayer of thanksgiving in 2 Sam. xxii.!) When, now, David says in this connexion : " I trust (also farther) in *him*," the ἐγώ here has its antithesis, not in the unbelievers, but in Jehovah ; the anointed of God in these words enters into a close union with God ; he expresses the feeling of the purest sonship to God; it is God who has anointed him, in whom he has trusted in the extremity of need, who as a faithful father has extricated him, in whom he will henceforth also rest all his hope.—The subject of Ps. xxii. was David's relation to his subjects, that of 2 Sam. xxii. is David's relation to God. We thus see how these two citations are connected together, supplement each other, and only when taken together form the entire proof, just as in the first chapter vers. 8, 9 and vers. 10--13 formed the two connected members of one argument. Let it be remembered, that in chap. i. 8, 9 it was shown that the Messianic salvation must needs come through a human ruler and not through an angel, and in vers. 10—13 that the Messianic salvation was to be brought about and accomplished immediately by God and not through angels. Here also, in like manner, we find two propositions similarly related to each other : *a*, the anointed of God must raise his subjects to his own position of faith and grace, must educate them so that they shall stand in the same relation to God as he does, and *b*, the anointed of God stands in the relation of closest unity with God. Or, more shortly and precisely: the Messiah makes his subjects to be *his brethren* (his fellows in as far as respects the relation to God); he himself, however, is the *child of God.* The Ergo is easily supplied : he makes his subjects to be children of God, υἱοί.— Here, again, it is not words but ideas on which the force of the reasoning rests.—

As in chap. i. 6, in addition to the passages cited to prove that the Son has received a more excellent name than the angels, other passages are at the same time brought forward which say nothing more of this *name,* but in which the description of the Messianic salvation is continued, so, here also, in the course of the 13th verse, to the two citations in which it is shown that the Messiah raises his subjects to the place of brethren and partners, with him in his sonship,[1] a *third* is added in which nothing further is said specially on this point, but in which a new independent proof is adduced of the principal proposition in ver. 10, that the Messiah makes his people to be *children.*—The third citation is taken from Is. viii. 18. Just as it was natural for the author to pass from the 22d Psalm to the corresponding prayer of thanksgiving in 2 Sam. xxii., so naturally must the passage 2 Sam. xxii. 3 have brought to his mind the parallel passage in Is. viii. 17, and thus led him to Is. viii. 18. We must again carefully consider this passage in its connexion, in order rightly to understand it. Ahaz, immediately after his accession to the throne, being threatened by Ephraim and Syria, despises the offered help of the Lord (vii. 11 s.), and relies on the help of the Assyrians. The rebuke is addressed to him ver. 13 ss.: O house of David, why dost thou offend God? Behold, O maid (O woman), thou shalt have yet to conceive (the well-known symbol of an affliction which is necessary in order to a salvation), and shalt come through suffering to bear a son whom thou shalt call " God with us" (the promised second David.) God, then, will bring the self-trusting house of David by means of afflictions to this—that it will feel as a woman, as a maid; then first is it capable of bearing the promised one, when in humility it places itself in a *receptive* relation to God.[2] For, before the time arrives when the promised one can as a grown up man bring the Messianic salvation, Judea *shall be laid waste* (ver. 15 comp. ver. 22.) An unprecedented calamity shall first befall *both kingdoms*, Ephraim and Judah (ver. 17), before the promised period of glory, and that from the same Assyrian power on which the foolish Ahaz relied for help (vers. 18 and 20).—After this revelation had been made to Ahaz, Isaiah receives the command from God to write upon a roll the symbolical name " haste to the spoil, speed to the prey." He does this taking two men as witnesses. After this, he begets a child, when the child is born it is a boy, and he receives

[1] Nothing of course is said here of the eternal Sonship of Jesus Christ. To a participation in that eternal Sonship none of the *sanctified* are exalted; they are however exalted to a participation in *that* Sonship spoken of in ver. 10, *i.e.* the Sonship commonly so called.
[2] We see then the house of David, purified by affliction, matured in the person of the Virgin Mary to a purely womanly receptivity for the promised salvation.

the command to give to this boy the name "haste to the spoil, speed to the prey;" the boy was to be a living witness and pledge, that the prophecy given to Isaiah nine months before would in its first part (that Samaria and Damascus should be laid waste by the Assyrians) be soon fulfilled (ver. 4); with like certainty, also, would the other part be fulfilled, that Judah should be oppressed by the Euphratean power (which must here still be regarded as the "Assyrian," as it was first under Hezekiah revealed to the prophet that Babylon should take the place of Assyria.) That the prophet, immediately after having written on the roll, goes in to the prophetess, leaves us to conclude that he did this according to divine direction. Thus we have here a series of signs, of which one always points to the other. His writing on the roll is a sign that a *boy* should be born to him, to whom he is to assign that name written on the roll. That the boy is in reality born, and receives that name, is a sign that Samaria and Damascus are to be laid waste by the Assyrians; the overthrow of Samaria is a sign that the after part of the threatening also, chap. vii. 17, that concerning Judah, shall be fulfilled, and with this the coming of the promised Son of David rendered possible.

The "haste to the spoil, speed to the prey" was, however, not the first son of Isaiah who bore a symbolical prophetical name. In chap. vii. 3 it is purposely mentioned that already an older boy existed with such a name, the "Shearjaschub." The younger son was a living prophecy of the judgments which were to come upon Juda, the elder, a living prophecy of the future salvation, of the conversion in which these judgments were to issue (comp. Is. x. 21.)

But it is not merely on the existence of these *sons* who were prophetic in their names that Isaiah, in his address viii. 18, rests that trust which bears him up amid all the agitations of the people, for he goes on to say, "Behold I and the children whom thou hast given me." In like manner as his trust rests upon his sons does it rest also upon himself. His sons give him faith and hope by the *names* which they bear; in himself, also, it must be the *name* which he has received from his parents, and which appears to him—in connection with the names of his sons—to be significant and consolatory. He is called "Jehovah's salvation," and, as

David in his character as the anointed king was a type of the New Testament king, so is Isaiah, as the anointed prophet and servant of God, a type of the New Testament Messiah, the *Saviour;* Isaiah is the Saviour of the Old Testament as David was the Messiah of the Old Testament. *That not he alone, however, but that he, together with his sons, forms the type of Christ*—this is important to our author. The sons of Isaiah were certainly not merely living *pledges* that the " salvation of Jehovah" would at one time come after " calamity" and " conversion ;" but the future salvation was also *typified* in this father together with his sons. Certainly, however, there must be added to this the other element,—that the children of Isaiah in their character as *pledges* (personal living prophecies) *were with him received into the prophetical calling of their father, into the dignity of the prophetical office;* in other words, that they were not merely children of a prophet (of a man who was besides a prophet), but prophetical children, or that *their relation to their father as children was itself a prophetical relation.* And the Isaiah of the New Testament, the Saviour, the Joshua (יְשַׁעְיָה and יְהוֹשׁוּעַ are synonymous), must not be inferior to him in this : was the one not merely a prophet in word, neither must the other be so ; did the one beget children which like their father were prophets, then must the other also beget children who, like him, stand in a Messianic union of grace with God.

Thus the three citations do in reality prove exactly what they ought to prove. It belongs to the calling of the Messiah to raise *others* to a participation in his *sonship.*

Ver. 14—18. Our author now passes to a new application of the idea, closely connected, however, with the third of the citations which we have just been considering. He had, *a,* laid down in ver. 5 the thesis, that the place of ruler in the future kingdom of God is assigned not to the angels (but to man) ; he had, *b,* shown in vers. 6—8, that even in the Old Testament this place is promised to the family of man ; he had, *c,* observed in vers. 9, 10, that as yet indeed Jesus alone had been exalted to the glory, but it is only as the first-fruits and as leader to bring *many sons* after him ; and here, by way of appendix, he had in ver. 11—13 called to mind how, already, the Old Testament considers it as a part of the Messiah's office, to lift up the members of his kingdom to the same relation of grace and unity in which he stands to God. Now, however, in ver. 14 he begins to show, that as *means* to this end—the exaltation of man to the rank of sons of God and this glory—it was necessary that the Son of God should come down to be a son of man, a son of Adam. As in ver. 9, 10 he affirmed, that the (already present, as it were already perfected) Messiah must needs *suffer* in order to make others to be *sons*, so in vers. 14—18 he shows that it was necessary the Son of God should *become* man in order to *become* the Messiah.

The proof of this which he adduces connects itself so naturally with the third of the preceding citations, that ver. 14 just presents the same idea as is contained in that citation, only in another point of view. In ver. 13 the principal thing was to show, that to the office of the Old Testament יְשַׁעְיָה belonged *not merely the uttering of words but also the begetting of children;* in ver. 14 he *lays* stress on this—that those children *must also be actually born*, in order to be living prophecies; in ver. 13 he shows, that the children of Isaiah *had part* in the prophetical spiritual calling of their father, in ver. 14, that that participation was rendered *possible* by the *actual birth* of those children. And that this new application of the passage is warranted, appears already from the interpretation we have given of it above. The mere uttering or writing down of the words " Schearjashub, Mahershalal-hashbaz" was as yet no sign, no testimony, no prophetical ratification of the deliverance; the gracious sign imparted to the prophet, and through him to the people, was only then given when God *actually sent* these children to him, when they *actually came into the world*, when they *partook of flesh and blood* (for these words contain the antithesis to the mere giving of the names). It must not, however, be thought that our author avails himself of this view of the case as containing properly a proof, that it was necessary the Son of God should be born as man. He could not mean this, for that case contains no such proof. For, it is not with the children of Isaiah, but with the father Isaiah himself, that Jesus is represented as parallel. He had, however, no such argument in his mind. Even the ἐπεί does not express properly a causal relation, but serves only to introduce *that parallel* which the author himself by adding the word παραπλησίως "in a similar way"—has denoted as one which does not hold *fully and in every point of view*. Indeed, he makes use of the citation in ver. 13 not as a proof of the idea contained in vers. 14—18 (he never applies one and the same citation to prove two different trains of thought), but merely by way of *transition*. According to that passage, it was necessary that the children should be actually born, and we perceive a relation in some measure analogous to this in Jesus; *he also has assumed flesh and blood*, he, in order to make us partakers in his sonship to God, has first taken part in our sonship to Adam. This *new thesis* is laid down, and it is not *proven* from Is. viii. 18, but that citation only served as a *transition* to it introduced in the elegant manner peculiar to the author. The proof follows in the sentence beginning with ἵνα, and then in ver. 16. Σὰρξ καὶ αἷμα— designates the *human nature* in opposition to the incorporeal uncreated *God* (comp. Matt. xvi. 17; Gal. i. 16) not the body in opposition to the soul, nor the mortal body in opposition to the glorified (Grotius, Tholuck)—an antithesis which could not be urged in this context.

That through death, &c. The author now proceeds to specify the *internal ground* upon which the thesis rests. That which stands in the way of our becoming sons of God, and which must first be removed, is *death*, or—as the author here more specially describes it—the being subject to the kingdom of darkness and the prince of this kingdom, who has the power of death. This bondage of death could be removed only by our guilt being atoned for through the sacrificial death of Christ. In order to this, however, it was necessary that he should become a member of that humanity which took its rise from the first Adam.

So much in reference to the train of thought in general. To come to particulars, καταργεῖν is an expression frequently used by Paul, but occurring in the New Testament only in Luke xiii. 7, and in our passage (but also in profane writers.) It is equivalent to ἀεργὸν ποιεῖν to render ineffective, to deprive of efficacy. The author certainly might have expressed his meaning thus: ἵνα διὰ τοῦ θανάτου τὸν θάνατον καταργήσῃ. But he has, with good reason, avoided doing so. For Jesus by his death has not freed us from death, absolutely, and in every respect; the death of the body still remains, but its sting has been taken away; it is no longer a judgment before which conscience trembles and which keeps men in incessant fear; to the Christian the death of the body is rather only a deliverance from the "body of this death" (Rom. vii. 24), a final putting off of the last remnant of the old Adam with which we have still to contend, in other words, the completion of sanctification, for, as the Heidelbergh catechism so admirably expresses it in the 42d question: "Our death is not a payment for our sin, but only a dying to sin, and an entrance on life eternal." Therefore the author speaks not of a taking away of death absolutely, but only of a cessation of the *power of death*. In the words κράτος τοῦ θανάτου the genitive is not the gen. objecti ("power, to kill"), for κράτος never denotes a mere facultas; it is the gen. subjecti. It is the power which death exercises over us, the violence which it offers to us. The best explanation of this is to be found in ver. 15, the consideration of which we shall here anticipate. Christ has delivered those who *through fear of death* were, *i.e.* showed themselves, to be all their life time subject to bondage. The man who, however well he might ward off repentance and the knowledge of sin, and by this pretended self-righteousness keep his conscience at rest, yet, when the thought of death comes home to him, cannot divest his mind of anxiety, testifies by this very anxiety—these irrepressible stirrings of conscience in the prospect of death—that he is *guilty*, and that as yet he can lay no claim to freedom from the power of death.

But the author is not satisfied with saying merely that Christ has rendered ineffectual the *power of death;* he goes a step farther back and says: Christ has rendered ineffective him who had this power of death over us—the devil—who held this power as an instrument in his own hands, and made use of it as a means to vanquish us. The time is now happily gone by when it was customary to explain away the Satan of whom we read in the Bible, by changing him into an "evil principle." An "evil principle" implies in itself nothing less than an absurdity. The very essence of evil consists in the absence of principle, in a contradiction to principle. If the idea of an "evil principle" were conceivable, then might it also be conceived that God was evil! But evil is only conceivable as a perverted selfish quality of the will of the personal creature, to be accounted for by the formal freedom of this creature; evil as such has no existence (nullam habet *substantiam*), but we give the name of evil to the quality of that creature-will which, in opposition to God's will, and to man's own inner nature, refuses to stand in a *receptive* relation towards God, and will be its own independent lord, its own God. (Hence, also, evil is not a mere negation of good, but its direct, positive opposite.) Now, we learn from the Scriptures that this evil quality of the will is to be found not merely in the human race, but also in the sphere of that other class of personal creatures, the angels, only with this difference, that because, in the angels, sin cannot be divided into sins of pride, and sins of the flesh, which strive against each other, and because it cannot be driven out of the centre of the soul into a circumference, the σάρξ, —the fallen angels are sunk *irrecoverably* into corruption. The sinful man is in his corruption half beast and half devil, the fallen angel is all devil. Farther, it is evident, that as the sinful man devotes his spiritual and corporeal powers and capacities to the service of sin, so the fallen angels, subject to the permission of God, spend the energies with which as creatures they are endowed, and employ their greater freedom from the restraints of body and space, in the service of sin.

Experience fully corresponds to what we learn on this subject from revelation. It is manifest in the history of the kingdom of God, that that kingdom has to contend not merely with individual weakness, or with the wickedness of individual men, but with great anti-Christian powers (Eph. vi. 12), to which the men who are engaged in their service are for the most part related merely as *blind* instruments. The workman, who lets himself be persuaded to join in a rebellion through the false representations of insurrectionary communists, commits *knowingly* only the sin of covetousness and of disobedience to the law; the citizen, who allows himself to be drawn by the prevailing spirit of the time into unlawful transactions, commits only the unconscious sin of folly; neither the one nor the other has discovered the great plot against the kingdom of God which they are helping to advance, nay, they are often surprised when they see the fruits which ripen on the field that has been wrought by them. The blinded man often aims at the *very opposite* of that which the prince of darkness, whose instrument he is, strives and manages to accomplish by him; in the hands of that prince of this world, parties professedly opposed to him often unwillingly help forward the same cause, and bring about the same victory. In short, there is actually a *providence of evil*, only relative, it is true, and in the end always subject to the absolute providence of God, which, however, stretches far beyond the conscious aims of its human instruments.

Now, the man who has not attained to freedom in Christ, or has fallen back from this freedom into the *bondage* of sin and death, is not merely a slave of his individual sins and sinful infirmities, but becomes, at the same time, a slave and tool of the prince of darkness; he has a price at which he is saleable, and for which the wicked one gets possession of him. He becomes a slave of that power which is at once a seducing, a conscience-accusing, and a corrupting power (corrupting the body as well as the soul, destroying all happiness, recompensing with poison and death.) It is the prince of darkness who holds in his hands the power which death exercises over us; who employs the power of spiritual death, of sin, to make man his tool; who employs the power of bodily death to spread death and murder and destruction; who employs the power of guilt to accuse us before God, and, *above all, before ourselves*, to rob us of rest, to quench in us the hope of the possibility of grace; who insultingly rejoices to see us condemned before the judgment seat of God. He has, indeed, (as Anselm of Canterbury has already shown in opposition to a false theory of his time) no *legitimate claim* as the seducer to the possession of the seduced; but he exercises a *real objective power* over those who, through their own sin, have surrendered themselves to his power. From him must the Messiah redeem men, —and he showed that he *acknowledged the debt in the manner in which he removed it*. Men seek to redeem themselves, either by *not at all acknowledging* the guilt and the necessity of a real atonement for the sin, but by trifling away and disowning this last remnant of truth in the sinner—the deposition of an evil conscience—and thus putting a self-invented idol in the place of the holy God; or, they seek to do this by acknowledging the necessity of an atonement, but setting themselves at the same time to effect this atonement by external works which they regard as meritorious, but which have no foundation to rest on. Christ, by giving himself up to death, has *acknowledged* the guilt and *truly atoned for it;* he has, in one act, atoned for the sinner and judged the sin.

The 15th verse has already been explained above. Something only remains to be said on the words τούτους, ὅσοι. Τούτους does not point backward (as if it were intended to express an antithesis to διάβολος: Christ has taken the power from the *devil*, but *these* —scil. men—he has set free); it evidently points forward to ὅσοι, and is almost equivalent to " those who." Ὅσοι, however, is of course not to be taken in a *restrictive* sense, as if it were denied that all needed this deliverance, but in a *comprehensive* sense: " but those who were always subject," = " as many as" quotquot. Ὅσοι is similarly used in Acts xiii. 48. The meaning of that passage is : of the Jews (who also were ordained of God to the salvation in Christ) only a small number believed; but of the Gentiles, *as many as* were ordained to salvation believed, *i.e.* a great number.

Ver. 16. To the internal proof derived from the nature of thing, the author now—in accordance with his former procedure —adds a proof taken from the Old Testament. But it was not necessary here that he should cite a particular passage, it was enough to allude to a generally known fact of the Old Testament. *God has assisted not the angels but the seed of Abraham.*[1] By means of an explicative γάρ, this idea is added as a *further explanation* of the clause beginning with ἵνα, &c. The force of the proof lies precisely in the generality of the idea. On the part of the human race there is the need of redemption, but also the capability of being redeemed; the good angels need no Saviour, the fallen are incapable of being saved (because they are not merely slaves of sin, but wicked rulers in the kingdom of death.) But the author, in giving expression to the antithesis evidently implied in οὐκ ἀγγέλους, shows, that his object in the 16th verse is not merely to prove positively that the Messiah must of necessity become man, but, *returning to the point from which he set out in ver. 5*, that not the *angels* but *man* has been chosen to be exalted through the Messiah to that glory and honour described in vers. 8 and 10, and *from this* the inference

---

[1] The Church Fathers and the theologians of the 16th and 17th centuries supplied a φύσιν to the genitive, and rendered thus: "he has not assumed the nature of angels, but that of the seed of Abraham." Castellio was the first to oppose this monstrous interpretation; after him the Socinians and Arminians. Since 1650 the right interpretation has been the general one.

is then indirectly drawn (in ver. 17) that the Son of God must become *man*—not angel.

Seed of Abraham denotes in itself not man, but the theocratic Israel. He, however, who entered into the *species*, entered at the same time into the *genus* to which this species belonged. The expression here is to be understood in a different sense from that in which Paul uses it in Gal. iii. Paul in that passage means by the *seed of Abraham* not the bodily posterity of Abraham into which Christ *entered* by his incarnation, but the spiritual Israel which is *born* of Christ and of which he is the *leader*.

Vers. 17, 18. In the 17th verse the author first states the amount of what is contained in the argument given in ver. 16. His object was to prove that the New Testament Messiah must needs take part in the human nature; he has appealed in proof of this to the well known Old Testament fact, that God entered into a gracious and covenant relation not with the angels but with the seed of Abraham, consequently that the seed of Abraham stands in need of salvation and is capable of receiving it; he now repeats the quod erat demonstrandum : therefore he (the subject is to be brought down from vers. 14, 15) must be made in all things like to those who (ver. 11—13) are ordained to be exalted through him to be his brethren. The vis conclusionis depends on the idea which has already been expressed, ver. 14, in the sentence beginning with ἵνα. The author, however, does not merely close the series of arguments begun in vers. 14—16, but at the same time makes a transition to a *new idea*. He *repeats* the idea already expressed in the words ἵνα διὰ τοῦ θανάτου, &c., ver. 15, but repeats it so as to open up an entirely new perspective. The idea in ver. 14 s. was this : Christ must become man in order by his death to free us from the power of death and the bondage of Satan—in other words to make atonement for us. Now, however, this idea appears in the new form : Christ must become man, because only thus could he execute the office of a High Priest. In showing that man is exalted through the Son to the place of sons, and thus made superior to the angels, the author is led to show the necessity of the incarnation and the atoning sufferings of Christ, i.e. his office as the Redeemer, the high priestly atoner. In this office, the type of Christ is not the מַלְאַךְ יְהוָה but the ἀρχιερεύς, and thus the author shows in ver. 17 that the New Testament Messiah is exalted above the מַלְאַךְ יְהוָה and the angels in general, conclusively and principally on this account, that he *unites to the office of a messenger of God to men that of a priestly representative of men before God*, to the office of a מַלְאָךְ (ἀπόστολος chap. iii. 1) that of an ἀρχιερεύς.

This idea is most clearly expressed in the additional clause τὰ πρὸς τὸν θεόν. Hitherto, the Messiah of the New Testament was regarded from that point of view in which like the Old Testament מַלְאָךְ ו״י he was a messenger of God to men; but this does not comprehend his whole Messianic office. He is not merely a more perfect messenger of God to men than the Old Testament messenger of the covenant; but he is this, precisely because he is *not merely* the perfect *apostle*, but at *the same time* also the perfect high-priestly representative of men *in their relation to God* τὰ πρὸς τὸν θεόν. This simple explanation is confirmed by the analogous conjunction of the *apostle* and *high priest*, in the first verse of the next chapter.

Ἐλεήμων is not to be understood as an independent predicate along with ἀρχιερεύς as a second predicate, but like πιστός belongs as an adjective to ἀρχιερεύς. (Otherwise πιστός must have been placed after ἀρχιερεύς.) Further, these two epithets do not express a differentia specifica, by which Christ, as the compassionate and faithful high priest, is to be distinguished from the Old Testament high priests as unmerciful and unfaithful,— the author does not, and indeed cannot, enter here on this comparison which he afterwards draws, and in which he shows that Christ was superior to Aaron,—but those adjectives are rather to be understood as simple epitheta necessaria. The idea is this: every high priest must, on his part, feel compassion toward those who are represented by him, and on their part again, must enjoy their confidence; now, as the New Testament Messiah must unite with the office of a *messenger* that of a *high priest*, he must also be merciful and faithful, and as this would not be possible if the high priest were not in all things like to his brethren, so must he become like to them in all things. Or more concisely expressed: "He must become like to his brethren in all things—wherefore he was a merciful and faithful high priest for them, in their relation to God."

And he must be a high priest "in order to make atonement for the sins of the people." Ἱλάσκεσθαι comes from ἵλαος. The idea expressed in ἵλαος we will explain by the following observations. God is love; out of love he created the world and its crown, the personal creature. In this act, his love is one with his holiness. In creating man such as he is, in forming him so as that in his inmost nature he is led to love God, and, through the love of God and holiness, to become happy, *and only thus to be capable of happiness* and harmony within himself—in this, God showed as much his love as his holiness. This might be called the *legislative grace of God* (צֶדֶק and חֵן.) But after man had fallen, God did not cease to love him; he loves him still with *saving grace*, Rom. iii. 24. The first act and manifestation of this saving grace consists, however, in this—that God *maintains unimpaired* also in the fallen man that 'fundamental law of man's nature, according to which he cannot be happy without holiness, —does not take conscience from him, in other words, takes *happiness* from him, displays himself as not *propitious* towards him, and turns against him his *wrath*, Rom. i. 18. This is the *conservative*, or, which is the same thing, the *chastising* grace of God. The second act of that saving grace consists in the sending of his Son and then his Spirit,—in the *saving* grace properly so called (ἔλεος, רַחֲם, תַּנְחוּם Luke i. 72), and more especially, the ustifying and sanctifying (juridical and medicinal) grace. When man does not resist this grace, then it becomes again possible for God to let man taste his friendship, enjoy his blessed presence, and to conduct himself again as propitious towards him. Ἵλαος then denotes not the internal disposition of God towards man, but the actual, positive *expression* and *radiation* of that feeling which first becomes again possible towards the redeemed; and ἱλάσκεσθαι means to *make* it again possible for God to be ἵλαος, i.e. to make a real atonement for real guilt.

In ver. 18 an explanation is given of why the being *compassionate*, and *faithful* and, with this, the being *made like to his brethren*, necessarily belongs to the office of the high priest.

First of all, however, it must be settled how this verse is to be construed. Erasmus, Bengel, Storr, Kuinoel, Böhme, and Tholuck take ἐν ᾧ as a simple argumentative particle " because."

It is true that it is not a relative limited *temptation* that is here spoken of—it is not "*in as far as* he was tempted, *in so far* is he able to save,"—as if Christ was tempted only up to a certain point, and was able to succour only up to a certain point. It is true also, that it is not the aorist that is here used ἔπαθεν. But precisely because it is not the aorist, we think that every obstacle in the way of taking ἐν ᾧ in its proper signification is removed. It is no historical or special statement that is here made, but one of a general kind. It is not: "Christ *was* tempted in certain points but in others not, and in so far as he *was* tempted he has been able to succour;" but it is, "in so far as he *has been* tempted *he can* help," or, to separate the two ideas which are here conjoined: A high priest can help in so far as he has been tempted, and so also can Christ,—he therefore must be tempted in all things, in order to be able to help in all things.

But of those critics who rightly and literally translate ἐν ᾧ, some have still had recourse to artificial constructions. Casaubon and others have referred ἐν ᾧ not to πειρασθείς but to πέπονθε: "in that which he has suffered, and suffered as one who was tempted, he is able to help those who are tempted." Here the πειρασθείς becomes an accessary idea, while it evidently stands parallel with πειραζομένοις as a principal idea. Bleek takes the words ἐν ᾧ πέπονθεν as a relative clause dependent on πειρασθείς; "as one who was tempted, namely, in the things in which he had to suffer, he is able to help those who are tempted;" but it is difficult to see either what necessity there was for this accessary idea in the relative clause, or why the relative clause should have been placed first, or what is to be made of the αὐτός. The idea which Bleek thus obtains would in Greek be expressed thus: πειρασθεὶς γὰρ ἐν ᾧ πέπονθεν, δύναται, &c.

The only natural construction is that which refers ἐν ᾧ directly to πειρασθείς, which is placed after precisely for the sake of emphasis. Quibus in rebus tentatus ipse (est et) passus est, iis tentatos potest adjurare. The πειραζομένοις stands opposite to the πειρασθείς, and the βοηθῆναι to the πέπονθεν. With *grammatical* exactness the sentence would be expressed thus: "In all things Jesus could help those, who were tempted (in those things), in which being tempted, he has suffered;" so that ἐν ᾧ belongs to πειρασθείς, and ἐν τούτῳ to be supplied belongs to δύναται. *Logically* ἐν ᾧ refers also of course to πέπονθεν, and ἐν τούτῳ also to πειραζομένοις, so that the parallelism becomes perfect. For as Christ was tempted precisely through suffering, and suffered in the being tempted, so it is evident that he " has suffered" in the same respects in which he was " tempted." And again, he who succours one who is tempted, just helps him to overcome the temptation; the helping, therefore, refers just to those things in which the state of *being tempted* manifests itself.

In this 18th verse we have the deepest internal ground on which the doctrine of the *vicarious satisfaction of Christ* is based. How true and scriptural soever the dogma is, it cannot be denied that in the ecclesaistico-scholastic development of it, the depths of the Scripture doctrine were far from being thoroughly penetrated. The view taken by the scholastics of the middle ages and those of the evangelical school, was, for the most part, merely the juridical. They thought of the multitude of single human *individuals* together with the *individual* Jesus, standing as it were upon one level before the Judge. Those individuals have each a debt which they cannot pay; that individual Jesus pays the debt for all the others. The inadequacy of this representation lies not in the idea of the objective substitution as such, but in this,—that no inquiry is made into the ground of the *possibility* of this substitution, that the substitute is viewed merely as an individual beside individuals, consequently as absolutely *another* and *different* person from them, as this particular individual. Our author teaches us to look deeper than this, when in vers. 10—18 he closely connects the necessity of the incarnation with that of the substitutionary high-priestly sufferings; he teaches us to regard man not as a *mass of individuals*, but as one *organism*, as a tree, so to speak, which has grown out of one root, out of Adam. In the man Jesus, the pure and ripe fruit of humanity, so to speak, has stood before God—a fruit, however, which has not *developed* itself out of the race of Adam, but was *given* to this race, *engrafted* upon the diseased tree—and thus in Jesus the *organism of man* has done all that was required to be done. But though this fruit did not *develope* itself out of the diseased life of the diseased tree, it was yet necessary that it should grow upon this tree; by the incarnation of Christ a *sound branch* was engrafted on the tree, which, as a branch of the tree bore blossom and fruit, so that blossom and fruit, although not products of the life-power of this tree, still in reality belong to it. But, to speak without metaphor, the proto-adamitic humanity could not *beget* a sinless man, but it could *receive* the Son of God becoming man and sinless man, so that he *as a real member of this race*, partaking in its nature and in the consequences of death, could bear the fruit, nay could be himself the fruit, which the race ought to have borne. Accordingly it is manifest that what is here spoken of is not merely a satisfactio vicaria passiva, but chiefly a satisfactio vicaria activa, which again forms the basis of the satisfactio passiva.

PART SECOND.

(Chap. iii.—iv.)

THE SON AND MOSES.

From what is said in chap. ii. 17—18, the author might have proceeded forthwith to the comparison of the New Testament Messiah as the perfect High Priest, with the imperfect High Priest of the old covenant. But after a brief recapitulation in chap. iii. 1 of what is proved in the preceding, namely, that Christ unites the office of a *high priest* with that of a perfect *messenger* of God to men, he suddenly breaks off in ver. 2 into a *comparison of Christ with Moses*. This is not the result of caprice, but of an intrinsic necessity.

First, the place held by the organs of the Old Testament covenant themselves, rendered it necessary that he should pass first of all to Moses. The instruments employed in the *institution* of the law were not the מלאך and Aaron, but the מלאך and Moses. Not till the third line of succession did the permanent office of the high priest appear. Then secondly, the intrinsic suitableness of the above arrangement of the principal parts, depends on the *carrying out of the second part itself*. The manner in which this second part is carried out is exactly parallel with the arrangement of the first part, so that the author also at the end of the second part, (iv. 10), recurs again to the idea of the *high priest*. And thus, after having been conducted from the two terminal points to this idea as the *central idea* of the Messianic office, he can then proceed—in a third part—to develope this acknowledged central idea (chap. v.)

The angel of the covenant appeared in the name of God before the people of Israel, Moses in the name of Israel before God, the high priest stood in the name of God (with the name *Jehovah* on the front of his mitre) before Israel, and in the name of Israel (with the names of the twelve tribes on the breast-plate) before God (Ex. xxviii. 9—29, and 36—38.)

Now the New Testament Messiah is, according to chap. i. 2, superior to the angels, a, because in himself as the Son he is higher than the angels, and b, because in him also, the whole human race is exalted above the angels to dominion in the οἰκουμένη μέλλουσα, and this because the Messiah is not merely מַלְאָךְ, but at the same time ἀρχιερεύς, not merely the messenger of God to man, but, at the same time, the atoning priestly representative of man before God.

With this, now, the second part runs quite parallel. The fundamental thesis iii. 3 : *for this man was counted worthy of more glory than Moses*, is, even in respect of form, evidently analogous to the fundamental thesis of the first part, i. 4 : *being made so much better than the angels*. The New Testament Messiah is superior to Moses, because, a, as a Son in the house (iii. 6) he is superior to *the mere servant* of the house (comp. with iii. 5, θεράπων, chap. i. 14, λειτουργικὰ πνεύματα), and, b, because the work of conducting Israel to its rest, which Moses had not completed, was first completed by him (chap. iv. 1, ss.) This work Christ has accomplished, in virtue of his not having been merely a Moses, a leader and lawgiver, but at the same time an atoning representative, a high priest (chap. iv. 14, ss.)

But so exact is the parallelism between these two parts even in minute details, that as the two sections of the first part, so also those of the second, are separated from each other by an intermediate passage of a hortatory kind:

I. THE SON AND THE ANGELS.	II. THE SON AND MOSES.
a, The Son of God is, in himself, superior to the *ministering spirits* of God, i. 5—14.	a, The *Son* of the house of Israel is, in himself, superior to the *servant* of this house, iii. 1—6.
(Hortatory passage, ii. 1—5.)	(*Hortatory passage*, iii. 7—19.)
b, In him *man* is raised above the angels, ii. 6—16. *For*: he was *at the same time high priest*.	b, In him *Israel* is conducted to its rest, iv. 1—13. *Therefore* he was *at the same time high priest*, iv. 14—16.

SECTION FIRST.

(Chap. iii. 1—6.)

THE NEW TESTAMENT MESSIAH IS IN HIMSELF, AS SON, SUPERIOR TO MOSES.

Vers. 1, 2, form the transition. This transition takes the form of an exhortation. This exhortation, however, is not, as some have thought, connected by means of the πιστός, iii. 2, with the idea expressed in the πιστός, ii. 17 ; for in chap. ii. 17 πιστός denotes one who is the object of another's confidence, the "trustworthy;" while in iii. 2 it denotes active "faithfulness;" the link of connection is rather in the words ἀπόστολος and ἀρχιερεύς, in which the substance of the train of thought in chap. i.—ii. is recapitulated, in order from this point to proceed further. Κατανοεῖν does not mean to lay anything to heart, but to submit anything to the νόησις, to consider, to weigh. The more proximate object of this verb is Ἰησοῦν, which, however, is already provided with the attribute τὸν ἀπόστολον καὶ ἀρχιερέα τῆς ὁμολογίας ἡμῶν. Its more remote object are the words πιστὸν ὄντα, &c. "Consider the (this) messenger of God and high priest of our profession Jesus, (as him) who is faithful in his house to him who appointed him, as Moses was faithful." The attribute *messenger and high priest*, &c., thus serves to *recapitulate* the attributes which the readers *already knew* to belong to Jesus ; the appositional clause *who was faithful*, &c., serves to introduce a new attribute which is now predicated of Jesus, and which is henceforth to be the object of their attentive consideration. The imperative κατανοήσατε does not, however, in this context involve an *independent practical exhortation* which flows from the theoretical passage chap. ii., but a mere charge to the readers now immediately to accompany the author to a new idea.

But this charge, at the same time, certainly implies the *moral* duty of laying permanently to heart what is further to be said. This is evident from the manner in which it is introduced, *holy brethren, partakers of the heavenly calling*. On the idea expressed by ἅγιος see chap. ii. 11. The mention of the *heavenly calling* entirely corresponds, in the place it occupies here, with the mention of the *so great salvation* in chap. ii. 3. The motive to the earnest consideration and heed which is enjoined, lies in the excellent and heavenly character of the object which is to be considered. By the κλῆσις is meant the calling explained in chap. ii. 6—8 to the dominion in the οἰκουμένη μέλλουσα. It is idle to inquire, whether this *calling* is designated *heavenly* because it proceeds from heaven, or because it calls and conducts to heaven. The two things are inseparable. A calling which comes forth from heaven to man, has, eo ipso, for its *object and import* the relation of man to heaven. Moreover, what is spoken of here specially is that call which has come to men through the eternal Son himself, the incarnate one, who has come from heaven, and which invites men to become *children*, fellow heirs with him of the heavenly inheritance. He who is a *partaker* of this calling, that is, in whose ears soever this call has been sounded, is thereby laid under obligation attentively to consider and give heed to all the elements of this *calling*.

Let us now consider more particularly the attribute τὸν ἀπόστολον καὶ ἀρχιερέα τῆς ὁμολογίας ἡμῶν. Jesus is called ἀπόστολος, from the analogous relation in which he stands to the מַלְאַךְ יְיָ as *messenger of God to men*, ἀρχιερεύς, from the analogy between him and the כֹּהֵן הַגָּדוֹל as *representative of men before God*. This signification of ἀπόστολος, following so simply from chap. i.—ii., would certainly not have been missed, although the author had written ἄγγελος instead. It is, however, easy to see why he was not at liberty to use ἄγγελος. In the Old Testament מַלְאָךְ there lies a double signification,—first, the etymological appellative, according to which it means messenger, and according to which, whosoever held the place and office of a messenger of God to men might be called מַלְאָךְ; and, secondly, the usual Gentile signification according to which it means *angel*, and denotes only a certain *kind or class* of beings (viz. the angels). Now it is true, that these two significations belong also to the Greek word ἄγγελος (comp. 1 Tim. iii. 16, where ἄγγελος, *messenger*, is used of the disciples). But after the author had in chap. i.—ii. used throughout the word ἄγγελος in its Gentile sense, to denote the *species* angel in opposition to the human species, he could not well, without causing confusion, apply the same word to denote the mere *vocation* of a messenger of God. After having in chap. i.—ii. so strongly urged, that Jesus has perfectly and absolutely fulfilled the calling of a messenger of God, just in virtue of his not belonging to the species ἄγγελοι, it was necessary that here, when he again ascribes to Jesus that calling, the office of a messenger of God, he should choose a word which expresses only the appellative, and not at the same time also the Gentile sense of מַלְאָךְ, a word which might without ambiguity be rendered only by "messenger," and not at the same time by "angel." For this, no better, and generally speaking no other word offered itself than ἀπόστολος, formed from the verb ἀποστέλλειν, which is so often employed by John (iii. 34; v. 36; vi: 29; x. 36; xx. 21), and elsewhere also in the New Testament (for example Gal. iv. 4), as the *technical term* for the sending of the Son into the world.

All the difficulties which critics have hitherto found in the expression ἀπόστολος, from their not observing the relation of chap. i.—ii. to chap. iii.—iv., thus fall of themselves to the ground, and we are also saved the trouble of considering one by one, and refuting the many unsuitable explanations of ἀπόστολος that have been given. Some have expressed their surprise that Jesus should be placed on the same level with his Apostles—but it is the sending of Christ by the Father that is here spoken of, not the sending of the twelve by Christ, and consequently, not the special signification of the word ἀπόστολος as the official name of the twelve. Others thought that the author should rather have said προφήτης or διάκονος, but the analogy of the office of Jesus to that of the מַלְאָךְ יְיָ could be expressed neither by προφήτης nor by διάκονος. A third class sought to explain the idea expressed in ἀπόστολος by that of the ὁμολογία, or (as Olshausen) by that of the κλῆσις; a fourth, to which Bleek belongs, thought that Jesus is called ἀπόστολος on account of his analogous relation to Moses, &c., &c. Even the signification "high priest" was contended for by some, because, in a passage of the Talmud, the high priest is on a single occasion called שְׁלִיחַ בֵּית דִּין!

The genitive τῆς ὁμολογίας ἡμῶν has for its object, simply to distinguish Jesus as the New Testament messenger of God and high priest, from the Old Testament מלאך י׳ and הכהן. He is the ἀπ. and ἀρχ. of *our* confession. This does not require that with Thom. Aquinas, Luther, Calov., Storr, &c., we should grammatically resolve the genitive into the clause ὅν ὁμολογοῦμεν. The same sense is obtained without this procedure, if we take the genitive simply as expressing the idea of "belonging to." The messenger of God *belonging to* our confession is thereby also the *object* of our confession.—The rendering of ὁμολογία by "covenant," which some have proposed, is contrary to the grammatical usage.

Let us proceed now to the appositional sentence ver. 2, in which is specified the *new* quality and office to which the attentive consideration of the readers is to be directed, πιστὸν ὄντα, &c. Ποιεῖν here, as in Acts ii. 36, Mar. iii. 14, is used to express not the calling into *existence*, but the appointing to an *office*, here the office of Messiah, which is represented under the figure of the establishment and government of a household. In this his office Jesus was faithful to him who had called him to this office.

The words ἐν ὅλῳ τῷ οἴκῳ αὐτοῦ are referred by Chrysostom, Theoph., Böhme, Kuinoel, and De Wette to the words ὡς καὶ Μωϋσῆς, so that no comma is placed after Μωϋσῆς, and the sense is as follows: "Jesus was faithful to him who appointed him, as also Moses was faithful in all his house." The genitive αὐτοῦ can, in this case, be referred either to Moses, or to Jesus, or (as the majority are of opinion) to God. But this construction appears unnatural, especially when we compare it with vers. 5—6, where the idea is more fully brought out, that as Moses in his (Moses') house was faithful as a *servant*, so, in like manner, was Jesus faithful in his (Jesus') house as a *son*. We, therefore, with Calvin, Seb. Schmidt, Paulus, Bleek, and others, place a comma after Μωϋσῆς, and refer the words ἐν ὅλῳ, &c. to πιστὸν ὄντα. "Who is faithful in his house to him who appointed him, in like manner as Moses was." *Logically*, the sentence would of course have to be extended thus: Ἰησοῦς πιστός ἐστιν τῷ ποιήσαντι αὐτόν ἐν ὅλῳ τῷ οἴκῳ αὐτοῦ, ὡς καὶ Μωϋσῆς πιστὸς ἦν ἐν ὅλῳ τῷ οἴκῳ αὐτοῦ.—The genitive αὐτοῦ is already, on account of the parallel accusative αὐτόν, not to be referred to God, but to be taken in the *reflexive* sense. Christ was faithful in his (Christ's) house, as Moses in his (Moses' house.) Only, the difference between the two houses is not yet *urged* here. All that is meant to be said is, that each was faithful in the sphere of office assigned to him. Hence also the genitive is not a gen. possess., according to which, the house of Christ would be represented as Christ's *property*, and the house of Moses as the *property* of Moses—this would, indeed, be in contradiction to ver. 5, where it is plainly said that Moses was not lord but only servant in his house— but the genitive αὐτοῦ is (just as in the words ἐν ὅλῳ τῷ οἴκῳ αὐτοῦ, ver. 5) merely a genitive of *appertainment or locality*. "His house" signifies "the house to which he belonged, in which he was placed."

What house, or what two houses, are here meant will more particularly appear in ver. 5 s. In the meantime, the simple answer will suffice with reference both to Moses and Christ, that the author had in his mind the בֵּית־יִשְׂרָאֵל.

Ver. 3. As the author in chap. i. 4 introduced the principal theme of the first part in the form of an appendix, an apposition, so here, he introduces the principal theme of the second part in like manner, in the form of an appendix, namely, an *explanation*. Γάρ is not argumentative; for the statement that Christ excelled Moses in *glory*, contains no argument for the statement that he was like him in faithfulness. Γάρ is explicative; it is not, however, the idea in ver. 2 that is explained, but a new motive is adduced for the exhortation in ver. 1. So much the more must the relation of Jesus to Moses be considered and laid to heart, as Jesus excelled Moses in *honour* (whom he resembled in faithfulness ver. 2.)

Ἠξίωται. The *subject* here is, no more than in chap i., the Son of God *qua* pre-existent logos, but here, as there, the Son of God manifest, incarnate. The author does not set out from the eternity of Christ, and come down to his incarnation, but sets out from his historical appearance upon earth, and ascends from this to his eternal being with the Father (ver. 4.) Here, first of all, it is predicated of the human historical person of the New Testament Messiah, Jesus, that he has been counted worthy by the Father of higher honour than Moses. *Wherein this higher honour consisted*, it was not necessary for the author to bring to the remembrance of his readers. This had already been done implicitly in chap. ii. 9, 10. Moses has not risen again, Moses has not ascended to heaven, Moses has not been crowned as *leader*, and first-fruits in the kingdom of exalted and glorified humanity; Moses, in the transfiguration of Christ, rather took a subordinate place next to Christ. All this was so familiar and so clear, that the author could feel satisfied in laying down the proposition, that Christ has been counted worthy of higher honour than Moses, as one which would be unquestioned by all his readers. (And what an argument have we in this silence for the historic truth of the evangelical history!)—But *upon what this elevation to higher honour was founded*, the author proceeds to mention in the words καθ' ὅσον πλείονα τιμὴν ἔχει τοῦ οἴκου ὁ κατασκευάσας αὐτόν. It is founded on this, that Christ was the incarnate eternal Son, he by whom are all things, by whom also the house of Israel, the theocracy, was established. The train of thought thus runs exactly parallel with that of chap. i. The train of thought in the 4th verse of that chapter we found to be this: Jesus the incarnate, was (after his sufferings) made higher than the angels, because he is the incarnate eternal *Son*.

The καθ' ὅσον is to be explained precisely in the same way as the similar, ἐν ᾧ ii. 18. The author does not mean to say that Christ is superior to Moses only in a certain respect, or only in a certain degree; he does not mean to deny that Christ *is absolutely* superior to Moses; in short, he does not intend to limit the thesis, *Christ has more honour;* but he draws out the three logical propositions of which the proof of this thesis consists—the *universal* or major proposition: " the founder of a household has more honour than the household founded by him"—the *particular* or minor: " Christ was founder of the household to which Moses belonged as a part or member"—and lastly, the conclusion: " therefore Christ has more honour than Moses." Or to express this in one sentence: " Christ has so much the more honour than Moses, by how much the founder of a household has more honour than the household founded by him." The καθ' ὅσον thus serves merely to compare a particular case with a general principle.

We have, in this explanation—following the Peschito, Chrys., Theodoret, Calvin, Beza, Erasmus, Capellus, Bengel, Bleek, Olshausen, &c.—understood the genitive τοῦ οἴκου as the genitivus comparativus, and referred it to πλείονα. The conclusion thus arrived at may, however, appear unwarranted, as the intermediate idea, namely, that Moses was a part of the *house* itself, seems to be not so easily supplied. Many, indeed, (with the Vulg., comp. Luther, Michaelis, Heumann, Semler, Erneste, Paulus) have appealed to ver. 5, where Moses is spoken of not as part of the house, but as θεράπων in the *house*, and have therefore construed τοῦ οἴκου as dependent on the verb ἔχει, and rendered thus: "by how much more honour from the house the founder of it has," where we must supply: "than the servant in it." But this supplement is exceedingly harsh, and all the more so, as the idea that Moses took the place of a *servant* has not yet come before us. Besides, it is not even true to say, that Jesus bore so much honour in, or from the house of Israel; for, from the house of Israel in which he was placed, he bore nothing but shame and contempt; he had his *honour* not (ἀπὸ) τοῦ οἴκου but ἀπὸ τοῦ πατρός. But, finally, the text gives not the slightest occasion for this forced construction. Let it be observed that the author does not speak of the οἰκοδομεῖν, but of the κατασκευάζειν of a house. The κατασκευάζειν, the founding and equipment of a house, comprehends not merely the setting up of the stones and beams, but also the entire regulation of the *household;* the οἰκοδομεῖν is an act of the builder, and the οἶκος οἰκοδομούμενος is the aedificium; on the other hand, the κατασκευάζειν is an act of the young husband or householder, who not only builds or causes to be built an aedificium, but sets up a familia in it, and the οἶκος κατασκευαζόμενος is the *household;* hence οἶκος here may be translated "household." But that Moses belonged to the *household* of God was no far fetched idea, an idea to which the subsequent designation of Moses as a θεράπων is nowise contradictory, but which rather confirms and explains it.

Ver. 4. The further explanation which is added in ver. 4 by a γάρ is somewhat strange. It is impossible that the design of this can be, to bring before the readers the two trivial ideas, that every house is built by some one, and that God is the creator of all things. Wherefore such undisputed truisms in this connexion? The contents of ver. 4 must evidently rather be fitted in to the reasoning, and must form a necessary organic member of the argument. One would expect a priori to find in ver. 4 the minor proposition, that Christ was in reality the *founder*. And, indeed, all the more ancient theologians explained the ver. in this sense. In support of it, the absence of the article at θεός has been urged, and θεός taken as a predicate. The proposition contained in the words ὁ δὲ τὰ πάντα κατασκευάσας θεός (scil. ἐστιν) would accordingly not be declaratory, but descriptive, not an answer to the question: *who* he is who has founded all things, but an answer to the question, *what* he is who has founded all things. It would be said that Christ who has founded all things is God, that divinity belongs to him.

But there are weighty objections against this interpretation. What is desiderated as the explanation of ver. 3, is not the statement that Christ as the founder of all things is God, or an answer to the question whether he is God or a mere man, but that Christ is related to the *house of Israel* as its founder. Moreover, the substitution of *all things* in this verse for the house of Israel, ver. 3, would be a doubly perplexing interruption to the train of thought. But above all, the words ὁ δὲ πάντα κατασκευάσας viewed as the *subject*, would, in this context, be an exceedingly *indefinite* designation of the person of Jesus, as thus, between ver. 3 and ver. 4, those necessary middle terms would be entirely wanting. And, moreover, it would be impossible to perceive in this case what could be intended by the preceding statement, *every house is founded by some man;* this would only have meaning on the supposition that the author's intention was to represent both Moses and Christ as *founders* of houses, and, accordingly, to represent only the houses themselves as differing in honour. This he certainly *might* have done (for Moses might quite properly be considered as the founder of the Old Testament economy); this, however, he has not done, but rather has farther carried out in ver. 5, 6, the opposition introduced at ver. 4 between Christ as the *son* of the house, and Moses as the *servant*. If, then, we would not bring total confusion into the author's train of thought, we must depart from that interpretation, and determine with Olshausen, &c., to understand θεός as the subject (the article, it is well known, is often wanting at θεός), and ὁ πάντα κατασκευάσας as the predicate. "He, who has founded all things, is God."

The old difficulty, however, here recurs,—what these apparently trivial statements have to do in this context. Meanwhile, their purport and significance becomes clear, *whenever we understand ver. 4 not as an explanation of ver. 3 alone, but of vers. 2, 3 taken together.* In ver. 2, the faithfulness of Christ towards him who had appointed him was spoken of, and then in ver. 3, Christ was called the κατασκευάσας τὸν οἶκον. This might appear to involve a contradiction. It might be asked: how can Christ have been a faithful *curator* if he filled the place of a *master and founder*? Now the author shows in ver. 4, that the one does not exclude the other, that it is true every house has a founder, but that above all such founders God ever stands, consequently that Christ, *although κατασκευάσας, was yet in a situation in which he might exercise faithfulness towards one still superior to him.*[1]

In ver. 5—6 there follows a second proof of the thesis laid down in ver. 3, namely, that Jesus is superior to Moses. It was said quite generally in ver. 2, that Christ was faithful in his house (*i.e.* the house entrusted to him), as also Moses was faithful in his house (*i.e.* the house entrusted to him.) *Nothing was determined in ver. 2* as to whether the house entrusted to Christ is identical with the house entrusted to Moses. There was not a single word to indicate that two different houses were meant, so that it was still in ver. 2 left open to the reader to understand *one* house as meant, which had been entrusted for administration first to Moses, and subsequently, to Christ. The sole difference which as yet, namely at ver. 3, has been spoken of is, that Christ in the house entrusted to him filled the place of the κατασκευάσας, but Moses that of a part of the familia. And herein, lay the first proof of the greater *honour* of Jesus.—A second proof of this is now adduced, namely, a second point of comparison or difference, so stated, however, that the first is again repeated along with it. Now also in ver. 5—6, the two *houses* themselves are distinctly represented as two different houses; in the one house, Moses serves *for a testimony of the future revela-*

---

[1] Similarly, but less exactly, Bleek : God is indeed the *proper* κατασκευάσας, the primus autor, but still the place of a κατασκευάσας belongs also to Christ. This is inaccurate. What is meant to be said in ver. 4, is not that a kind of κατασκευάζειν might be predicated of Christ although *his Father* was the κατασκευάσας, but that the *being faithful* might be predicated of Christ although he was the κατασκευάσας.

tions of God (so that this house itself exists εἰς μαρτύριον), the other house, the house of Christ *are we;* the other οἶκος is a *living* house, built of *living* stones. Thus there is a twofold difference which appears in ver. 5—6; to the difference in the place occupied by the two *curators* is added the difference in the dignity of the *houses themselves*. Moses is θεράπων in the house committed to his care, and this house is of a *typical* nature; Christ is υἱός in the house committed to his care, and this house is a *living* house composed of *living* stones. (Olshausen gives the train of thought in like manner thus: "Moses is a servant in the tabernacle, but Christ is lord over the new temple.")

This second proof, taken from the essential nature of the Old and the New Testament economy, bears the same relation to the first proof which was drawn from the abstract dignity of the persons, as (in chap. i. ver. 7—12) the proof drawn from the essential nature of angelic revelations bears to that drawn from the name *angel* and *Son* (ver. 5—6.) Here, however, in this passage, as has been already observed, the first proof is at the same time recapitulated. The designation of Moses as a *servant*, explains in what respect Moses belonged to the *house* (according to ver. 3) and formed a part of it (of the familia); in the designation of Christ as a son, a son of the house, are comprehended the two statements in ver. 3 and ver. 4, namely, that Christ in relation to the *house* filled the superior place of the *founder*, but that nevertheless in relation to *God*, he occupied the subordinate place of a *faithful* fulfiller of the divine commands. Both these are involved in the idea of the *son of the house*,—the superiority over the familia, and the inferiority to the Father as the supreme lord of the house.

Many commentators, however, have been of opinion, that a third antithesis between Christ and Moses is indicated in these two verses, namely, between αὐτοῦ, ver. 5, and αὐτοῦ, ver. 6. Either the second of these words was read αὑτοῦ, in which case αὐτοῦ, ver. 5, as the direct antithesis of αὑτοῦ, ver. 6, would have to be rendered by *ejus* and referred to God, and *could* not be taken in a reflexive sense—or else (so Bleek), while the reading αὐτοῦ was retained in both places, in the former it was rendered by *ejus*, in the latter by *suus*. The meaning was held to be, that Moses was a servant in the house of God as a house *not his own*, but Christ a son in *his own* house.—First of all, it is evident that in reality no new idea results from this; for if Moses was a servant and Christ the son, it is implied in this that the house in which Moses exercised his office was not in the same sense *his* house, as the house of Christ was *Christ's* house. The only question is, whether the author when he wrote αυτου, αυτου meant, by means of these two genitives, to *express* and *give emphasis* to this idea which was *already apparent* without them. We think this question must be answered decidedly in the negative. Had the author meant this, he must at least have used the emphatic ἑαυτοῦ at ver. 6, and not have left the choice of the spiritus asper or lenis to chance, or the caprice of the reader. But even a mere ἑαυτοῦ at ver. 6 would not be sufficient for this. At ver. 5 the idea of *not his own* would necessarily have to be expressed positively and explicitly, not merely implicitly by an αὐτοῦ (in itself, moreover, ambiguous, and capable of being understood reflexively); it must have been said distinctly that Moses was servant in a house *not his own*. Of all this, the author has said nothing and indicated nothing. But finally, in addition to this, that interpretation would involve us in a positive difficulty. If the author means to say, that Moses acted in God's house as a house not his own, but Christ in God's house as his own paternal house, this would imply that the house in which Moses acted is *presupposed as identical* with that in which Christ acted. This, however, would do away with that second point of difference on which the author purposely lays special emphasis in ver. 5—6. His design, evidently, is to distinguish the house of Christ " which we are," as one different from that in which Moses served, εἰς μαρτύριον τῶν λαληθησομένων.

All these considerations lead us to the conclusion, that no such opposition is intended between αὐτοῦ, ver. 5, and αὐτοῦ, ver. 6, as would represent the house of Moses as one not belonging to him, ver. 5; and the house of Christ, ver. 6, as his own property. We understand αὐτοῦ in both places reflexively and precisely in the same sense as at ver. 3, the genitive being neither with respect to Moses or Christ a gen. possessoris, but only a genitive of relation in both cases. Moses was faithful as a *servant* in his house, *i.e.* in the house the care of which was enjoined upon him, Christ as a *son* in his house, *i.e.* in the house the care of which was enjoined upon him. The difference in the place occupied by both is first expressed in the words θεράπων and υἱός.

This entirely new idea in ver. 5, 6 is introduced by καί—μέν, and is thus connected with what is said in ver. 2, so as to appear to be a limitation of what is there said. In ver. 2 it was said that both Christ and Moses, each in the house committed to his management, were faithful. In ver. 5, 6 it is shown what differences obtained in respect to this.

The words θεράπων and υἱός in which the first difference (already specified in ver. 3) is repeated, need no further explanation than they have already received. On the other hand, we must consider more particularly those words in which the new, the second difference, that which obtains between the *houses*, is represented—namely, the words εἰς μαρτύριον τῶν λαληθησομένων and οὗ οἶκός ἐσμεν ἡμεῖς. Λαληθησόμενα does not, as some expositors have unaccountably explained it, denote those revelations which Moses was still further to receive. This explanation could only have any meaning, if in the context, mention were made of a certain period in the life of Moses from which the "still further" was to be reckoned. The word rather denotes those revelations (on this wide sense of λαλεῖν comp. what is said on chap. i. 1) which God purposed to give *after the time of Moses*; in particular, the revelation in Christ is meant. The whole office and service of Moses was comprised in laying down *a testimony*, which pointed to the necessity of a future, more perfect, revelation of God.—To what extent was this testimony given? The author himself replies to this in the subsequent chapters of the epistle. At present, we may be allowed to make only the following observations. Through Moses God gave his law, first the ten commandments, and then the laws respecting the tabernacle and sacrifices. The ten commandments, even in the Pentateuch itself, bore the name of the *testimony* (עֵדוּת), and they were to be deposited in the ark of the covenant, in the presence of God, as a testimony bearing witness before God against the sins of the people. But that the holy and righteous anger of God might not be provoked by the sight of the testimony to visit the people with just punishment, that testimony must be *covered* (כָּפַר) before the eye of God; and for this the golden mercy-lid (כפרת) alone was not sufficient, but God's eye must ever rest on the blood of the propitiatory sacrifices, sprinkled with which the mercy-lid could then only truly " cover" the sins of Israel. But the necessity of always from time to time offering these propitiatory sacrifices anew, *testified* most clearly that those animal sacrifices could not take away guilt, and that a future more perfect priest and sacrifice was necessary. Thus was the service of Moses, and at the same time also, the *house* itself in which Moses ministered—the tabernacle—*a testimony of the things that were afterwards to be spoken*. In a grammatical point of view, indeed, the words εἰς μαρτύριον belong, of course, not to οἴκῳ but to θεράπων. But logically, they are placed so as to form the antithesis to the words οὗ οἶκός ἐσμεν ἡμεῖς. If Moses as lawgiver and builder of the tabernacle served *for a testimony*, this implies that the entire tabernacle itself existed *for a testimony*. It was not yet the true perfect house in which God could truly dwell with men, but was a dead, a symbolical, house in which was represented the relative approximation between God and the people of Israel which was preliminarily possible, and in which was *testified* the necessity of a more perfect revelation and atonement.

Christ's house on the contrary *are we*. (Comp. Eph. ii. 19—22 ; 1 Pet. ii. 5.)—The reading ὃς οἶκος is not warranted critically, but would yield the same sense. The absence of the article at οἶκος is analogous to the passages Luke x. 29 ; Heb. xi. 10 ; LXX. Ps. cxliv. 15, and is explained by the unconscious style of expression peculiar to the native Hebrew, who would think the noun sufficiently determined by the accompanying genitive. It is quite as unnecessary, therefore, as incorrect and contrary to the sense, to render the words: "a house of him are we," as if the author meant to ascribe more than one house to Christ, one identical with that of Moses (!) and another besides. No, the one and the only house of Christ is the true, New Testament Israel, and this is meant to be expressly *distinguished* from that house in which Moses served *for a testimony* &c.

The threefold difference between Christ and Moses, ver. 5, 6, entirely corresponds in the arrangement of the epistle, to the threefold difference between Christ and the angels, chap. i. 7—12.

The limitation expressed in the words ἐάν περ τὴν παρρησίαν, &c., forms the transition to the exhortation in ver. 7—19 (which, again, in the place it occupies, corresponds to that exhortation, in chap. ii. 1—4, which stands between the two sections of the first part, inasmuch as it comes in between the two sections of the second part). This limitation is not necessary to the completion of what is said in ver. 5. The house of Christ is *in itself, objectively*, and in its very nature—not conditionally upon our continuing faithful—different from the house of Moses, as a living house; it has this superiority unconditioned. But whether the author can *express* this in itself unconditional superiority under the *subjective* form : " whose house are we"—whether he must not rather say : " whose house are *Christians* (to which class, however, *you* do not belong"—this depends on whether the readers of the epistle continue in the *confidence* and in the *rejoicing of the hope*.—Παρρησία is nothing else than the πίστις itself in its most direct and most practical expression, manifesting itself as the inward power of the peace which dwells in the heart, in circumstances of outward difficulty. While, therefore, ἡδονή denotes rather that felt gladness and joy the experience of which is awakened within a man by means of favourable circumstances *from without*, παρρησία is precisely the reverse, and denotes that joyful boldness which flows *from within* and is victorious over *unfavourable* circumstances; it is joyfulness felt in situations in which *others would despair;* hence it is the immediate fruit of the objective peace obtained with God through the atonement. But why does the author so emphatically require the maintenance of this παρρησία? If we compare the admonitions in chap. ii. 1—4, iii. 7—19, vi. 1 ss., &c., we find in them all, earnest warnings not so much against direct apostasy, as against the *neglect of the doctrine that the institutions of the old covenant have found their fulfilment in the new covenant and by it are made superfluous.* The readers do not appear to have been already suffering persecution, but as likely soon to encounter dangers and persecutions. Now, in the introduction (to chap. i. 1) we have found it to be probable, that the Epistle to the Hebrews is not an epistle properly so called, and was not addressed to a church, but is a treatise intended for a circle of Jews who were about to pass over to Christianity, perhaps, according to chap. vi., in part already baptised, but who were still *catechumens*, and were now, through fear of being excommunicated from the temple, and the temple worship, in danger of being estranged and turned aside from their resolution to become Christians, because, namely, they had not yet accustomed themselves to regard the Old Testament institutions as things that might be *dispensed* with, and had not yet been able to convince themselves that they were *superfluous*. Hence the author everywhere shows, how all that is peculiar to the Old Testament is inferior in excellence and in internal significance to the New Testament revelation in Christ, and is related to it merely as the imperfect, the typical, is related to the perfect fulfilment. The same circumstance also accounts for the regular alternation of purely doctrinal and purely hortatory passages, such as we find in none of the *epistles* properly so called. Perhaps also, it would not be too bold in us to explain the words μέχρι τέλους—which some have most unsuitably referred to the end of the world, and others, better, to the death of the individual—as referring rather to the end of the *crisis of decision* in which the readers were placed at that time. For, if he only were truly a stone in the house of God who had held fast his *confidence* until death, then none of the living would be at liberty to regard themselves as such. It occurs to me therefore, that the author intends rather to say, that the readers would only then have a right to consider themselves as belonging to the house of Christ when they had kept the παρρησία *to the conclusion, i.e.* until the final resolution were taken to go over to Christianity.

The second thing in which they are to continue stedfast is the καύχημα τῆς ἐλπίδος. The Jews also had a καύχημα; they boasted of their descent from Abraham (John viii.), of their temple and priesthood, of their being the chosen people of God, all palpable and manifest advantages. The poor Christians had nothing of the kind in which they could glory. Regarded by the Gentiles as a Jewish sect, by the Jews as apostates from the people of Israel, forming no state, no people, without rulers, without a head except one who was crucified, the refuse and offscouring of the people, they had nothing of which to boast but the glory which they hoped to receive. Since that period the same has been substantially true of Christians. Hence, it is their duty now, as it was then, to hold fast the hope in which they glory.

INTERMEDIATE PASSAGE OF A HORTATORY KIND.

(Chap. iii. 7—19.)

In vers. 7—19 follows the *exhortation* itself, for which we are prepared by what is said at the end of ver. 6. The particle διό closely connects it with ver. 6. Because salvation and sonship are to be obtained only under the condition mentioned in ver. 6, *therefore* must they not be obstinate and disobedient, as the Scripture says, or the Holy Ghost, through whose impulse it was that the holy men of God spake. The passage in Ps. xcv. 7—11 is here cited according to the Sept. The Sept. has given substantially the right rendering. In it the two names of places מְרִיבָה and מַסָּה are rendered by the appellatives παραπικρασμός and πειρασμός not improperly, but rather with happy tact, as, indeed, these names were not properly nomina propria which belonged to those places before the time of Moses, but appellative designations of otherwise unknown localities, and designations which owed their origin and occasion to the actual occurrence of a *temptation* and *provocation* (comp. Ex. xv. 23, xvii. 7.) The words אַרְבָּעִים שָׁנָה are referred by the Massorites (doubtless with reason) to the 10th verse, "אָקוּט, by the LXX. (not so well, although of course without any substantial alteration of the sense) to "רָאוּ, verse 9.—The meaning of the passage here cited is evident, and needs no further explanation than is furnished in Ex. xv. and xvii.

The citation, as has been already observed, is connected grammatically with the end of the 6th verse by means of διό, but is nevertheless so selected as in its entire contents to form an inference from the whole train of thought ver. 3—6. Not merely from the statement that without holding fast the *confidence* and *hope* no sonship and participation in the Messianic salvation is possible, but also from this, that Christ is superior to Moses, it follows, that if obduracy towards the *servant* was already so severely punished, all the more earnestly should men beware of obduracy towards the *Son*.

The σήμερον ἐὰν, in like manner as the הַיּוֹם אִם of the original text, has the general meaning which our author ascribes to it (chiefly in ver. 13 in the words καθ' ἑκάστην ἡμέραν, ἄχρις οὗ τὸ σήμερον καλεῖται.) Even the Psalmist evidently does not indicate any particular day in the calendar on which the people should not be obdurate; still he might presuppose that on the same day on which he composed the psalm they would hear it; with him also —more manifestly even than in the Greek translation—the הַיּוֹם אִם has the more general sense : " the day, when" = " what day ;" הַיּוֹם אִם is = בַּיּוֹם, Gen. ii. 17, iii. 5. The sense is, that if any one receives an admonition from God he should comply with it *without delay*, and not put off the required obedience till the morrow.

Ver. 12. It is somewhat inconsistent with the spirit of the Greek diction, that βλέπετε here is not connected with ver. 11 by an οὖν or δέ, and the more surprising in our author, as he generally studies elegance of style. The difficulty is not helped by supposing, with Tholuck, that the words of the citation from σήμερον, ver. 7, on to κατάπαυσίν μου, ver. 11, are dependent on the words καθὼς λέγει τὸ πνεῦμα τὸ ἅγιον, and thus making καθώς the *protasis* to which an *apodosis* is to be supplied : μὴ σκληρύνητε. (" Therefore, as the Holy Ghost saith, be not obdurate," &c.—so be not obdurate.) For a new period begins again with βλέπετε without any connecting particle, and, moreover, the supplement which is proposed is very forced and tautological. Much more preferable is the explanation proposed by Erasmus, Calvin, Grotius, Bengel, Wetstein, Carpzov, Ernesti, and others, to which Bleek also inclines. These join the whole citation also with καθώς, so as to form one member which they regard as the *protasis*, and do not supply an *apodosis*, but consider this as given in ver. 12, " Therefore, as the Holy Ghost saith, be not obdurate, &c.—so take heed." Meanwhile, it may reasonably be asked, whether so long a citation attached to the protasis, which cannot be read in one breath, not to speak of a raised breath (as the nature of the protasis requires)—whether such be not a greater offence against good style than the want of an οὖν or δέ in a newly begun sentence. The latter may rather be explained satisfactorily enough by supposing, that the author here purposely leaves the smoothly flowing train of thought, and with intentional liveliness and directness interrupting himself, as it were, breaks in on the flow of the address by exclaiming: "Take heed, brethren," &c.[1] I hold it, therefore, more natural, with Schlichting, Capellus, Heinrichs, Kuinoel, Klee, &c., to understand the citation as dependent, not on λέγει but on διό, and to explain the words καθὼς . . . . ἅγιον, not as a protasis, but as a parenthesis—" therefore (as the Holy Ghost saith), harden not your hearts," &c.—and then to begin a new period with ver. 12.

Βλέπειν, in the sense of prospicere, occurs also in Mark viii. 15, xiii. 9. Of what are they to take heed? Of this, that none amongst them have an evil heart of unbelief. The genitive ἀπιστίας serves to determine the manner in which, and in how far, the heart is evil; the words ἐν τῷ ἀποστῆναι express the manner in which this *unbelief* manifests itself. In departing, namely, from the way of conversion to Christ once entered upon.

In ver. 13 a positive admonition is added by way of *warning*, the admonition, namely, that they should daily exercise the παράκλησις. This word denotes both the practical application of the law in admonitory discipline, and that of the gospel in quickening, refreshing comfort. The author, especially at this part of his exhortation, avails himself of the word σήμερον in the passage from the Psalms (the sense of which is given above on ver. 7.) He directs attention to the importance of the *daily, ceaseless,* practical application of the Christian doctrine to the heart and mind. And what avails all speaking and studying, where this powerful, living purification of the *heart* through the law and gospel of God is neglected?

Ἵνα μὴ σκληρυνθῇ, &c. The idea expressed by σκληρύνειν is to be explained from the figure involved in the word. The figure is derived from a circumstance in physical nature, namely, from

---

[1] In ver. 15, where the absence of a δέ cannot be explained in this way, Bleek nevertheless admits that a new period begins.

the gradual stiffening of bodies originally soft. Still more beautiful and striking is the figure involved in the corresponding German expression *verstocken*; it is taken from a circumstance connected with organic life, namely, from the growth of trees, in which the pliant branch becomes by degrees an unbending bough or stem, a stock. The stiffened body no longer takes on any impression, the bough now grown into wood can no longer be drawn and bent at pleasure. Just as the living plant grows until it reaches some fixed limit of development, so does the soul of man, by its ceaseless development of life, form itself into that fixed state to which it is destined. In itself, and in general, there is nothing bad in this progressive development of the soul; in the season of youth and education a certain germ will and must shoot forth in the soul, the personal *character* and destined life-vocation of the individual will and must form themselves ; in his twentieth year the man should already *be* something, should be not merely a single individual, but one who has *become* of such or such a nature or disposition. Nay, the last and highest step which the Christian takes from the stage of formal freedom to that freedom of the children of God, in which holiness has become altogether another nature to him, can be explained from that general fundamental law of the progressive growth of the soul. But this growth and development can take place also *in reference to what is evil*, and it is this to which the word σκληρύνειν—as a vox mala non ambigua—is specially applied in the Holy Scripture. Such a process, by which the soul becomes firm and unbending, can take place, firstly, in the sphere of the *will*, as a wilful obdurateness against particular commandments of God, as in Pharaoh (Ex. iii. ss), then, in the sphere of the entire disposition and moral character, as an abandonment to sins and vices, in which case the man has no longer *in himself* any strength to effect a change in himself, but there remains for him only that salvation which is offered through the quickening and electrically kindling influence of grace and redemption ; or finally, a hardening of the heart may exist also in reference to this offered salvation itself, the obduracy of *positive unbelief;* this is its absolute form, in which the last power of the soul to substantiate itself is exhausted, the last possible step in the kingdom of freedom is taken, and this is properly the most limited idea expressed by σκληρύνειν as it appears in the *New Testament.*

It is, moreover, a fine proof of divine wisdom that this figure of *hardening* is applied only in malem partem, and that nothing is ever said in Scripture of a σκληρύνεσθαι in what is good. For although that development of the soul, as we have seen, takes place also in the sphere of the good, it could yet be but very inadequately expressed by the figure of a *hardening*, as the good even when as perfect holiness it implies the *impossibility* of sinning, consequently the highest degree of internal fixedness, still preserves throughout the character of the *free, loving* will, and therefore of the highest *internal* moveableness and movement.

This state of obdurateness is not always reached by one leap, and through intentional wickedness, but quite as often, nay oftener, through ἀπάτη, *i.e.* through being deceived and self-deception. Thus the readers of the Epistle to the Hebrews, by their foolish, one-sided attachment to the Old Testament forms of the theocracy—by overvaluing what was relative, and regarding it as absolute—were in great danger of making complete shipwreck of faith, and sinking into this miserable state of obduracy. The remark may here be made, that in our own day an analogous overvaluing of things in themselves important, but still only relatively so, as, for example, of differences in confessions, or, it may be, of the extraordinary gifts of the apostolic time, is possible, and may possibly lead to the same issue.

This ἀπάτη, however, is never such as that, under it, the man is *guiltless* and purely passive, purely one who is deceived. On the contrary, our author speaks with good reason of an ἀπάτη, τῆς ἁμαρτίας, consequently of a being deceived, which implies guilt on the part of him who is deceived, a *self-deception.* The convictions of men are, in general, only apparently determined by arguments which address the reason alone; in reality, they are always substantially determined through the will. Man's power of perception does not resemble a mirror which *must* take up all the rays that fall on it; it rather resembles the living eye, which can open and shut itself, turn itself hither and thither; which also, on account of its being a relative light, can let itself be *blinded* and *dazzled*, and rendered incapable of receiving the light of the sun, the absolute truth. In ver. 14 the author recurs to the idea contained in the 6th verse, in order from it to pass in ver. 15 to a new element in the practical application of the passage from the Psalms, cited in vers. 7—11, namely, to the application of the word παραπικρασμός (in vers. 12, 13 he had chiefly availed himself of the word σήμερον.)

In ver. 14 there is a repetition of the idea, that because the salvation in Christ is so great, it is of so much the more importance to keep hold of it; or more exactly, mention is made here, as in ver. 6, of the greatness of the salvation; and as in ver. 6, the condition is here stated under which alone we can be partakers of it. We are μέτοχοι Χριστοῦ—the meaning of this expression is explained by what was said on chap. ii. 10—13—but we are so only *if we hold fast the beginning of the confidence firm unto the end.* The word ὑπόστασις signifies (comp. i. 3) base, bottom, foundation, then substance; lastly, also (principally in the usus linguae of the LXX.), fiducia (the act of resting one's self on or confiding one's self to anything.) This signification, also, best suits the passage xi. 1; faith is there described as a confident trusting in unseen future things which we cannot yet grasp, but for which we must hope. So also here, it denotes the confidence of faith. The readers have already a *beginning* of this. If, as is commonly supposed, the Epistle to the Hebrews were an epistle addressed to a circle of churches in Palestine, it would be impossible to explain how the author should have been able to say of his readers collectively, that they had a *beginning* of faith. For in the churches in Palestine, where indeed were the congregations of longest standing, there must have been a number of persons who had reached the maturity of the Christian life— individuals who had belonged to the personal circle of Jesus' disciples, and in reference to whom it would, to say the least, have been harsh to put it down as *questionable* whether they would continue in the faith stedfast to the end. For the ἐάν περ does not, as εἰ, express a simple objective condition, but places before us a decision according as either of the two events shall happen, and thus puts both events seriously in question. On the other hand, this style of address finds a perfect explanation, if, as we have supposed, the Epistle to the Hebrews was directed to a certain circle of catechumens and neophytes, in regard to whom it was really a matter of serious question whether they would eventually join themselves to the Christian Church, or would let themselves be estranged, through fear of being excommunicated from the temple worship.

Ver. 15. The chief difficulty is in the construction. On what verb does ἐν depend, in the words ἐν τῷ λέγεσθαι? Chrysostom, Grotius, Rosenmüller, and others, have taken vers. 16—19 as a parenthesis, and connected ἐν τῷ λέγεσθαι with the words φοβηθῶμεν οὖν, chap. iv. 1. But in this case we should expect to find a particle, a δέ, or some such, at ἐν τῷ λέγεσθαι, although no great weight can be laid upon this, as at ver. 12, also, the transition particle is wanting. A stronger objection is, that according to that interpretation, a particle (namely, the οὖν) at chap. iv. 1 would be too much. (For it cannot be explained as a *resumptive* οὖν, as it could only be so in the case of the words ἐν τῷ λέγεσθαι being again taken up at chap. iv. 1, thus: ἐν τῷ λέγεσθαι οὖν τοῦτό φοβηθῶμεν.) But the strongest objection of all to this mode of construction is, that it would entirely destroy the train of thought, seeing that in chap. iv. 1 the author, as we shall soon find, passes from the intermediate hortatory part to an entirely new didactic section, so that chap. iv. 1 cannot be joined into one period with chap. iii. 16. Others, as Flacius, Capellus, Carpzov, Kuinoel, have been of opinion that only the half of the words cited in ver. 15 are dependent on λέγεσθαι, and that the other half, from μὴ σκληρύνητε onwards—which clearly forms a part of the citation—is the principal clause on which the ἐν must be made to depend! (When it is said: "To-day if ye will hear his voice:" then harden not your hearts.)—Semler, Morus, Storr, de Wette, Bleek, Olshausen, &c., supply λέγω before ver. 16. (Seeing that it is said: "To-day, &c.," I ask, who then has hardened himself?) This rendering, also, and the connection of thought which results from it, no one will affirm to be natural, besides that in this case, if the author in ver. 15 s., passes to a new turn of thought, the δέ at ver. 15 could not be dispensed with. Bengel, Michaelis, Zacharia, and others, explained ver. 14 as a parenthesis, and construed ἐν τῷ λέγεσθαι with παρακαλεῖτε, as if the author meant to prescribe the forms of words with which they were to admonish one another daily: "to-day, harden not," &c. Not much better is the connection with κατάσχωμεν proposed by Luther, Calvin, Beza, and Tholuck; they will hold fast the faith most effectually by repeating to themselves at times the words in Ps. xcv. 7.—It is certainly preferable to all these artificial constructions, to suppose a simple anacolauthon; as if the author had begun a new period at ver. 15, but had not finished it, having allowed himself to be interrupted by the question τίνες γὰρ, &c., and thus led to another idea. But here, likewise, we stumble at the want of the δέ, which cannot, in the case before us, as at ver. 12, be explained by the emphasis of the address.

It appears to me the most natural way to take ἐν τῷ λέγεσθαι as dependent on *the whole of the* 14*th verse*, i.e. as grammatically dependent on μέτοχοι γεγόναμεν, and to render " as it is said." We are partakers of Christ if we keep the faith, *inasmuch as it is said*, &c. Ver. 15, therefore does not (as according to the interpretation of Luther, Calvin, &c.) lay down the manner in which we *must act* in order to keep the faith, but simply a *reason* or *proof* that we must keep the *faith*, in order to be partakers of Christ.

This proof is now developed in ver. 16—18, and then in ver. 19 the same thesis as we have in ver. 14, only in a negative form (that the Israelites on account of their *unbelief* came not into the rest), is repeated as a quod erat demonstrandum. The carrying out of the proof connects itself with the word παραπικρασμός, on to which the author had quoted the passage from the Psalms at ver. 15. Still, only the *first* link in the chain of proof is connected with this word. It forms only the point from which the writer sets out. Afterwards he deals in like manner with the other ideas and words of the passage in the Psalms, chiefly specifying the forty years' murmuring (προσοχθίζω from προσοχθέω from ὀχθέω, indignari, this again from ὄχθη, a cliff, a place of breakers, hence ὀχθεῖν, to surge against, to be vehement against any one), and the words εἰ εἰσελεύσονται εἰς τὴν κατάπαυσίν μου.

The following are the successive steps in the proof. At Marah (Ex. xv. 23), and at Massah and Meribah (Ex. xvii. 7), *certain* sins were committed; the people had murmured on account of the want of water; it was not, however, these sins, but sins committed at a later period at Kadesh (Num. xiv.) that brought upon the people the punishment of the forty years' wandering in the wilderness, which the Psalmist poetically connects with those sins at Marah and Meribah; nor was it at these places, but at Kadesh, where it is *expressly* recorded that the *entire* people, with the sole exceptions of Joshua and Caleb, murmured and sinned. Therefore our author finds himself necessitated to form a bridge, so to speak, from those particular sins mentioned in the passage in the Psalms, to the general sin of *unbelief*. He asks therefore first : "Who[1] were they who did provoke God? (Was it those only who had sinned at Meribah?) Did not all do this who came out of Egypt by Moses?" Thus he remembers that that special act of sin taken by itself, does not find its fit and proper designation in the word *provocation*, but the *disposition* as a whole, which all Israel everywhere manifested. Hence, secondly, it is evident, that the Psalmist was justified in connecting the punishment of the forty years' wandering with the sin of the "provocation." "But with whom was he angry forty years?"[2] Was it not with them that had *sinned?*" From this it was to be inferred that all must have *sinned*. Finally, in the third place, he must notice the chief and fundamental sin, that *disobedience* which refuses to be led in the gracious ways pointed out by God, that disobedience which is therefore substantially one and the same thing with *unbelief;* for in Kadesh nothing was said of a disobedience against the law, but of the disobedience which—as was well known to all the readers of the Epistle to the Hebrews—had its source in the *unbelief* described in Num. xiv., which led the people to think that, in spite of God's help, it would not be possible for them to conquer the land. Thus the author, in ver. 18, adds the third member of the proof, and returns again in ver. 19 to the thesis which was to be proved.

[1] It is evident, even from the train of thought, that the true reading is τίνες, τίσι, and not (with Oecum., Theoph., Vulg., Luther, Calvin, Grotius, &c.) τίνες τισί (" only some.") Comp. Bleek on this passage, p. 471. ss.) The author could infer only from the universality of sin in the time of Moses that the Israelites entered not into their rest, and therefore that the promise still awaited its fulfilment; he could not have inferred this from the fact, that " only some" had sinned at that time and had been punished.

[2] Here he shows, by the way, that he was well acquainted with the original text of the passage. He here connects ארבעים שנה with אקוט just as is done in the original.

In speaking, however, of the *entrance into God's rest*, the author has introduced to his readers a new element of which he further avails himself as the theme of the following *didactic section*. It was to be ascribed—he shows in chap. iv.—not merely to the subjective unbelief of the Israelites, but also to the objective imperfection of the Old Testament revelation, that Israel could not enter into the true rest. He then shows, how the highest fulfilment of the promise of rest still lies in the future, and is offered through Christ, and that we have therefore now to be doubly on our guard against *unbelief*, as this is now doubly inexcusable.

SECTION SECOND.

(Chap. iv.)

IN THE SON ISRAEL HAS ENTERED INTO ITS TRUE REST.

This section belongs to those of which, as Tholuck justly remarks, "few commentators have succeeded in clearly tracing out the connexion of the ideas." The fault of this, however, belongs not to the passage, but to the commentators, who have brought too much their own ideas with them, and have not had the self-denial simply to surrender themselves to the words of the writer.

For example, it has been taken for granted at the very outset vers. 1—3, that the author here proceeds to warn against the subjective sin of unbelief. It is all one whether the words can bear this sense or not,—this *must* be their meaning! nor does it alter the case, although what follows in ver. 4 ss. should in no way be suitable to such a sense.

Ver. 1. In the sentence $\mu\acute{\eta}\pi o \tau \epsilon$, &c., it is self evident that $\tau\iota\varsigma$ is the subject, $\delta o\kappa\hat{\eta}$ the predicate, $\dot{v}\sigma\tau\epsilon\rho\eta\kappa\acute{\epsilon}\nu a\iota$ the object to $\delta o\kappa\hat{\eta}$, as also that the words $\epsilon\acute{\iota}\sigma\epsilon\lambda\theta\epsilon\hat{\iota}\nu$ $\epsilon\acute{\iota}\varsigma$ $\tau\grave{\eta}\nu$ $\kappa a\tau\acute{a}\pi a\upsilon\sigma\iota\nu$ $a\dot{\upsilon}\tau o\hat{\upsilon}$ are dependent on $\dot{\epsilon}\pi a\gamma\gamma\epsilon\lambda\acute{\iota}a\varsigma$. Further, it appears pretty clear on a comparison of chap. ii. 11 with 18, that $a\dot{\upsilon}\tau o\hat{\upsilon}$ here is not to be understood in the reflexive sense, but as pointing back to God, who was the subject at chap. ii. 17—18. The only thing about which there can be any question is, upon what the genitive καταλειπομένης ἐπαγγελίας depends.

The great majority of commentators understand this genitive, without more ado, either (so Cramer and Ernesti), as a genitive of relation dependent on the verb ὑστερηκέναι ("that no one among you appear to remain behind the promise which is still left," *i.e.* appear as one who neglects the promise which is still left, *i.e.* the fulfilment of it)—a construction which is impossible owing to the position of the words, and the absence of the article at ἐπαγγελίας—or, they take the words καταλειπομένης ἐπαγγελίας as a *gen. abs.*, but still regard this genitive abs. as dependent on ὑστερηκέναι, while ὑστερηκεναι is considered as the principal idea, and δοκῇ, which is taken in the sense of *videri*, as a pleonastic accessory idea (so Bleek, Olshausen, and the greater number.) The sense then is: "Let us take heed, that no one amongst you show himself as *one who comes too late*, seeing that a promise is still with us," *i.e.* that no one amongst you appear, in reference to the promise still existing (still to be fulfilled), as one who comes too late.[1] In support of the purely pleonastic use of δοκεῖν which is here supposed, the only authority that can be adduced is a passage of the bombastic Josephus (art. ii. 6—10.) The signification putare, opinari, which δοκεῖν usually has (for example chap. x. 29 ; Acts xxvii. 13), we are assured will not suit the context here; as the author evidently intends to warn his readers not against the *thought* of being too late, but against the actual coming short itself.

Meanwhile, this is not so clear and manifest as for example Bleek himself thinks. First of all, apart from the purely pleonastic use of δοκῇ in that interpretation, the use of the verb ὑστερεῖν already strikes us as strange. If it is the aim of the author to warn against trifling away the fulfilment of the promise still left *i.e.* the *subjective participation* in this fulfilment, why does he select a word for this purpose which in nowise contains the idea of a subjective trifling away, but of a purely objective being too

[1] Still more unsuitably, Erasmus, Luther, Calvin, Gerhard, de Wette explain καταλ. ἐπαγγ. by contemta promissione = promissionem contemnens. Καταλείπειν might indeed have this meaning (Acts vi. 2), but in this case, the article could not be omitted before ἐπαγγελίας. The only natural way of expressing this idea in Greek would be this: μήποτέ τις ἐξ ὑμῶν καταλείπων τὴν ἐπαγγελίαν κλ. δοκῇ ὑστερηκέναι.

late? Whether the readers lived before or after the fulfilment of the still remaining promise was not a matter depending upon their choice; how then could the author admonish them to take heed, lest they came some time after this promise, which was still left, was also fulfilled? Did this fulfilment then take place in one definite moment of time?—We must therefore take the verb ὑστερεῖν in a very weakened signification, somewhat in the signification of "neglect," and in addition to this suppose a double figure in ἐπαγγελίας; in the first place, "promise" must stand for "fulfilment of the promise," and, secondly, the words "subjective interest in the fulfiment of the promise" must be supplied at ὑστερεῖν. Take heed—this would be the idea—seeing that the fulfilment of a promise still remains, lest any of you should lose by delay his interest in this fulfilment, (or should neglect the right time at which to obtain an interest in it.)

But a second inconvenience now presents itself, namely, the perfect ὑστερηκέναι. Ὑστερεῖν already means "to come too late;" and why should the perfect be used in a passage where warning is given against a *future* coming to late?

For all these reasons, we agree with the interpretation given by Schöttgen, Baumgarten, Schulz, Wahl, and Bretschneider, according to which δοκῇ receives its proper and natural signification, which beside the inf. perf. is the only suitable one (as in Acts xxvii. 13), while the *principal idea* is in δοκῇ, and the gen. abs. is regarded as dependent on δοκῇ. "Let us take heed, therefore, lest while there is still a promise to be fulfilled, any one of you should nevertheless imagine that he has come too late" (namely: that he lives in a time when all promises are long since fulfilled, and that no further salvation is to be expected, or has any claim on our earnest endeavours to attain it.) The author says purposely not μὴ δοκῶμεν οὖν, but φοβηθῶμεν οὖν μήποτέ τις δοκῇ; he will represent this error not merely as a theoretical one, but (chap ii. 12) as one that was practically dangerous. This idea harmonizes exactly with the context. The author here, as indeed everywhere throughout the epistle, designs to impress upon his readers the consciousness that the new covenant is not worse than the old, that Christianity is not something superfluous, something with which, at any rate, they might dispense if only they have their beloved Judaism, but that the latter rather has been made dispensable by Christianity. He, therefore, in ver. 1, and in the beginning of ver. 2, places Christianity *on a level* with Judaism,—we too wait for a promise to be fulfilled—then in the second half of ver. 2, he begins to show how Christianity is even far superior to Judaism.

Ver. 2. The first words are clear. We too, as well as those who lived in the time of Moses, have received a blessed message, a promise that we shall be introduced into a promised land of rest. Nay, we have received this in a higher and better sense than they. The word which has been given to us is infinitely better than the word which the Israelites received by Moses. In the first place; the word spoken by Moses could not bring the hearers to the faith; it remained something external to them, it proffered a promise indeed, and annexed a condition to it, but it imparted no strength to fulfil this condition (ver. 2—5 comp. ver. 12, 13); and secondly, the promise contained in that word even in respect of its import, was not the true and right promise, for it was an earthly rest that was there proffered, whereas it is a spiritual and eternal rest that is now promised to us (ver. 6—10.)

Let us look, now, at the first of these two arguments which begins with the words ver. 2. ἀλλ'. οὐκ ὠφέλησεν, and is afterwards repeated more fully in ver. 12—13. It is not to be wondered at, that a false interpretation of ver. 1 should have led the majority of commentators into an entire misunderstanding also of ver. 2. They conceive that here (as in chap. ii. 16—19) it is still the *subjective unbelief of the Jews* that is adduced as the reason of their not having attained to the rest, whereas, in the passage before us, it is rather the *objective imperfection of the Old Testament revelation* that is given as the ground of the imperfect fulfilment of the promises. Only thus, too, can the connecting particle ἀλλά be accounted for. In the words καὶ γάρ ἐσμεν, &c., the new covenant is only placed on a level with the old, and in the purely objective point of view, that in the one, as in the other, a gracious message is given. The statement now made, that the word of God in the old covenant *did not profit* or was inefficacious, stands in an antithetical relation to that which precedes it. (Had the writer meant to say, that the Israelites under the old covenant were unbelieving, as also many under the new covenant are inclined to unbelief, he would have used only the connecting particle δέ, or better still καὶ—μέν.)

But the view which we have given of the train of thought finds its justification chiefly in the words themselves. The reading of these words, however, wavers, and that in three points. Firstly, in one portion of the codd. the attic form συγκεκρ-αμεν.... is found, in the other the later form συγκεκερασμεν...; that the latter is the true reading, while the form owes its origin to a correction, is self-evident. Secondly, a single *cursive* manuscript (Griesbach Nro. 71) has ἀκουσθεῖσι, instead of ἀκούσασι; and more recent critics, on the authority of the Vulg., have conjectured a reading ἀκούσμασι (dat. plur. of ἄκουσμα); here again it is self-evident that the reading ἀκούσασι, confirmed by all sources, considered merely as the more difficult, is the genuine reading; and we shall soon see that ἀκουσθεῖσι, as also the rendering of the Vulgate, ex illis quae audierant, owes its origin to the embarrassment arising from not being able to extract any suitable sense from the other. The difficulty is greater in the third point. The Peschito (ܡܠܬܐ ܕܠܐ ܡܙܝܓܐ ܒܗܝܡܢܘܬܐ ܠܗܢܘܢ ܕܫܡܥܘ) and the Vulgate (sermo auditus non ad-admixtus fidei ex eis quae audierant) point to the reading συγκεκ-ρασμένος, which is found also in Chrysostom, and has been retained in several cursive MSS. On the other hand, the codd. A B C D E, the versio Copt., Aeth, Armen, Philoxen, Slav., have the accusative plural συγκεκερασμένους (resp. συγκεκρα-μένους). Almost all the more recent commentators (with the exception of Olshausen and Tholuck) consider the latter as decidedly the true reading, on account of these weighty external proofs. But the point is not, therefore, to be regarded as summarily settled. The fact of the nom. sing. occurring only in the cursive MSS., while the uncial MSS. have the acc. plur., by no means proves that the nom. sing. is not the ancient reading. Let us take into view the authority of the primitive Peschito, certainly the most ancient source of the New Testament text which we possess, the circumstance that Jerome, who, with the utmost care, compared good manuscripts which already in his time were old, gave the preference to the nom. sing.; finally, that Chrysostom read the nom., and we shall have no difficulty in coming to the conclusion, that the nom. sing. is a reading of primitive antiquity, beside which, however, there stood already in the first centuries another reading, and which was soon almost entirely supplanted by this other reading.

We have now only to ask which of the two readings is, upon internal grounds, the more suitable; and if we find, moreover, that this internally more suitable reading might, as the more difficult one, be easily misunderstood, we will then have an explanation of the early origin and the subsequent general acceptation of the false reading. The acc. plur. yields the more flat and less suitable sense; the nom. sing. yields a finer sense, which, however, might easily escape recognition on a superficial reading.

If we adopt the reading συγκεκερασμένους, the passage must then be rendered thus: "The word heard (comp. 1 Thess. ii. 13) did not profit those persons, because they did not unite themselves in the faith with those who obeyed,"—viz., with Joshua and Caleb. According to this, it would still be the *subjective unbelief* of the contemporaries of Moses that is here blamed —a view inconsistent with the context. (So Oecum., Photius, Hammond, Cramer, Matthai.) But as before, at chap. ii. 16—19, no distinction whatever was made between those who believed not, and Joshua and Caleb who believed, and, in general, no reference at all was made to these two men,—such an explanation of the passage as that just mentioned would be unintelligible and arbitrary. Besides, it is inadmissible to take ἀκούειν in the particip. ἀκούσασιν, in the pregnant signification of "obey," which it never has in the Epistle to the Hebrews; and this is doubly inadmissible here, where it stands so close beside ἀκοή. Others have proposed, moreover, to connect the dat. ἀκούσασιν as *the dative of possession* in the sense of a *genitive* with πίστει (through the faith belonging to the hearers, or becoming them), which is a grammatical monstrosity. Even Bleek can find no other way of escape than to conjecture ἀκούσμασι, and in this he at least shows from what view the reading ἀκουσθεῖσιν has originated.

The reading συγκεκερασμένος offers an exceedingly fine and suitable sense, but one indeed which might easily be overlooked. The author, in chap. iv., no longer speaks of the subjective unbelief of Moses' contemporaries, but of the objective imperfection of the Old Testament institutions. The word which was given by Moses to the Israelites—consisting, *a*, of the *promise* that they should come into the earthly *rest*, and, *b*, of the *law* as the annexed *condition*—could not be *united to the hearers* by faith. (So also Olshausen.) This idea finds its clearest explanation in its opposite ver. 12, where, according to the context, the New Testament *word of God* is spoken of, and where it is described as *penetrating into the innermost marrow and joints of the man*. The law remained as a cold command external to the man, the will of God and the will of man were not united; therefore the Mosaic word of God could not profit. The law, with its "thou shalt," could never bring about that surrender of the heart, that disposition and attitude of loving *receptivity*, which can be awakened only by the love of Him "who hath first loved us," and which is called "faith," and leads to a fellowship of being and of life with God.

How easily now might this idea have been overlooked, as it lies not on the surface of the words! How easily may it have happened to interpreters and transcribers, in the very earliest period, as it has to the majority of commentators till the present day, to fall into the error of supposing that the writer still continues, in chap. iv. 1, 2, to speak of the subjective unbelief of Moses' contemporaries! It will not be disputed that the early origin, and the subsequent wide extension of the false reading συγκεκερασμένους, may in this way be fully accounted for.—The antithesis, therefore, to *faith*, ver. 2, is not *unbelief*, but *works*, and this antithesis is, in fact, expressed in ver. 3.

Ver. 3. "For we enter into the rest as *believers*." It is quite evident that those are wrong who paraphrase the words thus: "If we do not merely *hear*, but also *believe*." The πιστεύειν has its antithesis in the ἔργοις. It is not a condition *equally* belonging to the old and the new covenant that is here described, but the *difference* of the condition of the New Testament covenant from that of the Old Testament. In the words, *as he said*, the author proceeds to show in how far even the Old Testament itself points to the insufficiency of the law and its *works*. For this end he again cites a verse from the 95th Psalm, which he had already cited in chap. 3 (although with a different object), namely, the words: "As I have sworn in my wrath: they shall not enter into my rest." These words, however, in themselves contain no proof of the statement, that through *faith alone* we can enter into the rest of God, but they derive their argumentative force from the clause which is added: "Although the works were performed from the creation of the world." It is self-evident that the *works* here are antithetically opposed to *faith*. It is surprising how all critics should have supposed that the works *of God* are here meant, and especially his works of *creation*. Γενηθέντων is understood in the pregnant sense of a part. pass., and γίγνεσθαι, moreover, in the sense of τελεῖσθαι; and the words are thus rendered: "Although the works (of God) were already completed from the moment of the (finished) creation of the world"—*i.e.*, in other words: "Although the creation of the world was already finished from the moment at which it was finished!!" A strange idea! And when was it that the concluding moment of an action came to be denoted by ἀπό? Had this been the meaning of the author, he must have expressed himself thus: καίτοι τῶν ἔργων τῆς καταβολῆς κόσμου ἤδη τετελεσμένων. Works which are done ἀπό καταβολῆς κόσμου, can be no other than such as are done *since* the creation of the world, *from* the creation of the world onwards.

And, if the above interpretation is ungrammatical, it is no less irreconcileable with the context and the train of thought. The meaning which it yields would be this: Although God already rested, men did not yet rest. But the "although" is about as suitable in this place as it would be in the sentence: Although Quintus is already very old, Cestius is still young. From the fact that God has already completed the creation of the world, to infer directly, and without any intermediate proposition, a warrant for expecting that the Israelites shall be introduced into the *rest of God*, is about as valid a sequence as, from the fact that Quintus is old, to infer the expectation that Cestius also shall be old. The commentators, too, have not been insensible to this impropriety, and have sought to lessen it in various ways. Many of the older interpreters gave to καίτοι for a change the signification et quidem—of this nothing further need be said. Others of more recent date, following Calvin, have sought to remove the difficulty by ingenious supplements. Tholuck, for example, supplements the idea in the following terms: The Israelites were not permitted to enter into the *rest;* and yet

God rested *in heaven* after the work of creation was finished, so that an objective *resting-place* already existed. But what reader could find all this in the words καίτοι, &c.? Bleek has shown most ingenuity in filling up the idea, and if we have rightly understood him, it is in the following way: God rested from the *creation;* but God's rest is reciprocal in its nature; then only does God *really* rest, when he has completed the work of his *manifestation* to the *creatures*. And, accordingly, it is remarkable that for God *the Sabbath* has already begun; and there are, nevertheless, *creatures who do not keep the Sabbath with him,* nay, who *cannot* keep it with him. But however true this train of thought may be in itself, we read nothing of it in the text; and no one who reads this chapter, without beginning at the middle, and coming backward, could possibly have in his mind, in reading ver. 3, these intermediate ideas about the Sabbath (which are to be found in ver. 9 s, and in a similar form to that in which Bleek has given them.) But, in addition to this, no indication is given, even in what follows, of the antithesis implied in the words, that God rests *indeed* from the creation, *but* that he has not yet finished the *work* of the manifestation of himself to his creatures. We must therefore reject this explanation also, on account of the *context,* even although the *interpretation* on which it rests had been less untenable in a grammatical point of view. The true and most simple explanation is to be drawn from ver. 2. The author had there affirmed of the word spoken by Moses, that it was not *mixed* or amalgamated with the hearers *by faith,* that it remained external and strange to them, and therefore that it could profit them nothing. He had, in opposition to this, laid it down in ver. 3, that we, the members of the New Testament Israel, enter into that *rest* into which the Old Testament Israel entered not, and that we enter *by faith*. What more natural, now, than that the reader should think of the well-known opposition of faith and works, which indeed had already been implicitly indicated in ver. 2? It was almost an example of the rule of three: the New Testament word of Christ is related to faith as the word of Moses, the law, is to—the works.

Only we must guard against limiting the idea expressed in ἔργα to *good* works. Of such works, indeed, *none* were performed from the creation of the world. Nay, this is rather what the apostle intends to bring out—that as "the works" were done from the beginning, and yet notwithstanding Israel did not enter into the rest, these works were none of them good, but evil, and at least imperfect, works tainted with sin.

In like manner, we must guard against another improper restriction of ἔργα to the works of the law, fulfilments of the Mosaic commands. These were, of course, not performed from the creation of the world, but only after the giving of the law from Sinai. No; the author speaks quite generally of the works of men, of the *work* of the human race, of all activity, all endeavours better or worse. The idea is, in general terms, as follows: *All that can be comprehended under the term works, has been performed from the time of the creation of the world onwards, but has never been sufficient to bring man to the* κατάπαυσις, *to a state of satisfied rest.* The inference from this is, that an entirely new way of salvation, not that of human doings and human endeavours, but that of faith in the salvation which God hath provided, is necessary in order to attain to the *rest*.

Ver. 4, 5.—This idea is in these verses more fully explained. The author shows here, that by ἔργα he meant not the works of God, but the works of men in opposition to those of God. "*God*, indeed, rested already on the seventh of the days occupied in the creation of the world: and still he says of *men*, they are not yet capable of entering into his rest." God's works, then, were finished—internally perfect, and therefore externally complete— but the works of men were internally imperfect, and hence, externally there was no mention of a resting of men; the work and labour still continued, and could not cease until the result was arrived at; the result, however, remained ever unattained.

The first part of this idea is introduced by the words: εἴρηκε γάρ που περὶ τῆς ἑβδόμης. On που compare our remark on chap. ii. 6. The author here refers beforehand to the ἑβδόμη, because he intends afterwards to graft a further idea on this preliminary mention of it, which he does in ver. 9 s.

In ver. 6—8 the author passes to a *new* sentiment, a new point of comparison between the work of Christ and the work of Moses. The opposition between the work of both is twofold, just as was that in chap. iii. 2—6 between the persons. The first imperfection in the work of Moses consisted in this (iv. 2—5)—

that his work imparted no power for the fulfilment of it, did not unite itself to the hearers through faith, and therefore could not conduct to the promised rest; the second consists in this—that the rest itself into which the Israelites could be introduced by Moses and were actually introduced by Joshua, was only an earthly, a typical rest, while Christ conducts to a real a substantial rest, which in its nature corresponds to the Sabbath rest of God. But, as in chap. iii. the first point of difference was repeated in the developement of the second (Moses was a *servant* in the *typical* house, Christ a *son* in the *living* house), so here also, when the author shows the opposition between the Old and New Testament rest, he repeats at the same time the first point of difference, that, namely, between the not being able to enter into the rest, and the being able to enter into it, nay, he finds in the second the full confirmation of the first.

Ver. 6, 7, form a somewhat complicated period. The *protasis* consists of two parts, which depend on the verbs ἀπολείπεται and οὐκ εἰσῆλθον; the *apodosis* consists of the statement, that God, in the old covenant, indicates by the Psalmist a future rest. The connecting link between the two is the particle ἐπεί, since.

The words, *it remains that some enter into it*, are evidently only a repetition of what is said in ver. 1 (a promise being left of entering into his rest), and express, therefore, the fundamental thesis, that the promise of a rest was not fully or really fulfilled in the entrance of Joshua into Canaan. The second member: *those to whom it was first preached entered not in because of unbelief* form, again, only the negative reverse side of the first member, and who are the persons meant by those to whom it was first preached is explained in ver. 2, where it is said of the Christians in opposition to the Old Testament Israel: *for to us hath the gospel been preached as well as to them.* The τίνες, therefore, whose entrance into the rest is still impending, are the Christians, while *those to whom it was first preached* are the Jews, and those, especially, to whom in the time of Moses the gracious call to enter into the land of rest was addressed. The words *through unbelief* serve to remind us at once of the subjective fault of the Jews mentioned in chap. iii. 16—19, and of the objective impotency of the law mentioned in chap. iv. 2—5.

The principal question here, however, is, in what logical relation do the protasis and the apodosis stand to each other. The view generally taken of this relation is, that the apodosis contains the final conclusion at which the author aims, and which he wishes to prove, while the protasis contains the proof. The entire passage is viewed as containing an answer to the question, why God *must* needs have defined and mentioned a second day of rest. The necessitating cause of this was, that the Israelites were disobedient the first time.—To this interpretation the words *since they to whom it was first preached entered not in because of unbelief* are certainly agreeable, but not the words: *seeing it remains that some enter into it.* That *at present* (in the author's time) a farther entering into the rest is about to be accomplished, cannot be the reason why God has, in the time of David, defined a more distant day of rest. (The most that can be said is, that $ἀπολεί-πεται$ might be related to $ὁρίζειν$ as a kind of *end* or *aim*.)

We think, however, that the protasis contains the answer to the question, why it was *possible* for God to determine a second day of rest. We may give the sense periphrastically for the sake of clearness thus: only for this *reason* could God define a second day of rest long after the time of Moses, because, namely, as was said above in ver. 1, 2, the original promise still waits for its fulfilment, and the Israelites at that time did not in general enter into the rest. The thing therefore to be proven lies in the protasis, the proof in the apodosis (as if, for example, I wished to prove that one is a spendthrift and said to him: " because you are a spendthrift your father has not entrusted you with any money = if you were not a spendthrift he would not have withdrawn his credit from you). It is only *formally* and *apparently*, that the protasis contains any reason for the apodosis; the sinew of the proof lies in the conclusion drawn backward from the apodosis to the protasis. Had the author written logically he would have said: " Only if the case so stands as was said in ver. 1, 2, can we comprehend how God could again define a day of rest; but, as he has actually done this, the case must stand so; there *must* still be a rest to be entered into, and Israel at that time must not have entered the rest." (Quite a similar form of logical inversion occurs in chap. v. 1; see infra.)

This absolute non-entrance of the Israelites ($οὐκ\ εἰσῆλθον$) now prepares the way for the second point of difference between the work of Christ and that of Moses. All that was said in chap. iii. was, that the *single generation* consisting of Moses' contemporaries did not come into the rest, but died in the wilderness. There was still room in that chapter for the supposition, that the following generation did enter into the rest. But, already in chap. iv. 1, the author has tacitly presupposed, that even after the time of Joshua, even now, the fulfilment of that promise of rest is yet at least in part to be accomplished, and in the 6th verse he speaks quite unconditionally of an οὐκ εἰσελθεῖν on the part of those to whom it was first preached, while in ver. 8, which is explanatory, he directly denies disertis verbis that Joshua brought the Israelites to the rest—denies that the rest into which Joshua brought the people was the *true* rest. *Thus, in ver. 6, ss., the Old Testament rest is opposed to that of the New Testament as the merely typical to the substantial* (just as in chap. iii. 5, the *house* in which Moses served for a testimony of future revelations, is opposed to the *house* of Christ, whose living stones we are.)

Now this proposition thus modified and thus expanded, that the Old Testament rest was in general not the true rest, is in ver. 7 proven from the Old Testament. Only thus can it be explained, that God could point to a second future day of rest. And this God has done in the 7th verse of the 95th Psalm (cited in chap. iii. for a different purpose).

Three questions present themselves here. First, how the apodosis, ver. 7, is to be construed; secondly, whether the 95th Psalm is one of David's, and thirdly, whether the passage proves what the author intends it should prove. With regard to the first of these questions, the words ἐν Δαυιδ . . . . προείρηται are a parenthetical insertion, with which the author interrupts himself after he had begun the citation itself, and which, grammatically, stands in the relation of apposition to the subject involved in ὁρίζει. The words μετὰ τοσοῦτον χρόνον determine the time of the λέγων, and intimate that God spake thus so long after the time of Joshua, namely, by the mouth, and therefore in the time, of David; and the words καθὼς προείρηται likewise connect grammatically with λέγων, and indicate to the reader that the words here cited had already been cited above in chap. iii. 7, s., and 15.[1] As regards the *third question*, it must be acknowledged that the argumentative force of the passage is very apparent. The Psalmist refers back to the time when Israel was called to enter into its rest, and when Israel neglected this call by its disobedience; then he exhorts the Israelites, on what day they should hear the voice of God again, to give a different response to it from what they did then, and to obey it without delay (according to the Greek translation: if ye again hear his voice *to-day*, obey it *to-day*.) The Psalmist therefore presupposes the possibility of Israel's being again placed in an analogous situation to what it was then, and admonishes it not to forfeit again the entrance into the offered glory.

And this, too, involves the answer to the *second* question. Whether David was the author of the psalm or not, is a question on which no important result depends; the 95th psalm is not like the 2d and 110th, grafted on a special promise made to David, but contains only the general expectation of future gracious calls from God, which, if Israel had already been conducted by Joshua into its absolute rest and satisfaction, would no longer have been possible. All that needs to be insisted on is, that the passage in the psalm was written "so long afterwards" (namely after Moses and Joshua); its force of proof lay, not in its antiquity, but rather in the lateness, of the time when it was written. In the Old Testament the psalm has no superscription, the Sept. which was in the hands of the readers of the Epistle to the Hebrews ascribed it to David, and this comparatively late period was sufficient for the argument which the author would draw from it, and therefore he could without hesitation adopt the statement of the Sept. Critical investigations into the genuineness or spuriousness of the superscription which the psalm bears in the Sept., would certainly have been just as little in place here, as, in the address of Stephen, Acts vii. 14, an investigation into the accuracy of the number 75. It must not, however, be over-

---

[1] Others take the first σήμερον as the object of λέγων, "inasmuch as in David he calls it (the day) a to-day." Others, as Calvin, Beza, Grotius, Bleek, take σήμερον as *apposition* to ἡμέραν τινά, "he defines again a day, a to-day." This entire treatment of σήμερον is *modern*.

looked that our author, inasmuch as he says merely "in David" (= in the book of David, the Psalms) and not *by the mouth of David*, shows plainly enough his intention, that no weight at all should here be made to rest on the person of David. In ver. 8 we have an extension of the proof contained in ver. 7, and, with this, an explanation of ver. 7, in the clear and simple statement, that such a reference to a future call of God and *word of God* would not have been possible, if Ἰησοῦς (*i.e.* in this context of course *Joshua*) had already truly led the Israelites into the rest. This, however, involves the inference, that Joshua did not truly lead the Israelites into the rest; the earthly possession of the land which was not even completely conquered under Joshua, which under the Judges was oppressed by heathen kings, which had in Saul a bad king, in David one who had little rest from war, in Solomon one who fell from wisdom into folly, and which, after the death of Solomon, sunk down from its high eminence of typical glory—that earthly possession of the land such as was brought about by Joshua, was not yet the true *rest of God*. Thus has the writer returned to the thesis contained in ver. 6 : *The Old Testament had no true rest*, and therewith to the thesis in ver. 1, 2 : *We have still to expect the entrance into a rest, and that the true rest.*

This last inference is now drawn in ver. 9. The author, however, does not here say merely that there is still a κατάπαυσις, a state of rest to be looked for, but he denotes this κατάπαυσις by the higher name σαββατισμός (a word which occurs besides only in Plutarch de superstit. 3), *as the celebration of a Sabbath*. And thus he carries out here an idea which he had indicated in ver. 4; he carries it out here, after having in ver. 6—8 shown, that the rest into which Joshua led the Israelites was no true rest. Now, he shows, on the other hand, that the rest into which the people of God were to be led at a future time, and therefore by Christ, is true, because it bears the character of a *Sabbatical* rest, and thus truly corresponds to the rest of God, after the work of creation was finished. *Here, therefore*, after having suitably prepared the way, the author *first* brings out the idea which the commentators have thrust into ver. 3, where it could have suggested itself to the mind of no reader.

God rested on the seventh day of the creation, because he had finished his work not merely outwardly, but because his work was, internally and qualitatively, a finished and perfect work (ver. 4.) But men could not in Moses', nay, even in Joshua's time, attain to any rest from their activity, labour, pains, and exertion (ver. 3), because their work and activity were internally imperfect, stained with sin. The true rest lies in the future; this must be the rest analogous to the rest of God, a *holy*, a *Sabbath rest*; it must consist in this, that man is able to rest from his works, in like manner and in the same way, as God did from his, in other words, that man has finished his work internally, and can appear before God with the result of his work undefiled by sin.

Ver. 10. And this work man has accomplished in the person of his Saviour and substitute, Jesus Christ. This verse is generally understood as containing a general statement ("he who, quisquis, enters into his rest, rests from his works"), and it is supposed that the aorist κατέπαυσεν is used here, by way of change, instead of the present, or (Bleek), that the aorist is occasioned by the aorist to be supplied at ὥσπερ. But with all this artifice, nothing more is gained than a statement in great measure tautological. When we translate the words with grammatical exactness as they stand ("for he who has entered into his rest, himself rested in like manner from his works, as God from his") they yield the finest and the most striking parallel to the corresponding member in the first principal part of our epistle at chap. ii. 9. In the second section of the first principal part the three members of the argument were the following.

1. Man is destined to the dominion over the universe.

But 2. Man is not yet so highly exalted.

But 3. Jesus is already exalted.

Quite analogous to this (with a difference only in the formal logical connection of the three members) is, what we find in this, the second section of the second principal part:

1. Man has received the call to enter into his rest.

2. He has not yet been led into this rest by Joshua; there is still a rest to be expected.

3. And that a *Sabbatical rest*, for: Jesus, who is entered into his rest, rests in a Sabbatical manner as God does.

The statement in ver. 10 is therefore not general, but special; by the words ὁ γὰρ εἰσελθών the author meant Jesus, and every unprejudiced reader must also, on account of the aorist κατέπαυσεν understand the verse in the same way. The author does not expressly add the name Ἰησοῦς, because in ver. 8 this name was used to designate Joshua. In evident opposition to the Joshua who could *not* bring the people to the rest, the author speaks in ver. 10 of " that one who hath entered into his rest." (Αὐτοῦ refers to θεοῦ, according to the analogy of chap. iii. 11, 18.)

Jesus has internally finished his works, nay, the works of all mankind, and therefore has brought them to an external completion. With the Sabbath of the resurrection, on which, after his work and humiliation was ended, he entered into his state of exaltation and glory, on which he left the state in which the soul was separated from the body, the Sheol, and entered into the life of glorified body; with this Sabbath began the *second Sabbath of God*, the Sabbath of God the *Son*, as with the future setting up of a new heavens and a new earth, the Sabbath of God the Holy Ghost will begin. When, therefore, in accordance with the eternally binding command which requires that after every six days of activity in our earthly calling, one day of rest should be devoted to the sacred Sabbath activities of our heavenly calling, Christians everywhere reckon the seven days not from the creation-Sabbath of God the Father, but from the creation-Sabbath of God the Son—this mode of reckoning finds its justification in the passage before us.

Ver. 11. Man has not yet entered into the rest, but Jesus has entered into the true Sabbath rest; what, remains, then, but that *we also* should seek *by him* to enter into this σαββατισμός. This exhortation follows in ver. 11: *Let us strive, therefore, to enter into that rest*, with the accompanying warning not to let it be with us as with those contemporaries of Moses, who, because they listened not through *unbelief* and *disobedience* to the gracious call which was then addressed to them, were afterwards held up by the Psalmist as an example of warning to us. Let us beware, therefore, says the author, lest we neglect the second more excellent and more powerful call of grace, and lest we also should, in our turn, become a sad example of warning to others. Ὑπόδειγμα, a later Greek word instead of the attic παράδειγμα. Ἐν ὑποδείγματι "as an example," a proleptic use of the ἐν, "that we do not turn out to be an example."

Ver. 12. The warning, however, is rendered still more pointed and impressive by the statement, that the excuse which (according to ver. 2) the contemporaries of Moses had, no longer remains for us. The ground of *unbelief* in their case lay, not merely in the perverse will of the men, but in part, also, in the objective impotency of the *word* brought by Moses, the law, which could awaken no confidence of faith, no joy, no love, and which could not open the heart. This extenuating circumstance, however, does not hold in our case; in our case, there is nothing weak or deficient in the word of God; for the word of God is quick, powerful, penetrating into the soul; if we fall into unbelief, the blame rests *with ourselves alone.*

By the *word of God* is therefore clearly to be understood, as the context shows, the word of the New Testament revelation. Only, it is not to be supposed that in the genititive τοῦ θεοῦ is expressed the antithesis to the λόγος τῆς ἀκοῆς of ver. 2. The genitive τοῦ θεοῦ forms rather merely the antithesis to the first person plural σπουδάσωμεν. "Let us strive to enter into that rest, for nothing any longer fails on the part of *God*—the word of *God* is powerful." Only from the context is it to be inferred as a thing self-evident, that the author speaks here of the word of God which we have heard, and not of the law of Moses.

And thus ver. 12 certainly forms a supplementary antithesis to ver. 2 in respect of the *matter* (though not in a formally logical connection.) This deep and fine connection has, however, by all commentators hitherto been overlooked. A portion of these commentators (many of the Fathers, Clericus, Bertholdt) have understood ὁ λόγος in the sense in which it is used by John of the Son of God as pre-existent, and find in ver. 12 a reason why we ought to fear—because Christ, who as the pre-existent λόγος punished the Israelites, is so severe; an explanation which is not consistent with the usus linguae of the Epistle to the Hebrews (comp. i. 6, where Christ as pre-existent is denoted rather by πρωτότοκος.) Another section of the critics (almost all from the Reformation downwards,) understood by the λόγος τοῦ θεοῦ the Word of God in respect of its minatory declarations,[1] and find in the verse this sentiment: We must therefore beware of becoming an example, because the threatening predictions of God were so surely and powerfully fulfilled. But, according to this, we should rather expect to find in ver. 12 the words: " for the word of God is *killing* and *wounding* as a sword.". Instead of this, we read of the quickness and *penetrating sharpness* of the word, a sharpness penetrating into the innermost joints and marrow, into the soul and spirit. These predicates form evidently an antithesis to the words of ver. 2 μὴ συγκεκερασμένος τῇ πίστει τοῖς ἀκούσασι.

The predicates, now, according to our interpretation, explain themselves without great difficulty. The word of God (with which we have to do in the New Testament), the word of the revelation of the gospel in Christ, is *living*, chiefly in opposition to the stiff, dead law, comp. Gal. iii. 21. The law is a dead fixing of the commands of God upon us,—as it stands, so it is. The gospel is nothing but an embodying of living love itself in living words, words which immediately take captive the heart. The law kills because it is itself a dead letter, because it makes demands which it does not give strength to perform, the gospel is itself a living breath of love, and therefore it makes alive, therefore it works out what it aims at, it is ἐνεργής.

The nature of its efficacy is now more particularly described as an innermost penetration of the innermost man, as a genuine συγκεράννυμι (comp. ver. 2.) It is sharper than every two-edged sword (δίστομος that which has two mouths, then that which has two fore-sides and no back, thus used of a sword: two-edged comp. Rev. i. 16, ii. 12, LXX., Is. xi. 4, &c.) Not the deadly efficacy but the penetrating sharpness, is that which is meant to be set forth. This appears somewhat more clearly in the following member διϊκνούμενος, &c. " It (the word of God) penetrates even to the dividing asunder of soul and spirit, of the joints and the marrow." The first question that presents itself here is,

---

[1] Only Grotius says: Convenit hoc omni verbo Dei, sed praecipue evangelio, still without explaining more particularly the connection with ver. 11.

whether this language is to be understood as figurative or not; *i.e.* whether in what is here predicated of the λόγος τ. θ., we are to understand the language as properly a continuation of the figure of the sword (so that logically it would have to be extended thus: it penetrates *as a sword which penetrates* to the dividing asunder of soul and spirit, of joints and marrow), or whether we are to understand a real and literal efficacy of the word of God as such to be set forth in the words: the word of God pierces into soul and spirit, into marrow and bone (in which case only the latter expression would have to be taken as metonymical, or better still as a proverbial expression). Now, prima facie, it seems to be decisive against the latter and in favour of the former interpretation, that according to the latter, the author would be guilty of the inelegance of passing from a statement which is proper and definite, viz. that the word of God penetrates soul and spirit, to one which is vague and proverbial—that it penetrates marrow and bone. But the former interpretation also is attended with a difficulty by no means inconsiderable. Namely: can the figure of a sharp sword be, generally speaking, represented in the words: the sword penetrates even to the dividing asunder of *soul and spirit* ? Swords have to do surely with bodies, not with souls and spirits! The most that can be said for this sense is, that the expression "separation of soul and spirit" may be understood as something equivalent to the separation of the body from the soul, and therefore as a mere designation of bodily death. In this case, we must either suppose that the expression is to be extended thus: "to the separation of the soul and the spirit *from the body*" (which, however, would destroy the parallelism with the following member ἁρμῶν τε καὶ μυελῶν, while it cannot be perceived why the author should have named the spirit together with the soul, and why he did not rather simply say: ψυχῆς τε καὶ σώματος.) Or, we must, with Olshausen, have recourse to the conjecture that the author, under the idea of bodily death, had in his mind the consummation of a trichotomy, the separation of the soul from the spirit as well as from the body.

This leads us, however, to a *second question*, the determination of which is indispensable, ere we are at liberty to return to the first. The question is this: must we understand as connected by τε καί two things closely united with each other by nature, or two things which have grown up together, between which the sword (or the word of God as a sword) penetrates, and which it is to separate *from each other*? So that the soul should be viewed as having grown upon the spirit, the ἁρμός on the μυελός, somewhat in the same way as the bark on the wood, and the sword cuts through between them somewhat in the same way as a knife separates the bark from the wood. Or, are we to understand τε καί as connecting two things lying deep, of which, however, the second lies still deeper than the first, so that the sword (or the divine word as a sword) first of all, generally speaking, penetrates to them, and then, moreover, penetrates through the first to the second? Thus the spirit would be viewed as being in somewhat the same relation to the soul, as the innermost kernel of a fruit is to the core, and the sword as a knife which cuts into the core, nay, into the innermost kernel itself. The word μερισμός is not at all decisive in favour of the first interpretation; what is spoken of is a separation *as well* of the soul as of the spirit, *as well* of the joints as of the marrow, but not a separation of the soul *from* the spirit, of the joints from the marrow. This very τε καί is rather in favour of the second interpretation.

But a certain solution of the question must be obtained, first of all, from a closer consideration of the two pairs of things themselves. Could the author have had before his mind a separation of the soul *from* the spirit in general? In support of this, reference is made to the biblical trichotomy of body, soul, and spirit which meets us in 1 Thess. v. 23. There is undoubtedly a trichotomy in that passage; but whether by this is to be understood any such *mechanical* construction of man out of three parts or substances; whether it involves the possibility that the soul and the spirit can be cut asunder from each other, so that each may stand by itself, is indeed very much to be questioned. The Holy Scripture certainly distinguishes the soul from the body, and the spirit from the body, and the soul from the spirit. But nowhere does it represent the body as *outwardly separable* from the soul. The present body is a σῶμα ψυχικόν (1 Cor. xv. 44), and the ψυχικὸν εἶναι belongs to its essence. Separated from the soul, it is no longer "body," but "corpse;" every atom in it is qualitatively different as soon as the soul is severed from it; the body is throughout a quickened, animated, living, active material; the corpse is but a material subject to chemical laws. Now, as a "body" separated from the soul is a nonentity, much less can we conceive of a soul separated from the spirit. The same ψυχή which, by its separation from the body, has changed it into a corpse, is called as such also πνεῦμα (Luke xxiv. 37), a sure proof that soul and spirit are still more identical than soul and body. But how are we to explain the circumstance, that in 1 Thess. v. 23, and Heb. iv. 12, soul and spirit are *distinguished* from each other? Soul is the designation of that *life-centre* of individuality *given by nature*, proceeding from natural generation, and bringing with it from nature (as being a thing *not free*, but subject to the influence of nature) certain definite qualities and dispositions. The irrational animal has also this physical centre of life. But that of man is, according to his nature, immortal; the chief endowment which he has brought along with him is that of self-consciousness in the higher sense, and with this, the consciousness of God; thus his nature possesses the internal necessity of developing itself on the basis of *individuality* given by nature, to a self-determining *personality*, to *fill* itself with an endless existence. And thus the same *centre of life*, viewed as self-conscious, bears the name of πνεῦμα. The πνεῦμα is ψυχή in respect of its fundamental quality derived from nature, the ψυχή is πνεῦμα in respect of its personal development. This then affords also a complete explanation of the passage in 1 Thess. v. 23. The whole man,—spirit, soul, and body, is to be preserved blameless. The keeping blameless of the soul can certainly be distinguished from that of the spirit, without its being necessary to infer from this, that the soul is a second substance separable from the spirit. The body is kept blameless, when it is shielded from disease and preserved from vicious defilement, the soul, when it is preserved from insanity (distraction of the soul, frenzy), and pollution through unregulated instincts and passions, the spirit, when it is protected against error and sin.

We cannot, therefore, speak of a separation of the soul *from* the spirit (and with this the possibility falls to the ground of comprehending the μερισμός, &c., under the figure of the sword.) On the other hand, an excellent sense is evolved when we regard the soul as something lying deep within man, the spirit as lying still deeper, and the word of God as *penetrating into the soul, and thence still deeper, even into the spirit*. For, the first and more superficial effect of the gospel is, that it in many ways stirs and moves the mind,—the complex assemblage of feelings derived from nature,—it involuntarily seizes the mind, binds and disturbs it. This stirring and arresting effect on the ψυχή it exercises in wider circles also among the unawakened, it exercises this effect in national churches upon the nation, sinks itself into the heart as a still slumbering seed-corn, keeps hold of the man although he may not yet, by any free act of his own, have decided in favour of the gospel and its reception, and works on in the sphere of the *soul*, produces a strange and unaccountable uneasiness, and again gives comfort like a soft balm; in all this, it is only the ψυχή which has experienced its *power*. Soon, however, it penetrates still deeper, works no longer merely in the sphere of the involuntary activities of the soul, where no conscious resistance is made to it, but penetrates into the watchfully conscious life of the thoughts, passes from the ἐνθυμήσεις to the ἔννοιαι, obtains for itself a place in the sphere of the conscious will and voluntary thought, and carries on its plea with the old Adam in the clear light of day, until the man is driven to a final decision for or against the gospel.

The second member ἁρμῶν τε καὶ μυελῶν serves most fully to establish the interpretation we have given. With as little reason can it be said that the ἁρμοί have *grown* upon the μυελοί, as the soul upon the spirit. Μυελός is the marrow, μυελοί are the pieces of marrow in the cavities of the bones. Ἁρμός, literally joint, can be taken either in the signification of limb or of joint. The marrow grows neither together with the limbs nor the joints, but forms the inmost kernel of the limbs, and if we adopt the signification limb, we have, here again, two things named which are concentrically related to each other. It is not meant, therefore, that the marrow and the limb are severed from each other, but something is spoken of which cuts not merely into the members, but through the bones into the innermost marrow. Or, if we prefer the signification *joint*, something is spoken of, which not merely pierces as a common sword into the place of the cartilaginous joint, and in this way separates, for example, the under from the upper part of the arm at the elbow, but which penetrates also through and through to the marrow tubes.

But what is this something which has this penetrating power? The *separation of soul and spirit* must, as we have seen, be taken in the proper sense, and referred to the *word of God*, not, in a figurative sense, to the sword. Can, then, this *separation of joints and marrow*, which is grammatically included with the foregoing in a single μερισμός, be referred to anything else than to the *word of God?* And yet can it with any propriety be said of the word of God, that it cuts into the joints, nay even into the marrow? This brings us back to the *first question* which, as it will be remembered, was left undetermined.—I do not think we are warranted in charging the author with an inelegant recurrence from the thing to the figure; but the words in question seem capable of the easiest explanation, by supposing a rhetorical intermixture of two ideas which are logically to be separated, such as we have already observed in chap. ii. 18, iii. 3. With logical precision, the idea would be expressed thus: "The word of God is still sharper than a sword; for a sword cuts generally only into the soft flesh (soft, offering less resistance), but the word of God cuts not only into the (passive) soul, but even into the (free and conscious) spirit; it therefore resembles a sword which penetrates not merely into the members, but (through the bones) into the marrow." This chain of ideas the author puts into a more concise form thus: "The word of God is sharper than every two-edged sword, inasmuch as it penetrates to the dividing asunder as well of spirit as of soul" thus resembling a sword which pierces even to the separation of the parts), "as well of the marrow as of the joints."

Κριτικὸς ἐνθυμήσεων καὶ ἐννοιῶν καρδίας—in these words lies the explanation of what was meant by the *cutting asunder of soul and spirit*. Ἐνθυμήσεις are the natural desires and passions (not the evil only) which involuntarily and undisturbed find play in the natural man. The word of the gospel falls into these like a leavening, a λόγος κριτικός. *i.e.* not as a κριτής, a judge, but as having a *critical or separating* effect upon them. It causes a movement, a fermentation, an unavoidable disquiet among the more unconscious and slumbering impulses and passions; the man feels himself no longer happy, no longer innocent in the indulgence of inclinations to which he yielded before with undisturbed pleasure; he feels himself no longer satisfied with enjoyments and delights, which before were the ideal after which he strove. The word of God, however, exercises this sifting, rebuking, awakening, and comforting power, not merely on the ἐνθυμήσεις, but also on the ἔννοιαι (1 Pet. i. 12), the opinions, the maxims and principles which have been formed on the basis of the natural man, as the result of the conscious and free exercise of the mind. This power it has, because, as the word of that *grace* in the highest manifestation of which the *holiness* of God remained altogether unscathed, it both forgives and judges the same sin in the heart of man, at one and the same time, and by one and the same act. On the cross of Christ the guilt has been atoned for, and the sin which brought Christ to the cross at the same time condemned, and held up as an object of abhorrence to all who love the propitiator. Thus has this word of wonder, the wonder of all words, the power to comfort without seducing into levity, to shake without plunging into despair. It draws while it rebukes, it sifts while it draws; the man cannot set himself free from it who has once heard it; its gentleness will not allow him to cast it from him, and as he holds it fast he escapes not also from its sifting severity. It has in one word—a barb. The law of Moses rebukes the deed done; the word of the gospel works upon the source whence actions proceed, the mind, the heart; it judges *before* the deed is done not *after*; it is living; its judging consists in making better, in sanctifying the inner man of the heart, and thus extending its efficacy to the outward life.

Ver. 13. In these words, in which a power of *vision* is ascribed to the word of God (" nothing is hid from its eyes"), we have an instance of that familiar tropical application of this faculty, which is wont to be made to any *illuminating body*, and are by no means under the necessity of recurring to that unsuitable interpretation which explains the *word of God* of a *person*. We can say with perfect propriety: " the sun looks on us, before the sun everything lies open, nothing is hid from it; the stars look into the night"—we can say this without representing the sun and the stars as personal beings. So here: all things lie open before the word of the gospel, simply because this word *throws its light* upon and illuminates all things, even the most secret motions of the heart.

Τραχηλίζω, to bend the neck, is said, according to the view of the later critics (since Perizonius), to have received the signification "to put in the pillory" (because those who were put in the pillory had their neck bent downwards), and from this came the signification : to lay open. There is no necessity, however, for such an explanation. The explanation given by old Greek scholiasts is the true one: *τραχηλίζω*, to bend any one's neck *backwards*, and thereby to lay bare the throat, hence in general: to lay bare.

Αὐτοῦ refers, of course, back to λόγος, not to θεοῦ, by which the thought would be entirely destroyed. With as little reason can it be regarded as pointing forwards to πρὸς ὅν (in the sense of ἐκείνου), so that we should have to translate the words thus: "all things are open to the eyes of that with which we have to do," and as if this were to be distinguished from the λόγος τοῦ θεοῦ ver. 12, as something different. It is self-evident that both genitives αὐτοῦ point *backwards* to ὁ λόγος τοῦ θεοῦ.

The relative clause πρὸς ὅν ἡμῖν ὁ λόγος is therefore dependent on an *αὐτοῦ already sufficiently definite in itself*, and does not serve the purpose of giving a definiteness to αὐτοῦ, but contains a new and additional idea. That λόγος does not here again denote the word of God, but has a different signification from what it has in ver. 12, is likewise evident. Luther, Schulz, Vater, and others take it in the signification "speech, address," and πρός in the signification "in reference to," and the whole clause is analogous to the words in chap. v. 11 περὶ οὗ (πολὺς) ἡμῖν ὁ λόγος. They rendered it, accordingly, thus: "before the eyes of the word *of which we speak*." But this additional clause would be altogether insipid, superfluous, and useless. Others therefore sought to find a weightier meaning in the words. Following the Peschito Chrys., Theophyl., Theodoret, Schmid, Michaelis assigned to the word λόγος the signification, "reckoning," which it has in the phrase λόγον ἀποδιδόναι (for example xiii. 17), and rendered: "of which we have to give account." This sense is not even suitable to the right explanation of ὁ λόγος τ. θ., nor is it consistent with the right explanation of ver. 12, in which, as we have seen, it is not the judicial threatenings of God's word that are spoken of. Moreover, this sense will not admit of being justified on grammatical grounds, as λόγος ἐστί alone cannot stand for λόγος ἀποδοτέος ἐστί. With much more reason, Calvin, Kuinoel, and De Wette take λόγος in the general signification, res, negotium, and render: "with which we have to do." This explanation is doubly recommended if we were justified in finding in ver. 12 a material antithesis to ver. 2, the antithesis, namely, between the λόγος τῆς ἀκοῆς which was spoken to the *contemporaries of Moses* and could not profit them, and the λόγος τοῦ θεοῦ ver. 12, which is living and powerful, and by which, *according to the context*, is to be understood the New Testament word of God in Christ. We have just observed in ver. 12, that this antithesis is in no way *expressed* in the words λόγος τοῦ θεοῦ (inasmuch as the genitive θεοῦ must be referred to a totally different antithesis); we see now, however, that the author has by no means left that antithesis without marked and definite expression. With intentional emphasis, he places quite at the end (and this very position gives it a peculiar force) the relative clause πρὸς ὃν ἡμῖν ὁ λόγος, "with which *we* have to do," in which the emphasis must be laid on the ἡμῖν. (In the German translation the αὐτοῦ must be rendered not by "desjenigen" by only by the possess. pron. On this, however, no relative can, according to the rules of the German language, be dependent, so that this relative clause, even in order rightly to express the emphasis which rests upon it, must be connected with the subject of the clause in ver. 12.)

Ver. 14—16. In the last verses the striking comparison between the *dead, outward, legal word* of Moses, which could not take away the *disobedience* of the Israelites, nor lead them to the true rest, and the *living penetrating word of the new covenant* was brought to a close. From this now flows as a direct consequence, that we have therefore (οὖν) in Christ not merely a second Moses, that we have in him more than a lawgiver, that we have in him who has gone for us and before us into the eternal Sabbath rest of the heavenly sanctuary, a *High Priest*.

This conclusion of the second section of the second part is, as we have already observed, on chap. ii. 17 completely parallel with the conclusion of the second section of the *first* part. In the first part it was shown that *the Son is superior to the angels*;

a, in his *person*, because in him the eternal πρωτότοκος became man ; *b*, in his *work*, because in him as the first-fruits man is raised to the dominion over the universe, and over all heavens; and. *c*, this is effected because Christ as the *messenger of God* (ἀ...στολος) in things pertaining to men, united with this the office of *high priestly representative of men* (ἀρχιερεύς) in things pertaining to God. In the second part, it has now been shown that the *Son is superior to Moses; a*, in his *person*, as the *Son* in the perfect *house* to the *servant* in the typical *house; b, in his work*, because he first opened up the way for man to the true Sabbatical rest into which he himself entered before ; and from this it follows, *c*, that he joined to the office of a second Moses— a divinely commissioned leader *out of captivity*—the office of a *high priest*. The author having thus been led from these two different starting-points to the idea of the ἀρχιερεύς, now proceeds to place upon the two first parts which may be viewed as the pillars of the arch, the third part which forms the key-stone, chap. vi., vii.

It will appear from what has been said that the particle οὖν, ver. 14, is to be taken in its usual signification, as marking an *inference* to be drawn from the foregoing, and as closely connecting ver. 14—16 with ver. 10—13. Those err furthest from the right understanding of the passage, who think (as Tholuck and Bleek) that the author left his *proper theme* at chap. iii. 1, lost himself, so to speak, in a digression which had *no proper connexion with the subject*, and that he now takes a sudden leap back to the path he had left, so that οὖν here is to be taken in a *resumptive* signification, and as referring to the end of chap. ii. ("Seeing then that we have, as has before been said, an high priest," &c.) With more reason it was already perceived by Calvin, that the author has compared Christ first with the angels, then (according to his plan) with Moses, and that he now intends to pass to a third point ; only he failed to perceive that the idea with which the 14th verse begins, really follows as an *inference* from ver. 10—13, and thought therefore that οὖν must be taken in the signification atqui; " now further," which the word never has, and of which, as has been already said, there is no need.

Now it is not, of course, to be thought that all the epithets which are assigned to Christ in ver. 14—16, are enumerated with the view of exhibiting the *dissimilarity* between Christ and the Old Testament high priests, and the inferiority of the latter; for a comparison of this kind between Christ and the Old Testament high priest first begins at the third principal part, which immediately follows, and is there (chap. v. 1, ss.) expressly introduced by the general enumeration of the necessary requisites for the high priesthood (*for every high priest*, &c.). Here, on the other hand, we have simply the inference drawn from ver. 10—13, that to Christ belongs in general the high priestly calling (together with that of a second Moses.) All the epithets that are here assigned to him have rather the object, therefore, of showing the *similarity* between Christ and a high priest, or in other words, to vindicate the subsumption of Jesus under the idea of high priest. Ver. 14—16 do not at all belong to the third part, but quite as much to the second as chap. ii. 17, 18 to the first part; and Hugo von St Cher showed a much truer and deeper insight into the meaning and aim of the passage than the majority of later critics, when he commenced a new chapter with the words πᾶς γὰρ ἀρχιερεύς.

Ἀρχιερέα μέγαν; ἀρχιερεύς signifies by itself "high priest;" μέγας does not therefore serve to complete the idea of high priest (as is the case when it stands along with a mere ἱερεύς, when ὁ ἱερεὺς ὁ μέγας = הכהן הגדול is to be rendered by "the high priest," as for example chap. x. 21), but μέγας has here the independent force of an attribute. It follows, however, from what has before been said, that Christ is not here by the adjective μέγας, as by a diff. specif., placed in opposition to the Old Testament high priest, as the great high priest to the small, but that μέγας here simply takes the place of an epitheton naturale (just as in chap. xiii. 20, in the words τὸν ποιμένα τῶν προβάτων τὸν μέγαν.) In like manner, the words διεληλυθότα τοὺς οὐρανούς, which point back immediately to ver. 11 (comp. however also chap. vii. 26, ix. 11), serve simply to indicate an act of Christ wherein he appears analogous to the high priest; which also justifies the author in calling him an ἀρχιερεύς. These words διεληλυθότα, &c., contain therefore a supplementary explanation of the vis conclusionis indicated by οὖν. Because Christ has gone before as the first-fruits of humanity through the heavens into the eternal substantial rest, there to prepare a habitation for us, therefore, *and in so far*, was his act *analogous* not to what was done by Moses, but rather to the business of those high priests who in like manner entered into the earthly holy of holies. (That the entrance was again also *different* from that of the Old Testament high priests is indeed *implied* in these words, although it is not here *urged*. It is rather the difference between Christ and Moses that is here urged; all that is here urged is, that Christ in virtue of his being at the same time also a high priest, is superior to Moses.)

On the οὐρανοί comp. our remarks on chap. i. 3. The οὐρανοί in the *plural*, through which Jesus has passed to the right hand of God, are here the different spheres of the creature, the atmospheric, the planetary heavens, the heavens of the fixed stars and the angels. He is gone into the dwelling-place in space of the absolute, finished, absolutely undisturbed revelation of the Father.

Jesus the Son of God, a brief repetition of the idea unfolded in chap. ii., that in the person of the incarnate πρωτότοκος, who as incarnate is called the *Son of God*, man is exalted to the right hand of God.

Because, therefore, we have in the person of this Jesus an high priest, and not a mere Moses redivivus, because he is, in virtue of this, so much superior to Moses, we must " hold fast the New Testament confession, and are not at liberty to give this an inferior and subordinate place to that of the Old Testament. Κρατεῖν, not " seize," but " hold fast," the opposite of παραρρεῖν ii. 1, παραπίπτειν vi. 6.

In ver. 15 there follows not an argument or motive for the exhortation κρατῶμεν; for this has already its motive in the words *having an high priest*; besides, the circumstance that Christ sympathises with our weakness, and was tempted like us, contains no motive for that exhortation; for this being tempted is not a peculiar characteristic of the New Testament high priest, not a prerogative of the new covenant, but a quality which belongs to him in common with the Old Testament high priests. In ver. 15 we have rather an explanation of the clause, *We have an high priest*. The author shows that Christ was not wanting in the chief requisite necessary to an high priest in general. (In ver. 15, therefore, there is no such thing as a comparison between Christ and Aaron. The Old Testament high priests were in like manner *able to sympathise.* Comp. chap. vi. 1. *" Every* high priest enters into office as one taken from among men, for the benefit of men in their relation to God.")

But to what extent Christ was able to sympathise with our infirmities, and what is to be understood by these infirmities, appears most clearly from the words which follow : *Having been tempted in all things like as we are, without sin.* (At ὁμοιότητα the ἡμῶν which of course is to be understood, is omitted, as in Ephes. iii. 18.) We must here, first of all, endeavour to obtain a clear idea of what is meant by *being tempted.* Being *tempted* is, on the one hand, something different from being *seduced;* on the other hand, however, it is something different from mere *physical suffering.* He who is seduced stands not in a purely passive relation, but with his own will acquiesces in the will of the seducer; he who is tempted is as such, purely passive. This, however, is no merely physical passivity; headache as such is no πειρασμός. In order rightly and fully to apprehend the idea involved in πειρασμός, we must keep in view the opposition between nature and spirit, between involuntary physical life and freely conscious life, natural dispositions and culture, original temperament and passions and personal character, a given situation and the manner of conduct. Christ as true man had a truly human physical life, experienced the affections of joy and sorrow, of pleasure and aversion, of hope and fear and anxiety, just as we do. He was capable of enjoying the innocent and tranquil pleasures of life, and he felt a truly human shrinking from suffering and death; in short, he was in *the sphere of the involuntary life of the soul passively susceptible* as we are. But there is a moral obligation lying upon every man, not to let himself be mastered by his natural affections *which in themselves are altogether sinless,* but rather to acquire the mastery over them. This will be most evident in reference to temperaments. That one man is naturally of a sanguine temperament is no sin; but if he should allow himself to be hurried into rage by his temperament, instead of laying a check upon it, this is sin. To be of a phlegmatic temperament is no sin; but to fall into habits of sloth, by giving place to this temperament, is sin. Thus *every* temperament involves peculiar temptations. The case is similar with reference to the affections. That I feel joy in an innocent and quiet life is no sin; but were I placed in a position in which such happiness of life could be acquired or maintained only by the neglect of a duty, then it is my duty to suppress that feeling which is sinless in itself,—that innocent sensation,— and to sacrifice my pleasure to duty. And in as far as I shall still be susceptible of that natural affection of pleasure which I have sacrificed, in so far will it be to me in my peculiar position a *temptation*. That a poor man loves his children, and cannot bear that they should perish of hunger, is in itself a natural sinless affection; but let him be so placed as that without danger of discovery he could steal a piece of money, then that natural affection becomes to him a temptation.

Now, it is quite clear that a man may, in this way, find himself in the situation of *being tempted*, without its being necessary to suppose that there is therefore in him any *evil inclination*. The poor man may be a truly honest Christian man; the objective temptation is there; the thought is present to his mind in all the force of the natural affection: "If I were at liberty to take this gold, how I might appease the hunger of my children;" but at the same time he has an immediate and lively consciousness of his duty, and not a breath of desire moves within him to take the gold; he knows that he dare not do this; it is a settled thing with him that he is no thief.—So was it in reference to Christ's temptation; he was tempted "in every respect," in joy and sorrow, in fear and hope, in the most various situations, but *without sin;* the being tempted was to him purely *passive*, purely *objective;* throughout the whole period of his life he renounced the pleasures of life for *which he had a natural susceptibility*, because he could retain these only by compliance with the carnal hopes of the Messiah entertained by the multitude, and he maintained this course of conduct in spite of the prospect which became ever more and more sure, that his faithfulness and persecution would lead him to suffering and death, *of which he felt a natural fear*. That susceptibility of pleasure and this fear, were what tempted him—not sinful inclinations but pure, innocent, natural affections, belonging essentially to human nature.[1]

[1] Hence the error of the Irvinites in thinking that it is impossible to

It is evident, that a distinction is to be drawn between this *being tempted without sin* and that temptation in whith the sinful, fallen man " is drawn away of his own lust and enticed" (*i.e.* the *subjective* operation of a *sinful desire*, in an objective situation which demands the suppression of a natural affection in itself good.) That this species of temptation found any place in the sinless one, is denied in the words : *without sin*. Christ, as Olshausen well observes, possessed in his estate of humiliation not indeed the non posse peccare, but certainly like Adam the posse non peccare.

Ver. 16. brings the second section of the second part, and, therewith, this part itself to a full and formal conclusion. We have here, however, not merely the old admonition of mercly general import : not to lose the benefits of the *new* covenant from a false attachment to the forms of the *old* covenant ; the admonition is given here in a special form, namely, to hold fast the *grace* of God, and to come with joyfulness to the throne of *grace*. In speaking of this throne of grace, the author had certainly not in his mind the כַּפֹּרֶת (which indeed is called " mercy-seat" *only* in Luther's translation, but not in the original, nor in the Sept., and which was in reality a simple " cover" or " lid") ; the author in an exhortation to hold fast the specifically Christian element in the atonement of Christ, would assuredly not have expressed himself in a form peculiar to the *Jewish* cultus. The throne of grace is simply the throne of God, but of God as a reconciled father in Christ : They are to draw near to God not as a judge but as a gracious father for Christ's sake.

῞Ινα λάβωμεν ἔλεον καὶ χάριν εὕρωμεν εἰς εὔκαιρον βοήθειαν, that we may receive mercy and find grace to a seasonable help (as seasonable help.) Εὔκαιρος, opportunus, not " in time of need," but simply the opposite of an ἄκαιρος βοήθεια, a help which comes too late. Εἰς cannot, grammatically considered, introduce the *time* of the *receiving* and *finding*, but only the *end* and *result* thereof. (" That we may receive mercy, &c. to a seasonable help" = that the mercy which we receive may take the form of a help coming still at the right time ; *i.e.* to give the sense in

---

hold the real temptation of Christ without the supposition of an inward evil inclination.

other words : that we, so long as it is yet time, and we have something still to help us, may receive mercy and find grace.)

This concluding exhortation to have recourse to *grace*, forms also at the same time the transition to the following part. " Let us come to the throne of grace," the author has just said. Forthwith he himself follows his own admonition, and goes with his readers before the throne of grace, and begins the consideration of the *high priestly* calling of Christ.

PART THIRD.

(Chap. v.—vii.)

CHRIST AND THE HIGH PRIEST.

Hugo von St Cher has, here again, shown a happy tact in making a new chapter begin with the words πᾶς γὰρ ἀρχιερεύς. On the first superficial view, one might be tempted to connect chap. v. 1—10 with chap. iv. 14—16, because in both passages we find a comparison between Christ and the Old Testament high priest (a comparison, too, which has respect to the points of similarity.) But, to say nothing of the formal conclusion in iv. 16, a closer view of the contents will show us that a new part begins with v. 1, which (as before at ii. 17 s.) was merely intimated, and for which the way was prepared in iv. 14 ss. In chap. iv. 14 the writer had already come to speak of the highest and last point in the high-priestly work of Christ; the comparison with Moses and Joshua had led him to the high-priestly entrance of Christ into the Sabbatical rest of the heavenly sanctuary. In chap. v. 1, on the contrary, he begins again, so to speak, at the lowest point and goes upwards, specifying one by one the requisites for the office of High Priest, and proving whether these requisites are found in Christ. (Every high priest must, in the first place, be taken from among men ver. 1—3, secondly, however, must be called of God to his office ver. 4. Christ was truly called of God ver. 5, 6, but at the same time he was true man, ver. 7—9.) These points of similarity, however, lead him of themselves to the points of difference between Christ and Aaron, to the Melchisedec-nature of the priesthood of Christ, which new theme he intimates in ver. 10, and, after a somewhat lengthy digression of a hortatory character, treats it in detail in chap. vii. In chap. vii. he then takes up the threads of argument laid down in chap. ii. and chap. iv., and is at length led back to the idea, which was already only briefly intimated in chap. iv. 14 (the entrance of Christ into the *heavenly* the *true* holy of holies) as the highest point at which he aims. The entire part, therefore, chap. v. 1—chap. vii. 28, forms the exposition of the theme that was merely intimated in chap. ii. 17, and chap. iv. 14. And thus we are convinced that chap. iv. 14—16 forms in reality the *conclusion* of the second principal part, in like manner as chap. ii. 17, 18 that of the first part, and that the true and proper commencement of the third part is to be placed at chap. v. 1.

We infer also from what has just been said, that the third part is, as a whole, parallel in its arrangement with the two first parts. It, too, falls into *two sections*, (1, chap. v. 1—10, similarity between Christ and Aaron; 2, dissimilarity between Christ and Aaron, similarity with Melchisedec), and here also, these two sections are markedly separated from each other by an admonitory piece inserted between them (chap. v. 11—vi. 20.) That this hortatory piece in the third part is longer and fuller than in the two first parts can create no surprise. Already was that of the second part (extending from the 7th to the 19th verse of chap. 3) longer than that of the first part (chap. ii. 1—4); in this third part it extends to twenty-four verses, and thus shows itself even outwardly as the last part of an admonition, which from its commencement onwards, gradually becomes more urgent and more full. But in its internal character also, as we shall see, it stands in very close connexion with the chapter which follows. And a longer resting-place was necessary before this seventh chapter, not merely on account of the greater *difficulty* of its contents, but chiefly also because chap. vii. does not connect immediately with chap. v. 10, but at once points back to the train of thought in chap. i.—ii., iii.—iv., and weaves into an ingenious web all the threads formerly laid down. Chap. vii. is not merely the second section of the third part, but forms at once the key-stone of the first and second parts, and the basis of the fourth part (the argument that the sanctuary into which Christ entered is the true sanctuary, of which the Old Testament temple and worship were only a type.) Nay, the seventh chapter may thus be said to form properly the kernel and central point of the whole epistle.

SECTION FIRST.

(Chap. v. 1—10.)

CHRIST AND AARON.

Ver. 1. Γάρ is not argumentative, but explicative, and introduces the exposition of the theme intimated in iv. 14—16, to the closer consideration and laying to heart of which a charge was implicitly given in ver. 16.—Other interpreters have understood γάρ as argumentative, and entirely misapprehending the clear structure of thought in these ten verses, have taken ver. 1 as helping to prove what is said in iv. 15. " Christ must have sympathy with our infirmities, for even human high priests have sympathy with sins." Thus the high priests taken from among men would here be opposed to Christ as one not taken from among men, and an inference drawn a minori ad majus. But if this interpretation is to be received, we miss here, first of all, a καί or καίπερ before the words ἐξ ἀνθρώπων λαμβανόμενος ; then the words ὑπὲρ ἀνθρώπων καθίσταται and τὰ πρὸς τὸν θεόν would be quite superfluous ; thirdly, we should expect ληφθείς, and finally, the words ἐξ ἀνθρώπων λαμβανόμενος would not even form a clear antithesis to Christ, who also was to be included among those born of woman. Nay, even the vis conclusionis in that argum. a minori would be very doubtful ; from the fact that sinful men are indulgent towards the ἀγνοήματα of others, it cannot be all at once inferred that the sinless one must have been much more indulgent.

We therefore understand the proposition in ver. 1 not as a special, but as a general one. Nothing is intended to be said of the human high priests in opposition to Christ, but the intention rather is to enumerate the requisites which *every* high priest must have. That these requisites were found in Christ, and in how far they belonged to him, is then shown in ver. 5—10. Thus then ver. 1—4 form a sort of major proposition, ver. 5—10 a minor proposition (which implicitly contains the self-evident conclusion.)

Of course, the words ἐξ ἀνθρώπων λαμβανόμενος cannot be the *attribute* belonging to the *subject* of the sentence, but must be viewed as in *apposition* to the predicate. The right rendering is not: "Every high priest taken from among men is ordained for men," but "Every high priest is as one taken from among men, ordained for men in their relation to God." And it is further to be observed, that the words *taken from among men* express the *principal idea,* while the proof of the *necessity* of this is given in the words *is ordained for men*. The form in which this proof is given is, that the being *taken from among men* expresses the *ground of the possibility* of the being *ordained for men*. Expressed in a logical form, it would stand thus: Every high priest can appear before God for men, *only in virtue of his being taken from among men*. (We found precisely the same logical form at chap. iv. 6, 7.)

It is *men* whom the high priest is to represent, and that " in their relation to God," τὰ πρὸς τὸν θεόν (comp. chap. ii. 17, where the same idea was briefly hinted which is here ex professo carried out;) therefore must every high priest himself be taken *out of men*, out of the number of men; this is the *first requisite of every high priest*. This requisite is now further explained. He is ordained or appointed for men as their representative before God, not as Moses, to receive the law in their stead, but to offer sacrifices for them. Δῶρα is not the more general, and θυσίαι the more special term, for ὑπὲρ ἁμαρτιῶν refers to προσφέρῃ, and therefore also to both δῶρα and θυσίαι. These two terms are (just like τέρατα and σημεῖα) only two designations of one and the same thing, regarded from different points of view. Sacrifices are called δῶρα, because the person for whom the atonement is to be made gives them to the priest for God; they are called θυσίαι, because they must be slain in order to have an atoning efficacy. The person whose guilt is to be atoned for must take the victim from his own *property*, that it may appear as a representative of himself; and then the victim must suffer the death which its owner had deserved.

In vers. 2, 3 this first requisite of the high priest is still further illustrated. Every high priest is set up as one taken from among men, that he may offer sacrifices *as one who can rightly judge respecting the sinners who bring them*. The mechanical offering of the sacrifices is not enough; a psychologically just estimate of the particular case of him for whom the atonement is to be made, must precede the offering.

Now, this is a point which, so far as I know, no commentator has rightly understood. To look at the passage, first of all, grammatically, the word μετριοπαθεῖν is a term invented by the Peripatetics, which afterwards passed into the general language. The best explanation of the term is given by Diog. Laert. v. 31, when he represents Aristotle as saying that the wise man is not ἀπαθής but μετριοπαθής. The term involves an antithesis at once to the want and the excess of the passions; it denotes the application of Aristotle's cardinal virtūe μεσότης to the sphere of the πάθη. Hence, it may quite agreeably to the context signify : "firm" in relation to suffering, "mild" in relation to the offender, "indulgent" in reference to the erring. (So in Appian, Josephus, especially in Philo and Clem. Alex.) Many commentators would therefore, without more ado, understand the term here also as signifying "to be indulgent," but, as we shall soon see, improperly so. The term ἀγνόημα does not denote sin in general, but a particular class of sins. It is well known, that by no means all trespasses and crimes were, under the old covenant, atoned for by sacrifice, but wilfully wicked transgressions of the law (παραβάσεις) were required to be punished, and could be expiated and atoned for only by the endurance of the penalty. Those sins alone which had been committed בִּשְׁגָגָה, *i.e.* without the purpose to do evil, in which the man had been hurried into evil by his nature, by the ebullition of passion, could be atoned for without punishment, by sacrifices or sin-offerings (according to the degree of the trespass.) Now, ἀγνοοῦντες καὶ πλανώμενοι in our passage corresponds precisely to the idea of the שְׁגָגָה. (Some wrongly explain ἀγνόημα of "sins of error." Such sins are not meant as proceed from *habitual* errors, but such as *in the moment of their being committed* were not accompanied with a clear consciousness of their culpability.)

We have now the explanation of the idea as a whole. A priest was not at liberty all at once to receive and slay a sacrifice which one brought to him; but he must first make inquiry into the act that had been committed, and must examine whether it belonged to the category of the שְׁגָגָה to which sacrifices were appropriated. This, of course, he could do only by knowing from his own experience the passions of human nature; *i.e.*, ἐπεὶ καὶ αὐτὸς περίκειται ἀσθένειαν. (Περικεῖσθαί τι, to be clothed with anything, to be burdened with.)[1]

The third verse contains a farther explanation. In order to demonstrate how necessary it is that a high priest should partake in the infirmity of the men whom he represents, the circumstance is added, that according to the ordinances of the Mosaic law, the high priest was required to offer sacrifice for his own sins. It is this idea chiefly that has given occasion to the false interpretation of ver. 1. Such a thing, it has been thought, could be said only of "human high priests." But this is altogether unnecessary, for the author in ver. 1—4 speaks just as little of human high priests in opposition to Christ, as of Christ specially. He simply lays down the two requisites which belong to the idea of *high priest*, as historically represented in the law, and ver. 3 contains a proof of the first requisite taken from the law. Let us leave it to the author himself to inquire in ver. 5 ss. how far these requisites were predicable of Christ. He will himself know the proper time and place, ver. 8 (and later, chap. vii. 27), for showing in what respects Christ was *unlike* those Old Testament high priests.

In ver. 4 we have the *second requisite qualification* of every high priest. He must be taken *from among men;* he must not be ordained *by men,* nor usurp the office himself, but must be one *called of*

---

[1] The idle question why the author does not use συμπαθεῖν instead of μετριοπαθεῖν, as well as the false solution of this question connected with the false interpretation of ver. 1, namely, that a pure sympathy can be ascribed only to Christ, but a weak "indulgence" to "human high priests"—both fall of themselves to the ground. Συμπαθῆσαι *could* not be used; we might say συμπαθῆσαι ταῖς ἀσθενείαις, but not συμπαθῆσαι τοῖς ἀγνοοῦσι; the latter would mean: to partake in the feelings of sinners—therefore, for example, in those of an evil conscience.

God (at ἀλλὰ καλούμενος ὑπὸ τοῦ θεοῦ is to be supplied simply λαμβάνει τὴν τιμήν, "as one called of God he receives this honour"), as was the case also with Aaron (and therefore with his posterity who were called with him.)[1]

At vers. 5, 6, the inquiry begins whether, and in how far, these two requisites belonged to Christ. The words in themselves are clear. At ἀλλ' ὁ λαλήσας is, of course, to be supplied ἐδόξασαν αὐτόν. The sentiment, however, is variously interpreted. Some, as Grotius, Limborch, Tholuck, &c., understand the cited passage Ps. ii. 7, as if the author intended to adduce it as a proof that Jesus was called of God to be an high priest. The words ἀλλ' ὁ λαλήσας would accordingly have to be logically resolved thus: "But God, inasmuch as he has spoken to him." Others, however, object to this, that in the passage of the psalms neither is the person of Jesus addressed, nor is anything said of the high priestly dignity. Now, that in the psalm Jesus is not personally addressed, would of itself have little weight; the verse that is cited contains an address to that Son of David who came soon to be identified with the Messiah; and that Jesus is the Messiah was, as we have before seen, a thing undoubted by the readers. If then it was said in the Old Testament that the Messiah must be an high priest, this was eo ipso true also of Jesus, because he was the Messiah. But another question is, whether in Ps. ii. 7 there is any mention of a high priestly dignity as belonging to the Messiah? In the most ingenious way has it been attempted to introduce this into the words, while the expression, *This day I have begotten thee*, refers, as we have seen at chap. i. 5, to the prophecy of Nathan, 2 Sam. vii., which is regarded by the Psalmist as, so to speak, a generation of the future *seed*. Grotius, Limborch, Tholuck, &c., would accordingly understand this statement, arbitrarily as I think, of the future installation of the second David into his kingdom; and with this again the resurrection of Christ is said to be denoted, and this again is said to involve a calling to the office of high priest. It is therefore not to be wondered at that others, as Carpzov, Bengel, Bleek, &c., have renounced that interpreta-

---

[1] Tholuck begins a new section with ver. 4. But ver. 7—10 refers to ver. 1—3 precisely in the same way as ver. 5, 6 to ver. 4. Ver. 5—10 forms the logical minor proposition to ver. 1—4.

tion of ἀλλ' ὁ λαλήσας as a whole, and following Theophylact and Erasmus, have taken these words, together with the citation from Ps. ii. 7, as a *mere circumlocution* for ὁ πατήρ. Jesus did not make himself an high priest, but he who has called him his Son. The same who, in another place (Ps. ii. 7), called him his Son, has called him also priest (Ps. cx. 4.) But convenient as this escape from the difficulty is, it can still hardly be justified. The author must in that case have said at ver. 6: λέγει γὰρ ἐν ἑτέρῳ, or at least (with the omission of the καὶ) : καθὼς ἐν ἑτέρῳ λέγει. But as it stands, the passage cited in ver. 6 from Ps. cx. is clearly added as a *second* proof to the passage from Ps. ii., the *first* proof of the divine calling of the Messiah (consequently of Jesus) to the honour of the priesthood.

And, in reality, the second psalm will be seen to involve such a proof, whenever we look at it in its historical connexion. The Messiah was called, 2 Sam. vii., to build an house for the Lord more perfect than the tabernacle built under the direction of Moses and Aaron; through him, nay in his person, God was really and perfectly to dwell with men; through him, mankind was to be exalted to the honour of being children of God; he himself was to be raised to the honour of being a son of God. To this Ps. ii. refers. Thus was given to him indeed the calling to be *more than a mere ruler;* by a truly priestly mediation he was to transact the affairs of men in their relation to God.

This is expressed undoubtedly more plainly and distinctly in the passage Ps. cx. 4 which is cited in ver. 6. The emphasis in this passage rests on the words *thou art a priest,* not on the words *according to the order* (Hebr. דברה) *of Melchisedec.* Some wrongly suppose that the author, here already, designs to pass to the dissimilarity between Christ and Aaron, the Melchisedec-nature of the priesthood of Christ. How can such an assertion be made in the face of the fact, that the author first in ver. 10 formally lays down the comparison between Christ and Melchisedec as a new theme *(of whom we have much to say),* to the detailed treatment of which he does not proceed, until he has prepared the way by an admonition of considerable length v. 11, vi. 20? In our passage, those concluding words of the 4th verse of the psalm are cited, simply in passing, along with the rest of the verse, partly, for the better understanding of the verse in general, partly, because the author has it in his mind afterwards (ver. 10) to bring into the fore-ground this new element involved in the name Melchisedec, partly, in fine, because, in general, Melchisedec offered a suitable example for the element of which he treats here in the 6th verse—the union of the priestly with the kingly dignity of the Messiah. Here then, as already observed, all the emphasis lies on ἱερεύς. That to the promised seed of David (to that form which was then, so to speak, obscure and wavering, but which afterwards consolidated itself into the definite form of the Messiah) it was said: " Thou art a priest"— in this lay the most sufficient proof of the statement that he who was the Messiah was therewith, eo ipso, also called of God to the honour of the priesthood. We have already seen (on chap. i. 13) that Ps. cx. refers to that same prediction of Nathan 2 Sam. 7. And that the Psalmist could not but see in that promise of Nathan the promise of a priest-king, has appeared from our remarks on the 5th verse. A king who was called to build God a temple, was called to something more than the kingly office,—to something more than the government of men in their human and civil relations; he was called to a direct interest in the sacred relation of men to God. Now in Ps. cx. 1 it was expressly said, that that *seed* shall sit with God upon his throne, take part in the dominion of God, be the most immediate fulfiller of the will of God among the Israelites, and thereby serve the Lord in a priestly character, not, however, in that of the Aaronitical priesthood. What better form could present itself to the Psalmist as combining all these features, than the form of that Melchisedec who had been at once king and priest on the same hill of Zion, and in whose name even was expressed all that was expected of the future second David? (comp. Ps. xlv. 6, and our remarks on chap. i. 9 ss.) Thus came the Psalmist to the designation of the Messiah as a *priest*.

Therefore: *Jesus, who is the Messiah, is in the first place similar to Aaron in this, that like him he is called of God to the high priesthood*, called in the prophecy of Nathan itself, and in the two psalms which refer to that prophecy, which represent the future Messiah as *mediator of men with God*, and the second of which even *names* him " priest." In ver. 7—9 the author now proceeds to prove that the first requisite also—*taken from among men*—belonged to Christ. The farther treatment of this requisite carries him naturally to the point in which Jesus is superior to Aaron, to the theme of the second section (hence he has given this requisite which stands first in the major proposition the last place in the minor,)

By means of ὅς this sentiment is loosely connected with ver. 5, 6. Grammatically, ὅς refers back, of course, to ὁ Χριστός or (πρὸς) αὐτόν, ver. 5. The whole period vers. 7—9 can be construed in two ways. We may either, A, take the participles προσενέγκας and εἰσακουσθείς as appositions to the first principal verb ἔμαθεν alone (consequently to the first part of the predicate); or B, those two participles may be taken as appositions to the subject ὅς (in which case the two verbs ἔμαθεν and ἐγένετο are logically to be referred to the two ideas expressed by προσενέγκας and εἰσακουσθείς.)

A. ὅς 1, ... προσενέγκας καὶ ... εἰσακουσθεὶς ... ἔμαθεν
    2, καὶ τελειωθεὶς ἐγένετο αἴτιος

B. ὅς, προσενέγκας καὶ εἰσακουσθεὶς
    1, ἔμαθεν
    2, καὶ ἐγένετο αἴτιος

In order to be able to decide which of these two constructions deserves the preference—for, grammatically, both are equally possible—we must look more closely at the meaning of the several parts of the period, and we begin with the *first part of the predicate*, i.e. the words καίπερ ὢν υἱὸς ἔμαθεν ἀφ' ὧν ἔπαθε τὴν ὑπακοήν, "Who .... although he was a son, learned obedience in that which he suffered." The concession in καίπερ refers not to ἔμαθε as if what is strange consists in this, that a *son can learn*;[1] but it evidently refers especially to ὑπακοήν. Although a *son* he must learn to *obey*. Of course, however, ὑπακοή cannot be used here in its general sense, as denoting obedience *to the commands of God in general*, but finds its natural limitation in the words ἀφ' ὧν ἔπαθε beside which is the verb ἔμαθε. What is spoken of is obedience to the *special* decree of the Father who laid upon the son the necessity of *suffering;* or, otherwise expressed,

---

[1] This would be admissible only if υἱός were used by our author in the sense of the Nicene creed to denote the Logos *qua* pre-existent, which, however, as we have seen in chap. iv. 1, is not the case. Ὑιός in the Epistle to the Hebrews always denotes the son of God *qua* incarnate.

a special manifestation of general obedience to the Father consisting in this—that Christ swerved not from that general obedience even when it entailed upon him inevitable suffering. And thus the ἔμαθε explains itself. By this cannot of course be meant a gradual transition from disobedience to obedience, but only a development of the virtue of obedience itself, the progress of which runs parallel to the difficulty of the situation in which Jesus was placed; consequently, the transition from easy obedience to more difficult, and thereby, more perfect obedience. In proportion as the choice for Jesus either to become unfaithful to the will of his Father, or firmly to encounter unavoidable suffering, became more definite and critical, did he decide with ever increasing firmness and clearness of consciousness on the side of suffering, and against that of disobedience. Thus was every successive step rendered more easy by that which preceded it. When, at his entrance on his public labour, there was objectively set before him in the temptation (Matth. iv.) the possibility of his yielding to the carnal expectations of the Jews with reference to the Messiah, the choice which he then made was, outwardly indeed, (as no definite suffering threatened him as yet) easier, but, inwardly, more difficult than that which he made at the temptation in Gethsemane, when indeed his impending suffering appeared to him in its most definite and threatening form, but when he had already made such progress in the way of *obedience*, that he must have cast aside and negatived his whole past history had he now chosen the path of disobedience. With every step which he took in the way of *obedience* this became more and more a part of his nature, the law of his being. This is what the author will express by the words, *he learned obedience*.

The next question now is, on what word the determination of time ἐν ταῖς ἡμέραις τῆς σαρκὸς αὐτοῦ depends, whether on προσενέγκας or on ἔμαθε, whether therefore we are to place a comma after ὅς or after σαρκὸς αὐτοῦ. If ἐν ἡμέραις, &c. is referred to ἔμαθε, then ἐν ἡμέραις as the chronological determination of the first principal verb ἔμαθε corresponds to τελειωθείς as the chronological determination of the second principal verb ἐγένετο. We should then have to adopt the construction above denoted by A, [ὅς 1) ἐν ταῖς ἡμέραις, &c. προσενέγκας καὶ εἰσακουσθείς, ἔμαθεν, 2) καὶ τελειωθεὶς ἐγένετο αἴτιος.] For, if ἐν ταῖς ἡμέραις, &c. belongs to ἔμαθε, then προσενέγκας καὶ εἰσακουσθεὶς cannot of course be in apposition to ὅς, but only to the predicate contained in ἔμαθε. If, on the other hand, ἐν ἡμέραις, &c. be referred to προσενέγκας, in this case both the constructions A and B are possible. But against this reference of ἐν ἡμέραις, &c. to προσενέγκας is, in general, the circumstance, that the words προσενέγκας δεήσεις καὶ ἱκετηρίας, &c. evidently point to the struggle which Christ underwent in Gethsemane, for the chronological determination of which, however, the words ἐν ταῖς ἡμέραις τῆς σαρκὸς αὐτοῦ would be too vague and indefinite.

Σάρξ, different from σῶμα, denotes the creature in contradistinction to the immaterial, invisible God,—then in its opposition to God,—finally corporealness, as lying under the effects of sin, subject to death. In the future kingdom of glory there will be, according to 1 Cor. xv., σώματα, but no longer σώματα σαρκικά.[1] The ἡμέραι τῆς σαρκὸς αὐτοῦ are, therefore, the days of the life of Christ even to his death. They form indeed the most suitable antithesis to τελειωθείς, and quite as suitable a chronological determination of ἔμαθε ὑπακοήν, but on the other hand, not so suitable a chronological determination of the particular event denoted by the words προσενέγκας δεήσεις, &c. For this reason, even if there were no other, the reference to ἔμαθεν recommends itself as the preferable, and with it, that construction of the whole period which we have denoted above by A.

This is confirmed, however, when we turn to consider the two participles προσενέγκας and εἰσακουσθεὶς with that which is dependent on them.

That in the first of these participles there is a reference to the suffering of Jesus in Gethesmane, is unmistakeable. (So Theodoret, Calvin, Bengel, Carpzov, Paulus, Tholuck, Bleek, and the most of commentators.) On κραυγή comp. Luke xxii. 44, although κραυγή is a rhetorico-hyperbolical expression descriptive of the *inward* intensity of that struggle. It is doubtful,

---

[1] It has been justly doubted, on the other hand, whether the expression "resurrection of the flesh" in the Symb. apost. of Luther, &c., is one that altogether corresponds to Scripture phraseology. And in the oldest recensions of the Symb. apost. it is not an ἀνάστασις τῆς σαρκός, but πάσης σαρκός that is spoken of (= כל־בשר, all men, righteous and ungodly.)

however, whether θάνατος here denotes death in the wider sense, —the danger of death—or death as having already actually taken place; whether therefore the sense is, Jesus prayed to him who could save from death, *preserve from death*, or : Jesus prayed to him who could save from death *i.e. raise him up*. (Estius, Baumgarten, Schulz, suppose the latter; Michaelis and Bleek take both; the most of commentators the former alone.) In as far as that prayer of Jesus contains simply the request that he may be saved from the threatened cup of suffering, but has no special reference whatever to a future resurrection, in so far does the first interpretation recommend itself prima facie.

This is confirmed again by the following words : καὶ εἰσακουσθεὶς ἀπὸ τῆς εὐλαβείας. Critics are, indeed, here also, not agreed as to the way in which these words are to be explained. Chrys., Phot., Œcum., Theophylact, Vulgata, Luther, Calov, Olshausen, Bleek, and some others, understand εὐλάβεια in the sense of *fear of God, piety*, ἀπό in the sense of pro, propter = διά c. acc., and make the sense to be—that Jesus was heard on account of his piety. (In this case, σώζειν ἐκ θανάτου must be referred to the *resurrection* of Christ; for his prayer to be preserved from death, as every one knows, could not be heard.) But the meaning here given to ἀπό is unnatural, and the sentiment itself much more unnatural. In this place, where the design of the author is to show, that the first requisite of every high priest—that namely of being *taken from among men*, and *clothed with infirmity*—was not wanting in Christ, there was assuredly no occasion for mentioning the special piety of Christ. More correctly the Peschito, Itala, Ambrosius, Calvin, Beza, Grotius, Gerhard, Capellus, Limborch, Carpzov, Bengel, Morus, Storr, Kuinoel, Paulus, De Wette, Tholuck, and a whole host of critics besides, render εὐλάβεια by *fear, anxiety*, which signification has been vindicated on philological grounds by Casaubon, Wetstein, and Krebs. Εἰσακουσθεὶς is now, of course, to be taken in a pregnant sense, which pregnancy (this Bleek has entirely overlooked) is here fully explained by the foregoing words : προσενέγκας δεήσεις πρὸς τὸν δυνάμενον σώζειν. Christ was, *in reference to his prayer to be preserved*, heard, and thus saved ἀπὸ τῆς εὐλαβείας. But then there is in these very words ἀπὸ τῆς εὐλαβείας a limitation of εἰσακουσθείς. He prayed to be preserved from the death which threatened him, and was *heard* and saved from the fear of death.[1]

At all events, it would be altogether unnatural to explain εἰσακούεσθαι ἀπὸ τῆς εὐλαβείας of the resurrection ("to save from all anxiety and trouble.") For this would certainly be a very indistinct way of denoting a thing for which many distinct expressions were at hand.

If, however, εἰσακουσθείς ἀπὸ τῆς εὐλαβείας is still explained of the resurrection from the dead, then must also the words σώζειν ἐκ τοῦ θανάτου be, of course, explained of the same. In this case, things that were done *in the days of his flesh* would be spoken of not in *both* participles, but only in the first (προσενέγκας, &c.) Then must the chronological determination *in the days* be referred to προσενέγκας *alone*, and thus we should come to the construction B.

Who,
After he, *a*, cried in the days of his flesh to him who could raise him up from death,
and, *b*, was then freed (by the resurrection) from all distress,
1, learned obedience by his suffering, and :
2, after he was perfected, is able to save others.

But against this interpretation there are all possible reasons; first, the unsuitableness indicated above of the second chronological determination *in the days*, &c., to this single event; secondly, the circumstance that Jesus did not pray in Gethsemane with reference to his restoration from death; thirdly, that the words εἰσακ. ἀπὸ τῆς εὐλαβείας cannot be understood as denoting with any distinctness the resurrection.

If, on the other hand, we abide by the explanation given above, and understand εἰσακουσθεὶς, &c., of the strengthening of Jesus by the angel, there results a far finer and more suitable sentiment. Jesus prayed to be preserved from death. This was not sin, but *infirmity*. His prayer was not unheard; it was so heard,

[1] Perhaps it would be still more simple not to take εἰσακουσθείς in a pregnant sense, but to give ἀπό the signification *on the side of*, "in reference to." He was heard in so far as regards the fear of death.

however, as that Jesus was divested of the *fear of death*.[1] What a significant example of *learning obedience !*

According to this interpretation, things are spoken of in *both* participles which were done " in the days of Christ's flesh." We can now refer *in the days* to that to which alone it is suitable, and to which it is more suitable than to προσενέγκας, namely to ἔμαθεν. Accordingly, we render the passage thus:

Who,
  1, In the days of his flesh,
    a, when he prayed for the warding off of death,
    b, and was heard in as far as respects the *fear* of death,
      learned obedience in that which he suffered, and :
  2, after he was perfected,
    became the author of eternal salvation, &c.

What a beautiful harmony and symmetry does the sentiment thus receive!

On ver. 9 only a little remains to be observed. Τελειωθείς finds its explanation in its corresponding antithesis : *in the days of his flesh.* In the days of his flesh he was a member and partaker of humanity still lying under the effects of sin and not yet arrived at its destination, and he himself had therefore not yet come to the destined end of his actions and history. This was first attained when, raised from the dead, he entered in a glorified body into the heavenly sanctuary, as the first-fruits of exalted humanity (chap. ii. 9.) Thither he draws after him all who allow themselves to be drawn by him, and who reproduce in themselves his priestly *obedience* in a priestly form, as the *obedience of faith* (Acts vi. 7 ; Rom. i. 5.) But as Christ himself was not saved from bodily death, but from the *fear* of death, so also is the *salvation* which he gives to his followers not a preservation from bodily death, but an *eternal salvation,* a deliverance from the *fear of death* and the power of him who has the *power of death* (ii. 14), from eternal death.

Ver. 10. Some hold with great incorrectness that Ver. 10 contains an *explanation* of ver. 9, and is designed to show how, and in what way, Christ is the *author of salvation,* namely, by

[1] This would do away with the objection of Bleek (ii. p. 78) : " that Christ was freed from his solicitude, stands in no intelligible connexion with the principal clause, that he learned obedience by suffering."

his priestly intercession with the Father. Not a word is here said of the priestly *intercessio* in opposition to the priestly *satisfactio*. Nor does the comparison with Melchisedec point to this, as Melchisedec never interceded for any one. The truth is, that the first section of our third part has at ver. 9 fully reached its conclusion, and at ver. 10, just as at i. 4, iii. 2, the *intimation of a new theme* is grammatically (but not logically) connected with what precedes. Logically, ver. 10 points back only to ver. 6, inasmuch as a word which formed part of a passage there cited, but the import of which has not yet been developed, is now placed in the foreground as the title of a new section. That the author intends in ver. 10 not to give an explanation of ver. 9, but to intimate a new theme, appears plainly, indeed, from the relative clause ver. 11.

INTERMEDIATE PART OF A HORTATORY KIND.

(Chap. v. 11—vi. 20.)

Ver. 11 connects grammatically as a relative clause with ver. 10. Περὶ οὗ πολὺς ἡμῖν (scil. ἐστιν) ὁ λόγος, the use of the article in this manner is familiar. But why is this comparison of the priesthood of Melchisedec with that of Christ *hard to be understood?* The *first reason* lies evidently in the subject itself. The thesis of the similarity of Christ with Melchisedec is, as we have already seen, not merely a third principal clause beside the two foregoing, but is an inference from these two. From the fact that the Messiah must, on the one hand, be more than an angel, on the other hand, more than Moses—from the fact that his priesthood is grafted, in like manner, on his immediate oneness with the Father, as on his humanity, it follows of itself that he is not merely equal to Aaron, but that he is more than Aaron; that as the perfect high priest he is partaker of the *divine* nature. Thus the author rises in chap. vii. 1, 2, directly to the doctrine of the *divinity* of Christ.[1]

---

[1] The Epistle to the Hebrews thus affords, at the same time, an important testimony in a critical point of view, for the original and intimate organic connexion of the so-called "Johanneic" doctrine of

A *second reason*, however, why that λόγος was δυσερμήνευτος *difficult to be made intelligible*, is given in the clause which follows, and was of a subjective nature. The difficulty lay not certainly in the fitness of the writer to set it forth, but in the capacity of the readers to understand it. Νωθροὶ γεγόνατε ταῖς ἀκοαῖς, they had *become* obtuse and dull of hearing. Those are wrong who take γεγόνατε in a weakened sense = ἐστέ. From the words of ver. 12: πάλιν χρείαν ἔχετε and γεγόνατε χρείαν ἔχοντες, as well as from the admonition in chap. x. 32: αναμιμνήσκεσθε τὰς προτέρας ἡμέρας, it is evidently to be inferred, that the readers had exposed themselves to the charge not merely of a want of progress in the development of their knowledge, but were even on the point of making a melancholy retrogression.

What was the nature of the retrogression we are told in ver. 12. "According to the time ye ought already to be teachers, but now ye must be taken again under instruction." The majority of commentators have passed very cursorily over these important words; only Mynster (Stud. u. Krit. 1829 p. 338) has deduced from them the right *negative* inference that the Epistle to the Hebrews cannot possibly have been addressed to the church in Jerusalem. How is it possible that the author could have written in such terms to that mother-church of Christianity, containing several thousand souls, among whom were many who had grown old in Christianity, and certainly individuals still who had known the Lord himself, who since the period referred to in Acts vii. had undergone a multitude of persecutions? How could he then have written to a large church which must necessarily have had in it many teachers, to whom the words *ye have need that we teach you*—and again many Neophytes, to whom the words *ye ought according to the time to be teachers*—would be altogether unsuitable? We agree, therefore, with Mynster when he finds that the Epistle to the Hebrews cannot have been written to the church in Jerusalem, and are of opinion that the suggestion of Bleek that James was then no longer alive weighs nothing against this, while the supposition " that the author had not before his mind at the time the whole circumstances of the

Christ's person, with the "Pauline" doctrinal system of Christ's work, and of the influence of both on the Jewish Christians.

church to which he wrote," weighs less than nothing. Mynster should only have gone a step farther and perceived, that our epistle can have been designed in general for no church whatever, consequently for no church in the neighbourhood of Jerusalem. For *every* church, from the very nature of the case, consists of earlier and later converts; our epistle, on the contrary, is addressed to quite a definite circle of readers who had passed over to Christianity together at the same time, and because they had let themselves go astray from the faith *had been taken anew under instruction*—for that the words *ye have need again that some one teach you* are not mere words, but indicate a fact, should not certainly be doubted. The author does not mean to say : ye had almost need that one instruct you again ; but upbraids his readers with this as a thing of which they ought to be ashamed, that those who, considering the time, might already be teachers, yet need to receive instruction from others. That, then, which we have already, at an earlier stage, seen to be probable finds here its fullest confirmation : *the Epistle to the Hebrews was written for a definite circle of catechumens, who, upon their conversion, having been perplexed by a threatened excommunication from the communion of the Jewish theocracy, had been subjected anew to a careful instruction.* The author had received information of this, and had doubtless been specially requested by the *teacher* of that people to prepare a writing that might serve as a basis for this difficult instruction.

This defect of knowledge related to the στοιχεῖα τῆς ἀρχῆς τῶν λογίων τοῦ θεοῦ. Λόγιον means a "saying," then an "oracular saying," then in biblical and christian usage "revelation" (Acts vii. 38), hence at a later period λόγια is used to denote the theopneustic writings generally (Iren. i. 8 ; Clem. Al. Strom. vii. 18 p. 900, s. ; Orig. comm. ad Matth. v. 19 ; Joh. Presb. in Euseb. iii. 39). Here, it has the quite general signification "revelation of God" = the doctrine revealed by God; the same as, in chap. iv. 12, vi. 1, is termed ὁ λόγος τοῦ θεοῦ, τοῦ Χριστοῦ. According to the context, it is of course the New Testament revelation that is meant (as at iv. 12), not the Old Testament as Schulz will have it. Τὰ στοιχεῖα τῆς ἀρχῆς is a cumulative expression similar to the Pindaric σκιᾶς ὄναρ, or as at Eph. i. 19, ἡ ἐνέργεια τοῦ κράτους τῆς ἰσχύος. Στοιχεῖα means by itself "beginnings," "elements." The idea of beginning is, however, intensified. "Beginnings of the beginning," = the very first beginnings.

Τινὰ is acc. of the subject "that some one teach you" = that one should teach you. (Luther, Bleek, Olshausen, &c.) The Peschito, Vulg., De Wette, &c., accentuate τίνα, ":that one teach you *which* be the first elements." But this is unsuitable. In the first place, an accusative of the subject would thus be wanting to διδάσκειν, and, secondly, the readers were not ignorant of what doctrinal articles *belonged* to the στοιχεῖα, but did not rightly understand the *import* of these στοιχεῖα.

The author repeats the same idea by means of a figure in the words: *and are become such as have need of milk and not of strong meat.*

Ver. 13, 14 contain an explanation from which it already begins to appear what doctrines the writer understood by the milk. Πᾶς γὰρ ὁ μετέχων γάλακτος, whosoever still partakes of milk, still particeps lactis est, still receives and needs milk for his nourishment. Of every such one it is said that he is uninformed, and has no share in the λόγος δικαιοσύνης. Calvin, Grotius, Morus, Schulz, Olshausen, Kuinoel, De Wette, &c., take the genitive δικαιοσύνης as the *genitive of quality*, and δικαιοσύνη = τελειότης, so that λόγος δικαιοσύνης would be equivalent to "the perfect doctrine," the completed, higher knowledge (or according to Zechariä, Dindorf, and others, "the proper, true instruction.") But apart from the intolerable tautological circle which would thus be introduced into the train of thought between ver. 13 and ver. 12, apart, further, from the insipid triviality of the 13th verse, as thus explained, the author would assuredly have used and applied other and less far-fetched expressions for the "perfect doctrine" than the strange expression λόγος δικαιοσύνης.[1] The majority of commentators have therefore rightly understood δικαιοσύνης as the *genitive of the object*, "the word of righteous-

[1] The Hebrew זִבְחֵי־צֶדֶק (θυσίαι δικαιοσύνης) Deut. xxxiii. 19, &c., would not even form an analogy. For זבחי־צדק are in reality such sacrifices as *correspond to the statutes*, to which therefore the property of צדק, *i.e.* of perfect legality, can be ascribed, while, on the contrary, in our passage δικαιοσύνη must be taken in the altogether heterogeneous sense of "perfect *development*," which it never has.

ness," in which, however, δικαιοσύνη is not (with Theophylact, Chrysostom, Oecumenius, a Lapide, Primasius, Bretschneider, &c.) to be explained of the perfect morality, and consequently λόγος δικαιοσύνης of the moral law, but, as in the whole New Testament, of the righteousness before God in Christ; and λόγος δικαιοσύνης is the doctrine of justification (Beza, J. Capellus, Rambach, Bengel, Storr, Klee, Tholuck, Bleek, &c.), which, as is well known, is also not strange to the Epistle to the Hebrews (comp. chap. xi. 7, xiii. 9.)

This explanation, however, is accompanied with a difficulty in respect to the logical connection with ver. 12. We should rather expect as an explanation of ver. 12 the words in an inverted form : Πᾶς γὰρ ὁ ἄπειρος λόγου δικαιοσύνης γάλακτος μετέχει. This would explain in how far the persons addressed are as yet babes. The train of thought would be this: "You still need milk; strong meat does not agree with you. For whosoever (like you) has not yet apprehended even the fundamental doctrine of righteousness in Christ (whosoever still makes his salvation to rest on the services and sacrifices of the temple), needs as yet milk, being yet a *babe*, and standing still at the first elements of Christian knowledge." This is what we should naturally expect the author to say.. Instead of this, however, he says: "Every one who still needs milk, has as yet no part in the doctrine of justification." Bleek thinks that ver. 13 contains an explanatory repetition of the words *not of strong meat*; "you could not yet bear strong meat, for whoever still nourishes himself with milk cannot yet understand the doctrine of justification." According to this, the author must have meant by the strong meat the doctrine of justification. But this is plainly against the context. By the strong meat, of which the readers were not yet capable, is rather to be understood that λόγος δυσερμήνευτος concerning the similarity between the priesthood of Melchisedec and Christ, the deep insight into the Old Testament type, the doctrine of the divinity of Christ. On the other hand the doctrine of justification, the doctrine of *repentance and dead works*, of *faith*, and of *baptism*, are rather reckoned as belonging to the *elements*, chap. vi. 1, s.; the doctrine of justification is itself the milk which must first be taken into the heart and the understanding, in order that a foundation may be laid on which the more difficult theologoumena can be built. Bleek's explanation is therefore not fitted to remove the difficulty.

This difficulty is rather to be removed simply by regarding the proposition in ver. 13 not as descriptive or declaratory, not as determining the import, but the extent or comprehension of the idea expressed by μετέχων γάλακτος. It is not an answer to the question: "What are the characteristics of him who still nourishes himself with milk?" but an answer to the question: "*Who* nourishes himself with milk?" The words contain a conclusion backwards from the consequence to the presupposed condition. Whosoever still needs milk, *of him it is presupposed* that he must not yet have rightly apprehended the doctrine of justification: = whosoever has not yet apprehended this doctrine is still at the stage at which he needs milk. We found similarly inverted conclusions at chap. ii. 11, iv. 6. This interpretation also affords a most satisfactory explanation of the words, *for he is still a babe*. Not without a stroke of irony does the author explain in these words, in how far it must be *presupposed* of a spiritual suckling that he will be *unskilled in the word of righteousness*.

The 14th verse also now runs perfectly parallel with the 13th. He who still needs milk will doubtless not yet have comprehended the doctrine of justification; but that strong and more difficult meat (of the higher typology) is adapted not to such, but only to mature Christians who have come of age, and who are exercised in distinguishing between the true and the false way. Τέλειος, as the opposite of νήπιος, is a term familiar to the Apostle Paul (1 Cor. iii. 1, xiii. 11; Rom. ii. 20; Eph. iv. 14.) Τελείων finds here its special explanation in the words which stand in opposition to it, τῶν διὰ τὴν ἕξιν αἰσθητήρια γεγυμνασμένα ἐχόντων, &c. "Εξις is a term proceeding from the Aristotelian school-phraseology; denoting the given natural condition or habitus, in opposition to the διάθεσις (πρᾶξις), the sphere of self-determination. In general use, it denotes frequently the condition as respects age—hence age = ἡλικία; and so in our passage the spiritual age, the degree of inward maturity. Αἰσθητήρια are the organs of feeling, the nerves of feeling. Γυμνάζειν, in the well-known sense of "exercise," occurs also in chap. xii. 11, further in 1 Tim. iv. 7; 2 Pet. ii. 14. The distinguishing between the καλόν and κακόν does not, as some strangely suppose, belong to the *strong meat;* but the habit already acquired of distinguishing the true from the false, is rather the immediate fruit of the right understanding of the λόγος δικαιοσύνης, and forms, together with the latter, the indispensable *condition* which must be fulfilled ere *strong meat* can be once thought of. He who has taken the milk of the Gospel, *i.e.*, the fundamental doctrine of justification so in succum et sanguinem, that he can spontaneously, and by immediate feeling, consequently without requiring any previous long reflection or reasoning, distinguish the right from the wrong, the way in which the Christian has to walk from the Jewish by-paths, the evangelic truth from the Pharisaic righteousness of the law, so that he could, as it were, find out the right path though asleep—he who has so thoroughly seized and digested these *elements*, that he no longer needs to be instructed in them (the milk), consequently is no longer νήπιος, but τέλειος—may now have strong meat offered to him—the difficult doctrines of the higher typology of the old covenant, and of the eternal Melchisedec-nature of the New Testament high priest.

In chap. vi. 1, therefore, the author admonishes his readers to strive after that *perfection,* and to exert themselves in order finally to pass beyond the *elements.* Ἀφέντες τὸν τῆς ἀρχῆς τοῦ Χριστοῦ λόγον—this, of course, signifies (as appears already from v. 12) not "the doctrine of the beginning of Christ," but "the beginning or elementary doctrine of Christ." Τῆς ἀρχῆς is an adjectival genitive, and to be closely connected with λόγος, so that τοῦ Χριστοῦ is dependent not on ἀρχῆς, but on λόγον. The great majority of interpreters do not take φερώμεθα as the *insinuative* first person plural, and the whole passage as *hortatory,* but understand the first person plural as *communicative,* and the whole as an *intimation* on the part of the author that he now intends to pass to the consideration of the *strong meat.* But that which, first of all, is opposed to the common interpretation, is the particle διό. How, from the fact that the readers, according to chap. v. 12—14, could as yet bear no strong meat, but needed the milk of the *elements,* could the author with any appearance of reason draw the inference: "Therefore, let us lay aside these elements, and proceed to the more difficult doctrines?" Secondly, that interpretation leads itself ad absurdum, for, according to it, τελειότης must be taken in a completely different sense from τέλειος, chap. v. 14. In chap. v. 14 τέλειος denoted the *subjective* state of those who are already exercised in the *word of righteousness*, and in the *discerning between good and evil*, in order to be able to understand what is more difficult; in chap. vi. 1 τελειότης is suddenly made to denote the *objective* difficult doctrinal statements respecting the similarity between the priesthood of Melchisedec and Christ! Hence Chrysostom, Theodoret, Photius, Gennadius, Theophylact, Faber, Stapul., Calvin, Schulz, Böhme, and Bleek, have with reason understood the first person plural as insinuatory, and the whole as an *admonition to the readers ;* they are to strive to get at length beyond the elements (in the partic. ἀφέντες there lies then, at all events, a prolepsis: strive after the τελειότης, so that you may then be able to lay aside the ἀρχῆς λόγος), and to arrive at that τελειότης described in chap. v. 14.

If, however, this explanation is right, then by consequence must the words μὴ καταβαλλόμενοι, &c., be understood differently from what they have been by all commentators hitherto (Calvin, Bleek, &c., not excepted.) All take καταβάλλεσθαι in the sense " to lay a foundation," a sense in which this verb also actually occurs. (Dion. Halic. iii. 69, Ταρκύνιος τούς τε θεμελίους κατεβάλετο; see other passages in Bleek ii. p. 149.) Now this sense would certainly suit well that false interpretation of the preceding words (" I design, laying aside the fundamental elements, to hasten to what is more difficult, and not again to lay the foundation of repentance," &c.) But, on the other hand, this sense of καταβάλλεσθαι does not suit the true and only possible explanation of φερώμεθα. If the readers were still deficient in the *elements*, in the apprehension of the doctrine of justification, the true means of attaining to the τελειότης did not assuredly consist in their neglecting to gain anew the foundation which they had lost, but, on the contrary, in their using the most strenuous endeavours to secure again that foundation of all knowledge which they had lost. We are therefore reduced to the necessity of taking καταβάλλεσθαι in another sense, in the signification which is the original one and the most common, namely, " to throw down, demolish, destroy," which the word has in all the Greek classical writers, and which it cannot surprise us to find in our author, who writes elegant Greek. "Strive after perfection, while you do not again demolish the foundation of repentance and faith, and the doctrine of baptism, the laying on of hands, the resurrection, and the judgment." The genitives μετανοίας πίστεως are also suitable to this explanation. The author does not speak of a foundation of the *doctrine* of repentance and faith—διδαχή is first introduced in connexion with the third member—but of the foundation of repentance and faith themselves. The apostle would assuredly not have dissuaded from laying again the foundation, in the case of its having been destroyed! According to the right explanation, he rather advises them not to destroy whatever of it may still remain. Πάλιν means, of course, not iterum "a second time," but is used here in the privative or contradictory sense, as at Gal. iv. 9; Acts xviii. 21. That the article is wanting at θεμέλιον cannot cause surprise; it is in like manner wanting in chap. v. 13 at λόγου δικαιοσύνης; chap. vi. 5 at θεοῦ ῥῆμα, &c. The word is sufficiently determined by its genitives. Now, the foundation which the readers are to preserve from destruction, in order to attain to *perfection*, consists of *three parts*. The first is the μετάνοια, the subjective turning of the νοῦς, the mind, the conversion from selfishness to the love of Christ, from self-righteousness to the consciousness of guilt, from contempt of the will of God to the accusation of self. And this μετάνοια is here called a μετάνοια ἀπὸ νεκρῶν ἔργων, because that state of the natural man had, in the persons addressed, taken the special form of a Jewish pharisaism which led them to believe that, as regards their relation to God, they might rest satisfied with certain works which were severed from the root of a heart right towards God, and were therefore "dead." (It is, moreover, not to be forgotten, that not merely the Jew, but every one has the tendency to stamp certain actions outwardly praiseworthy as meritorious works, and with this dead coin to discharge the demands of his conscience, and to still the accuser in his breast.) The positive and supplementary part to this μετάνοια is the πίστις ἐπὶ θεόν. That faith is here denoted not in the historico-dogmatic form of faith in Christ, the Messiah, but in the philosophico-religious form of faith in God, is not undesigned, but belongs to the fineness and delicacy of the thought. That the author means the *Christian* faith, was already self-evident, and needed not to be expressed by circumstantial description; on the other hand, this he would and must say, that the Christian, as by the μετάνοια he renounces dead works, so by the πίστις he enters into a living relation to the *living God*.

The third member is the διδαχή, *i.e.* not here, of course, the act of instruction, but the object gained by instruction, the knowledge of doctrine thereby acquired. On διδαχῆς are dependent the four genitives βαπτισμῶν, ἐπιθέσεως τε χειρῶν, ἀναστάσεώς τε νεκρῶν καὶ κρίματος. It is evident of itself, that the three last of these genitives cannot be directly dependent on θεμέλιον, for as the *resurrection* and the *judgment* are things to be looked for in the future, the readers cannot be admonished to retain these things themselves but only the doctrine respecting them. (Those interpreters who understand φερώμεθα, ver. 1, as an *intimation* of the author's design, and who render καταβάλλεσθαι by "lay," as they would supply διδαχῆς at μετανοίας, πίστεως, ἐπιθέσεως, ἀναστάσεως and κρίματος, must then as a matter of consequence supply a second διδαχῆς at βαπτισμῶν διδαχῆς, which would be nonsense. To make διδαχῆς dependent on βαπτισμῶν—" the doctrine of baptisms," in opposition to mere lustrations—as is done by Bengel, Winer, and Michaelis, yields no meaning whatever, as it is not the doctrine which forms the distinguishing feature between the sacrament of baptism and the mere lustrations, but the forgiveness of sins and regeneration. (With as little reason can we with Oecumenius, Luther, Hyperius, Gerhard, take διδαχῆς as an independent co-ordinate genitive beside βαπτισμῶν; for what then would be the meaning of ἀναστάσεως and κρίματος?) The right construction has been given by Calvin, Beza, Schlichting, Storr, Böhme, Paulus, and Bleek. They supply διδαχῆς at ἐπιθέσεως, ἀναστάσεως, and κρίματος respectively.

The writer therefore specifies *four principal objects* of the διδαχή, baptism and laying on of hands which belong to the beginning of the Christian life, and with which are connected the forgiveness of sins and bestowal of gifts of the Holy Spirit, and the resurrection together with the judgment, in which the life of the Christian Church finds its consummation, and which form the object of the Christian *hope*.

Ver. 3. Those who understand φερώμεθα, ver. 1, as an intimation of the author's intended plan of teaching, must, as a matter of consequence, understand ποιήσομεν, ver. 4, also in the same way, and refer the τοῦτο to the intimated transition to more difficult subjects, so that the author would here say, he designs, "if God will," now in fact to pass to what is more difficult. But it will be difficult to see how what he says in ver. 4 —6, namely, that whosoever has fallen away from the faith cannot be again renewed, is subservient to this design either as argument or illustration. We who have understood φερώμεθα, ver. 1, as *insinuative*, *i.e.*, as an exhortation, understand, of course, ποιήσομεν also in the same way, and refer τοῦτο to the whole of what precedes, as well to the "striving after perfection" as to the not destroying the foundation of the μετάνοια, πίστις and διδαχή." We thus obtain a sentiment with which ver. 4 connects in the closest and finest manner. The author seriously considers it as still a problematical thing whether the conversion to faith and the attainment of perfection be as yet possible for his readers. For, he says, he who has once *fallen from* the state of grace, can no more be renewed. Still, he adds ver. 9, the hope that with his readers it has not yet come to an entire falling away. He therefore sets before them in ver. 4—8 the greatness of the danger, but gives them encouragement again in ver. 9 ss. Both taken together—the danger as well as the still existing possibility (but only the possibility) of returning—form the exegesis of the ἐάνπερ. The thing rests upon the edge, but it is still upon the edge.

Vers. 4—6. The impossibility of being *renewed* is declared of those who, *a*, were enlightened, who had tasted the heavenly gift, had become partakers of the Holy Ghost, and had tasted the gospel together with the powers of the future world, and then, *b*, have again fallen away. The first four particulars describe the various steps from the beginning of conversion, on to the perfect state of faith and grace. The beginning is described in the words ἅπαξ φωτισθέντες, the general designation for the knowledge of the truth. Conversion begins with this, that the man who *was blind as regards himself*, blind in respect to his relation to God, his obligations to God, his undone state, his need of salvation, and *therefore all the more blind in respect to the offered salvation* which he knew not and wished not to know, is now *enlightened* as to his own condition and the truth of the salvation in Christ; that he begins to perceive and to feel, that there is something more than deception and superstition in what is declared to him of the Nazarene. Has this knowledge been once gained; then it must be progressive—or the man must be lost; for this light arises upon any one only *once*.—The second step is, that the man taking hold of the salvation, now has the *actual experience* in and for himself, that in Christ a heavenly gift—grace, forgiveness, and strength—is offered to him.—If he accepts these *gifts* in humility and faith, he receives, thirdly, the *gift of the Holy Ghost*; his Saviour begins by his spirit to be a living principle within him; and this has as its consequence a *twofold fruit*. He learns and experiences in himself the καλὸν θεοῦ ῥῆμα (= דבר־טוב Josh. xxi. 43, xxiii. 14 ; Jer. xxix. 10, &c.)—God's word of promise, *i.e.* of course the fulfilment of this word, consequently the whole riches of the inheritance of grace promised to the Messianic Israel—peace, joy, inclination to what is good, a new heart, &c.; and then, as a second fruit, he experiences in himself *the powers of the world to come.* To these powers belong not merely those extraordinary miraculous gifts of the apostolic age (which may certainly be viewed also as anticipations of the final victory of the *spirit* over the *flesh*), but all those gifts of sanctification and glorification which, even here below, give to the Christian the victory over the old Adam, and death.—This passage repels the slander of the young Hegelians and their associates who hold, that the Christianity of the Bible is a religion of the future world and not of the present. No! because it is a religion of the future state, it has power to elevate the present and to free it from the evils of sin which is the ruin of mankind. But the young Hegelians and their associates, because they have no future world, cannot do otherwise than corrupt and destroy the present.

Now, of him who has already passed over those stages in the Christian course and then falls away, it is here said that "it is impossible again to renew him," *i.e.* the state of grace out of which he has fallen (the μετάνοια conversion,[1] cannot be again

[1] Others foolishly think that the state of Adam before the fall is here meant.

restored in him; he is and remains lost. We must not shrink from these words or attempt to explain them away. The author assuredly does not mean (as some of the more ancient commentators thought) that such a one is not to be again *baptized*, although he may notwithstanding be saved; just as little does he mean that only men cannot save him, but God notwithstanding may. He lays it down quite absolutely, " it is impossible to renew him again to conversion."

This is one of those passages which speak of the so-called *sin against the Holy Ghost*, or more correctly of a fall that leads into irrecoverable perdition. It is well known, that on this subject there was a difference between the predestinarian Calvinists and the Lutherans, a difference extending even to the exegesis itself. The Calvinists founded their view on the passage in Matt. xii. 31, s., in which Christ warns the *unbelieving Jews* against committing the sin against the Holy Ghost which can never be forgiven; further, on the passage 1 John ii. 19, where John says of certain individuals who had fallen away from Christianity to Gnosticism: " They are gone out from us, but they were not of us; for if they had been of us they would have continued with us." Both passages were used by the Calvinists as a proof of the theorem that, *a,* one who is really born again cannot fall away, *b,* consequently he who falls away cannot have been really born again—a theorem which, we may observe, is not *necessarily* a consequence of the absolute doctrine of predestination, but is also conceivable independent of it. But how now is this to be reconciled with our passage Heb. vi. 4—6 ? with this passage in which we are taught, that there may be a falling away from a state of faith in the fullest and most proper sense of the term. Calvin laid emphasis on the word γευσάμενοι; individuals are here spoken of who had *but tasted a little* of the gifts of grace, and had received only " some sparks of light." But whoever is not blinded by dogmatical prejudices must perceive, that the aim of our author is evidently and assuredly not to say: *the less* one has tasted of the gifts of grace the more easily may he be irrecoverably lost, but precisely the reverse: the *more* one has already penetrated into the sanctuary of the state of grace, by so much the more irrecoverably is he lost in case he should fall away.

Our passage, therefore, unmistakeably declares the possibility that a regenerate person may fall away. But does it not herein contradict what is said in 1 John ii. 19. Not in the least! If in our own day a Christian preacher should write or say of people who had been corrupt members of the Church, and had become the prey of Ronge and other lying apostles: " They have fallen away from us because they never belonged to us," &c., who would infer from this, that that pastor virtually denies the possibility that those who are really regenerated may also fall away? So it is with John. Of him who could become the prey of such *manifest* babblers and lying prophets as the Gnostics were, it must be inferred, that he had not penetrated far into the substance of Christianity. From this, however, it does not at all follow, that one also who has really attained to a state of grace in the fullest and most proper sense, may not, by becoming indolent in the struggle with the old Adam, and allowing a bosom sin to get the mastery over him, suffer shipwreck of faith.

In opposition to Calvin, then, we must lay down the following as the doctrine of the Holy Scripture on the sin against the Holy Ghost.

There are three *different ways* specified in Scripture in which a man may be eternally lost. 1. The sin against the Holy Ghost properly so-called, Matth. xii. 31, s. when a man obstinately resists the *call* of grace, and repels all the *first motions* of the Holy Spirit in his heart and conscience; 2. 1 John ii. 19, when one embraces Christianity outwardly and superficially without being truly born again, and then becomes a prey to the seducing talk of some vagabond babbler; and 3. Heb. vi. 4—6, when one has been truly born again, but gives place to the evil principle in his heart, and being worsted in the struggle, suffers himself to be taken captive by some more refined temptation of Satan, some more refined lie (as here by a seemingly pious attachment to the institutions of the old covenant.)

Why such a one is irrecoverably lost, we learn from the words in apposition to those we have considered: $\dot{a}\nu a\sigma \tau a\nu\rho o\hat{\nu}\nu\tau a\varsigma$, &c. Such a one commits, in a more aggravated degree, the sin which the unbelieving Jews committed against Christ. The Israelites crucified in their madness a pseudo-Messiah, or at the worst a prophet. But he who has *known* and *experienced* Jesus as his Saviour and Redeemer, and yet after all falls away from Christianity, actually declares *him whom he has known as the Son of God* to be a pseudo-Messiah, and contemns him.

If now by δυνάμεις are meant the gifts communicated by the laying on of hands, then (as the laying on of hands took place after baptism,) the readers must have been *baptized*, and only taken again *under instruction* afterwards. Still δυνάμεις may mean also the powers of sanctification in the wider sense. The former is however the more probable.

Ver. 7, 8. The apostle here remembers Christ's parable of the different kinds of ground. In this parable, however, we find the best refutation of the Calvinistic exegesis of vers. 4—6. The fruitful as well as the unfruitful soil received the same rain and blessing; it is the fault of the soil if the seed is choked by thorns or *evil lusts.* The cause of the falling away lies not in the want of an abstract donum perseverantiae withheld by God, but in a shortcoming in the struggle with the old man. In the words κατάρας ἐγγύς the author cannot intend to say that the curse is *still uncertain* (this is forbidden by the words that follow), they simply mean "it goes towards the curse," "the curse is impending over it." (Comp. chap. viii. 13.)—'Εἰς καῦσιν for the nominative καῦσις is a Hebraism = לבער with the ל substantiae, comp. LXX. Is. xl. 16; xliv. 15. The meaning of the author is, of course, not that the thorns and thistles merely, but that the whole land itself shall be burned up with fire and brimstone (comp. Deut. xxix. 22.) This is, then, a type of the eternal destruction of the individual who was compared with an unfruitful field.

Vers. 9—12. The author now turns to the other side of the subject, to the comforting hope that in the case of his readers it has not yet come to a falling way. "If we thus speak to you (in this style of earnest warning) we are yet persuaded of better things concerning you, of things that pertain to salvation." ('Εχόμενα σωτηρίας a classical amplification of the adjectival idea = haud insalutaria. Ἔχεσθαί τινος, pertinere ad aliquid, to be connected with any thing, to have part in any thing. The expression is purposely left indefinite, and it is wrong to attempt to find in it one or another precise sense. 'Εχόμενα σωτηρίας forms only the general antithesis to κατάρας ἐγγύς. The change here from severity to gentleness reminds us of the pauline passages Gal. iv. 12 and 19; 2 Cor. x. 11.

Ver. 10. The more that the new life has already shown itself to be efficacious in a Christian, the more that the fruits of holiness have already been visible in him, so much the more safely may it be concluded that his has been a true central, fundamental, and deep conversion. The more that his Christianity consisted only of theory and head orthodoxy, so much the more reason is there to fear that the whole man has not been converted, so much the greater danger is there of a seeming conversion and a subsequent falling away. What the man has gained by mere dialectics may again be entirely lost by mere dialectics, amid the temptations of the flesh and the trials of suffering. The only sure mark of conversion is the presence of sanctification; the only sure mark of continuance in the state of grace is progress in sanctification.

Upon this truth the sentiment of ver. 10 is founded. Because the readers have already evinced, and do still evince, the visible *fruits* of faith in works of love and of service, the author cherishes the persuasion that God will not let them fall, will not withdraw his Spirit and the help of his grace from them. It is striking, however, that he here appeals to the *justice* of God. The Roman Catholic theologians have made use of this passage by way of confirming their theory of the *meritum condigni*. The natural man can indeed perform no good and meritorious works; but the converted man can, by the assistance of the Holy Spirit, perform works perfectly good and therefore meritorious, which God rewards by the communication of new gifts of grace. The evangelical theologians have justly opposed to this theory the truth, that the best works of the regenerate are still stained with sin and imperfect, and, in fact, that nothing is said in our passage of *rewarding particular works*. But the evangelical theologians have, in general, been able to find no other way of explaining this passage than by supposing, that the good works of the regenerate, *although imperfect*, yet received a reward *of grace* from God. This, however, is a *contradictio in adjecto*; what God gives out of grace in spite of our imperfection wants precisely for that reason the quality of a *reward.*—The truth is, there is another righteousness besides that which *recompenses*, or *rewards*. The righteousness of God spoken of in our passage is that which leads, *guides*, and *governs*, every man according to the particular stage of development which he occupies. It is here affirmed of God that he does not give up to perdition a man *who can still in any way be saved*, in whom the new life is not yet entirely extinct, and who has not yet entirely fallen away; but that he seeks to draw every one as long as they will allow themselves to be drawn. This is not a judicial or recompensing righteousness towards man (for man has no right to *demand* the assisting grace of God as a thing deserved), but it is *the righteousness of the Father towards the Son who has bought men with his blood, and to whom we poor sinners still belong until we have fallen away from him.* Not towards us but toward Christ would the Father be ἄδικος, were he to withdraw his gracious assistance from a man ere he has ceased to belong to the *peculium* of Christ.

Ver. 11. The writer now expresses his earnest wish that his readers may advance in the Christian life with renewed zeal; that " each one of them may now manifest, even to perfection, the same zeal in striving after the full assurance of hope," as they had hitherto shown in the ἀγάπη. The *full assurance of hope* is opposed to the wavering and uncertainty which they had hitherto shown, as to whether they might rely entirely and undividedly on the salvation and promise of Christ, or whether they required, together with this, the temple service, and Levitical priesthood.

Ver. 12. The result of that *zeal* which the readers are to show is, that they may be no longer νωθροί (as they have been hitherto chap. v. 12), but may be equal to other Christians, not only in the ἀγάπη διακονία but also in the πίστις and μακροθυμία. Μακροθυμία, however, by no means denotes merely passive patience, the passive endurance of suffering, but as at Rom. ii. 7 even ὑπομονή serves to denote active constancy, this is still more denoted here by μακροθυμία.

Vers. 13—15. Here commences a somewhat more difficult train of thought which, by means of the particle γάρ, is connected with the foregoing as an explanation. The question presents itself: What is *said* in vers. 13—15, and what is intended to be *proven* by it or to be *inferred* from it as an explanation of ver. 12 ? What is said, and said in words grammatically quite clear, is: God has sworn to Abraham (comp. Gen. xxii. 16 ss. with chap. xvii. 1 ss.) that he will bless him and multiply him. And from this it is inferred in ver. 15, that that ancestor of the covenant-people was thus also made a partaker of the promise through μακροθυμία. This idea of the μακροθυμεῖν is evidently the connecting link between ver. 12 and vers. 13—15. On the other hand, the words *God hath sworn by himself*, ver. 13, are at first only cited as *an accessary circumstance* which is afterwards brought into prominence in ver. 16, and made use of as a new and independent idea. (The words κατὰ τὴν τάξιν Μελχισεδέκ, chap. v. 6, are found to be cited quite in a similar way, and then, afterwards in chap. vii., made to form properly a new theme. Similarly also the citation chap. iii. 7—12 compared with ver. 15 ss. and chap. iv. 3 and 7.)

The principal question then in the explanation of the three verses under consideration is, how far does the fact that God has sworn to Abraham that he will bless him and multiply him involve the inference, that Abraham attained to the (fulfilment of the) promise by μακροθυμία? Bleek is certainly wrong when, in spite of the καὶ οὕτω, he will still not allow ver. 5 to be an *inference* from vers. 13, 14, but finds in it a statement to the effect that Abraham deserved that promise of the blessing and multiplying, by his constancy (in the faith) evinced at *another time*, namely, in the offering up of his son Isaac according to the command of God. The writer, indeed, does not in a single word point to the *strength* of faith shown in complying with the command to offer up Isaac; but from the circumstance that God *sware* to Abraham to bless him and to *multiply* him, he infers that Abraham obtained the promise (namely the fulfilment of it) through the *constancy* of his faith. Now, whoever ascribes to our author a rabbinical method of exegesis which cleaves to words and to the letter must, here again, find himself greatly embarrassed; for here, as always, the vis argumentationis lies not in the letter, but in the thought. There are two particulars on which the force of the proof rests. First, God promised to Abraham *with an oath;* this already implied that the fulfilment of the promise was to be looked for at some future time, for there can be no need of confirming with an oath the promise of a gift which is forthwith and immediately bestowed; an oath is then only necessary, when the fulfilment is so remote as to make it possible that doubts might spring up in the mind of the receiver of the promise from the long delay. Secondly, the subject-matter of the promise, *the promised object itself*, was such as from the nature of the case could only be realised after the death of Abraham. He was to be blessed, and that by an immense multiplication of his seed; this could, from the nature of the case, be fulfilled only many generations after Abraham. Thus Abraham throughout his whole life saw nothing of the fulfilment of the promise which had been made to him (comp. chap. xi. 39); he was directed to continue until death in the *constancy of the hope of that which he saw not.* So also are the readers of the Epistle to the Hebrews admonished not to rely on the earthly, visible, Jewish theocracy and its institutions, but with the constancy of Abraham's faith to build their hope of salvation on the crucified Jesus who has gone into the heavens, whose followers still form a scattered flock, and who have nothing on earth but the *hope* of what is promised for the future.

Vers. 16—19. The author now brings into prominence the *accessary idea* indicated in ver. 13: that God can swear by none greater than he is himself, and makes use of it for a new turn of the thought, namely, for the inference that, just because God is in himself unchangeable, a promise which he has not only given, but has, moreover, sworn by himself in confirmation of it, is absolutely sure and settled. In this certainty of the promises of God there lies a second motive for the readers to continue stedfast in the *hope* of the glory promised to the Messianic Israel (already in Abraham's time.) And from this the author, having inwardly prepared his readers and opened their *hearts*, dexterously retraces his steps to his theme respecting the similarity between the New Testament Messianic priesthood and that of Melchisedec.

Ver. 16. " Men swear by one who is greater (than themselves), and the oath is for certainty beyond all strife" (for indisputable certainty.) This idea is in itself plain. Men swear by a being who is greater than they, who possesses omniscience enabling him to know the perjured person, and power and justice to punish him. The oath consists in this, that the person who swears calls the higher being to witness at once the promise and its fulfilment or non-fulfilment, and to be the eventual avenger of the latter. (Hence with the purified Christian every word is a tacit oath; inasmuch as it is spoken in the consciousness of the testimony of the all-present and all-knowing God. And hence Christ forbids swearing by inanimate things (Matth. v. 34), and puts that state of mind in which every yea is a yea—*i.e.* in which every word, whether God be expressly called to witness or not, is spoken in the consciousness that God is witness—in the place of that swearing which was alike superstitious and false. Christ therefore does not forbid the oath, but he wills that the Christian should speak *only oaths*, and that in this way the difference between swearing and not swearing should find an end.)

Ver. 16. Now *in God*, the possibility of wavering, or the want of veracity, and thus the necessity of a higher guarantee, falls absolutely to the ground. He is true, not on account of another or from fear of any other, but by his own nature. Therefore he can swear only *by himself*, he can produce only himself and his own nature as the witness and guarantee of his veracity. It is true that for this very reason God's swearing by himself is an anthropopathism, or more correctly a condescension to human infirmity. On his own account he needs not to swear; on his own account the form of swearing, the form of a promiser and a witness, might be dispensed with. But so long as to *man* the knowledge of the unchangeableness of God was still hidden or imperfect, God condescended to swear. With wonderful wisdom he stooped to the human presupposition of the possibility of change in God, therefore he sware; but inasmuch as he sware by himself, he in the same act lifted man upwards to the knowledge that *he has that in his own nature* which hinders him from change. This idea, which was already briefly indicated in ver. 13, is further developed in ver. 17.

'Ἐν ᾧ, literally "in which circumstances," = in these circumstances, quae cum ita sint. Hence it may be rendered by "therefore" (Theophylact, Erasmus, Schlichting, Grotius, Kuinoel, Olshausen, De Wette, Tholuck, Bleek, &c.) 'Ἐν ᾧ does not, however, belong to βουλόμενος ; Rambach and others have explained thus: as now by this (by conforming to the practice among men of swearing) God would show, &c. ; the swearing of God is evidently, however, not placed parallel with the swearing of men, but in opposition to it, as already appears from the words ἄνθρωποι μὲν γάρ. 'Ἐν ᾧ belongs rather to ἐμεσίτευσεν.

" Therefore (because *men* swear by one superior to themselves) *God*, when he would show to the heirs of the promise the immutability of his will in a superabundantly *sure* way, placed *himself* in the middle" (between himself qua the promiser, and men.)—Μεσιτεύω, se interponere, to place one's self as mediator between two parties. Then specially in promises in the form of an oath, to place one's self as warranter, as fidejussor or security between the promiser and the receiver of the promise, in order to undertake the security for the fulfilment of the promise. God does this when a man swears by him; he then lets himself be called by both men as a witness and guarantee. When, however, God swears by himself, he then as it were comes in between himself and men. In other words, he is *his own* witness.

Ver. 18. "Therefore we have firm consolation by two indestructible things, in both of which it is impossible for God to lie—we who flee for refuge to lay hold on the hope at the future goal." As God is in himself unchangeable and true, and needs not to swear, *so his promise is in itself alone* already sure and indestructible. But when, moreover, he appears not merely as promiser, but (inasmuch as he swears) also as μεσιτεύων, as his own witness and security, then must the fulfilment be doubly sure, or, more precisely, a double testimony is given to the divine immutability.

In the words which stand in apposition to the subject οἱ καταφυγόντες, &c., the author repeats the condition upon which a subjective interest is obtained in the promise which is in itself and objectively sure. Nothing is wanting on God's part; but we on our part, forsaking all false consolation, must flee to lay hold on the ἐλπὶς προκειμένη. (On the partic. aor. comp. chap. iv. 3.—Others less naturally understand καταφυγόντες as an absolute idea, and make κρατῆσαι dependent on παράκλησις, and give this latter the signification "admonition, injunction.") The *hope* involves here both the object of the hope (comp. the adjective προκειμένη) and the act of it (comp. κρατῆσαι.) Καταφυγόντες is well explained by Calvin thus: Hoc verbo significat, non aliter Deo vere nos fidere, quam dum praesidiis omnibus aliis destituti ad solidam ejus promissionem confugimus. The readers were to flee from all false Judaistic props of hope in the concern of their salvation, and to direct their eye alone to the invisible goal of future glory promised in Christ.

Ver. 19. This firm hope resting solely upon Christ is "a sure and firm anchor of the soul, and such as enters into the inner place behind the vail." Two figures are here, not so much mixed as, in a very elegant manner, combined. The author might compare the world to a sea, the soul to a ship, the future still concealed glory to the covered bottom of the sea, the remote firm land stretching beneath the water and covered by the water. Or he might compare the present life upon earth to the forecourt, and the future blessedness to the heavenly sanctuary, which is still, as it were, concealed from us by a vail. He has, however, combined the two figures. The soul, like a shipwrecked mariner, clings to an anchor, and *sees* not where the cable of the anchor runs to, where it is made fast; it knows, however, that it is firmly fixed behind the vail which conceals from it the future glory, and that if it only keeps fast hold of the anchor, it will, in due time, be drawn in with the anchor by a rescuing hand into the holiest of all. Thus there is in the *hope* itself that which the *fulfilment* certainly brings about.

Ver. 20. The holy of holies is now more particularly described as that "into which Christ is entered as our Forerunner." In these words the author touches on the second section of the first part (chap. ii. ver. 16, comp. with ver. 17), and at the same time on the second section of the second part (chap. iv. vers. 10 and 14.) In both passages, but with more distinctness in the second, the inference was drawn from this going before of Christ as the first fruits and preparer of the way to heaven, that his office is a *high-priestly* office. Thus the sentiment of ver. 20 leads the author naturally and without constraint back to the theme begun at chap. v. 1—10, namely, the *comparison of Christ with the high priest*; and now, after having prepared the hearts of the readers for what he is about to say, he proceeds exactly from the place where he broke off at chap. v. 10; he repeats the new theme already intimated there: *Christ is a priest after the order of Melchisedec*, and this similarity between his priesthood and that of Melchisedec culminates in the *eternity* of it.

SECTION SECOND.

(Chap. vii.)

THE MESSIAH, AS A HIGH PRIEST AFTER THE ORDER OF MELCHISEDEC, IS A SUPERIOR HIGH PRIEST TO AARON.

The train of thought in this chapter is most clearly arranged. First, it is shown in ver. 1—10 that Melchisedec's priesthood was of a higher order than the Levitical; then, in vers. 11—19, the inference is drawn from this, that the Levitical priesthood, and, in like manner also, the Mosaical law upon which it was grafted was imperfect, and finally in vers. 20—28, that the Messiah, because according to Ps. cx. he must be a high priest after the order of Melchisedec, was greatly superior to the Levitical priesthood as well as to the Mosaical law.

The first of these three parts divides itself again into two lines of thought; in vers. 1—3 it is shown that the priesthood of Melchisedec is an *eternal* priesthood, in ver. 4—10 that Melchisedec *took tithes from Levi.*

Vers. 1—3. Οὗτος points back to chap. vi. 20. This Melchisedec, namely, he who is spoken of in Ps. cx. The principal nerve of the passage lies, of course, in the principal verb μένει εἰς τὸ διηνεκές (not as Storr would have it in the words ἑρμηνευόμενος βασιλεὺς δικαιοσύνης.) It was already intimated in chap. vi. 20, that Christ is like Melchisedec an *eternal* high priest. And, now in vers. 1—3, it is explained in how far Melchisedec's priesthood was eternal, and in like manner it is then shown in vers. 20—28 in how far Christ's priesthood was eternal. It can therefore not be doubted that the words μένει εἰς τὸ διηνεκές contain the principal idea of the sentence. All the other parts from vers. 1—3 are only accessary members of an explanatory kind.

The question, however, still remains in what relation does this principal idea stand to the thesis chap. iv. 20. Are we to take the γάρ in an *argumentative* sense, and is it the intention of the author to prove in vers. 1—3 that Christ was a high priest after the order of Melchisedec? And does the proof consist in this, that Melchisedec was an eternal priest, and that, in like manner, an eternal priesthood belongs also to Christ, so that in virtue of this tertium comparationis—eternity—Christ can be called a high priest after the order of Melchisedec? This cannot possibly have been the author's intention. He must in this case have left out the words εἰς τὸν αἰῶνα in the thesis chap. vi. 20, and, instead of this, must have introduced immediately after ver. 3 what he says from vers. 20—28. (The train of thought must then have been: Christ is a high priest after the manner of Melchisedec; for, Melchisedec's priesthood was eternal, Christ's priesthood was also eternal, ergo.)—In reality, however, the author was under *no necessity* whatever of proving that Christ's priesthood was and must be after the order of Melchisedec. This had already been settled at chap. v. 1—10, and settled on the ground that the prophetical psalm, Ps. cx., contains the calling of the Messiah to the priestly dignity, and that the Psalmist had therefore before-hand ascribed to the Messiah the priestly *in conjunction with the kingly honour.* No, it is not the aim of the author to *prove* in chap. vii. 1—3 that the priesthood of Christ is of the same order as that of Melchisedec, but, from the thesis already established, chap. vi. 20, to *draw inferences,* the inference, namely, that the *priesthood of the Messiah is superior to the Levitical priesthood.*

We must therefore take γάρ in an *explicative* signification in the sense of *namely.* The weighty import of the thesis, chap. vi. 20, is now to be evolved, the author will, so to speak, unfold to the reader the fulness of meaning that lies in the simple expression *after the order of Melchisedec,* and show him with what important results it is fraught.

A series of clauses in apposition follows the subject of the sentence, which, however, do not all belong to the subject, but in part to the predicate. Those which belong to the predicate begin with *first being by interpretation;* that they begin here and nowhere else is evident from this, that the first two attributes are *here repeated by way of being explained.*

Melchisedec, ... first being by interpretation king of righteousness,
king of Salem, ... then king of Salem, *i.e.,* king of peace, priest of God, &c.

We have therefore to render the sentence thus: " This Melchisedec, king of Salem, priest of the most high God, who met Abraham, &c., and blessed him, *abideth for ever* as one whose name signifies king of righteousness, &c." The first group of appositional clauses serves to denote and to describe the subject; the second serves to show, what ground there is for ascribing to this subject the predicate *abideth for ever*.

Let us consider the first group. *Melchisedec*, the well-known king of the Amorites, Gen. xiv. The conjecture of Jerome, Luther, &c., that Melchisedec was no other than Shem the son of Noah, is now with reason universally rejected. Equally untenable is the view of Molinäus, Hottinger, &c., that Melchisedec was no man, but a temporary incarnation of the Son of God. Melchisedec was doubtless, according to the Scriptures of the Old and New Testament, none other than an Amoritic prince of a tribe among whom (just as in the house of Laban) the ancient primitive monotheism was still preserved, and who, according to the old patriarchal fashion, still offered sacrifices as the priest of his tribe to the invisible God in heaven.—The words *who met* &c. as also the words *to whom he gave a tenth*, &c. serve here, first of all, to recall to the minds of his readers the few incidents that have been preserved from the life of this man, and to give them a more distinct presentation of the form of Melchisedec, although these incidents are afterwards, vers. 4 and 6, again taken up and made use of for farther inferences (just as at chap. vi. 13 the words ἐπεὶ, &c.)

Pass we now to the *second group* of clauses in apposition. Melchisedec *remains* a priest *for ever*, he whose name being interpreted is *King of righteousness*, whose title signifies *King of peace*. The author was fully entitled to lay stress on these names, as they were not merely arbitrary, but were really expressive of the nature and character of that man. If our author had drawn similar inferences from the name of the later king Adonizedec of Salem (Josh. x.), this might justly have been characterized as a rabbinical proceeding; but every reader of sound sense will feel how impossible such a proceeding would be to the author of the epistle to the Hebrews, how harshly it would contrast with the usually profound character of his reasonings. In Melchisedec, the nomen et omen truly met and harmonised. The tribe of people which had built Salem must have been *really* a peaceable

tribe, otherwise they would not have given to the city the name
"Peace," "city of Peace," and, in fact, the king of this city had
not involved himself and his people in that war which, considering
the times, was a pretty extensive war. This king himself showed
really a sense of justice in sympathising with the righteous cause
of Abraham, and he showed more than this, in coming to meet
Abraham in a friendly spirit with presents of refreshment.
Abraham, the champion of faith, offers to him gifts of homage;
nay, in giving him the tenth, he thereby places himself under his
sovereignty, he takes refuge beneath the sceptre of this king
who served the living God, in order that under his protection
he may henceforth live unmolested by hostile bands of heathen.
The names מלכי צדק and מלך שלם, therefore, really express only in a concise way the *features of character and form*
which distinguished that priest king. And when David (Ps.
110) in the spirit of prophecy sees and expects of the seed promised to him, that, like Melchisedec, he will unite the priestly
with the kingly dignity, he surely does not predict in these words
a merely outward and mechanical *conjunction* of the two dignities,
but he has before him the figure of a man in whom, as in Melchisedec, the kingly power would be consecrated and penetrated
with the sanctifying virtue of the priestly dignity and work, the
form, therefore, of a king who would truly govern in *peace*
(comp. 2 Sam. vii. 11) and *righteousness* (comp. Ps. xlv. 8.)

From this alone, however, it does not follow that Melchisedec's
priesthood is eternal. In order to prove this other attributes are
still necessary. Melchisedec is *without father, without mother,
without descent.* What does the author mean by this? Schulz
and Böhme have imputed such absurdity to him as to suppose,
that he really meant to say that Melchisedec came into the world
without parents, and with some this strange idea even yet finds
acceptance. But is it seriously believed that the author meant
to ascribe to Melchisedec a *really* eternal priesthood? Christ
then was not the only eternal priest! Such an interpretation as
this which cleaves to the letter, carries only in itself that rabbi-
hical narrowness which those who employ it think they find in
the Holy Scriptures.

Our author reasons in quite the reverse way. He turns

entirely away from all investigation respecting the other unknown events in Melchisedec's life, and views him only in so far as David in the 110th psalm has made use of him, and *could* make use of him as a type of the Messiah. The individual Melchisedec who met Abraham had indeed a father and a mother, possibly a brave father and a gentle mother—for all we know. But just because we do not know this, and because David also could know nothing of it when he used the words, " Thou art a priest after the order of Melchisedec," he cannot have intended to say : the Messiah will have a brave or not brave father, a gentle or ungentle-mother, &c.,—in other words, he could not mean to set forth the *individual* with his *other* characteristics as a figure of the future Messiah, but must have referred to the figure of Melchisedec only *in so far as it stands out from obscurity in Gen.* xiv., when he said of the promised seed that he shall be a priest after the manner of Melchisedec.

But this and this alone is justly important to our author. The Levitical priest had to legitimize himself as a priest by his descent from Levi and Aaron; Melchisedec's priesthood had certainly nothing to do with his race and his descent, as nothing at all has been recorded of his descent. Melchisedec stands altogether outside of the great theocratical lineage, which runs from Abraham upwards to Adam and downwards to Levi and Aaron, &c. He comes forth from the darkness, like a streak of light, only to disappear immediately in the darkness again. And yet—although he cannot have been a priest by theocratical descent—the Holy Scripture adduces him, Moses himself adduces him as a " priest of God on high," and acknowledges him as such. If now the Messiah is to be a priest after the order of Melchisedec, then to him also is ascribed not the Levitical hereditary priesthood but an *independent priesthood having its root in his own person.*

That the words ἀπάτωρ, ἀμήτωρ mean here really nothing more than parentibus *ignotis* appears partly, from the analogy of profane writers (for example, *Horace* serm. 1, 6, 10 : Multos saepe viros nullis majoribus ortos. *Liv.* iv. 3 : Servium Tullium, captiva Corniculana natum, patre nullo, matre serva, *Cic.* de oratore II. 64 : Quid hoc clamoris ? quibus nec pater nec mater, tanta confidentia estis ?)—partly from the explanatory ἀγενεαλόγητος, which, as is well known, signifies not "without generation" but " without pedigree."

Now this also points already indirectly at the eternal nature of the priesthood of Melchisedec ; the full proof, however, is first given in the words *having neither beginning of days nor end of life,* but ἀφομοιωμένος τῷ υἱῷ τοῦ θεοῦ. How this is to be explained appears from what has just been said. The individual Melchisedec had, in truth, a beginning and an end of life; but of this nothing is recorded in the Pentateuch, and therefore David could not refer to it in the 110th psalm. It is of importance to the author that nothing is *recorded* of Melchisedec's birth and death. As he has explained *without father and without mother* by the term *without genealogy,* so now he explains *having neither beginning of days nor end of life* by ἀφομοιωμένος, &c. Calvin has already observed with reason that the author does not say ὁμοῖος. Melchisedec was not like to Christ, but was *represented* in a manner like to Christ. But that nothing is recorded in the Pentateuch of the beginning and end of Melchisedec's life, and that, notwithstanding, Melchisedec is acknowledged as a priest of God, and that this his priesthood—without predecessors and successors—was set forth by David as a type of the future Messianic priesthood—this, again, has properly for our author a *positive* significance. This is to be explained by *the antithesis to the Levitical priesthood;* for all these characteristic features of the priesthood of Melchisedec are adduced as bearing on the comparison with the Levitical priesthood, and in proof of the inferiority of the latter. The Levitical priest or highpriest became a priest by his birth, and left the priesthood at *his death* to his son; his office was, from the nature of him who held it, not a continuing one, but one that moved onwards from member to member, and *this succession was expressly prescribed and regulated in the law.* When therefore the Psalmist will describe the priestly glory of the promised *seed,* and seeks to concentrate this in a corresponding type, he selects not that of a ritual Levitical high priest—one of those high priests who, from generation to generation, ceased from their office and gave place to each other—but that of Melchisedec who, *a,* was a priest not by formal, legal investment, but because his internal character, his qualities of *righteousness* and *peace* impelled him to bring sacrifices to God, and to consecrate the power of the king by the internal qualities of the priest; who, *b*, was a priest not by descent but in himself; and who therefore, *c*, was not a link in a chain of predecessors and successors, but is represented as alone in his order, and thus far as one who continues a priest (yields up his priesthood to no one).

It is therefore truly no play upon words or artifice of ingenuity, but the divine wisdom and illumination of the Holy Spirit, by which our author obtains the inferences which he builds on those particulars in the form under which Melchisedec is represented to us. The vindication of his procedure lies in this, that Melchisedec does not appear as in himself (Gen. xiv.) a type of Christ, but is first stamped as a type of Christ by David in Ps. cx., who in this could not certainly refer to all that Melchisedec was, but only to the little that was recorded of him in Gen. xiv.—Seeing then that David when he would describe in its highest form the glory of the seed promised to him, selects not the form of a Levitical high priest, but that of Melchisedec as represented in Gen. xiv., our author must needs inquire, wherefore and on what grounds this of Melchisedec appeared to the Psalmist the most glorious form, more so than that of a Levitical high priest. These reasons were not difficult to discover. The Levitical high priest was such by investment; altogether apart from his personal character, but the Messiah was to be a high priest (comp. i. 9, ii. 17, iv. 15) from his own internal character, through his personal holiness, compassion, righteousness, and truth, just as Melchisedec was a high priest through his own independent free act and piety. The Levitical high priest held his office in virtue of his descent from Levi and Aaron; the Messiah was to descend not from Aaron but from David; like Melchisedec he was to stand outside of the hereditary Levitical succession of priests. The Levitical high priest must give place to a successor; the Messiah was to be a priest-king without end (2 Sam. vii.; Ps. cx. 4); to this corresponds in Melchisedec the circumstance, that we are nowhere told of his successor in the priestly office. In the manner then in which the account respecting Melchisedec is given Gen. xiv. lies the reason why he must have appeared to the Psalmist as more exalted than the Levitical high priest. None of those *limitations* which were *essential* to the latter are ascribed to the former. It is precisely in the mysterious way in which the Pentateuch represents him as emerging from the darkness, and standing above the theocratical race, that we are to seek the ground of that impression of more exalted majesty which induced the Psalmist to set him forth as a type or example of the priest-kingly glory belonging to the future Messiah. It will, accordingly, be evident that those expositors are entirely mistaken who maintain, that the words *remaineth a priest for ever* intimate merely that the priestly office of Melchisedec was everlasting. The office was also in the case of the *Levitical* high priests abiding and lasting. No! the *person* of Melchisedec—not precisely his person in its individual reality but in the outline of it which was presented to the Psalmist— wore the aspect of a priest whose priesthood had its root *in himself,* and who *resigned his office to no successor.* The substance of ver. 1—3 is therefore this: Already the Holy Scriptures of the Old Testament ascribe to the Messiah a priesthood which, in virtue of its internal and external independence and freedom from limitations, is far superior to the Levitical priesthood.

Ver. 4—10. A second proof now follows of the superiority of the priesthood of Melchisedec to the Levitical priesthood. This second proof is drawn from the incidents in the history of Melchisedec already mentioned casually in ver. 1, s., *who met Abraham,* &c. The whole argument in ver. 4—10 moves in the form of a sorites. This sorites consists of two principal parts. In ver. 4—7, from the circumstance that Abraham gave to Melchisedec the tenth and received his blessing it is inferred, that Melchisedec was superior to Abraham. In ver. 9, 10 from the fact that Levi was then yet in the loins of Abraham it is inferred, that Levi also was subordinate to Abraham.

The first part of the sorites will in a scholastico-logical form stand thus:—

Major: The receiver of tithe and bestower of the blessing is superior to the giver of tithe and receiver of the blessing.
Minor: But Abraham gave tithe to Melchisedec and received the blessing from him.
Conclusion: Therefore Melchisedec is superior to Abraham.

The author does not, however, merely omit the conclusion according to the form of the sorites, and forthwith proceed to the second principal part, but he makes the omission of the conclusions still more easy by the simple process of placing the major after the minor proposition.

Ver. 4 is *the first half of the minor*: Melchisedec received from Abraham the tenth. In ver. 5 a subsidiary remark follows, to the effect that Melchisedec received the tenth from Abraham in a much more striking and distinguished manner than the Levites now receive it from the Jews. In ver. 6 the *first half of the minor*, enlarged by the antithetical reference to ver. 5, is *repeated*, and *the second half of the minor*: that Melchisedec *blessed* Abraham, is added.

In ver. 7 the *major proposition* (already involving the conclusion) now follows the minor; formally, however, it is adduced only in reference to the blessing. (The same thing was already self-evident in reference to the levying of the tithe chiefly from ver. 5.)

After it has been shown that Melchisedec is superior to Abraham, the receiver of the promise, and the progenitor of all the Levitical and non-Levitical Jews, the author, now glancing back to ver. 1—3, makes the transition in ver. 8 to the second principal part of the sorites, ver. 9, 10, ver. 9 containing the *thesis*, ver. 10 the *proof*.

Ver. 4. The particle δέ serves simply to denote the transition to another subject. "But now observe further." Πήλικος how great, how highly exalted, namely, in comparison with the Levitical high priests. The ᾧ does not serve first to determine who is meant by οὗτος; but οὗτος refers backwards to the Melchisedec named in ver. 1—3, and ᾧ is confirmatory, cui = quum ei. The apposition ὁ πατριάρχης is, on account of the emphasis, placed at the end of the period. He who, as the progenitor of all Israel, also of the Levites, is superior to Israel and to the Levites, nevertheless paid the tenth to Melchisedec, and thus placed himself in a subordinate position to him. This finishes the first part of the minor proposition (placed before the major in ver. 7.)

Before, however, the author adds the other part in ver. 6, he must first meet an objection. The objector might say, Why is so much stress laid on the circumstance that Melchisedec took tithes? Did not the Levitical priests also take tithes? The author must needs show, therefore, what an important difference there is between the two cases. He does this in a subsidiary remark at ver. 5. He first of all introduces the objection itself in the form of a *restriction*, " and indeed the Levites also take tithes ;" he, however, at the same time, joins to this restriction or concession all the particulars in which the inferiority of the Levites in this respect shows itself, so that he can then forthwith set forth, in opposition to this, the higher form of tithe-taking in the case of Melchisedec, and with this can, at the same time, repeat in a more enlarged and more definite form, in the 6th verse, the idea of the minor proposition of ver. 4.

We must first of all consider more closely the *subject*: οἱ μὲν ἐκ τῶν υἱῶν Λευὶ τὴν ἱερατείαν λαμβάνοντες. That οἱ λαμβάνοντες is really the subject, and that the words ἐκ τῶν υἱῶν Λευὶ depend on λαμβάνοντες, is evident of itself. If οἱ ἐκ τῶν υἱῶν Λευὶ by itself were taken as the subject, and τὴν ἱερατείαν λαμβάνοντες as a more special determination of the idea in the predicate, we should then obtain the unsuitable sense that the Levites *then* take tithes *when* they receive or enter upon the priesthood. This, however, would not be agreeable to historical fact. With as little reason can we, with Bleek and others, render thus: *those* among the Levites who receive the priesthood (in opposition to those who were Levites merely without being priests)—for, according to the Mosaic law, all Levites received tithe. (Lev. xxvii. 30.) The emphasis rather lies on λαμβάνοντες, and the Levites are placed in a twofold antithesis to Melchisedec; first, as those who were descended from Levi; secondly, as those who *received* the priesthood (in virtue of this their descent.) " Those who, being of the sons of Levi, *received* the priesthood," stand in opposition to Melchisedec, who, according to ver. 1—3, was *without genealogy*, and *had neither predecessor nor successor;* but whose priesthood flowed independently, as it were, from his own person. (So substantially also Reland, Pierce, Wolf.)

The word λαμβάνοντες, then, already indicates one point of inferiority in the Levitical receiving of tithes. A further point of inferiority is given in the words ἐντολὴν ἔχουσι. The Levites received by a command the right to lift tithes, and the rest of the Israelites give tithes because they *must* do so. Abraham, on the contrary, gave tithe to Melchisedec *voluntarily*. *There* there was a third party (namely, God) who is superior to the Levites, as well as to the rest of the tribes, to whom the tithe properly belonged, and who assigned it to the Levites. *Here* it was the personal dignity and majesty of Melchisedec that moved Abraham to give tithes. The same antithesis is repeated in the words κατὰ τὸν νόμον.

But the author does not overlook the circumstance, also, that the right of the Levites to exact tithes extends only to the λαός, τούτεστι τοὺς ἀδελφοὺς αὐτῶν, while Melchisedec's superiority stretches beyond his tribe, even to Abraham, who was quite a stranger to him. In like manner, also, that the descent from Abraham as, on the one hand (in the case of the Levites) it confers the right to take tithes, so, on the other hand (in the case of those who are not Levites), it does not protect from the burden of paying tithes. This latter lies in the words, *though they came out of the loins of Abraham*. Is Melchisedec, then, superior to the progenitor of the race whose members divide themselves into tithe-receivers and tithe-payers, it is therefore evident that the right of these latter (the Levites) to take tithes is of a far inferior nature to the right of Melchisedec. Or, in other words: that Melchisedec stood higher above Abraham, than among his descendants the Levites stand above those who are not Levites. The relation might be mathematically represented thus:

Melchisedec > > [Abraham > (Levites > not Levites)].

Then, in addition to this, comes the other difference indicated in the words ἐντολήν and κατὰ νόμον, between the right of the Levites to take tithes as a dependent right, and conferred by the lawgiver, and that of Melchisedec as independent and flowing from his personal dignity.

In ver. 6 the other side of the comparison between Melchisedec and the Levitical priests is presented, and special emphasis laid on this feature of it that Melchisedec received tithes from one who, in respect of descent, was not connected with him. In this the *first part of the minor proposition* is repeated, but in a more full and definite form. To this is added here the second part of the minor proposition, viz., that Abraham, although he had received from God the theocratical promise, was yet *blessed* of Melchisedec. The designation τὸν ἔχοντα τὰς ἐπαγγελίας corresponds in its logical position to the designation ὁ πατριάρχης, ver. 4. At both a καίπερ might be supplied instead of the article.

In ver. 7 the *major proposition* now follows the minor, and here we do not indeed find both parts of the minor referred with scholastic accuracy to corresponding general propositions, but only the second part of it, which was adduced immediately before. " Without all contradiction the less is blessed of the higher," = he who blesses is always superior to him who is blessed. The parallel member: The tithe-receiver is always superior to the tithe-giver was so self-evident (especially after what was said from ver 5 onwards), that the author might safely omit it.

Equally unnecessary was the formal statement of the *conclusion:* Ergo Melchisedec is superior to Abraham; and so much the more, as he had placed the major proposition, which involved this conclusion, behind the minor.

He therefore, in ver. 8, forthwith makes the *transition to the second principal part of the sorites,* to the argument, namely (for which also he had already prepared the way in ver. 5), that if Abraham is inferior to Melchisedec, so much the more inferior to him is Levi. He, however, makes this transition precisely in such a way as to introduce an *accessory remark* which connects substantially with the accessory remarks of the 5th verse.

The idea, namely, that *here* (under the Levitical law) it is dying men who receive tithes, but *there,* he of whom it is testified that he liveth—this idea forms no link in the syllogistic chain, does not follow from ver. 7, and proves nothing for ver. 8, but is in reality an accessory idea, serving only to lead the attention of the reader away from Abraham to the Levites. In respect of its import, this verse merely points back in a brief way to ver. 3, and only in this view is it, in general, intelligible. If ver. 3 had not gone before, ver. 8 might then really be so understood as if the author there meant to ascribe an endless life to the *individual Melchisedec* (for, with Justinian, Capellus, and others, to consider Christ as the subject of ζῇ, is mere nonsense.) But, after what was said in ver. 3 (as in the main Bleek also has rightly perceived) μαρτυρούμενος ὅτι ζῇ can be nothing else than a concise representation of the idea: μήτε ἀρχὴν ἡμερῶν μήτε ζωῆς τέλος ἔχων, and is therefore to be explained thus: "Of whom only his life is recorded, not his death" (Bleek); or, in other words: it is again not the individual Melchisedec who has the testimony *that he liveth*, but it is again the typical figure of Melchisedec, as it appeared to the eye of the Psalmist in the framework of Gen. xiv. Ver. 8, therefore, contains nothing new, but merely reminds the reader of the inferiority of the Levitical priesthood, already shown at ver. 3, and this with the view, as has been already observed, merely of turning in this way the attention of the reader from Abraham to the tribe of Levi.

Ver. 9, 10. In these verses we have now the *second principal part of the sorites* itself. In ver. 9 a thesis is laid down, a minor proposition to which the major proposition of the foregoing syllogism implicitly contained in ver. 7 (the tithe-receiver is superior to the tithe-giver) stands directly related; namely, the minor proposition : Levi also in a certain sense paid tithes to Melchisedec ; so that here, neither the major proposition nor the conclusion needed to be specially adduced. In ver. 10 the minor proposition of ver. 9 is proven. The words in both verses are perfectly clear. In the mode of reasoning, however, many commentators have, with a greater or less display of merriment, found here again a thoroughly crass specimen of the rabbinical manner of interpretation and reasoning, while others again (as Olshausen, Bleek) have sought to vindicate this reasoning by viewing it merely as an "argumentatio ad hominem directed against the Jewish estimation of mere bodily descent" (which might properly be called deductio ad absurdum), and thus to defend it against the charge of unsuitableness. Even Olshausen thinks that this argument is "not to be understood literally, and that the author means to indicate this by ὡς ἔπος εἰπεῖν ;" but how then is it to be understood ?—The argument would indeed be rabbinical, if the author had inferred from Levi's being still in the loins of Abraham that Levi participated in Abraham's giving tithes considered *as an individual act of Abraham*. For example, it would be strange and absurd were I to reason thus : "The Margrave George of Brandenburg with great courage protected the Reformation in Baireuth; but Frederic William IV. was then in the loins of

George, therefore Frederic William IV. with great courage protected the Reformation in Baireuth." Our author, on the contrary, infers from the fact that Levi was then in the loins of Abraham (*i.e.* let it be observed, that neither Levi, nor Isaac, nor Jacob were at that time begotten—for so soon as Isaac was begotten Levi was no longer, in Abraham's loins) only this, that the *legal relation* in which Abraham placed himself to Melchisedec held good also with reference to Levi. That he does not mean an *absolute* participation by Levi in the paying of tithes, but only such a participation *in a certain sense*, not a participation in the act as such, but only in the results and legal consequences of it, seems to me to be indicated by the clause ὡς ἔπος εἰπεῖν which is added to δεδεκάτωται. He therefore takes care not to say of Levi δεκάτην ἔδωκεν, and purposely makes use of the passive δεδεκάτωται. In this view the argument is fully justified. If, for example, I obtain the freedom of the city of Hamburgh, and have already a son arrived at majority, my investment with this right will not affect the position of this son; on the other hand, those of my children who are still minors, and those whom I may afterwards beget, participate in this right of citizenship which I have acquired. Or, if the Knight of Kronenburgh has placed himself in subjection to the Duke of Nassau as vassal, his already grown up and independent son does not participate in this act, but the children who are begotten after this act of subjection must acknowledge the sovereignty of the Duke of Nassau. So also here. If, at the period referred to in Gen. xiv., Isaac had been an independent man, he would have had a right to say to his father: You may, if it pleases you, subject yourself to this Melchisedec; that does not affect me; I am free. Isaac, however, was not begotten until after Abraham had entered into this relation of subjection. With perfect justice, therefore, is the inference drawn from the *dependent* character of the descendents to their participation in the act of subjection. Of course, however, it is not an outward political relation of subjection that is here meant (for such could only be spoken of, if the posterity of Abraham had continued all along to be subjects of the Amoritic kings of Salem), but an *ideal* subordination of the theocratical race to the priestly form of Melchisedec.[1]

[1] Strange to say, many commentators have found a difficulty in this,

In ver. 11—19 we have the second train of thought in this section. In ver. 1—10 the priesthood of Melchisedec was compared with the Levitical, and the inferiority of the latter demonstrated. In ver. 11—19 the author demonstrates, as a further inference from this, the *imperfection* and *incompleteness* not of the *Levitical priesthood* alone, but also of the *Mosaical law*.

Here again, the ideas of the writer move in the form of sorites. Ver. 11 involves the new thesis: in the Levitical priesthood there was no τελείωσις. This, however, is not laid down formally as a thesis but the transition is made in the following manner. In ver. 1—10 had been already shewn the *inferiority* of the Levitical priesthood. In ver. 11 the author now says: How too could this be otherwise? If a τελείωσις had been given by the Levitical priesthood, then in general there had been no necessity for that promise of *another* priest, a priest after the order of Melchisedec. He thus shapes the new thesis into the form of an *argument*. And as in ver. 1—10 he drew inferences from the import of the prophecy Ps. cx., so here, he draws an inference from the fact of its *existence*. He then in ver. 12 adduces a collateral argument, or rather he again disposes of an objection (just as above at ver. 5.) He has conceded in parenthesi ver. 11, that the Levitical priesthood forms the inner basis of the Mosaical law; from this the inference might have been drawn: by so much the more must the Levitical priesthood be perfect; for the law is perfect. This objection the author in ver. 12 removes by the explanatory remark that, *vice versa*, from the imperfection of the priesthood follows that also of the law. In this, however, there is implicitly contained a *second thesis* ver. 12.

This second thesis: *the Mosaical law has no perfection*, is proven in ver. 13—19. (For the first thesis there lay already an argument in ver. 11.)

   A, Ver. 13. The Messiah is *High Priest, and yet not of the tribe of Levi* (consequently the Messianic idea as such involves a going beyond the law.)

   Proof: *a*, Ver. 14. The *historical fact*: Jesus was of the tribe of Juda.

that Jesus as the descendant of David and Abraham must *also* have stood below Melchisedec. Did Jesus then proceed from the loins of a human father?

b, Ver. 15—17. The *christological necessity.*
  Major, Ver. 15 : the Messiah was to be a priest after the order of Melchisedec.
  Minor, Ver. 17 : Melchisedec is a priest *for ever.*
  Conclusion, Ver. 16 : the Messiah must not be born according to the law of the flesh.
B, Vers. 18, 19. From the fact that the law *could* be abrogated, it follows that it was *imperfect.*

Ver. 11. *Εἰ* with the Imp. expresses the abstract possibility of a case already known as not actual. "If perfection were." As the logical intermediate member between vers. 10 and 11, the idea supplies itself : " It follows that the Levitical priesthood was also imperfect. And how naturally ! For if, &c." Ἱερωσύνη, also in ver. 12, denotes originally the priestly condition, the priestly office, the priestly dignity, while ἱερατεία denotes originally the service to be performed by the priests. But in this chapter (comp. vers. 5 and 12) both words are used promiscuously to denote the priestly condition as a whole—person, office, and service taken together. The expression τελείωσις ἦν διὰ is purposely of a quite general character; it denotes not the perfected atonement nor the perfected sanctification, but, quite generally, the completion of the saving acts and saving ways of God, *i.e.* of the theocracy.

The parenthesis ὁ λαὸς γὰρ, &c., serves to explain how some might be led to see in the Levitical priesthood the completion of the theocracy. Upon the basis of this priesthood the people received their law. Ἐπ' αὐτῆς is the reading in A.B.C.D.E. Cyr. and the cursory manuscripts; in like manner, Grotius, Lachmann, Bleek; ἐπ' αὐτῇ is less authorized, and yields the trifling sense that the people received their law with the priesthood, *i.e.* either contemporaneously with it (Erasmus, Luther, Calvin, Beza, &c.), or over and above the priesthood (Gerhard, Bengel, Limborch, &c. Wolf, Storr, and others, interpret the ἐπὶ " on *condition* of the existence of a priesthood," which is equally unsuitable, grammatically and in point of fact.) If we adopt the reading ἐπ' αὐτῆς, then ἐπὶ is c. gen., and used in the same way as at ix. 17; 1 Cor. ix. 10, " upon it," " upon its basis." The Levitical priesthood, although, considered externally and in respect of time, it was first instituted in the law and through the law, yet formed, internally, the basis and presupposed condition *in* the giving of the law, nay *for* the giving of the law. *In* the giving of the law; for the entire plan and arrangement of it rests on the law of worship, on the representation of the people before God by the priests, and likewise all its other ordinances are most closely connected with the institution of the Levitical priesthood. *For* the giving of the law; inasmuch as this law was necessary only to awaken within the Israelites a sense of their need of a priestly representation before God; in itself the Mosaical law was not necessary, but only a pedagogical preparatory step correlative with the period of the Levitical priesthood. Some, therefore, might be led to infer, from the important part which the Levitical priesthood plays in the *Thorah*, that the Levitical priesthood was certainly complete in itself, in like manner as the Thorah was *considered* as perfect by the Jews. On this latter supposition, and the inquiry whether a τελείωσις was given by *the law*, the author does not yet enter here, but, in the first place, proves his *first* thesis—that no perfection was given by the *Levitical priesthood*—altogether independently of the other supposition; and he proves this simply by showing, that otherwise there would assuredly have been no promise of another priest, who should be a priest not after the order of Aaron, but of *Melchisedec*. The construction of the passage is as follows: Τίς ἔτι χρεία, ἕτερον ἱερέα κατὰ τὴν τάξιν Μελχισεδὲκ ἀνίστασθαι, καὶ (αὐτὸν) οὐ κατὰ τὴν τάξιν Ἀαρὼν λέγεσθαι; What necessity would there in that case have been, that another priest should arise after the order of Melchisedec, "and that he," (= "this one,") should not be called after the order of Aaron? (Schleusner and others take λέγεσθαι unnaturally in the sense of "to be chosen." Luther, Baumgarten, &c., construe: τίς ἔτι χρεία, λέγεσθαι· ἕτερον ἱερέα ἀνίστασθαι κατὰ τὴν τάξιν Μελχισεδὲκ καὶ οὐ κατὰ, τ. τ. Ἀαρών, a construction which necessarily presupposes a very unnatural arrangement of the words.) That καὶ λέγεσθαι stands for ὅς λέγεται will explain why the author—having ὅς λέγεται in his mind—has put οὐ for μή.

In ver. 12 the author now proceeds to obviate the objection contained in the parenthesis of ver. 11. Will some infer from the perfection of the law that the Levitical priesthood, which stood so closely connected with the law, was also perfect? He infers, vice versa, from the imperfection of the priesthood, that the law also was imperfect. As a proof of the imperfection of the former, he has just adduced in ver. 11 the fact, that the Levitical priesthood was to be superseded by one after the order of Melchisedec, and now he proceeds to say : " But where the priesthood changes, there of necessity also the law changes." This, however, involves the assertion that *the law also was imperfect*, as a *second* or auxiliary thesis ; and this is now in ver. 13—19 circumstantially proven.

Ver. 13—17 forms, as has just been said, the first principal part of the proof. In ver. 13 we have the argument, that he of whom this was said (namely, the promise mentioned in ver. 11 of a priest after the order of Melchisedec), *was* member of another tribe (than the tribe of Levi), a tribe none of the members of which had ever anything to do with the altar. The words are clear. The author does not say : It is *prophesied* in the *Old* Testament of the Messiah, that he should be of another tribe, but he simply lays down in ver. 13 the *fact*, that he to whom that prediction applied—therefore the Messiah—*was* of another tribe. Not till ver. 14 and ver. 15—17, does he separate the fact of the fulfilment from the prophetical christological necessity. In ver. 13 he still mentions merely the fact of the case viewed as a whole. The Messiah, the *Son of David* (consequently, one who was not a Levite), was to be priest. Thus a priesthood out of the tribe of Levi was ordained. A passing beyond the law, a μετάθεσις νόμου, was therefore predicted.

That Jesus is *he of whom these things are spoken*, the author does not prove, and needs not to prove. His readers did not doubt that Jesus was the Messiah ; the question only was, whether by this Messiah the Old Testament cultus was abolished, or whether it still continues.[1]

In ver. 14 the author, by way of confirming what is said in ver. 13, appeals to the *manifest historical fact* that " our Lord " (so he evidently designates *Jesus* as the *historical person*) " sprang

---

[1] I cannot understand how even Bleek (ii. 351) should still deny this grand practical aim of the whole Epistle to the Hebrews.

from the tribe of Judah." Those therefore are altogether wrong, who find in our passage a proof that the Christians had first inferred from the prophecy of the Messiah's descent from David, that Jesus must certainly have sprung from the tribe of Judah. No! the author introduces this inference first in ver. 15—17, after having previously in ver. 14 laid it down as a *manifest fact* not of the Χριστός, of the Messiah, but (as Bleek also rightly perceives) of " Our Lord," of the person of the Lord and Master historically known to the Christians, that he "has sprung" from Judah (ἀνατέταλκεν perfect). We have here therefore rather a most significant proof, that the descent of Jesus from the tribe of Judah was a well and universally known fact before the destruction of Jerusalem. In the same years in which the Gospels of Mark and Luke were written, the descent of Jesus from David was already universally known.

Πρόδηλον is stronger than δῆλον. Δῆλον is what lies open and manifest, πρόδηλον is what lies conspicuously manifest among other manifest things.—'Ανατέλλειν is a term. techn. for the rising of the sun; also in Luke i. 78 the expression ἀνατολή is used of the birth of Jesus. In the words εἰς ἣν φυλὴν, &c., it is again emphatically repeated that, according to the law, the tribe of Judah had no right to the office of the priesthood. The author here delicately expresses in the form of a *litotes*, the *strict prohibition* laid on all who were not Levites from serving as priests: "In reference to which tribe Moses has said nothing of a priesthood."

In ver. 15—17 the author shows that the Messiah, as he was in fact not a Levite, so in accordance with the prediction *could* not be a Levite. He adds the christological necessity to the historical reality. In proof of the former, he might simply have appealed to the predictions of the Messiah's descent from David already mentioned in the preceding chapters; but his manner is not to grasp at what lies nearest and what every reader must himself have been able to say. He goes deeper. He proves in ver. 15—17, not merely that the Messiah must in respect of his humanity spring from David (this was already implied in ver. 13), but that it follows from the nature of the priesthood of Melchisedec, that the Messiah must be born, *in general, not according to the law of a carnal commandment, but according to the power of an indestructible life.*

The sentence beginning with εἰ cannot, of course, form the subject to κατάδηλόν ἐστι, as εἰ cannot stand for ὅτι ; equally unnecessary and unjustifiable is it arbitrarily to invent a subject to κατάδηλον (as is done for example by Oecumenius, Limborch, Tholuck, Bleek, &c. : "that, with the priesthood, the law also is abrogated, is so much the more manifest," &c) ; all that we have to do is simply to bring down from ver. 14 the clause ὅτι ἐξ Ἰούδα ἀνατέταλκεν, &c. That Jesus sprang from Judah is already in itself an *acknowledged fact* (ver. 14) ; but this is all the more manifest, as (ver. 15) it follows from Christ's priesthood being after the order of Melchisedec, that he *could* not be born κατὰ νόμου. This reference is drawn syllogistically. From the major proposition ver. 15 the conclusion is directly drawn in ver. 16, and then, in ver. 16, the minor which connects the two is added in the form of an explanation.

The major proposition ver. 15 is clear ; it is a mere repetition of the prediction already adduced in ver. 11. In the idea which logically forms the minor premiss ver. 17, the emphasis lies on εἰς τὸν αἰῶνα. *Therefore* the inference follows from the nature of the Messianic priesthood (its being after the order of Melchisedec), that the Messiah must be born *according to the power of an indestructible life*, because the εἰς τὸν αἰῶνα belongs to the characteristics of that priesthood of Melchisedec. —Is now the conclusion thus made good? Does the word לְעוֹלָם, Ps. cx., form really the tertium comparationis in which the future heir of David is to agree with Melchisedec ? No ; tert. comp. lies rather in the union of the priestly with the kingly power. But neither (as Bleek thinks, ii. p. 62) has our author by any means adduced the εἰς τὸν αἰῶνα as a tert. comp., but only as an *inference* which appeared to the Psalmist to follow, and (as is proven in vers. 1—3) must follow, from the general idea of a priest like to Melchisedec. The promised posterity which was described to David, and was conceived of by him as a *priest-king*, and therefore as a Melchisedec-like figure, could not for this very reason be, like a Levitical high priest, a single member of a genealogically connected series of priests, but, as the *only one of his kind* excluding every possibility of succession, must consequently appear as holding his office *for ever*.

Ver. 16 contains the conclusion which follows from the everlasting duration of the Messianic priesthood. He who, differently from the Levitical priests, is to *remain* a priest for ever must have *been made* a priest differently from the Levitical priests. The latter were made priests according to the law of a fleshly commandment. Σαρκικός (good ancient manuscripts here, and in other passages, have the form σαρκινός, which, however, in like manner as the reading in the received version, forms the antithesis to πνευματικός, so that no difference is thus made out in the sense) is not to be understood as designating the commandment in so far as, in respect of its import, it refers to bodily descent (Theodoret, Grotius, Limborch, Tholuck, Bleek); for then those Messianic prophecies which say that the Messiah was to descend from David had also been fleshly! The term is rather to be explained (as already Carpzov and Kuinoel rightly perceived) from the antithetical word ἀκατάλυτος. The passage contains a threefold antithesis; δύναμις is antithetical to νόμος, ζωή to ἐντολή, and ἀκατάλυτος to σαρκικός. The meaning of these antithesis we shall best be able to explain by the following questions: *a*, How did the Levitical priest originate? First, and in general, according to a law which ordained that the posterity of Aaron should be priests, whatever might be their inward character and qualifications. How was the Messiah made priest? Independently of the law, nay contrary to the law (vers. 13, 14), purely *in virtue of the power* which dwelt within him personally, which entitled and qualified him to represent men before God.—*b*, What was the nature of that law?—It appeared as a single external statute, an ἐντολή. How did that δύναμις show itself? As a ζωή, as direct power and actuality of life.—*c*, What was the character of that ἐντολή? It belonged to that paedagogical preparatory stage which had as yet nothing to do with the *implanting of spiritual life* in man who was dead through sin, but only with the setting up of outward barriers against sin, and with types of salvation for the *natural, carnal, man*. (This is the meaning of σαρκικός comp. Gal. iii. 3.) What, on the other hand, is the character of that ζωή? Indissoluble, *i.e.*, possessing in itself the power of perpetuity. In the one case, therefore, that separation of men from their Maker, in which the divine being appears to man only *outwardly* in the form of *fixed commandment* without entering into inward fellowship with him (comp. chap. iv. 2) still continues; in the other case, on the contrary, God has united himself with man, implanted himself within man as the beginning and beginner of a new life, inasmuch as he has assumed the nature of men, and shown himself to be the true and perfect high priest, inasmuch as he proved his divine power in his vicarious sufferings, and in the victory of the resurrection.

In vers. 18, 19 the author now draws from the proposition laid down in ver. 12 and proven in ver. 13—17, viz., that the Mosaic law was destined to be annulled by the Messiah—this last inference: that this law was a mere pedagogical preparatory stage, and therefore not the final perfect consummation of the divine revelations. The mode of argumentation is retrogressive. That ἀθέτησις, the actual fact of which was already shown in ver. 13—17, is explained only on the presupposition of the ἀσθενὲς καὶ ἀνωφελές. The author might have logically connected in the scholastic form the separate ideas of vers. 18, 19 in the following way: " But (atque οὖν) now the *annulling* of a *commandment* only then takes place when the *commandment* in question has shewn itself to be *weak* and *unprofitable.* Consequently (ergo, ἄρα) that law must have been weak and unprofitable, must have left its task unfinished, and must only have been an *introduction* to a better hope." But, as always in such cases of reasoning in this inverted order, he despises this scholastico-pedantic form, and chooses the easier form of the explicative γάρ.

The principal sentence and the last inference lies in the words οὐδὲν γὰρ ἐτελείωσεν ὁ νόμος, ἐπεισαγωγὴ δὲ κρείττονος ἐλπίδος. At ἐπεισαγωγή we have not to supply γίνεται from ver. 18 (as is done by Theodoret, Luther, Gerhard, Bengel, Tholuck, Bleek, Olshausen, and others); for the words, in respect of their import, form no antithesis to ἀθέτησις μὲν γὰρ γίνεται—(what sort of antithesis would this be: " An annulling of a law is wont to take place only on account of the weakness and unprofitableness of that law; but an introduction of a better hope takes place."— Nothing is said as to how or why this introduction takes place !) Nor are we to supply ἐτελείωσεν (with Schlichting, Michaelis,

Semler, Ernesti, and others), for then, first of all, the article must have stood before ἐπεισαγωγή, and further, it is not possible that a τελείωσις can have been effected by the introduction to a hope. The right construction is that which supplies at ἐπεισαγωγή, either ἦν (Erasmus, Vatable, Calvin, &c.), so that ἐπεισαγωγή becomes predicate to νόμος, or ἐγένετο δι' αὐτοῦ (νόμου),—"the law has made nothing perfect, but an introduction was given through it to a better hope." That the omission of such a verb is not elegant Greek is of small moment; the supposition that our author, who usually writes correctly, has here again written with somewhat less care, must always be more tolerable than a construction which yields a senseless idea.

Something negative and something positive, therefore, is affirmed of the law. The negative is: οὐδὲν ἐτελείωσεν. Οὐδέν is not here in the sense of οὐδένα, as Theophylact and others have supposed. What is here said is, not that the particular individual could not be led to perfection by the law, but that the law in every respect opened up and imposed a number of problems without solving any one of them. It set up in the decalogue the ideal of a holy life, and yet gave no power to realise this ideal; it awakened, by means of its law of sacrifice, the consciousness of the necessity of an atonement, and yet could provide no true valid offering for sin; it held forth in the institutions of the priesthood the necessity of a representation of the sinner before God, and yet it gave no priest who was able to save men εἰς τὸ παντελές (as it is said ver. 25.) In short, "it left everything unfinished."—But one thing the law did accomplish; those who submitted to its rebuke, and did not allow themselves to be seduced into the base and delusive hope of a pharisaical self-righteousness, were led on by it to the better hope through which we (Christians) come nigh to God (in truth.) This is the positive thing which is affirmed of the law in the words ἐπεισαγωγὴ &c.

Ver. 20—28. In these verses we have the *third* part of this section. It was shown in ver. 1—10 that the priesthood of Melchisedec, which was represented in Ps. cx. as the type of the Messianic priesthood, is more exalted than the Levitical. In ver. 11—19 it was proven that this Levitical priesthood, together with the Mosaic law so closely connected with it, was destined to find its end and its abolition as an imperfect preparatory stage in the Messiah. In ver. 20—28 it is now shown that Jesus the Messiah, in opposition to the imperfect Levitical priesthood and Mosaic law, is the *perfect* priest of a *new* and *perfect covenant*. The mention of the imperfection of the Mosaic law, ver. 19, leads, by an easy transition, to this new thought.

In ver. 20 and 22, we have the principal sentence : " Inasmuch as Jesus (was made a surety) by an oath, insomuch was he made a surety of a better covenant (or, insomuch is the covenant, whose surety he was made, a better covenant.) There are here (just as at chap. ii. ver. 18, also ver. 17, chap. iii. 3) three members of a syllogism brought together in one sentence. The idea expressed in a strictly logical form would run thus : A covenant, whose surety has been made a surety by an oath, is better than a covenant in which this is not the case. Now Jesus was made such by an oath, but not so the Levitical priest. Therefore, &c. The minor proposition implicitly contained in ver. 20 and 22, is now further explained and confirmed by the parenthesis in ver. 21. Let us first look at ver. 20 and 22.

Only the terms διαθήκη and ἔγγυος need here any explanation. Διαθήκη, from διατίθεσθαι, has in classic Greek the signification *testament, last will;* then also the further signification *contract;* hence also *covenant,* also *foundation, institution*. If now we consider that the LXX. always renders by διαθήκη the fully developed Old Testament religious idea בְּרִית, it will be evident that the Greek διαθήκη must also have developed itself into a *fixed dogmatical idea,* and that, consequently, whenever the word occurs in a religious connexion in the writings of Jews and Christians, we must, as a matter of course, take it in this sense as = בְּרִית, *covenant*. It may appear as if the context imperiously forbids this interpretation in the passage before us. This, however, is by no means the case; on the contrary, the mention of a *surety* is strongly in favour of the rendering by " covenant," and against that by " testament." For, it is nowhere the custom for a testator to appoint a surety for the actual fulfilment of his last will; he himself is the surety for this, if, of course, he does not retract his will before his death, and he gives no security that he will not do this. On the other hand, when two parties enter into a covenant-agreement, in which the one party binds himself to an act which is not to be performed till some future time, there is then some reason in his appointing a surety who may give security in his person that the thing promised shall be truly and rightly performed. Luther, Böhme, Bleek, &c., would hardly have allowed themselves to be misled into the rendering "testament," had they not believed that the signification "covenant" would not correspond with a subsequent passage of this epistle (ix. 16), as, indeed, Bleek ii. p. 390, has quite frankly confessed. We must, however, interpret our passage in the sense in which alone every reader could understand it, who reads the epistle onwards from the beginning, and not in the reverse way. We will then have to deal with the subsequent passage in its proper place.

Ἔγγυος, denom. from ἐγγύη sponsio, signifies sponsor, fidejussor. Christ is called a surety here, not because he had stood *before God* as surety (that is, as the vicarious fulfiller of that which men ought to have performed), so Calov, Gerhard, Cramer, &c., but (so Schlichting, Grotius, Olshausen, &c.), because God on his part gave him to the human race as a surety for the actual fulfilment of his covenant promise. For this, and this alone, is what is spoken of in the context. Because *God* has made him a surety by an oath, he is therefore the surety of a better covenant. (Comp. the similar idea in chap. vi. 17, 18, where it is said that *God himself* interposed as fidejussor between himself and men.)—The author here, with good reason, calls Jesus not μεσίτης, but ἔγγυος. From the fact, that God confirmed with an oath the promise that he would send a *mediator* or *founder* of a covenant, it follows only that such a mediator would come, and that such a covenant would, in general, take place, but not that this covenant has already taken place, and will continue for ever. Has God sworn, on the other hand, that he will appoint a *surety?*—*i.e.*, a guarantee for the *maintenance* of the covenant—the permanent validity of the *covenant itself* has been thereby guaranteed.—In how far God has promised to appoint a *surety for the everlasting maintenance* of the covenant to be established, is now shown in the *parenthesis*, ver. 21. The subject is οἱ μέν ὁ δέ, the Levitical priest and

Jesus. The Messiah, Jesus, has been made priest (comp. vi. 16 ss.) by an oath of God—*i.e.*, God promised and swore that the Messiah should be a priest according to the order of Melchisedec. The descendants of Aaron were constituted priests in quite a different way, namely, in consequence, and by means of the carrying out of a simple, ordinary, legal command. If, then, God has, by that promise on oath, sworn that a priest-king after the order of Melchisedec (consequently eternal, comp. ver. 1—3, and ver. 17), should stand as representative between him and the people, he has thereby clearly promised, not merely one who shall set up a covenant, but one who shall set up and *everlastingly maintain* the covenant—a surety.

Ver. 23—25: As the superiority of the new covenant is manifest in the appointment of a surety by an oath, so also does it further appear in what is closely connected with this,—the unchangeableness of the New Testament priest as compared with the change of the Levitical priests. Ver. 23—25 is, in its position as well as in its form (οἱ μέν—ὁ δέ—), parallel with ver. 21 ; ver. 21 contains a first, ver. 23—25 a second illustration of what is said in ver. 22 : that Jesus is the surety of a better covenant.—Οἱ μέν—ὁ δέ is again the subject. Εἰσὶ γεγονότες is the copula of οἱ μέν, while ἱερεῖς is predicate, and πλείονες a more special determination of the subject. (Not : they were made several priests, but : they, as being more than one, were made priests, *i.e.* they were made priests in their plurality.) The author does not, however, allude here to the circumstance, that *cotemporarily* with the high priest there were also a number of subordinate priests; he has, up to this point, taken no notice of this difference between the ordinary priests and the high priests, but rather views the entire Levitical priesthood (the ἱερωσύνη, ver. 11) as a whole, in comparison with the priesthood of Melchisedec, although, of course, all that is said of the Levitical priesthood applies also and *pre-eminently* to the Levitical *high priest*. For this very reason, however, the πλείονες here refers not to those several priests who existed *simultaneously* with the high priest, but (as appears from the words διὰ τὸ κωλύεσθαι, &c.) to the *successive* plurality of priests who followed one another (and *chiefly* high priests.) The priesthood of Christ, on the contrary, is, according to ver. 1—3 and ver. 17, ἀπαράβατος, such as cannot pass to a successor, because he ever lives. On the one side, we see the weakness of mortality, on the other, the *power of an endless life;* comp. what is said in ver. 16.

From this now proceeds the inference ver. 25, that Christ, because he ever lives, is able *to save to the uttermost* all who come to the Father through him. Εἰς τὸ παντελές does not signify "evermore," but "to completeness," *i.e.* perfectly; it forms, both in its etymology and its place in the context, the precise antithesis to the words ver. 19, *the law made nothing perfect.* There is still another inference drawn from the *ever liveth;* Christ is therefore able to make intercession for them. (Εἰς c. inf. need not be understood in a final sense, comp. 2 Cor. viii. 6; Rom. vi. 12; Winer Gramm. § 45, 6.) Ἐντυγχάνειν is a genuine Pauline term, comp. Rom. viii. 34; to appear in the stead of another, in order to represent his interests, at the same time taking upon one's self his guilt.

In ver. 26—27 the author proceeds, now in conclusion, to state what was properly the material difference between Christ and the Levitical priesthood, inasmuch as he shows, wherein lay the οὐδὲν ἐτελείωσεν of the one, and the εἰς τὸ παντελές of the other. He states in a concise and condensed form the principal points of difference between the *person* and the *office* of both high priests, and thus the difference between the two *covenants.*

Καὶ ἔπρεπεν, he says, and thus ver. 26, 27 connects itself with ver. 24, 25, in the same way as ver. 15—17 with ver. 14. As, in ver. 14, the fact of the non-Levitical descent of Jesus was laid down, and in ver. 15—17 the christological necessity for this, so in ver. 24, 25, the fact of the singularity and perfection of the New Testament high priest is stated, while in ver. 26, 27 the *soteriological necessity* for such an high priest is declared.

It had been shown in chap. v. 1—10 that Christ, by taking part in human infirmity, was an high priest—that he had this *similarity* to the Levitical high priest. Here, it is shown, that, for the same end, the representation of men before God, he must also at the same time be *different* from the Levitical high priests, namely sinless. This sinlessness is expressed, however, by a series of attributes all of which are to be explained from the antithesis with the Levitical high-priesthood. The Levitical high priest was also all that is here predicated of Christ; he was, however, not perfectly, not truly so, but only in a symbolical way, and therefore imperfectly. The high priest bore upon the plate on his forehead the inscription *Holiness to the Lord* (Ex. xxxix. 30), he was, however, not truly holy, but had holiness in himself only in that symbol. Christ, on the other hand, was truly and inwardly holy; this is expressed by ὅσιος; for ὅσιος forms the antithesis to " sinful" (while ἅγιος, as we saw before, is opposed to " profane.") The Levitical high priest, farther, was, only as a sinless person, qualified for bringing the blood of the sacrifice of atonement into the holiest of all for the people; he *was*, however, not sinless, but required first to atone for his own sins by a sacrifice (Lev. xvi. 2—14), and this atonement too was no real one, but only symbolical, typical. Christ, on the contrary, was truly ἄκακος, therefore (comp. ver. 27) he needed not first to offer for himself. The Levitical high priest must, thirdly, be *undefiled and pure* in order to be able to represent the people before God; he was, however, not inwardly immaculate and pure, but had only the outward symbolical representation of purity, the Levitical purity. Christ, on the contrary, was inwardly and truly *undefiled.* The Levitical high priest required, finally, to be ever on his guard, lest by contact with one who was Levitically unclean he should himself become unclean, and therefore had always to keep at a distance from such, Lev. xxi. 22, especially xxi. 12. Nay, the Talmud ordains (tract. Jomah i. 1), that, for seven days before the sacrifice of atonement, he must refrain from all intercourse with his family. This separation was, however, again only *outward.* Christ, on the contrary, in his intercourse with sinners *remained inwardly free from all participation in their sinfulness,* inwardly untouched by its contagion; notwithstanding that he mingled with men in all their varieties of character and situation, he yet never let drop, for a moment, that inner veil of chaste holiness which separated him from sinners. This is what is meant by the expression *separate from sinners* (Theophylact, Calvin, Gerhard, Michaelis, Storr, Boehme, Kuinoel, Olshausen, &c.), which need not therefore (with Grotius, Bengel, Tholuck, Bleek, &c.) be made to refer to Christ's departure from the world, *i.e.* to his ascension, which comes first to be spoken of in a subsequent place. (Besides, his being separate from men *after* the ascension, would form no parallel with the separation of the Levitical high priest *before* the day of the sacrifice of atonement.) Not till the very last, is his *exaltation above all heavens* adduced as a sealing proof that he was holy, sinless, undefiled, and uncontaminated by the sin of the race,—that exaltation in which, as is then shown in chap. viii., his high-priestly work completed itself.

Ver. 27. The inner difference of his *person* showed itself also in the form and manner of his *functions*. The principal idea of ver. 27 lies in the words: "who needeth not daily as those high priests to offer up sacrifice. For this he did once." It is clear that the *this* here refers to the principal idea, the *offering up sacrifice*, and cannot refer, at the same time, to the words *first for his own sins*. There is, however, a subordinate idea inserted into that principal idea, namely, that Christ did not need to offer first for his own sins, ere he offered for those of the people. A twofold difference, then, is found to exist between his priestly service and that of the Levitical high priest. First, and chiefly in this, that Christ offered *only once*, whereby he has, once for all, ver. 25, εἰς τὸ παντελές saved all who come to God by him, while the Levitical high priests always atoned only for one generation, and this always but for a year, and this only typically. Secondly in this, that he needed not first to offer for his own sins.

A difficulty lies in the statement, that the *high priests* offered *daily*. For, the comparison with the *atoning* sacrifice of Christ offered once seems to require that, here also, in reference to the high priests, we should understand the *yearly*—not daily—*great sacrifice of atonement* as meant, and so it would be really doubly unsuitable to take οἱ ἀρχιερεῖς here in the weakened sense = οἱ ἱερεῖς; doubly unsuitable, as precisely here, for the first time, the author uses this expression. Two solutions of this difficulty have been attempted. Some have understood either, the daily *incense offering* (Ex. xxx. 6, s.) which the high priest had to present—but with this the expression θυσία will not at all correspond; or (as Gerhard, Calov, Michaelis, Bleek, Tholuck, &c.) the daily *burnt offering* (Ex. xxix. 38—42; Num. xxviii. 3)—this, however, was not brought by the high priest, although (according to Jos. bell. Jud. v. 5, 7) he might *sometimes* voluntarily take part in this offering, namely, on the new moons and Sabbaths; the expression καθ' ἡμέραν, however, would still be unsuitable. (One might rather suppose that the author intends to oppose to the one offering of Christ, not merely the *oft-repeated* offerings of the sacrifice of atonement, but also the *various* kinds of offerings—if only οἱ ἀρχιερεῖς did not stand here.) Others (as Schlichting, Piscator, Olshausen) are for taking καθ' ἡμέραν in the signification die statuto (= once every year), or else in a weakened signification (= frequently). The former will certainly not do; had the author intended to express the definite idea that the high priest brought the offering *yearly on a certain day*, he would have said (as at chap. ix. 25, x. 1—3) κατ' ἐνιαυτόν. On the other hand, I do not see what well-grounded objection can be brought against Bengel's view that our author here — where nothing depended on the bringing into view the *length of time that intervened* between each day of atonement, but where all the emphasis lies merely on the *repetition* of that sacrifice—should have used the somewhat hyperbolical expression καθ' ἡμέραν " one day after the other." Looking back on a series of centuries, he fixes his eye merely on a successive series of days, upon which the high priests again and again brought the appointed sacrifice. He takes no notice of the intervening days. Enough, that " day after day" such sacrifices were offered. In one word, the author intends here not to *measure* but to *count*. He does not lay before him the calender of the days in the year, and inquire upon what days an atonement festival fell, and how many days intervened between each, but he sets before him the immense number of days on which these fasts were observed, and lays stress upon this, that on one such day after the other the high priest must offer the sacrifice. (In like manner Olshausen.) He treats these days, in other words, as a discrete, not as a concrete quantity. So might a teacher say to an unruly pupil : " day after day" or " day by day I must punish you," without meaning by this, that he is wont, regularly every day at a certain hour, to punish him, but only, that, *again and again*, punishments are necessary, although not merely the Sundays, but, now and then, whole weeks should intervene between them. So much, at any rate, is beyond all doubt, that our author did not say καθ' ἡμέραν from any ignorance of the law ; for, in chap. ix. 7 (where he expressly distinguishes the yearly service in the holiest of all from the daily service in the sanctuary), he himself mentions, that the sacrifice of atonement was brought once in the year.

How far the once offered sacrifice of Christ was to consist in this—that he offered *himself ἑαυτὸν προσενέγκας*—is explained in the following principal part of our epistle, so that we do not need here to anticipate what is there said on this question by any subjective reasonings of our own.

Ver. 28 is a concluding explanation, but, at the same time also, a *recapitulation of the whole of our third principal part*.

As an *explanation and further development* of what goes before, this verse connects itself (by means of an explicative γάρ) with vers. 26, 27, the connecting link being the idea, that through the oath of promise the *Son of God* was made an high priest *for ever*.

It is, however, a *recapitulation of the whole part*, in virtue of the *antithesis* implicitly contained in it between ὁ νόμος and ὁ λόγος τῆς ὁρκωμοσίας.

Meanwhile it may be asked, whether ver. 28 is really a recapitulation of chaps. v.—vii., or merely of chap. vii. This verse is generally so understood as that the words ὁ νόμος γὰρ . . . . ἀσθένειαν refer to the Levitical priests, and accordingly, that something is here declared of the law as *no longer valid, as abrogated by and for Christ*, consequently, that we have only a repetition of what is said chap. vii. 11—19. The idea would be as follows: The (no longer valid) Mosaical law could make no better high priests than *men encompassed with infirmity;* on the contrary, by the promise, Ps. cx., a better high priest has been appointed, namely, the *for ever perfected Son* (scil. of God as at chap. i. 1 ss.) But there are serious objections against this interpretation. If this were the author's idea, he would then, *in the first place*, deny here what he himself had formerly maintained and taught chap. iv. 15; vii. 5—10, namely, that Jesus also was encompassed with infirmity. And, in addition to this, we are by no means warranted in understanding by ἀσθένεια here the imperfection of the Levitical priesthood, thus giving it a different signification from what it has in chap. iv. The solution given by Bleek is preferable to this, that in this passage Christ is regarded only in his state of *exaltation* in which he had laid aside the ἀσθένεια; as the one *who had ascended into heaven*, as the *perfected* one, there is no necessity for him to repeat his sacrifice. Meanwhile,—not to mention that the author had he meant to say this must of necessity have said it more plainly,—it would, even then, not be in accordance with his teaching elsewhere; since, according to chap. ix. 9—14 and 26, the sacrifice of Christ was a perfect one, excluding all repetition, not in virtue of the *exaltation which followed it*, and the laying aside of the ἀσθένεια, but already in virtue of *its own quality*. To this is to be added, that according to this the common interpretation of our verse, the author would not merely deny that Christ had *infirmity*, but, *secondly*, that he was ἄνθρωπος. For, he would plainly put the υἱός (in the sense of chap. i. 1) in opposition to the ἄνθρωπος. I am of opinion, therefore, that the whole verse must be taken in a different sense. The author does not intend to *deny* that Jesus was an ἀρχιερεὺς ἄνθρωπος ὢν καὶ ἀσθένειαν ἔχων; but he takes it for granted as known that Christ was both these things, on the one hand, ἄνθρωπος ἀσθένειαν ἔχων according to chap. v., and, on the other, υἱός τετελειωμένος εἰς τὸν αἰῶνα according to chap. vii.; and he recapitulates both here, the fundamental idea of chap. v. 1—10, and the fundamental idea of chap. vii. 1—27. He shows that Christ must have answered the requirements also *of the law*, and *in how far* he must have done so. That the legal requirements of Levitical descent, of daily sacrifice, &c., do not apply to him, that in these respects he abrogated the law—this is proven; but *one* requirement of the law had an internal, an everlasting validity, and, according to chap. v. 1—10, was applicable also to the New Testament high priest, namely, that he, as every high priest, must be a *man having infirmity*. To this of *humanity* and *infirmity* was added, in the case of the Messiah, a second requisite contained, not in the law, but in the promise, Psalm cx., that he must also be a *Son perfected for ever*. Thus, then, the words ὁ νόμος . . . ἀσθένειαν contain a *concession* pointing back to chap. v. The idea is this: The law (in so far as it has not been abrogated) requires of all high priests (consequently also, of Jesus,) that they be *men having infirmity*; the word of promise, however, confirmed by an oath given *after* the law and stretching far above it, constitutes the Son, who is perfected for ever an high priest.

Thus understood the 28th verse therefore contains really a recapitulation of the *whole third part*.

PART FOURTH.

(Chap. viii.—x.)

THE MOSAIC TABERNACLE AND THE HEAVENLY SANCTUARY.

From the nature of the two covenants is now shown the difference between their respective sanctuaries, their λειτουργίαι, and the result of their respective services. This, the last of the *theoretical* parts, as it introduces us to the *fifth practical* part in which all the rays from the hortatory parts are concentrated into one focus, is not itself interrupted by an intervening exhortation, as was the case with the three foregoing parts. And, as it does not stand parallel with these three parts, but (as is expressly intimated in chap. viii. 1) is placed as a *key-stone* upon them, so also the introduction to it does not run parallel with that of the foregoing parts, but is independent and peculiar. Our fourth part divides itself into *four sections*. In a *first introductory* section, chap. viii., it is shown, in general, that the two *tabernacles*, the Mosaic and the heavenly, correspond to the two *covenants*. In a *second section*, chap. ix. 1—11, the construction of the two tabernales is compared, and it is shown how, in the Mosaic tabernacle, there lies an imperfection in the separation of the holy place from the holy of holies. In the *third section*, chap. ix. 11—chap. x. 13, the two tabernacles are compared, *a*,—*similarity*: chap. ix. 15 ss., that for the fulfilment of the perfect covenant in general, the *death* of Christ was necessary,—*b*, *dissimilarity*: chap. ix. 25—chap. x. 13, that this death was a *perfect sacrifice once offered*, in opposition to the Old Testament animal sacrifices. Finally, in the *fourth section*, chap. x. 14—39, the *result* of these respective services is compared, and it is shown how, by the offering of Christ, the *perfect atonement* and *the access to God in the spirit* has been accomplished in a way which renders all auxiliary means of any other kind superfluous.

SECTION FIRST

(Chap. viii.)

THE TWO TABERNACLES CORRESPOND TO THE TWO COVENANTS

In chap. viii. 1, preparation is made for the theme which lies in ver. 2. Κεφάλαιον δέ is not to be taken as an apposition to the whole sentence that follows; it is better, as some do, to supply a λέγω τοῦτο (not an ἐστι, as Bleek does, for then it must have been τὸ κεφάλαιον).—Κεφάλαιον, used for the classical expression κεφαλή, signifies *sum*, or also *principal point*. Either signification will do here, provided that the rendering "sum" be not understood of a recapitulation of former particular points (this belongs rather to chap. vii. 28), but of an organic combination, a product resulting from all that goes before; and further, that the rendering "principal point" be not understood of a *particular* principal proposition which stands only side by side with the former propositions (much less of a "principal thing" taken from the ideas developed at the conclusion of chap. vii., upon which, as a point of special importance, emphasis is again laid), but of the principal point of the whole book, at which all the former parts aimed. The meaning of the word is best and most comprehensively rendered by the expression "key-stone." Ἐπὶ τοῖς λεγομένοις means, besides, not "*in* what has been hitherto said, *under* what has been hitherto said," (this or that is especially important); but "to what has been hitherto said," (the author will now add the key-stone.)

In the sentence τοιοῦτον, &c., all the emphasis lies, of course, on the words ἐν δεξιᾷ τοῦ θρόνου, &c. That Christ is *such* an high priest *as has entered not into the earthly but into the heavenly sanctuary*; or, as it is still more plainly repeated in ver. 2, fulfils his service in the *true* tabernacle,—this new sentence, with its further development in ver. 8—10, forms the key-stone of all that has gone before. The two *tabernacles*, together with their *services*, are forthwith compared.

What now are we to understand by the expression *on the right hand of the majesty in the heavens?* Instead of occupying themselves here with dogmatical discussions on ubiquity or non-ubiquity, the critics ought to have explained these words solely from the antithesis. The O. T. high priest went into the *earthly holy of holies as the place where God revealed his presence.* Still, this revelation of the presence of God in the holiest of all, was not such as if this compartment of the tent had been the true and proper dwelling-place of God; but only in gracious condescension to the wants of men did God, by means of theophanies and manifestations in the light-cloud, consecrate this abode as a place of his presence for men. The holy of holies, therefore, was not the place of *God's presence in itself*, but only the *abode of his presence for the Old Testament Israel*, and therefore, secondly, rather a place where God *symbolically represented* his nearness than one in which he really was. For, the entire distinction of profane places and holy places, the entire distinction of world, fore-court, holy°place, and holy of holies (as also the separation of a particular people—Israel—from the rest of mankind; or, again, the separation of the Levites from Israel, or of the Aaronites from Levi)—all this rested on the real truth, that God could not yet *in truth* dwell with men, because sin and the power of sin as yet hindered him from revealing himself among, and in, and before men, as he can already reveal himself in the sphere of the angels, and of the just made perfect, in that heaven where his will is perfectly fulfilled (Matt. vi. 10.) And therefore, thirdly, this same holy of holies, in which the *nearness* of God was emblematically represented, was, at the same time also, an emblematical representation of the *distance of God from men.* The need of *a special place,* where God revealed his presence, intimated that he was, in *general,* as yet *separated from men.* (Comp. with this John iv. 21—24.) This was the holy of holies into which the high priest might enter once every year, and in which he was not permitted to abide, but must immediately again leave it. In opposition to this, Christ has, *a,* sat down on the throne of the majesty on high; in him (comp. Heb. ii. 9) man has entered on the *everlasting, abiding* enjoyment of the presence of God; the state of separation, of banishment from God in which man was before, is now done away with; God is there in heaven truly present to man, because man is present to him, and thereby has a beginning been made *upon earth* of the *real* presence of God. *b*, Christ has *sat down at the right hand of the throne of the divine majesty;* he has not appeared before God, like the Levitical priests, as a poor sinner who must draw near to the presence of the divine majesty—even its symbolical representation—only with fear and trembling, but so, as that he himself fully participates in the divine majesty and dominion.[1] *c*, Christ has not entered into that symbolical holy of holies, where God represented quite as much his distance from men as his presence with them, and the latter only as a presence *for men* (more particularly for Isreal), but into that sphere where God, without hindrance or limit, *really* reveals before the sinless angels his entire being, and the entire presence not merely of his world-governing omnipotence, but of his whole being manifested on all sides.

This universal view which we thus take of the idea in the words before us, shows us, now already, that we must regard the expression to *sit down on the right hand of the throne* as figurative = enter on an abiding participation in the sovereign authority of any one, and that the author did not entertain the crude conception (as has most recently been laid to his charge by the young Hegelians), that a throne stands in the heaven, with a place on the right hand and on the left ! Such a conception would indeed be in direct contradiction to the ground-idea of the author, who makes the divine element of the New Testament high priesthood to consist in this, that Christ has done away with the limitations of place and time. Carefully, however, as we are here to guard against a crass materialistic exegesis, we must equally beware of a false spiritualistic exegesis in the explanation of the οὐρανοί, as if the heaven were the mere absence of space, and the state of being above or beyond space regarded as an at-

[1] The more recent deniers of the divinity of Christ, though they maintain that "nothing is to be found in the Bible about the divinity of Christ," are yet wont at least to acknowledge with the Socinians, that the *exalted* Christ participates in the Godhead according to the doctrine of the holy Scripture ! But he who acknowledges so much must, if he will not give up all claim to the name of a rational being, also acknowledge the eternal divinity of the Incarnate. For that a finite, created being should take part in the world-governing dominion of the Omnipotent and Omnipresent—this were indeed the very climax of unreason. An absolute being can limit itself, *because* it is absolute and its own lord; but a finite being can not be *made* absolute.

tribute of God. That this is never denoted by שמים we have already seen at chap. i. 3. The heaven is that *sphere of the creation* in which the will of God is perfectly done (Matt. vi. 10), and where no sin hinders Him from the full and adequate revelation of Himself. *Into that sphere of the world of space* has Christ ascended, as the first-fruits of glorified humanity, in order to bring us thither after him (chap. ii. 10).

Ver. 2. The principal idea of ver. 1 is now repeated with more distinctness, in the form of an apposition to the subject of ἐκάθισεν, and, therewith, the *proper theme* of the fourth part formally laid down. Christ has sat down on the right hand of the Majesty, as one who (in this) completes the service in the true sanctuary and the true tabernacle. Τῶν ἁγίων is, of course, not to be taken (with Oecumenius, Schulz, Paulus, &c.), as gen. plur. masculine (Christ a servant of the saints), but as gen. plur. neut., and τὰ ἅγια does not signify (as Luther and others render it), "the holy possessions," but (as at chap. ix. 8, 12, and 24, s.; chap. x. 19; chap. xiii. 11) "the holy place," or specially the "holy of holies," (Theophylact, Erasmus, Calvin, Bleek, Tholuck, and the most). As the author wished to place the adjective ἀληθινός after the noun, for the sake of the emphasis, he could only make it to agree in case and number with σκηνῆς; in respect of the sense, τῶν ἀληθινῶν is to be supplied also at τῶν ἁγίων (Bleek, &c.) A similar use of the adjective is made also in German, with the exception that it is placed before the noun. "Ein Diener des wahrhaften Heiligthums und der (scil. wahrhaften) Hütte."

The true sanctuary, the place where God is really and truly united with men, is "not made with men's hands." That tent, covered with curtains and skins, cannot, of course, be the place where heaven and earth are united.

In Ver. 3—4 the author now adduces the *first argument*, to prove that the *sanctuary* into which Christ entered is the *true* sanctuary, and different from the *tabernacle* of Moses. The steps in the reasoning logically arranged are the following:—A, Only the Aaronitic priests were qualified and permitted to offer sacrifice in the Mosaic tabernacle. Christ being not an Aaronite *could* not offer there. B, But he must offer (somewhere and something), because every high priest must offer sacrifice. Consequently, he needed another tabernacle than that of Moses, (the only one that existed *on earth*). The author now, however, (just as at chap. vii. 15—17), passes forthwith from the thesis to the second and more remote member of the proof (B), and then brings in after it the first member of the proof, in the form of an explanation (of how far there lies in B an argument in proof of the thesis). The idea, therefore, takes this form : Thesis : Christ is minister in the *true* (namely heavenly) tabernacle. Argument : For every high priest must offer sacrifice; therefore, Christ also must offer. (Supple :; from this follows, however, the above thesis, that Christ needed another tabernacle ;) *for*, had he been priest in that earthly tabernacle, he would then have been no priest, as there were already priests there, who brought their offerings in conformity with the law.

The words in detail have no difficulty. Δῶρα τε καὶ θυσίαι as a general designation of the offerings, we had already at chap. v. 2. The author does not, of course, say of Christ that it was necessary for him to bring δῶρα τε καὶ θυσίαι, different kinds of offerings, but only that he must have *somewhat* to offer.

Ver. 5. Although grammatically connected with ver. 4 by a οἵτινες (which, however, may be well enough rendered by "and these"), ver. 5 contains an independent idea, a *new argument* for the thesis ver. 2, so stated as that this thesis itself, only in a more definite form, is first repeated (the tabernacle in which the Levitical priests served is called an image and shadow of the heavenly things), and then the passage Ex. xxv. 40 is adduced as a new argument for the inferiority of the Mosaic tabernacle.

Λατρεύειν with the dative of the person whom one serves is frequent ; it more rarely occurs with the dative of the thing in which one serves (besides this passage comp. chap. xiii. 10.) To take the dative in an instrumental signification would yield no sense. The Levitical high priests served in a tabernacle which was an emblem and shadow of the heavenly things. Ἅγια is not (with Bleek and others) to be supplied at τὰ ἐπουράνια ; the author has evidently rather, on purpose and with good reason, avoided placing a heavenly *tabernacle* in opposition to the earthly. True, in ver. 2, where in stating the thesis he wished to make an evident antithesis, he spoke of a " true tabernacle," a " true sanctuary ;" from that place onwards, however, he avoids with intentional care every expression which might have led to the conception of a local sanctuary in heaven. Also in chap. ix., he again sets in opposition to the "holy places made with hands" only "the heavenly things" and "the things in the heavens," ver. 23. And, moreover, the whole reasoning in chap. ix. shows, that he considered as the archetype of the tabernacle not *heavenly localities*, but *heavenly relations* and *heavenly facts*. (The holy life of Christ, in his state of humiliation, is the heavenly sanctuary through which Christ must pass; the rending of his body is the rending of the vail that separates him from the holiest of all, &c. Comp. below on chap. ix. 11, and on chap. x. 20.) Now, to these *heavenly relations and facts of salvation* the Mosaic tabernacle stands in the relation of a ὑπόδειγμα and σκιά. The verb from which ὑπόδειγμα is derived, ὑποδείκνυμι, has two significations; first, it signifies to show something privately to any one, to let something be seen in an underhand way, hence ὑπόδειγμα, a private sign, secret token, and, in general, a mark or token; secondly, it signifies also to illustrate something by examples, to draw from a pattern, to copy, hence ὑπόδειγμα, a copy, or also (in the profane writers as well as in Heb. iv. 11) = παράδειγμα image, model, example. In this passage, however, it has not the less proper signification of image in the sense of παράδειγμα, *model, pattern*, but the proper signification of *copy*, so that it was not the Mosaic tabernacle that was the παράδειγμα (the original from which the copy was taken), but the *heavenly things*. The same idea lies in σκιά, but in a still stronger form. The shadow of a body represents not even a proper image of it, but only the colourless contour.

Now, that the Mosaic tabernacle was not *an original but the copy of a heavenly original*, the author proves from Ex. xxv. 40. In Ex. xxv. 40 Moses is told to build the tabernacle according to the תַּבְנִית, that is, *plan* (not model, comp. Is. xliv. 13, where, ver. 13, the draught is first sketched, and then, ver. 14, the wood is sought for completing it; also 2 Kings xvi. 10; 1 Chron. xxviii. 11, where the signification "plan, sketch," is perfectly suitable, better certainly than the signification "model")—according to the plan which God showed to him in the mount. These words already lead (as תבנית never denotes *an independent original building*, but always only a *plan on a small scale* by which one to be guided in the construction—and, even according to the common false explanation of the term, only a *model in miniature*)—these words, I say, already lead, not to the conception that there had been shown to Moses on Mount Sinai a large real tabernacle; still less, can the author's opinion of Ex. xxv. 40 be, that the original of the tabernacle stands permanently on Mount Sinai (as later Rabbins fabled), and least of all, that Moses looked forth into the heaven from the top of Sinai, and saw there in heaven the original structure. Either the words in Ex. xxv. 40 are to be taken as a figurative expression (so that the *description in words*, Ex. xxv. 4 ss., was called figuratively a plan which had been shown to Moses), or, there was really shown to Moses *in a prophetic vision* the draught of a building (comp. Ex. xxvi. 30) but still a draught or plan which, beyond his vision, had no existence.—The question now presents itself, whether our author understood the passage in this, the right way, or whether he misunderstood it after the manner of the later Rabbins. Now, it is first of all to be observed, that there are throughout no positive intimations that might necessitate our adopting this latter supposition. The whole reasoning retains its full force on the supposition, that he *rightly* understood the passage in question. The *heavenly things* themselves (the New Testament *facts* of salvation which were delineated in the tabernacle) were, indeed, not shown to Moses, but only a plan according to which he was to build that hypodeigmatic tabernacle, and he had as yet no consciousness of the prophetical signification of this building. But, indeed, the force of the author's reasoning depends in nowise on whether Moses understood the typical signification of the tabernacle or not. Enough, that *Moses himself did not make or invent the plan of the tabernacle*, enough, that *God gave him the plan*—God, who knew well the symbolical signification of this plan. That the plan for the tabernacle was given by God —in *this circumstance* lies the nerve of the argument; *for this reason* is the Mosaic tabernacle a reflection of *heavenly* thoughts, ideas, relations.[1]

[1] Faber, Stapulensis, Rivet, Schlichting, Storr, and Bleek, go still farther, and suppose even, that our author did not at all understand the word τύπος in the sense of *ground-plan* or model, but in the sense of *copy*, and that his object was expressly to say, that the model which was shown to Moses was itself the only copy of the true ἐπουράνια.

But *further*, there are even *distinct reasons* at hand for rejecting the supposition, that the author conceived of an original tabernacle standing permanently in heaven, or on Mount Sinai. If he had conceived of this as in heaven, then he must either have said more plainly, Moses was permitted to look forth into the heaven from Mount Sinai, or he must have said more plainly (comp. the remarks above) : that which Moses saw on Sinai was itself again only a copy of the heavenly original. If, however, he conceived of this as standing on Mount Sinai, then this tabernacle would not have been ἐπουράνια, but ἐπὶ τῆς γῆς, which was precisely denied in ver. 4. But that neither of these fantastic ideas had any place in the mind of the author, appears most evidently from the ninth chapter. If the separation of a holy of holies from a holy place is there expressly represented as an *imperfection*, in which the Mosaic tabernacle is *distinguished* from the heavenly original,—how, in all possibility, can the author have regarded that model shown to Moses—which corresponded with the Mosaic tabernacle even in the minutest detail, and therefore had also a holy place separated from the holy of holies —as that heavenly original itself? So much then is beyond all doubt—that those *heavenly things*, which in the Mosaic tabernacle were delineated in a faint shadow-sketch, did not themselves, according to our author's view, consist of a *locality*, a tabernacle with skins, curtains, fore-courts, holy place, and holy of holies.

Thus, then, the force of the reasoning in ver. 5 lies in reality only in the *negative* circumstance, that the tabernacle was not an *independent original*, but was built according to a *pattern* given by God, the object of which, therefore, must have been *symbolically to represent* divine ideas.

In ver. 6 the thesis, contained in ver. 2 and repeated in a more modified form in the beginning of ver. 5, is *once more repeated*, and this time in a form still more complete; so, namely, that not merely the two ideas contained in ver. 2 and ver. 5 are *united*, but a third is added. In ver. 2 it was said positively :

Accordingly, he intends to represent the tabernacle as the *copy of a copy*. This, however, could hardly be justified on exegetical grounds. The author would assuredly have expressed this idea more distinctly.

Christ is *minister* in the true tabernacle, in ver. 5 negatively: the Levitical high priests served in a tabernacle which was only an image and shadow. Now, in ver. 6 it is said: the *ministry of Christ is more glorious (than that of the Levitical high priests), and in so much more glorious as the new covenant is more glorious (than the old.)* Here, therefore, not merely are the two λειτουρ-γίαι compared with *each other*, but they are, moreover, placed parallel with the two διαθήκαις. Thus ver. 6 forms the proper thesis of the entire fourth part, and vers. 1—5 serves only as a preparatory introduction to this thesis. As the author in ver. 6 not merely combines the ideas in vers. 1—5, but, at the same time, also passes to a *new* idea, to the comparison of the services with the *covenants*, he has therefore connected ver. 6 with ver. 5, not by a particle of *inference*, but by a particle of *progression* (νυνὶ δέ.)

In respect of form, ver. 6 has the greatest resemblance to chap. i. 4. Here, as there, the comparatives κρείττων and διαφορώτερος are used in the comparison of what belongs to the Old Testament with what belongs to the New. Instead of λειτουργία the author might, by all means, have put σκηνή, but, as has already been observed at ver. 5, he henceforth industriously avoids placing a heavenly tabernacle in opposition to the Mosaic tabernacle.

The ground-idea of ver. 6 then is this, that the ministry of the Levitical priests in the Mosaic tabernacle stands related to the minstry of Christ in the *heavenly things* precisely as the old *covenant* does to the new. *In what* the old covenant is excelled by the new, we are informed in the relative clause ἥτις, which finds farther explanation in vers. 7—12. This explanation, at the same time, already contains the idea, that the old covenant was destined to *vanish* and to be *replaced* by the new. This idea is then in ver. 13 formally expressed as an *inference*. Does the Levitical priestly service in the temple bear the same relation to the ministry of Christ (according to ver. 6) as the old covenant bears to the new, and again, is the old covenant (according to ver. 13) to be *abrogated* by the new—in this lies already implicite the final inference (which is then in chap. ix.—x. explicitly developed in detail), that the Levitical temple service is *in like manner abrogated, rendered superfluous* by the *ministry* of Christ, as the old covenant by the new.

So much on the train of thought in general. Let us look now, first of all, at the relative clause: ἥτις ἐπὶ κρείττοσιν ἐπαγγελίαις νενομοθέτηται. Νομοθετεῖν, here evidently in the wider sense = to establish, to enact authoritatively; for that the new covenant also has to do with the *giving of a law* is expressly shown in vers. 8—12. The new covenant is founded on better promises; for (comp. vers. 9, 10) the old covenant promised salvation and blessing only to him who perfectly fulfilled the law; the new covenant, on the other hand, *gives first* before it *asks*.

Ver. 7 serves, first of all, to obviate an objection that might arise in the minds of the readers at ver. 6. They were wont to consider Moses, and the covenant of God with Moses, as the proper and most sacred kernel of the Israelitish true religion. Had not the Messiah himself, according to their view, been promised and given precisely to the members of the *Mosaic covenant people!* Now, to say that this covenant of God with Moses was lowered in value by another covenant, must have appeared to them as almost frivolous. Therefore the author explains to them, that he is at liberty to depreciate, nay, to find fault with the old covenant, and why he is so. "If that first covenant had been faultless, then there had been no room for desiring a second." This was certainly the author's idea, but instead of saying οὐκ ἂν τόπος ἦν τοῦ ζητεῖν δευτέραν, he has with unconscious conciseness (or by blending the two ideas: οὐκ ἂν ἦν τόπος and οὐκ ἂν ἐζητεῖτο δευτέρα) joined τόπος also with ἐζητεῖτο as the object. (The explanation of Bleek and others is not natural: then God would have had no need to seek in the hearts of men a better place for his covenant than was the place on the tables of stone. Equally unnatural is Olshausen's "τόπον τινὸς ζητεῖν = to will that something should take place.")—The turn of the thought in general is quite parallel with that in chap. vii. ver. 11 (and ver. 18.) As in that place, from the established fact that a new and different high priest is promised, the inference is drawn that the old high priesthood must have been insufficient (and similarly at vii. 18 of the law), so here, from the fact that God—as is shown explanatorily in vers. 8—12—has promised a new covenant it is inferred, that the old covenant was οὐκ ἄμεμπτος.

The meaning of this οὐκ ἄμεμπτος is well explained in the expressions used in quite a similar way in chap. vii. 18, ἀσθενὲς καὶ ἀνωφελές. The author does not mean to find fault with the old Mosaic covenant as being not of divine origin, or, although constituted by God as being insufficient even for its relative object, and unwisely framed; he only means, that it lies open to the charge of being faulty, when human folly, contrary to the divine purpose, gives it out as being *everlastingly sufficient*, while yet God himself, inasmuch as he has promised to give a *new, another* covenant, has thereby declared the old one to be imperfect. It is, therefore, not the author, nor generally speaking a man who presumed to find fault with the old covenant, but *God himself* has found fault with it. (Comp. the repeated λέγει κύριος, ver. 8 and 9. It was not the word of Jeremiah, but the word of the Lord to Jeremiah.)

Ver. 8—12. The author in these verses cites the passage in which God has promised a new and a different covenant, and thereby has found fault with the old covenant (not as one that was not divine, or not wise, but as insufficient and destined to cease). The passage is in Jer. xxxi. 31—34. The author quotes literally from the Sept., and the rendering of the Sept. is right.— In the whole of the Old Testament no passage is to be found in which the view is expressed more clearly and distinctly, that the law was only a παιδαγωγός, than in this. And, if some commentators have thought that in this passage no fault is found with the old covenant itself, but only with the Israelites, they merely show by this, that they have not understood the simple sense of the passage. It is true, that fault is found with the Israelites who "abode not in the covenant (of Moses);" but when the Lord is induced by this consideration to determine, that he will frame a different covenant, in which he will write the law not upon tables of stone but on the hearts of his people, he surely acknowledges thereby expressly and clearly, that a part of the fault belonged also to the old covenant. (In like manner Olshausen. Comp. also our explanation of the passage chap. iv. 2, in which we encounter a similar misunderstanding on the part of the critics.)

The train of thought in the passage Jer. xxxi. 31—34 is as follows. A *first principal idea* lies in the words ἰδοὺ .... γῆς Αἰγύπτου. The Lord announces to his people, that he will, at a future time, make a new covenant with them, ver. 8. He calls this covenant new, however, not in the sense of its being only a confirmatory renewal of the old covenant, but in precise and express opposition to the covenant which was made on their removal from Egypt, it is to be a new covenant not merely numerically, but qualitatively (ver. 9, οὐ κατὰ .... ἐκ γῆς Αἰγύπτου). Then follows a *second principal idea* (ὅτι αὐτοὶ οὐκ .... ἔσονταί μοι εἰς λαόν). We are now told what it was that was imperfect in the old covenant, and why there was need of a new covenant, and wherein this should be different from the old. The principal imperfection of the old covenant lies in its *inefficacy*, which has been demonstrated by actual experience. The cause of this is to be traced not merely to the Israelites not continuing in that covenant, but to the mutual relation that subsisted between the people and their God, which is expressed in the two members: *they continued not, &c., and I regarded them not.* The people, on their part, remained not in the covenant, fulfilled not the commands enjoined as the condition of the covenant, and God, on his part, punished the people, inasmuch as after, and in consequence of, the transgressions, he accepted them no more. *The conduct of God regulated itself then according to the conduct of men.* God first demanded before he gave; he first imposed his commands without regard to the capacity and power of men; then he rejected the people because they fulfilled not these commands. (It needs not, of course, to be shown here for the first time, how wise this stage of legal enactment in the training of Israel was, how necessary it was in order to awaken the knowledge of the infirmities of sin. Nor does our author deny that it was necessary *for its time*. But he proves from this announcement of God himself to Jeremiah, that this stage was only a preparatory one, which could not confer blessedness and brought no *perfection*.) It is different with the new covenant which God promises to make יָמִים הַבָּאִים. In this covenant God will not write his law outwardly, as a cold requirement, on tables of stone, but he will *write it in the hearts and in the minds* of his people; he will, therefore, *first give to the people and then ask from them;* he will first give them a new heart, a regenerate spirit, pleasure, love, and joy in God's will, and then he will require of them, nor will he then require in vain, for he will then be truly the people's God, worshipped and beloved by them, and, in consequence of this, the people can then also be truly his people, protected and blessed by him. In a *third principal idea* (ver. 11—12), it is now shown still more plainly, how the fulfilment of the law is under this new covenant to rest on the *inward* disposition, and on what ground this disposition is to rest. In the old covenant God had commissioned Moses and the priests to read the law to the people, and to lay before them the command to acknowledge Jehovah as their God. There is to be no such outward process under the new covenant. Then will every one personally, and from his own inmost experience, know and acknowledge the Lord,—and how? by what means? Because *he forgives their sins, and remembers not their iniquities.* The difference, then, between the old and the new covenant is traced even to this innermost centre-point in that evangelical announcement of God to Jeremiah. There it is the *law* that stands first, and lays down its requirements, which man cannot fulfil, because he wants the power and the spirit, the power of love and the spirit of love. Here it is *free grace*, the forgiveness of sins, and reconciliation that stands first, and in the heart whose sins have been forgiven love springs up, and from love springs the strength and the inclination for holiness, and the personal experience of the knowledge of God.

Ver. 13. The author has now shown that, according to God's own announcement, a new, a higher covenant was to be formed, which rests on better promises, (namely, promises not first conditioned by the conduct of men). From this is now drawn the further inference, that for the old covenant a time must also at length come, when it would no longer be merely relatively the old in opposition to the *new*, but also, the absolutely *weak through age* in opposition to the new covenant coming into operation with the *freshness of youth.*

Two ideas are to be distinguished from each other in this

verse. First, with the promise of God to make in general a (relatively) new, different, second covenant, the covenant made with Moses ceases to be the only one, and becomes a (relatively) old covenant. Secondly: But of two things, that which is the *relatively older* must also, at some time, become the *absolutely old*, be survived and pass away.

We have here, first of all, to obtain a clear idea of the two categories, *old* and *new*, *aged* and *young*. Καινός means *new*, new in the relative sense, that which is added to a thing already existing as a new, *i.e.* a different thing, *novus*. (In the same sense might one, who at an entertainment brings first wine of vintage 1846, and then of 1811, say he will now bring a *new wine*, that is, a new, another kind.) The opposite of this in Greek is παλαιός, that which was already there, πάλαι, the old = the earlier, (relatively old), antiquus (from ante), what does not come after something else. The application of παλαιός to old persons is secondary, and these also are so called, not in the sense of their being infirm through age, but only in the sense of their having been *earlier* in the world than those who are young.

Νέος, on the other hand, means *young*, fresh, *recens*, that which (at any given time) is still absolutely new *in respect of its existence*, (not in comparison with another), that which has not yet existed long, still stands in fresh vigour. (So is that wine of 1846 the *young* wine.) In opposition to this, γεραιός, as the Latin vetus denotes what is *absolutely old*, what has no longer in itself the strength to exist much longer. (Thus a man of eighty years of age may be a *new* member (καινός) of a legislative assembly, and still be a γεραιός, and one of thirty years of age may be an old (παλαιός) member of the assembly, and yet be νέος.)

Most unjustly, therefore, will Bleek, Tholuck, and others render παλαιοῦν by senem reddere, "to render antiquated." Only thus, Bleek thinks, can a natural connection of ideas be made out between the two members; it gives rise rather, we think, only to a tautology. Παλαιοῦν is rather simply "to make the older" antiquum reddere, (not to antiquate in the modern sense, which would be equivalent to "abrogate.") Inasmuch as God speaks of a καινὴ διαθήκη, he *has* (the use of the perf. is to be noted) thereby made the covenant of Moses the *old covenant*, *i.e.* the relatively older. That, however, which has been made the antiquum, the *older*, is, for this reason—*because* it is destined to be displaced by a novum—also far on the way towards an absolute point of *old age, i.e.* it is a γηράσκον, *it is old* in respect of its own capacity of existence, and approaches therefore, step by step, the impending ἀφανισμός. ('Εγγύς is used in the same way as at chap. vi. 8. As, in that place, ἐγγὺς κατάρας does not mean "nigh to the curse," but "approaching step by step *nearer* to the curse," so here, ἐγγὺς ἀφανισμοῦ, "approaching step by step nearer to dissolution.") Thus, from the fact that God has promised, in general, a new, *i.e. second* covenant, and has declared the covenant of Moses to be the *earlier*, it follows, that this earlier covenant must, at some time, be *old* and *cease*. Now, as, according to ver. 6, the relation between the *ministries* is the same as that between the *covenants*, ver. 13, therefore, already implicitly contains the idea (as has been already observed) that the Levitical λειτουργία is destined to become old, to be survived and to cease.

SECTION SECOND.

(Chap. ix. 1—10.)

THE CONSTRUCTION OF THE MOSAIC TABERNACLE.

According to the train of thought in the foregoing section, we are prepared to expect here two ideas which Zuingle has already well denoted in the words: Docet, ceremonias testamenti veteris nonnisi *typum* fuisse novi. Atque ita rursum probat, novum testamentum, sacerdotium videlicet Christi, *excellentius* fuisse levitico. First, the author will have to prove in detail the idea expressed in chap. viii. 1—5, that the Old Testament tabernacle, in general, was a copy of the heavenly things *i.e.* the *ministry* of Christ,—then, the idea in chap. viii. 6 ss., that, as a mere *copy*, it corresponds to the nature of the *old* covenant as *distinguished* from the new. And indeed we do find both of these things in this section, only (as was to be expected) not treated successively, but blended together.

In ver. 1 the first thing to be asked is, what substantive is to be supplied at πρώτη. The Complut. and Steph. editions read ἡ πρώτη σκηνή, but this σκηνή is not found in the majority of the oldest and best codd. and versions, it rests, therefore, merely on a conjecture, and this conjecture, moreover, is groundless. In chap. viii. 6—13 it was the *two covenants* that were spoken of throughout, and, even at ver. 13, the words *in that he saith*, a *new*, &c., pointed back to the citation in ver. 8 (I will make a new *covenant*), and thus, at ver. 13 also, the substantive, *covenant*, was to be supplied at the words—*he hath made the first old*. This of itself would show, that the same substantive must be supplied at ἡ πρώτη in the verse before us. And, indeed, σκηνή would in nowise be suitable. For, in ver. 2, where the expression ἡ πρώτη σκηνή actually occurs, it serves to denote not the *Old Testament* sanctuary in opposition to that of the *New Testament*, but the *fore-compartment* of the Old Testament tabernacle (the so-called "holy place") in opposition to the *hind-compartment* (the "holiest of all"), and, therefore, has a signification which would not at all be suitable in ver. 1. We have, therefore, to supply διαθήκη (so Peschito, Chrysostom, Luther, Calvin, Beza, Grotius, Bleek, Olshausen, and, in general, all the more recent commentators.)

Δικαιώματα λατρείας,—δικαίωμα denotes the result of the act expressed by δικαιοῦν, and signifies, therefore, the making just or right. In the New Testament it occurs in a threefold sense: first, it signifies the *fulfilling of righteousness* (as applicable to the perfect man Christ), Rom. v. 18, viii. 4; secondly, the *declaring of the sinner to be righteous* by God for Christ's sake, Rom. v. 16; thirdly, it denotes an act whereby certain things are declared to be right and therefore obligatory, *i.e. ordinance, law* = מִשְׁפָּט, חֹק, Rom. i. 32; Luke i. 6. Here, of course, only this third signification is suitable. To understand δικαιώματα of the holy vessels is contrary to all usage. Luther, Grotius, and others, take λατρείας as the accusative, and suppose a comma between δικαιώματα and λατρείας, so that the three things would be co-ordinated, "ordinances, services, and sanctuary." But, first of all, τε is mostly used in the case of things *connected by pairs*; besides, the use of the plural in λατρείας would be strange, and λατρείας, moreover, would express nothing else than the performance of the δικαιώματα, which would give rise to a tautology. We therefore agree with the immense majority of both ancient and modern commentators in taking λατρείας as the genitive to δικαιώματα. We thus obtain *two* ideas (" ordinances respecting the service," and " the sanctuary"), which correspond precisely to the two ideas of the foregoing chapter, *service* and *tabernacle*.

By τὸ ἅγιον, as already appears from the epithet κοσμικόν (which forms the antithesis to ἐπουράνιον), is to be understood the *entire* Old Testament *fanum* (not the " holiest of all," which in the Epistle to the Hebrews is denoted by τὰ ἅγια, vers. 3 and 8, or ἅγια ἁγίων, ver. 2; nor the so called "holy place," which our author always designates by the expression ἡ πρώτη σκηνή.) —The epithet κοσμικόν, as already said, finds its explanation in the antithesis to τὰ ἐπουράνια. The writer intends evidently to say this: " the old covenant, too, had indeed a *service* and a *sanctuary*, but it had a service determined by *ordinances*, and a sanctuary belonging to *this world*." These two things he has concisely put together in one clause. He, therefore (as already Olshausen has rightly observed), expresses by κοσμικόν nearly the same thing that he had already expressed in chap. viii. 4 by ἐπὶ γῆς, with this difference, that in κοσμικόν lies not merely the locality but also the quality. Some of the older critics have strangely mistaken the sense of these simple words. Luther and others take τὸ ἅγιον = τὴν ἁγιότητα; Hornberg rightly interprets τὸ ἅγιον, but renders κοσμικός = κόσμιος, " adorned ; " Chrysostom, Theophylact, Oecumenius, Kypke, explain κοσμικός = for the *whole* world, destined for all nations (but one of the principal imperfections of the Old Testament sanctuary lay precisely in this, that it was *not* destined for all nations, but only for one people); Theophylact, Grotius, Este, Wetstein, explain : " representing a type of the world-structure " (but the tabernacle represented this in no possible way.) Even among those commentators who rightly explain κοσμικός as antithetical with ἐπουράνιος (It., Vulg., Calvin, Beza, Cramer, Storr, Kuinoel, Tholuck, Bleek), it is still unnecessarily disputed, whether the writer intended by this to denote the imperfection or the materiality of the Old Testament sanctuary. Κοσμικός signifies neither "imperfect" nor "material," but "belonging to the world."[1] The Old Testament sanctuary was an integral part of *this world*, this κόσμος, which exists as a world separated from God, and in which, therefore, even when what was heavenly appeared, it must needs take the form of the limited, the particular, *i.e.*, under the distinction of fanum and profanum. In this is involved at once the material, local, external, and emblematic character of the Old Testament ἅγιον, and, at the same time, also, its imperfection.

Ver. 2—5. What is now to be proven is not that, in general, a *service* and a *sanctuary* existed under the old covenant, but that that *service* was one according to ordinances, and that sanctuary one pertaining to this world. In proof of this (comp. the γάρ), the principal idea is now laid down: "There was built the *first* compartment of the tent; behind the *second* vail, however, was the holy of holies." In this construction, which rendered it necessary to pass through two vails into the holiest of all, was plainly expressed that cosmical imperfection, that state of separation between God and the sinful world.

This separation was not, however, in any way merely accidental or outward, but was most closely connected with the entire nature, and with the collective symbols of the Old Testament cultus. The writer shows this by specifying the particular pieces of furniture in each of the two compartments of the tabernacle, and the acts of worship which were performed in each.

Before entering here on the explanation of the text, we must not omit taking a short survey of the local construction and symbolical significance of the tabernacle.

On entering by the door of the rectangular fore-court (which stood on one of its smaller sides) into the *fore-court*, one would then have had the tent immediately before him (again its smaller side), but in entering it, he would yet have to pass the altar of burnt-offering and the basin of water which stood just at the entrance to the tent. On entering into the *tent itself* (therefore

---

[1] Bleek renders the word by "worldly." But this word has acquired in common usage a different meaning. It no longer forms the antithesis to heavenly, but to spiritual, and has become almost synonymous with "profane."

passing through the first vail, which formed the entrance from the fore-court outwards), he would then have found himself in the *holy place* (πρώτη σκηνή), a rectangular space which, again, had greater depth than breadth. On the right hand, in this space, stood the *table with the shew-bread*, on the left, the *golden candlestick*, and furthest back, immediately before the entrance to the holiest of all (Ex. xxx. 6), the *altar of incense*. On entering (through the second vail, which separated the holy place from the holiest of all) into the *holiest of all*, he would then have found himself in a square space which had no other entrance but the one from the holy place. Here stood the *ark of the covenant*.

This holy of holies was the place where God sometimes manifested his presence in a bright light or a cloud of smoke. This was the place where God was to be conceived of as always present, even although he should not be visibly manifest. He was present here, however, not as the Creator and Governor of the world (as such he dwelt in heaven), but as the *covenant God* of his people. And therefore was the *act of the covenant* kept here in the *ark of the covenant*. This act of the covenant contained the mutual contract which God had made with his people. He *required* of the people the fulfilment of his eternal, absolutely holy will, which he had expressed in the " ten words ; " the decalogue was the *condition of the covenant*; if this was fulfilled, then would the Lord, on his part, fulfil the *promise of the covenant*, and be the God of this people.

But, not only did the people break that condition from the very first; they had never the power to fulfil a command in which even an evil desire was forbidden. Hence God had never given this law to the end that it should be fulfilled, but to the end that the people should by this testimony (עֵדוּת) be led to the knowledge of their sinfulness. And this is not an idea to be found first in the New Testament, in the writings of Paul, but one which had been, in the clearest manner, expressed in *the ceremonial law and worship*.

The " words of the testimony " (*i. e.* the decalogue) must needs be *covered* (כָּפַר), so that the eye of the God who was present in the holy of holies might not fall upon these words, which were an *act of accusation* against the people. (From this is to be explained the frequent form of expression " to cover sin.") A golden *cover* the כַּפֹּרֶת, was to be laid upon the ark; this dead cover, however, did not suffice of itself to turn away the eye of divine penal justice from the record which testified of the guilt of the people. For this there was necessary an *actual atonement for this guilt.* Therefore the high priest must, once every year, on the great day of atonement, slay the great sacrifice of atonement, and carry the blood into the holiest of all, and sprinkle it on the cover or lid of the ark, that the eye of God might fall upon this witness of the accomplished atonement. (Of course this atonement was, in like manner, only symbolical and typical, as was the representation of the presence of God, and the beholding of God.) Thus, then, there was represented in the holy of holies the *absolute* relation of the *absolutely holy God* to the sinful people. It will appear from what has been said, how very superficial is the view of those who would place the decalogue in the same category with the ceremonial law, and regard it as given only for the Jews. The whole ceremonial law had rather a significance only on the supposition, that the decalogue was not a relative thing suited to the capacity and development of the time when it was given, but the *purely absolute* representation of the *eternal, independent* will of God.

Let us now look at the cultus of the holy place, the πρώτη σκηνή. After the decalogue God gave, at the same time, to the Israelites (Ex. xx. 22, 23, 33), a *second law*, which did not require absolute holiness, but rather, on the contrary, was suited to an unholy sinful people, and which presupposed the non-fulfilment of the decalogue. In the decalogue it is said: thou shalt not kill; in chap. xxi. 12 ss. it is taken for granted that, notwithstanding of this, murder would occur, and ordinances were given how this should be punished. In the decalogue it is said: thou shalt not steal; in chap. xxii. 1, it is presupposed, that still, thefts would be committed, and the civil punishment for the thief is specified, and so forth. In short, the decalogue was a law which could not be kept by a sinful people; the law, on the other hand, chap. xx. 22 ss. was instituted precisely to meet the capacity of observance belonging to a sinful people. The decalogue required *absolute holiness;* the second (the civil) law required merely *civil* propriety of conduct, therefore only a holiness of a very relative kind, only a justitia civilis.—*Now, just* as this civil law stands related to the decalogue, so does the cultus of the holy place to that of the holy of holies. While, in the one, the absolute will of God as accusing the people needed to be, as it were, hid from the eye of God by the *lid* sprinkled with the blood of the sacrifice, so, in the other, the people brought before God the temporary fruits of the land,—bread and oil,—as symbols of their relative services, their relative holiness—they did not, however, present these immediately before the eye of God, but only in the fore-chamber of his house. The show-bread was no *lectisternium*, no meat for God (but as already the name לֶחֶם־פָּנִים intimates), was intended only to be looked upon by God; in like manner, in the candlestick which was filled with the other chief produce of the land, oil, the people made, as it were, their light to shine before God. In the holy place, therefore, were represented the symbols of the *temporary relative piety, which the Lord, in the meanwhile, until the people should become entirely and inwardly holy, graciously accepted*, and which he could graciously accept only because, at the same time, in the holiest of all, the sins against God's *absolute* requirements were, from time to time, covered by the sacrifices. Thus, then, we see how this *twofold* character of the cultus, really pointed to a future removal of the difference between the absolute requirements of the covenant and the merely relative services of the covenant.

The fore-court was the place for the sinful people. Here the sacrifices, namely, the atoning sacrifices were slain and burnt. This slaying and burning was a symbol of the death and the condemnation which the sinner properly had deserved, which, however, was transferred from him to the victim. Of course, therefore, neither the holy place nor the holy of holies was the fitting place for these acts of judicial punishment (the great sacrifice of atonement was therefore commanded to be burnt without the fore-court, nay, without the camp); only the *blood* of the slain sacrifice of atonement was brought before the eye of God, *i.e.* into the holy of holies, as a testimony that the atoning vicarious act of punishment had been executed. The general mutual relation between God and his people *resulting* from the sacred rites of the holy of holies, from those of the holy place and of the fore-court,—the result, that God in general still accepted the homage and worship of this people, was symbolically represented in the *incense-offering*. The incense-offering was burnt in the fore-court, in the fire of the altar of burnt-offering—only in virtue of this connexion with the expiatory side of the cultus was it acceptable—it was not carried into the holy of holies itself, but (just because it represented only the *temporary, relative* peace that subsisted between God and his people) into the *holy place;* but the altar of incense on which it was placed stood (Ex. xxx. 6) just before the entrance to the holy of holies "over against the ark of the covenant," and thus, the incense-offering referred to the God who was present in the holy of holies; the smoke of the incense was to penetrate into the holy of holies itself, and, because it belonged to the cultus of the holy of holies, it was offered not by the priests but by the *high priest.*

With this explanation of the symbolical meaning of the tabernacle and its worship in general, the question is already solved, why the author in vers. 2—5 names and enumerates these pieces of furniture (a question which, moreover, is answered by himself in ver. 6 ss.) But, at the same time also, a *difficulty* is thus by anticipation removed, which Calmet has declared to be the maxima totius epistolae difficultas. If, however, there existed no greater difficulties in it than this, then would the epistle to the Hebrews belong to the easiest books of the New Testament! It is the difficulty arising from the fact, that the *author in ver.* 4 *reckons the golden altar of incense as belonging to the holy of holies, while it stood undoubtedly in the holy place.*

Commentators have had recourse to a threefold solution of this difficulty.

First, some have directly expressed their opinion, that the author *was mistaken.* This, however, is too gross to be for a moment conceivable. The position of the altars must have been known to every Israelite from the book of Exodus, much more must he have known it, who set himself to reason from this against the Jewish Christians. This view has therefore been supported by *auxiliary conjectures.* Some say, the author may perhaps have lived and written in Alexandria, and therefore not have had an exact knowledge of the arrangements of the temple in Jerusalem. But the question, whether one lived in Jerusalem or elsewhere, is here altogether irrelevant, as, even in Jerusalem, the layman could not enter into the temple, and could only become acquainted with the internal arrangements of the temple from what he read *in the Pentateuch or in* 1 *Kings*. This information could be obtained, however, quite as easily in Alexandria as in Jerusalem, by a layman or a non-layman. Moreover, it is not the temple that is here spoken of, but the tabernacle, and specially *those* arrangements which found place *only* in the old tabernacle (thus in ver 4, Aaron's rod and the pot of manna are mentioned, both of which, according to 1 Kings viii. 6, even at the time of the building of Solomon's Temple were no longer to be found).—And this will, at the same time, afford an answer to a second auxiliary conjecture (that of a reviewer in Rheinwald's Repert. 1842 vol 9. p. 193), according to which, the author had in his mind, and before his eye, the arrangements of that temple which the Egyptian Jews, under Onias 150 B.C. built at Leontopolis. This conjecture is the more untenable when we find that Onias built his temple with *great exactness* after the pattern of that at Jerusalem, so that, at Leontopolis, the altar of incense assuredly stood nowhere else than it did at Jerusalem.

Side by side with the first solution is to be placed also that of Bleek, according to which, the altar of incense did really stand in the holy place, but the author allowed himself to be led into the mistake of placing it in the holy of holies by the passages Ex. xxx. 6 and 26; Lev. iv. 7, ss. (where it is said the altar of incense stands "over against the ark of the covenant.") This hypothesis is, however, simply refuted by the 7th verse of our chapter, where the author expressly and definitely says that the high priest entered into the δευτέρα σκηνή *only once in the year*, which he could not have said if, in his opinion, the *daily* offering of incense had been brought into the holiest of all.

With this also is refuted a second hypothesis (which has been put forth by Tholuck, only problematically, however, on the alleged ground of 1 Kings vi. 22; Ex. xxvi. 35), that, in reality, the altar of incense may have stood in the holy of holies. We are not under the necessity of having recourse to Ex. xxx. 6 ("thou shalt place it before the vail") in order to prove, that the altar of incense really stood in the holy place, and by no means in the holy of holies,[1] as it clearly appears from the 7th verse of our chapter that, in the opinion too of our author, it stood in the holy place and not in the holy of holies. The question, now, is no longer one of a contradiction between our author and the Pentateuch, but of a kind of contradiction into which he seems to have fallen with himself.

By how much the less conceivable such a contradiction of the author with himself is, by so much the more might the third principal solution seem, on a superficial view of the question, to recommend itself, the solution, namely, of those (as the Peschito, Vulg., Theophylact, Luther, Calov, de Dieu, Reland, Deyling, J. G. Michaelis, Böhme, Kuinoel, Stuart, Klee, &c.) who would translate θυμιατήριον here by *censer*. That θυμιατήριον may actually mean *censer* is proven (from Thucyd. vi. 46; Diod. Sec. xiii. 3; LXX. Ex. viii. 11; 2 Chron. xxvi. 19; Joseph. Ant. iv. 2, 4). It has even been maintained that it must be rendered here by censer; for the altar of incense is never denoted in the LXX. by θυμιατήριον, but always by θυσιαστήριον θυμιάματος. But this ground is not conclusive, as in Josephus, Philo, Clemens Alex., and Origen, the altar of incense, in spite of the usage of the LXX., is very often called θυμιατήριον. Moreover, our author, in the designation of the parts and vessels of the sanctuary, does not at all confine himself to the terms of the LXX.; he calls the holy place for example not τὸ ἅγιον (as LXX. Ex. xxvi. 33, &c.) but ἡ πρώτη σκηνή, while he uses τὸ ἅγιον (ver. 1) in a far wider sense to designate the *entire* sanctuary; to designate the holy of holies he uses, besides the expression of the LXX. ἅγια ἁγίων, also the expressions ἡ δευτέρα σκηνή (ver. 7) τὰ ἅγια (ver. 8), &c. It is thus quite *possible* that in the designation of the altar of incense he may have departed from the circumstantial term of the LXX., and followed the usage of Josephus and Philo. The word θυμιατήριον, therefore, in itself determines nothing.

Just as little is determined by the predicate χρυσοῦν. Some have understood this as a differentia specifica distinguishing a

[1] For the opposite opinion it has been contended, that Origen also (hom. 8 in Exod., 9 in Levit.) Oecumenius and Augustine (qu. 177, in Exod.) assigned the altar of incense to the holy of holies. But none of these three Fathers saw the temple themselves; they, all of them, drew their information solely from our passage, Heb. ix. 4, so that their testimony here is entirely without weight.

golden censer from a silver one, and in support of this, have appealed to a passage of the Talmud, according to which, there were many silver censers and only a single golden one—at the same time also, to the omission of the article at χρυσοῦν θυμιατήριον. But if the author had intended to distinguish that one particular censer from the many, he must precisely then have used the article. But the epithet χρυσοῦν can, just as little, be a differentia specifica as is the parallel epithet περικεκαλυμμένην πάντοθεν χρυσίῳ. Or, will the author distinguish the gilt lid of the covenant from a number of others, namely, of covenant lids not gilt!

The two following considerations are unfavourable to this third solution of the difficulty. In the first place, the holy of holies was no store-room in which all possible vessels were kept; though it were granted, then, that there was a particular golden censer which was specially set apart for the incense on the day of atonement in the holy of holies (Lev. xvi. 12, s.), this censer would still not be kept, the whole year through, in the holy of holies, as in that case, the high priest must needs have entered into the holy of holies *before* the formal presentation of the sacrifice in order to bring out the censer. But, in the second place, it is purely inconceivable that our author should have passed over the *altar* of incense, this *essential* part of the sacred furniture, and have mentioned, instead of it, any kind of incense-vessel whatever! Tholuck, it is true, observes that Josephus, in describing the entrance of Pompey into the temple (aut. xiv. 4, 4) mentions, among the objects which Pompey saw in the holy place, merely the table, the candlestick, and *censers;* these, however, were certainly not placed upon the ground, but standing on the altar of incense, so that, from this passage of Josephus, it can in no nowise be inferred, that at the time of Pompey there was no longer any altar of incense. But granted even, that there was then, in reality, no altar of incense, still our author speaks not of the temple, least of all of the temple as it existed after the captivity, but of the tabernacle. Aaron's rod and the pot of manna were no longer in the temple, (they were not there since the time of Solomon, 1 Kings viii. 6), and yet the author does not omit to mention them!

We need, in fact, to have recourse to none of these artificial expedients. The solution is exceedingly simple. The altar of incense *stood*, indeed, in the holy place, but *referred* to the holy of holies. (So, substantially, already Mynster and Olshausen.) The smoke of the incense was not intended to spread backwards, in order to dim the light of the candlestick, or to impart an aromatic flavour to the show-bread, but was intended to penetrate into the holy of holies, as a symbol of worship and homage. Now, our author, as has already been observed, mentions all these things, not with the aim of giving a local description, but in order to show (ver. 6, s.) how the entire cultus of the tabernacle divided itself into *two parts*, which pointed to a future union and reconciliation. Regarded from this point of view, the *table of showbread and the candlestick*, the cultus of which consisted in their being symbolical of the relative covenant services of the people—belonged to the holy place; the altar of incense, however, the smoke of which referred to the God present in the holy of holies, and in which the *total result* of the *entire* cultus of the tabernacle was represented, belonged most properly to the *holiest of all*, although it stood before the entrance to it, (just as the sign-board of a shop, although outside the shop door, yet belongs not to the street, but to the shop). Nor was this a refinement first invented by the author of this epistle, for in Ex. xxx. 6, it had already been expressly said, that the altar of incense, although without the vail, was yet to stand "before the ark of the covenant," (לִפְנֵי הַכַּפֹּרֶת); nay, in 1 Kings vi. 22, this connection of the altar of incense with the holy of holies is yet more strongly expressed in the words אֲשֶׁר לַדְּבִיר הַמִּזְבֵּחַ. By what other word could the author render this לְ than by ἔχειν? We are under no necessity to understand ἔχειν in a *local* sense. Being in a place locally, the author everywhere expresses, ver. 2—4, by the preposition ἐν (ἐν ᾗ); while ἔχειν is used in a local sense just as little in ver. 1 as in ver. 4. We therefore render the words thus: "the holy of holies, *to which* the golden altar of incense belonged." The author had the less reason to shrink from this use of the ἔχειν, as he might well take it for granted that the *local* position of those vessels was familiar to *all* his readers; and, moreover, ver. 7 showed that it was not unknown to himself.

Ἐν ᾗ στάμνος χρυσῆ, &c. It will be necessary to inquire here, first, whether the pot of manna, together with Aaron's rod, really stood in the ark of the covenant, and then, why these two objects, which had no significance in respect to the cultus of the tabernacle, are here mentioned.

With regard to the first of these questions, the passages Ex. xvi. 33.; Numb. xvii. 25; and 1 Kings, viii. 9, have been strangely referred to in support of the view, that those two things had their place not *in*, but *before*, or *beside* the ark of the covenant. The two first of these passages, it is said, expressly affirm that they were placed *before* the ark; the third as expressly denies that they were placed *in* the ark. But the very opposite of this is true. In Ex. xvi. 33, it is said, quite generally, that Jehovah commanded Moses to lay up לִפְנֵי־יְהוָֹה, a pot full of manna for a memorial. Now, so much, certainly, is true, that *this expression* does not possitively affirm that the pot of manna was to be laid precisely in the ark of the covenant, for לִפְנֵי־יְהוָֹה is often used of any one who enters into the holy of holies, nay, even into the tabernacle and its fore-court; and so, when it is said of Moses, he came לִפְנֵי־יְהוָֹה, it is assuredly not meant that he went into the ark of the covenant. But neither does that expression *forbid* our associating it with the holy of holies, and the ark of the covenant. And, if the pot of manna was kept at all in the holy of holies, it must have been kept in the ark of the covenant; for, placed on the ground, it would soon have been spoiled (it is not to be forgotten that the tabernacle was daily moved from place to place), and there was no niche in the wall, as the walls consisted of hangings. Now, as the ark was the only vessel in the holy of holies, it is reasonable to suppose, that the pot of manna would have its place nowhere else than in it.

If we are led to this conclusion already, a priori from Ex. xvi. 33, it is expressly confirmed, with respect to the pot of manna, by ver. 34, and, with respect to Aaron's rod, by Num. xvii. 25. For it is said there, of both these objects, that they were laid הָעֵדֻת לִפְנֵי "before the testimony." Expositors have yet to produce a passage in which the *ark* was designated by עֵדֻת. The ark is called אֲרוֹן הָעֵדֻת or אֲרוֹן־בְּרִית; on the other hand, הָאָרוֹן

עֵדֻת is always, and everywhere, used to designate the *decalogue* or the *tables of the law*, which, as is well known, lay in the ark. If now, for example, I have a microscope standing in a press, and I were to say, I have laid some article before the microscope, no rational man would understand me to say that I had laid it upon the ground, before the press in which the microscope stands, but every one would understand that I have laid it in the press, and before the microscope there. Just so is it with the pot of manna and Aaron's rod. If they were laid before the tables of the law, then must they have been placed on the same level with these, therefore on the bottom of the ark, not on the ground before the ark. Bleek himself admits it to be possible (ii. p. 458) that Ex. xxx. 6 may have the meaning, that the altar of incense, because it was לִפְנֵי הַכַּפֹּרֶת, stood in the holy of holies, notwithstanding of its being expressly said shortly before that it stood "before the vail," and yet, he all at once repudiates the very natural interpretation of Ex. xvi. 34, that the pot of manna and Aaron's rod, because לִפְנֵי הָעֵדֻת, had their place in the ark.

We have still to look at the passage in 1 Kings viii. 9. It is here said, certainly, that "there was nothing in the ark except the two tables," but what time is it that is here spoken of? The time of Solomon! Now, that in the time of Solomon the golden pot of manna and Aaron's rod should have been lost will not seriously surprise any one. Had not the ark been long in the hands of the Philistines, and carried about from place to place? Might not the Philistines have thrown aside the seemingly worthless rod of Aaron, and taken away the more valuable pot of manna? Let us now, however, inquire finally, why then in general the circumstance is mentioned in 1 Kings viii. 9, that in Solomon's time, when the ark was brought into the temple, "*nothing* was in it save the two tables." Certainly not for the purpose of obviating any idea that there might, perhaps, be in the ark, besides these, some bowls, plates, caps, &c., &c. It is quite evident that the statement has then only a meaning when it is supposed, that there was something else besides the tables *belonging properly to the ark*, which one might justly and reasonably *expect* to find in it. Now, let any one search through the whole of the Old Testament, and he will be able to discover no other objects that could be expected in the ark besides the tables, except the pot of manna and Aaron's rod mentioned in Ex. xvi. and Num. xvii. Thus, then, the passage 1 Kings viii. 9 speaks not of what belonged to the ark in Moses' time, but of what was found in it in the time of Solomon. With an emphasis expressive of surprise, it is observed, that "the tables only were found in it," *i.e.* that the pot of manna and Aaron's rod had been lost. This very passage, therefore, contains a decided testimony, that both of these objects, so long as they yet existed, had their place in the ark of the covenant.—The second question is, why the author, *in general*, mentions these objects which, in reference to the cultus, had no special significance? In ver. 5 he says expressly, that, in so far his object was concerned, he might pass over the more particular description of the cherubim; surely then, he must have had a special reason for not passing over the pot of manna and Aaron's rod. This reason consisted, on the one hand, perhaps in this, that he wished to show how, in the innermost sanctuary, there were not merely the tables of the law but also memorials of divine miracles of mercy;[1] on the other hand, however, and chiefly, in this, that the manna which fell from heaven, and the miraculously budding almond branch of Aaron formed a contrast with the ordinary earthly products of the land which were daily and weekly brought to the holy place.

The cherubic forms mentioned in ver. 5, which (two in number) which were brought to the mercy-lid, have no independent symbolical signification. They served only the aesthetical purpose of mediating between the accusing testimony which lay beneath them, and the cloud that hovered above them, in which God at times manifested himself. Thus, below, they formed, as it were, the guardians who kept watch over the records of the law, and, above, with their wings they formed, as it were, the throne upon which the cloud of revelation moved when it appeared. Hence, as Tholuck rightly observes, God is spoken of in the Psalms now, as "he who sitteth on the cherubim;" again, "a throne of the glory of the Lord" is spoken of, *i.e.* a throne of

---

[1] Olshausen finds in the pot of manna a symbol of the heavenly spiritual bread of life, in Aaron's rod (less happily) a symbol of regeneration. Comp. on this our remarks on the words τελειοτέρας σκηνῆς infra ver. 11.

that cloud,—from which it is evident that the cloud, when it appeared, appeared over the cherubim. (The rabbinical doctrine of the "Shekinah" is fabulous only in so far as they considered this cloud to hover *permanently* over the cherubim. In opposition to this comp. 1 Kings viii. 10, but on the other side also Ex. xxv. 22; Num. vii. 89; 1 Sam. iv. 4, and 22; 2 Sam. vi. 2.) The genitive δόξης is, therefore, also (with Hammond, Deyling, Braun, Schöttgen, Michaelis, Böhme, Tholuck, Bleek, &c.), to be explained of the cloud which, indeed, is in the Old Testament frequently called הַכָּבוֹד. They are called "cherubim of glory," because they bore "the glory of the Lord." Beza, Kuinoel, Olshausen, and others, have taken δόξης as the gen. expressive of quality ("glorious cherubim"), but to what purpose would be such a predicate here, as in its vague generality would not even be parallel with the descriptive epithets *golden, overlaid with gold,* ver. 4?

Ver. 6, 7. The author, having thus noticed the construction of the tabernacle, proceeds to consider the significance and destination of its two compartments. And in ver. 6, 7, he simply notices the acts of worship which were performed in each. Ἡ πρώτη σκηνή, as at ver. 2 the holy place. Διαπαντός is explained by the antithesis ἅπαξ τοῦ ἐνιαυτοῦ, and signifies, therefore, not continually, absolutely without interruption, but without *such* interruptions as, according to ver. 7, characterised the worship in the holy of holies, which was performed only once in the year. The acts of worship in the holy place were performed, in part, daily, and, in part, weekly. Daily the high priest presented the offering of incense on the altar of incense, daily was the candlestick supplied with the oil; while the show-bread was laid out weekly. The pres. εἰσίασιν (comp. ver. 9, καιρὸς ἐνεστώς, προσφέρονται) can be explained only the supposition, that when the Epistle to the Hebrews was written, the Old Testament temple worship was still in existence, consequently, that this epistle was written before the destruction of Jerusalem. In the description of the *construction* of the sanctuary, the author, for a very intelligible reason, has not had in view the Herodian temple, but has adhered to the description given in the Pentateuch of the original sanctuary, the tabernacle; here, however, when he speaks of the acts of worship, he describes them, with equal reason, *as still continuing;* for the acts had remained the same, and also the distinction between the holy place and the holy of holies, changed only in its outward form, had been maintained unaltered in the temples of Solomon, Zerubbabel, and Herod.[1]

The high priest went *once every year* into the holy of holies. It is needlessly asked, whether the high priest, on the great day of atonement, did not enter *twice in succession* into the holy of holies. He certainly did this, as we learn, not merely from Philo, but also from Lev. xvi. 12—14, and ver. 15 ;[2] but this is not in contradiction to our passage. Our author himself indicates in the words, *for his own sins and the sins of the people*, that this act, which was done once in the year, consisted of two parts.—On ἀγνοημάτων comp. what is said at chap. v. 2.

Ver. 8—10. From the fact that the worship of the tabernacle consisted of two parts, as described in ver. 6—7, the author *infers*, in ver. 8, that the *division of the tabernacle into two parts*, as described in ver. 1—5, implied an imperfection. This inference, however, finds its link of connection and its explanation in the relative sentence ver. 9, 10. The connexion of the thought as a whole is very subtle, and can be apparent and intelligible only to those who have understood all that lies in ver. 6, 7. For ver. 6, 7 has a twofold reference. In it, first of all (as is quite evident), the section v. 1—10 on the construction of the tabernacle is brought to a close, and an inference drawn backwards from the service of the tabernacle to its construction and destination. But in this verse, also, the way is prepared, at the same time, for the idea which follows, that the Old Testament sanctuary as a whole was merely of a *relative* character. In ver. 6, 7 then, first of all, notice is taken of the difference between the (relatively) *holy place* and (absolutely) *holy of holies*, and

---

[1] Bleek infers, on the contrary, from the connection of the pres. with the words τούτων δὲ οὕτως, &c., that the author must have believed that all the things which he names were still to be found in the temple! Why does Bleek not go just a step farther, and charge the author with believing that there was as yet no temple, but that the old tabernacle was still standing.

[2] The statement of the later Maimonides, that the high priest entered into the holy of holies *four times* on that day, is of no value against the testimony of Philo.

then it is at the same time also indicated, that, just on account of this distinction, the *tabernacle as a whole* was of a merely relative character in comparison with the New Testament fulfilment. First, notice is taken of the distinction between the (relatively) holy place and the (absolutely) holy of holies. In the one place there was a daily service; this service is not more particularly described here, but its general character appears from the antithetical expression in ver. 7, *not without blood.* The service in the holy place was *without blood;* the priest brought oil and bread, never an offering of blood. No atoning act was ever performed in the holy place, but always only a representation of the occasional relative holiness or conformity to the law.

But what follows from this distinction? That the people were *relatively* holy, but regarded from an *absolute* point of view, were *unholy,* and remained so in spite of the atonement which was repeated every year. (Comp. the preceding general observations on ver. 2.) It followed therefore, in other words, from the continued existence of a holy place (a symbol of relative holiness) side by side with the holy of holies, the place of atonement, that *the atonement itself was as yet merely relative,* that the true place of atonement had not yet been opened, or that "the place of atonement had not yet been truly opened."

What is subjoined to this by means of the gen. absolute ("inasmuch as the Holy Ghost thereby showed,") is easy and intelligible. That Holy Ghost, according to whose eternal plan (comp. chap. viii. 5), the tabernacle was built, intended to indicate by the separation between the holy place and the holy of holies, a *second,* a *further* truth (besides the distinction of relative holiness and absolute atonement), namely, that *here, in the tabernacle, the absolute also was as yet relative.*

This is the idea in ver. 8. Ἅγια (comp. ver. 3), the holy of holies; the genitive is the genitive of direction (as in Matt. x. 5; LXX., 2 Sam. viii. 23.) The way into the holiest of all was not opened (literally, not yet shown, revealed[1]), the holiest

---

The author seems here to allude to the event, recorded in Matt. xxvii. 51. Otherwise, he would have said simply: μήπω ἀνεωχθῆναι τὴν τῶν ἁγίων ὁδόν. But, in the manner in which he expresses himself,

of all was still shut; consequently the access to fellowship with God still prevented, the separation still subsisting, *man not yet truly reconciled.* Why so? How does this follow from what is said in ver. 6, 7? Various conjectures have been made in reply to this, instead of attention being directed to the fact, that the idea which is presupposed as the connecting link between the major proposition and the conclusion is first expressed in ver. 9. Some have found the vis conclusionis in this, that the existence of a holy place separate from the holy of holies pointed to the distinction between priests and the laity, (but the existence of a holy of holies, as distinguished merely from the fore-court, would have pointed to the same distinction, even had there been no πρώτη σκηνή between.) Others sought the vis conclusionis in this, that a chamber which has an antechamber, cannot be said to be an open chamber! or in this, that it was not open, because the high priest alone might enter into it (but the question still recurs, whether this had any connection with the existence of a πρώτη σκηνή.) Others, again, sought the vis conclusionis in the vail which separated the holy place from the holy of holies, (but this vail is only the manifest separation itself between the two σκηναῖς; nothing, therefore, is thereby explained.) The true reason is given by the author himself in ver. 9. *The holy place is related in respect of place, just as, in respect of time, the tabernacle as a whole is related to the priestly service of Christ:* πρώτη σκηνή : ἅγια ἁγίων = [πρώτη σκηνή + ἅγια ἁγίων] : Christ.

The holy place was a symbolical representation of relative holiness, outward conformity to the law, while the holy of holies was a symbolical representation of the re-establishment of the absolute relation between the merely sinful people and the absolutely holy God. If, now, the holy of holies had been a *true* holy of holies, if it had truly answered its purpose and *truly* opened the way of access to a real and true fellowship with God, then the people had been a *truly redeemed and sanctified* people, nor would there have been any state of merely relative, outward, typical holiness which needed to *be represented* in the holy place. From the

he points to a time when an event had not yet taken place, which, again, only emblematically indicated the opening up of the way. "At that time," he says, "it had not yet been shown by God (as has now been done) that the way into the holiest of all is open."

fact, therefore, that there was still a state of typical, relative holiness to *be represented*, *i.e., that there was such a state*, the author is fully warranted in drawing the inference, that the absolute restoration of the relation to God (the place of which was the holy of holies) had not yet been *really* and *truly* attained and wrought out, but that this absolute relation to God was even in the holy of holies *only represented*, only typically shadowed forth. Or, as he expresses it in ver. 8, the entrance to the presence and fellowship of God *was not yet truly open*.

The connexion of the ideas may very simply be made evident in the following way:

| Πρώτη σκηνή | : | ἅγια ἁγίων |
| Representation of *relative* holiness. | | Representation of *absolute* perfection. |

Mere representation : New Test. fulfilment. Or: because, in the holiest of all, the restoration of the absolute relation to God was merely *represented* (for the *relative* conformity to the law still subsisted *side by side with it*, and was still the object of representation *side by side with it*, namely, in the πρώτη σκηνή), the holiest of all itself was therefore not yet of an *absolute* but of a *relative* character. As the holy place, in a local respect, stands related to the holy of holies, so does the latter stand related, in respect of time, to the fulfilment in Christ.

Let us now see whether the author has really adduced this argument in ver. 9, 10.

In ver. 9 he says plainly and pointedly, the πρώτη σκηνή is a παραβολή—(*i.e.* likeness, comp. chap. xi. 19, denoting, however, as well the figurative representation of a thing in words as in things)—a παραβολή of the present time, in which the Old Testament sacrifices are still presented. That ἥτις refers to πρώτη σκηνή should never have been doubted.[1] What the author means by the "present time" is made plain by

---

[1] Erasmus and others, among whom is Bengel, have explained the ἥτις as connected by attraction with παραβολή, so that ἥτις would stand for ὅ, τι. The existence of a πρώτη σκηνή before the holy of holies is a figure of the time when the author wrote, in so far, namely, as at that time the Israelitish theocracy, which still subsisted, formed as it were the outward space for the Christianity that had arisen in its bosom. Ingenious but artificial!

the relative clause καθ' ὃν δῶρα, &c. A, B, and D, it is true, have the reading καθ' ἥν (scil. παραβολήν), and Lachmann, Olshausen, and Bleek, give the preference to this reading. But how forced would be the idea thus obtained: "the anterior tent which was a figure of the present time, according to which figure sacrifices were brought!" In what sense was the presentation of the sacrifices performed in accordance with the figure which was represented in the πρώτη σκηνή? There were no sacrifices at all offered in the πρώτη σκηνή! Moreover, the reading ἥν would deprive the expression ὁ καιρὸς ὁ ἐνεστώς of all its clearness and definiteness; for, separated from its relative clause, this expression might denote, as well the New Testament, as the Old Testament time. We may therefore confidently suppose that the reading ἥν owes its existence to an error in the writing, or a misunderstanding. We therefore adhere to the reading καθ' ὃν, and thus get the necessary determination of the idea ὁ καιρὸς ὁ ἐνεστώς. The author might have called the time of the Old Testament temple worship also "the past," and he would doubtless have so designated it had he intended to speak from *his own* point of view, but, with practical wisdom, he here speaks from the stand-point of his readers who still joined in the temple worship, and for whom, therefore, the period of the sacrifices did not yet belong to the past. (In another antithesis ὁ αἰὼν ὁ ἐνεστώς (Gal. i. 4) is used.

Thus, then, the holy place is called a figure of the Old Testament time, the time of the imperfect sacrifices of animals which could not make man perfect κατὰ συνείδησιν. Συνείδησις is used here in the widest sense; it denotes the inner part of man, his consciousness (including certainly the conscience specially so called); and finds its best explanation in the antithesis ver. 10.

At μόνον ἐπὶ βρώμασι, &c., it is simplest to supply the words δυνάμεναι τελειῶσαι. Ἐπί c. dat. denotes (as at Acts v. 35, and in our chapter ver. 15) the object on which, or in *reference to* which, the act in question is performed.[1] Those sacrifices

[1] Grotius, Bengel, Olshausen, Bleek, De Wette, and others, give to ἐπί the signification *together with*, which it nowhere has. It signifies *in addition to this and that*, but not *together with this and that*. And what could be meant by the μόνον? "The sacrifices which could not make inwardly perfect only in addition to meats, drinks and washings"—what does that mean?

could make the man complete and perfect, only in that which concerned meat, drink, and washing; *i.e.* the purity which was thereby obtained was no other than that Levitical, that typically outward purity which was acquired and maintained by observing the laws and ordinances about meats and washings.

Hence, those δῶρά τε καὶ θυσίαι are called also δικαιώματα σαρκός (comp. what is said at ver. 1) ordinances of the flesh, of the old natural man, the ἔξω ἄνθρωπος (comp. 2 Cor. iv. 16). That the reading δικαιώματα, authorised by all the versions (only cod. D reads δικαίωμα), deserves the preference before the received reading καὶ δικαιώμασι (so Olshausen reads), is already established on external grounds. (So also Mill, Bengel, Griesbach, Tholuck, Knapp, Lachmann, Schulz. How easily may the reading δικαιώμασι have arisen from a copier mechanically and carelessly putting it in the same case with the preceding words.) On external grounds, also, the reading δικαιώματα is the more suitable; for δικσιώματα is much too general an idea to form a fourth co-ordinate class along with *meats, drinks,* and *washings.* Besides, no one knew how ἐπικείμενα was to be construed; this nom. plur. neuter must be taken as an apposition to the nom. plur. fem. μὴ δυνάμεναι! If, now, we read δικαιώματα, the simplest way will be to understand this word as in apposition to δῶρά τε καὶ θυσίαι. (It is unnecessary to take it as an anacoluthic apposition to the datives.) Ἐπικείμενα μέχρι καιροῦ διορθώσεως, the ordinances of sacrifice were enjoined until the time of a better state of things. This time forms the antithesis to καιρὸς ἐνεστώς. The expression διορθώσεως explains itself from chap. viii. 8, s.; it is the time when God had promised to make a *better* covenant.

If now we look back on the connexion of the thought in ver. 9—10, and, tracing it backwards, resolve it into its particular parts, we will find them to be as follows:—

1. In the Old Testament time sacrifices and gifts were brought which do not make the inner man perfect, righteous and holy, but produce only that Levitical purity, that state of outward conformity to the law, which is especially shown also in the observance of the laws and commandments respecting meats and washings (ver. 10.)

2. The πρώτη σκηνή with its service is a figure of this *relative*, because typical, holiness (while, in the holiest of all, the restoration of the *absolute* relation to God is represented)—(ver. 9.)

3. The fact, however, of there being such a relative holiness to represent (consequently, that the absolute is not yet in existence, but is only *typically represented* even in the holy of holies), involves the inference (ver. 8), that the true way of access to God does not yet stand open, that the holy of holies itself still belongs to the category of the relative and the typical. Thus, we find that reason in proof of the proposition in ver. 8, which we mentioned above as the right one, actually expressed and developed by the author.

But, it having thus been made out, that the holy of holies itself also was merely relative and typical, this idea leads, forthwith, to a new theme, to the comparison of the New Testament *act* of atonement with the Old Testament *acts* of atonement.

SECTION THIRD.

(Chap. ix. 11—chap. x. 18.)

THE SERVICE OF THE TABERNACLE. THE BLOOD OF THE BULLOCKS AND THE BLOOD OF CHRIST.

In this section the author, first of all, lays down the *principal theme*, ver. 11, 12, namely, that Christ has offered *his own blood*.

From this it follows 1, vers. 13, 14, that his sacrifice was of an *internal, spiritual* character; 2, vers. 15—24, a sacrifice by which the new covenant promised, chap. viii. 8, ss., was ratified; 3, ver. 25—chap. x. 10, one which needed not to be repeated. In chap. x. 11—18 all the fundamental ideas of the whole part are recapitulated.

Vers. 11, 12. By means of the particle δέ the idea in ver. 11 forms an antithesis, first of all, certainly, to the immediately preceding train of thought ver. 7 ss.,—Christ is introduced in opposition to the high priest,—but thereby, at the same time, also an antithesis to the whole preceding section, vers. 1—10. Nay this δέ points not exactly to the 7th verse, where there is no μέν to correspond with it, but to the μέν of the *first* verse which logically corresponds to it. True, the old covenant *also* had a sanctuary; but (as was shown in ver. 1—10), even the holy of holies in this sanctuary was no true holy of holies. Christ, on the contrary, as the true high priest, has entered into the true holy of holies through a better tabernacle, in order to effect a not merely relative, and typical, but an eternal redemption.

This idea forms, however, only the *transition* to the new theme. This new theme lies in the words of the 12th verse: *by his own blood;* for it is this idea which is afterwards further developed, and which forms the proper subject of the section.

Three points are contained in the period ver. 11, 12 : *a,* Christ is the *present* high priest of *existing* good things; *b,* Christ has entered *through the perfect tabernacle* into the holy of holies, and that, *c,* by *his own blood*. The two first points form the transition.

Let us consider the first. Παραγενόμενος ἀρχιερεὺς τῶν γενομένων ἀγαθῶν forms an apposition to the subject Χριστός. Critics are not, indeed, agreed upon this construction. Tholuck, Bleek, and others place παραγενόμενος in apposition to the predicate εἰσῆλθεν, and resolve παραγενόμενος εἰσῆλθεν into παρεγένετο καὶ εἰσῆλθεν : " But Christ has appeared as a high priest of . . . good things and entered, &c." Meanwhile, not to say that such an emphatic announcement is more of a modern cast than in accordance with the plain and homely style of the New Testament, even in a grammatical point of view, it is to be objected to this construction that the παραγενόμενος, would then have to stand first, and the sentence to run thus : Παραγενόμενος δὲ ὁ Χριστὸς, ὁ ἀρχιερεὺς, &c. It will therefore be better, even on this ground, to connect παραγενόμενος with ἀρχιερεύς as an adjectival attribute, and to bring this again into apposition with the subject of the sentence. Still stronger reasons than this, however, are furnished by the sentiment itself. But before we can attend to these, we must first determine the reading. The reading wavers between τῶν γενομένων ἀγαθῶν and τῶν μελλόντων ἀγαθῶν. The former reading is found in cod. B and D, in Lat. D.E., in the Peschito, the Philoxen., and in Chrysostom and Oecumenius. It is certainly also a very ancient reading, which soon gave place generally to the easier reading μελλόντων. Bleek thinks that γενομένων may have easily arisen from a mistake of the transcriber, on account of the παραγενόμενος preceding, but would such a mistake have spread through so many families of MSS. (Peschito, B, D, Philoxen)? It is far more comprehensible that the more difficult γενομένων should have been misunderstood, and the copier have confidently put μελλόντων in its stead, because, in chap. x. 1 also, "future good things" are spoken of. But in chap. x. 1 μελλόντων is suitable; here, however, it is by no means suitable. In chap. x. 1 it is said of the Old Testament that this and that were types of the New Testament good things; here, on the contrary, it is meant to be said of *Christ* that he did not, like the holy of holies in the tabernacle, point *merely typically* to a *future* salvation, but that he brought about the *fulfilment* of this salvation. Μελλόντων ἀγαθῶν as said in reference to Christ would only then be tolerable, if here (as for example at chap. vi. 5) the antithesis were between the present sufferings of the church and its future glory, or between the present faith and the future vision. But nothing of this is said, even in the remotest degree, in the passage before us. The author does not speak here (as in chap. iv. 1 and 9) of this, that it is the privilege of the Christian to *hope* also for something *future*, but he mentions in vers. 12 and 14 only such good things belonging to the Christian as *had already been*, once for all, obtained for him. In one word, he places the true high priest who has in his hand the already *secured* and *existing* good things of grace, in opposition to the Old Testament high priest who had only to fulfil the emblems and types of *future* good things. We therefore give the decided preference (with Lachmann) to the reading γενομένων, and then it will be self-evident that we must connect παραγενόμενος with ἀρχιερεύς as its adjective. The Old Testament high priest was not present as regards the salvation to which his service referred, and as little was he present in rgeard to those for whom he was to make atonement; but he performed the duties of his office—separated, in respect of place, from the people, in respect of time, from the salvation—alone in the holy of holies. Nor was he present as regards God, but represented the people only in the place where God was symbolically present. Christ, on the contrary, is, in every respect, a *present* high priest, present, as regards his Father, to whom he has entered into the true heavenly holy of holies; present, as regards his people, with whom he is always, even unto the end of the world, after having once appeared on the earth for their salvation; present, as regards the salvation, which he does not need to look for from the future.

The second idea lies in the words διὰ τῆς μείζονος καὶ τελειοτέρας σκηνῆς, &c. We have here that use of the article which might best be termed the *proleptical;* the idea is properly this: by a tabernacle which (of the two) is the better. Similarly Acts ii. 47, προσετίθει τοὺς σωζομένους, "the Lord added *such* to the church as (then and on this account) belonged to the saved." John iii. 10, σὺ εἶ ὁ διδάσκαλος τοῦ Ἰσραήλ, "thou art *one* (such a one) who stands here before us as *the* teacher of Israel." Compare also Heb. xii. 25. The import of the clause is this: Christ entered into the holy of holies by a more perfect tabernacle than that was by which the Old Testament high priests entered into the holy of holies. (By the σκηνή is, of course, to be understood *specially* the πρώτη σκηνή, as it is distinguished from the holy of holies.) In what respects that holy place by which Christ entered into the holy of holies was better than the holy place of the Mosiac tabernacle, is now shown in the words *not made with hands, that is not belonging to this creation.* In opposition to the Mosaic, typical πρώτη σκηνή is placed a real πρώτη σκηνή, which bears the same analogous relation to the Mosaic as the New Testament holy of holies into which Christ entered, bears to the Mosaic holy of holies. This πρώτη σκηνή is not described positively, but negatively, namely, as one "not made with hands, that is, not belonging to this creation." If this last clause, *that is, not belonging,* &c., were not there, one might be contented to understand this τελειοτέρα σκηνή (witn Zuingle, Bucer, Tholuck, Bleek, and the most of commentators) of the *canopy of heaven,* (the sidereal heavens) through which Christ passed into the upper heaven, into the sphere of glorified corporality, subject to no death or change.[1] But that clause which is added

---

[1] Calov, Vriemont, and others explain it most unsuitably of the *New*

renders every explanation of this kind impossible. Moreover
the parallel itself between the heavens and the Mosaic πρώτη
σκηνή would be altogether without significance or meaning. In
what would the analogy between the two σκῆναι consist? At
most it might be said, that there is an analogy in the *outward*
circumstance, that the Mosaic πρώτη σκηνή stood *locally outside*
of the Mosaic holy of holies, and the visible heavens are outside
of the heavenly holy of holies! But such frigid parallelisms are
not in accordance with our author's manner. We must rather
seek the key to the solution of ver. 11 in the profound and subtle
thoughts of ver. 8—10. It was there shown that the Mosaic
holy of holies was itself *only typical; the antithesis between the
Mosaic and the heavenly holy of holies, is essentially not so much one
of place, as rather of time and quality;* it is not the heaven viewed
as a place that makes the true holy of holies, but the heaven and
throne of God as the *scene* of the *finished* true atonement and
reconciliation of God with man. *The true and proper antithesis
between the Mosaic and the heavenly holy of holies is that between
the prophetic type of an atonement and the actual fulfilment of it.*
Now the opposition between the Mosaic πρώτη σκηνή and the
τελειοτέρα (πρώτη) σκηνή must be analogous to this. We have
here, as it were, a question in proportion to solve
(Mos. holy of holies : heavenly holy of holies. = Mos. holy place : X.)

The Mosaic holy place symbolically represented that relative,
temporary, outward, purity, conformity to the law and holiness
which was described in ver. 10. The true, moral, inward holiness
must form the antithesis to the *symbolically holy place*—the *thing
to its emblem.* Is the holy of holies into which Christ entered
not the *place* in heaven viewed as a place, but the *act* of his exaltation and the *time* of his being exalted, then will also the πρώτη
σκηνή, through which he passed into his state of exaltation, be
not a *place* but an act and a *time.* In ver. 9 the Mosaic holy
place was actually called a *figure of the time of the old covenant.*
Through that *time* in which the old covenant with its ordinances
still subsisted Christ has passed, inasmuch as he was made under

---

Testament church. But this was rather first founded by Christ's
entrance into the holy of holies. How then can he have gone thither
through it?

the law; his *act* of passing through this state, his *act* of living in a state of humiliation, *i.e.* therefore, *his perfect inward fulfilment of the law*, or his *holy life*, was the τελειοτέρα σκηνή through which he passed into his state of exaltation.[1] The *real* fact of holiness (in the life of Jesus upon earth) stands opposed to the *symbolical representation* of holiness in the Mosaic πρώτη σκηνή. All that was *emblematically represented* in the Mosaic holy place has by him been *actually accomplished*. Was the earthly showbread laid out there—he was the bread of life that came down from heaven; did the candlestick burn there with earthly oil—*he was* the light of the world. Nay, we can now, for the first time, rightly understand why the author at ver. 4 has not omitted to mention also the pot of manna and Aaron's rod. Did the pot of manna in the holy of holies point to a better bread than the earthly showbread, to a bread from heaven—Christ was this better bread from heaven. Did Aaron's rod reviving again from a state of death point to a new life out of death—Christ brought, and was, this life which arose out of death, and gave life again to dead humanity.

The third idea *not by blood* &c. does not need here a more detailed explanation, as the author himself developes it, in the form of a new theme, in the verses which follow. The following points, only, are briefly to be noticed. Side by side with the absolutely holy *life* of Christ as the passage through the τελειοτέρα πρώτη σκηνή stands the holy *death* of Christ (together with his resurrection and ascension) as the entrance into the eternal *holy of holies*. The διά is, of course, not to be taken in a *local* sense here (as if Christ had passed to the Father through his blood poured out, and then everywhere diffused, as certain old Lutheran theologians have explained); this is inadmissible, already on the ground, that in the words δι' αἵματος τράγων καὶ μόσχων the διά cannot evidently be so understood. The διά is to be understood in an *instrumental* sense. Αἷμα stands by metonyme for "death" (as the Heb. דָּם); the death of the victim was the condition, and, in so far, the means, of being permitted

---

[1] Augustin, Calvin, Beza, Grotius, Bengel, and others, *approximate* the true explanation when by the τελειοτέρα σκηνή, they understand the body of Christ.

to enter into the holy of holies.—The adverb ἐφάπαξ introduces a natural consequence of what has been said. Types must, from their nature, be ever repeated until their fulfilment. The fulfilment itself needs no repetition, just because it is the fulfilment, *i.e.*, the adequate satisfaction of the existing need. An explanation of ἐφάπαξ lies in the words αἰωνίαν λύτρωσιν εὑράμενος. Εὑράμενος is a part. aor. 2 formed after the analogy of aor. 1; an Alexandrine peculiarity of dialect which had already passed into the LXX., and had thence been imparted to the idiom of the Hellenists (Jews and Jewish Christians who spoke Greek). Εὑρίσκω in the sense of " to discover, to bring to pass," occurs also at Rom. vii. 18. Λύτρωσις signifies literally ransoming, used of a slave who has no money wherewith to redeem himself, and, for whom, therefore, another pays the ransom in his stead (hence substitution is the principal idea in λύτρωσις).

Ver. 13, 14. The third of the ideas contained in ver. 11—12, namely, that Christ has *by his own blood* opened up the true entrance to the holy of holies, is now further explained. What is said in ver. 13—14 is mainly and substantially this: *The animal sacrifices give outward purity; the moral sacrifice of Christ purifies the conscience.* These two members, however, are not simply placed antithetically to each other, but in the form of an inference a minori ad majus (εἰ—πόσῳ μᾶλλον). The form of this inference is confirmed by this, that the Levitical symbolical purity followed from the sprinkling of the blood of animals *by an internal necessity far inferior* to that with which the real cleansing of the inner man results from the sacrifice of Christ. The causal connexion between the means of purification and the purification is, in the one case, much more loose, more arbitrary, because it is symbolical, while the cleansing of the *conscience* from dead works by the sacrifice of Christ is effected by a necessity of the inmost and strongest kind.

Pass we, now, to the particular parts of the first member of the sentence. Τράγοι, goats, were offered by the high priest for the people, ταῦροι, bulls, for himself (Lev. xvi. 6—11). Besides these, also, the ashes of the (reddish) cow are mentioned (Num. xix.), by the sprinkling of which such as had contracted uncleanness by contact with dead bodies were made Levitically clean. One reason why the author particularizes this ordinance was, that it afforded a special and manifest example of the *external* character of the relation subsisting between the means and the result. A deeper reason will appear from the antithesis in ver. 14. Of Christ it is said, ver. 14, that *he cleanses the conscience from dead works to serve the living God.* The idea expressed by συνείδησις finds its explanation in ver. 9, and the remarks there made. The opposition is that between what is really experienced in the consciousness, and what is only outwardly and in the outward man symbolically pourtrayed. The inmost religious consciousness is cleansed by Christ, and that *from dead works.* Many have all at once understood by these, sinful and evil works, and have explained this, either of the cleansing from the guilt of these evil works (justification), or of the cleansing from the sins themselves (sanctification). Others, on the contrary, as Bleek, understood by the ἔργοις νεκροῖς the outward works prescribed by the Mosaic law, and by the cleansing from these works conversion to Christianity. I think that both of these explanations are too narrow and too scholastic. The idea involved in the expression comprehends these two things, first, that in the state of mind of the person to be cleansed the whole question with him is one of *works* (therefore of a righteousness of the law), and, secondly, that all those works which a man does in order to acquire merit before God are *dead* (*i.e.* not merely "outwardly and symbolically," but "inwardly dead," "not proceeding from love," and therefore "tainted with sin." By the concise expression ἔργα νεκρά is denoted, *a*, not subjective sinfulness or guilt as such, *b*, nor the objective deficiency of the ceremonial law, but, *c*, the *state of heart in general* of him who, as yet, knows no other way to righteousness than that of works, and who, therefore, as a natural unregenerate man, is able to perform only *dead* works, *i.e.* works which are viewed separately from the disposition of the heart, works each of which by itself is considered as an objectively valuable legal tender to God, while, in reality, it is not only imperfect and tainted with sin, but also, on account of its standing isolated and by itself, a dead and worthless thing. The opposite of this state of heart is that of him, who does not at all imagine that he is able to pay God or to earn a reward from God by particular works and meritorious acts, but who seeks to become righteous only through Christ—who has died for him and now lives in him and whose member he now is—and who, *thereby*, receives the power to consecrate his whole self, his whole personal *life*, to God; and to let himself be penetrated and sanctified by the spirit of Christ. This state of heart includes both justification and sanctification in their organic combination. It is denoted by the words λατρεύειν θεῷ ζῶντι. Λατρεύειν is used in the Sept. of the holy service of the priests and Levites, and denotes, therefore, in the New Testament the *priestly consecration and offering up of the whole man to the service of God*. The idea expressed by λατρεύειν is therefore quite different from that of δουλεύειν; the latter signifies δοῦλος εἶναι and denotes simply subjection, obedience, be it slavish or willing; λατρεύειν, on the contrary, the willing priestly offering of oneself to God. The expression *living God* forms a logically proper antithesis to *dead works*. The unregenerate legally righteous man *sets not God before him*, but rather the *requirements and services of the law;* his eye is not directed immediately to the living God; he does not compare himself, his whole person, with the person of the living God, he sees not his personal organic corruption in the mirror of the divine holiness; but he measures and compares himself only with the particular isolated requirements of the law, and directs his regard and attention only to his particular, falsely supposed meritorious, works, and feels perfectly satisfied if only he has performed a certain number of such *works*. The regenerate man; on the contrary gives up his own *personality* to the *person* of the living God.

It will now, moreover, be evident why the author has in ver. 13 mentioned particularly the ashes of the heifer. There, it was a (Levitically outward) cleansing that was effected from contamination caused by contact with the dead bodies *of others;* here, it is an inward and real cleansing from *one's own inner death* that takes place, and a consecration of oneself to the living God.

What that act of Christ was, by which he has rendered this inward purification possible, we are now told in the relative clause, *who through the eternal spirit offered himself without spot to God*. Instead of αἰωνίου, the reading ἁγίου is to be found in D, Copt., Basm., Vulg., Slav. and Lat. D, E, and in Chrysostom. But there is still stronger external authority for αἰωνίου in A, B,

Peschito, Philoxen., Armen., Ambrosius, Theodoret, and Theophylact; for, besides the Alexandrine and Byzantine families, there is here the oldest authority, the Peschito, against the Italian family. Besides, it is easy to understand how the reading ἁγίου may have arisen, through a gloss or correction, in place of the more difficult αἰωνίου.—But what, now, does this mean: Christ has offered himself through the eternal spirit as a spotless sacrifice to God? These words have received some very strange interpretations; Nösselt has rendered πνεῦμα by victima.; Doederlein by status beatissimus; Storr and Olshausen understand by πνεῦμα αἰώνιον the heavenly life of Christ, the holy moving principle of love in Christ; Welcker has declared the whole passage to be inexplicable, and supposed that the author did not know himself what he would say, upon which Tholuck well observes: "It is bad, indeed, when the conceit of an interpreter leads him to impute the product of his own fancy to his author." But many, also, of the most judicious critics, go too hastily to work, when (as Bleek, Tholuck, and others) they all at once explain πνεῦμα αἰώνιον as synonymous with πνεῦμα ἅγιον. Bleek thinks that the Holy Spirit has here the designation of eternal spirit, "because he imparts to him in whom he dwells an eternal imperishable existence." But in ver. 14 it is not the eternal life with God as the *result* of the sacrifice of Christ that is spoken of; it is Christ's offering himself to death that is there spoken of. Tholuck and others think that the Holy Spirit is here designated as the impelling power which constrained Christ to offer himself to the death. But surely the author must have had a reason for not saying διὰ τοῦ πνεύματος ἁγίου! We shall most safely escape the necessity of having recourse to such guesses and conjectures by explaining the words in question from their own context, *i. e.* from the antithesis to ver. 13. Let us, first of all, suppose that the adjective αἰωνίου is not there, then διὰ πνεύματος forms the simple antithesis to διὰ σαρκός. The ashes of the heifer produced the *cleansing of the flesh*, because this heifer (so is the sentence to be extended) was offered διὰ σαρκός. In this sacrificial act it was merely the σάρξ of the priest, *i. e.* the natural man, that took part. A particular disposition or state of heart, a πνεῦμα θεοῦ, was not at all necessary in order to bring that offering. Whatever the priest's internal state might be, it was enough if he outwardly performed the prescribed ceremony. Christ, on the contrary, cleanses the συνείδησις, because he has offered himself διὰ πνεύματος. He was not slain through mechanical compliance with a carnal ordinance, *i.e.* an ordinance which every natural man is capable of fulfilling, he was not struck down by any priest, stabbed with a knife and burned; that which performed the sacrificial act in him was his πνεῦμα. His making himself by his holy life an object of aversion and hatred to the sinful and obdurate rulers, his patiently bearing this hatred, his not allowing himself to swerve—through fear of the persecution which threatened him on account of this hatred— from his fidelity to the will of his father, and from the fulfilment of the work committed to him ; all this was that through which he offered himself; consequently, it was by a moral act, an act of his πνεῦμα (where πνεῦμα is to be taken in the New Testament sense, in which it denotes not the understanding, but the disposition of mind or heart). And hence, in the sacrifice of Christ, the most important element, and that in which the atoning virtue lies, is not the outward physical shedding of that substance which we call blood, but it is that *inward act* by which Christ *willingly endured* unmerited *sufferings*. For the death of Christ is a holy death, precisely in virtue of its being *pure suffering*. Christ *did nothing directly* towards his own death, he did nothing *actively to bring this about;* he did not kill himself either directly or indirectly, *he merely forbore to withdraw himself from suffering by disobedience to his Father's will*. He did not offer himself as a fanatic does who, under the influence of some illusion, lets himself be nailed to a cross—this would indeed have been to offer himself διὰ σαρκός—but he offered himself as, for example, a faithful minister of the Gospel does, who faithfully declares the truth, notwithstanding that he thereby exposes himself to suffering and persecution, or as a martyr, when he is reduced to the choice between martyrdom and denial, and will not choose denial.

But, thus far, Christ is not the only one who has offered himself *through the spirit*. When a Codrus, a Leonidas, an Arnold of Winkelreid will rather give up life than prove unfaithful to his country ; when a Socrates does not choose to ward off the threatened cup of poison by denying that measure of truth to the knowledge of which he had attained,—these are likewise offerings διὰ πνεύματος. And yet there is an immense difference between Christ and all those, and also between Christ and the Christian martyrs. *This difference the author expresses by the adjective aἰωνίου.* Others, too, have offered themselves " through the spirit," but only in the struggle for good things of a *relative* nature; the triumph or downfall of a country, a relative knowledge of the truth was at stake in their case. In Christ, it was *the absolute salvation of the world,* it was *eternity itself* that was at stake. Hence, a *relative* πνεῦμα was sufficient for those others, the spirit of patriotism, or of the love of truth, &c.; but the sacrifice of Christ could only be offered in the power of *eternal* spirit. Only the eternal spirit of *absolute* love, holiness, wisdom, and compassion was capable of enduring that sacrificial death. Because, then, Christ's giving himself up to death was a moral act, and not a moral act of relative value and significance, but the absolute moral act, the act of all acts, the angle of the world's history, the finished manifestation of the fullness of the eternal being of God in time, the absolute fulfilment of the eternal decree of God—therefore, says the author, Christ has offered himself to God, διὰ πνεύματος αἰωνίου.

And he offered himself " as one who was faultless," ἄμωμον. The animal sacrifices under the law behoved also to be faultless, and so it may be said, there lies in ἄμωμον first of all, only a *similarity* between Christ and the animal sacrifices. But the words, *he has offered himself without spot,* cannot of course be separated here from *through the eternal spirit.* Has Christ offered himself without fault through the eternal spirit, he thereby obtains another and higher faultlessness, in comparison with which those animal sacrifices were οὐκ ἄμεμπτοι. (Comp. chap. viii. 7.)

The 14th verse is, in a practical point of view, one of the most important in the whole New Testament. For, as directed against the doctrine here taught concerning the value of Christ's sacrifice, all that calumnious talk of old Rationalists and new German Catholics about a theology of blood and wounds, and a tyrannical God, who "would look only on blood," is put to a shameful silence. The main thing in the sacrifice of Christ is not the blood, this red substance—for then might the blood of the animals under the first covenant have sufficed,—as little is it "the spirit" alone, if by the spirit be understood an abstraction, a misty ideal of virtue, or freedom, or of man-deification (in which case, it is too often the mere σάρξ that falsely boasts of possessing "the spirit of Christ")—but it is that *eternal spirit* of absolute eternal holiness and eternal love which has efficaciously manifested itself in time, inasmuch as it endured the real bloody death for the sinful world.

Thus much our author says, *in general*, on the opposition between the sacrifice of Christ and the Old Testament animal sacrifices. From ver. 15, onwards, he develops particular sides of this comparison.

In Ver. 15—23 he shows how, by the atoning death of Christ, *a new* διαθήκη also has been ratified. Thus this section points back, at the same time, to chap. viii. For, there, it was said, in general, that God has promised to make a new covenant, and that by this new covenant the old must be annulled. This, too, had already been said in chap. viii., that the priestly service (λειτουργία) of Christ bears the same relation to the Levitical priestly service as the new covenant bears to the old. The author then in chap. ix. entered more at large into the consideration of the *old* covenant, and had shown how the structure (vers. 1—10) as well as the service (vers. 11—14) of the tabernacle pointed to something future and more perfect; in vers. 11—14 he has shown how, in the death of Christ, the *more perfect* λειτουργία consists; now in vers. 15—23 he shows, that by this very death of Christ, *also the (promised) more perfect* covenant has been ratified.

Διὰ τοῦτο, in ver. 15, does not point backwards to ver. 14, but forwards to the clause beginning with ὅπως (although this final clause itself certainly involves substantially a repetition of the former idea. This final clause, is, however, differently construed.) First, it must be asked, whether the words εἰς ἀπολύτρωσιν belong to θανάτου γενομένου or to λάβωσιν. The former is the more natural according to the position of the words, and has also been acknowledged as the right construction by almost all critics. But, secondly, there is the question, whether the genitive τῆς αἰωνίου κληρονομίας is dependent on ἐπαγγελίαν or on κεκλημένοι. In the latter construction (Tholuck and others) not only must a strong hyperbaton be presupposed, but also the idea which it yields ("that those who are called may receive the promise of the eternal inheritance") is not quite suitable, seeing that this promise *as a promise* had already, according to chap. viii. 8, ss., been given to the members of the old covenant. It is better, with the majority of commentators, to take that genitive as dependent on κεκλημένοι. Those who are called to the *eternal* inheritance are, accordingly, those members of the old covenant who, according to chap. iv. 1 and 9, had hitherto only attained to a *temporary rest.* Τὴν ἐπαγγελίαν denotes not the act of promising but (as at chap. x. 36; chap. xi. 13 and 39) *the promised object*, the thing promised to them. The sentiment then is this: that those who are called to the *eternal* inheritance might receive the thing promised to them (the fulfilment of the promise.)

How this was done is shown in the words θανάτου γενομένου εἰς ἀπολύτρωσιν τῶν ἐπὶ τῇ πρώτῃ διαθήκῃ παραβάσεων. According to ver. 13, s., the animal sacrifices under the old covenant had not the power to redeem the sinner from transgressions (*i.e.* from the guilt of these.) They procured for him, not righteousness before God, but that relative outward purity or conformity to the law, which itself was only an emblem and symbol of the *righteousness of God*. In order truly to redeem from sins committed under the old covenant, a *death must be undergone* (a different one of course from that of bulls and goats.)

Now the entire sentiment becomes clear. *In order that* by a death —through which, at the same time, the sins committed under the *old* covenant first found their true atonement—those members of the old covenant who are called to the eternal inheritance might be enabled to receive the thing promised to them (namely, the eternal inheritance itself): Christ must establish a *new* covenant. The internal ground of this connection of ideas is manifest. It had already been shown in chap. viii. and ix. of the old covenant, that its *priestly service* could not blot out the guilt of sin. If the old covenant still continued to subsist, then its priestly service also continued, and thus, so long as it continued, there could be no *redemption*, no possibility of at length truly entering into the long promised *inheritance.* There is here, therefore, an *inference* drawn backwards from the necessity of a new priestly service (λειτουργία) to the necessity of a new διαθήκη.

But closely connected with these principal points is the second idea of the passage before us, θανάτου γενομένου εἰς ἀπολύτρωσιν, that it was possible to accomplish this *only by an atoning sacrificial death*.

This second point is further developed in ver. 16, ss. A covenant cannot be made without death; the sinner cannot enter into a covenant with the holy God without dying; hence, also, in the making of the first covenant, substitutionary burnt-offerings must needs be brought by the Israelites who entered into covenant with God.

This passage in itself so easy—easy whenever one has patience to read to the end of it, that is to ver. 22—has by most critics been regarded as a real *crux*. Many have been led by what seems to be said in ver. 16, to suppose, that the signification *covenant* here is by no means suitable, and thus have rendered διαθήκη either, already at ver 15, by *testament* (thus completely breaking the connection between chap. viii. and ix.), or, they supposed *a play upon the word*[1] in ver. 16, as if διαθήκη meant covenant in vers. 15 and 18, and *testament* in vers. 16 and 17; in other words, they here again imputed the product of their own fancy to the author. We will show that the signification *testament* is throughout the whole passage, not only *not necessary*, but even *unsuitable*.

Already, at chap. vii. 22, we found that διαθήκη, in the sense of the Heb. בְּרִית, was a *long-established religious idea* among the Jews and Jewish Christians. It is very doubtful, on the other hand, whether the Hebrews knew anything in general of testaments (comp. the 1760 of Rau's disput. de testamenti factione Hebraeis veteribus ignota). The passage Deut. xxi. 16 affords an argument against the possibility of there having been voluntary dispositions of inheritances, and the whole Mosaic right of inheritance was, in its nature and basis, an intestate right of inheritance. The most that can be said is, that, under the influence of the Romans, testaments may have come to be used here and there among the Jews, but it is still prima facie very improbable that the author should have selected a thing so foreign

---

[1] The rendering "testament" is given to διαθήκη throughout by Chrysostom, Vulg., Luther, and the older Lutheran theologians; that of " covenant" by the most of the Greek fathers, the most of the reformed theologians, especially Grotius, then by Michaelis, Tholuck, and others; a change in the signification, or a paronomasia, is supposed by Bleek, Olshausen, and several of the more recent commentators.

and so little known, with which to compare God's highest act of atonement. Now it is, moreover, a fact, that in that passage from Jer. xxxi. 31 ss. cited in chap. viii. 8 ss., which forms the foundation of the whole of this part of the epistle, διαθήκη is the translation of the Hebrew בְּרִית. It is also a fact, that chap. ix. 15 connects closely with the ideas of chap. viii.; and, besides, that in chap. ix. 15 a mediator of the διαθήκη is spoken of, while in a testament there cannot, from the nature of the thing, be a mediator; tnere may be such, however, in a covenant which two separated parties make. From all this, so much, at least, is evident, *that so long as the signification covenant can be shown to be suitable, we are not at liberty to depart from it.*

And why should this signification not suit in ver. 16? " Where a covenant is, there must, of necessity, the death of the person making the covenant be proven." (Φέρεσθαι never signifies existere, as Schulz and Böhme would have it; it certainly signifies versari, for example, ἐν τεταραγμένοις πράγμασι φέρεσθαι, *to find one's self in decayed circumstances;* but, when it stands by itself, it never has the independent substantial signification: to exist. Quite as little does it ever signify intercedere, as Beza understood it. But either: sermone ferri, fama divulgari, *i.e.* to be generally known; or, what suits still better here, afferi coram judicious to be proven, authenticated.) Therefore: where a διαθήκη is, there must the death of the διαθέμενος be proven. What had these commentators to do but to conclude, all at once, that it is evidently a testament that is here spoken of? But is it true, after all, that a testament cannot exist until the testator is dead? Would this inference be just: *where a testament is* (!), there must the death of the testator be shown? " It would be so if the author had said: where a testament is to be *opened* or *implemented!* The signification testament therefore is not even suitable. Let us try how it goes with the signification *covenant.* "Where a covenant is, there must of necessity the death of him who makes the covenant be proven." This idea is certainly not so self-evident as that of the testament *seemed* to be on a superficial consideration of it. This idea is rather enigmatical, obscure, almost paradoxical. But should we shrink from it on this account? Was it not also paradoxical, when the author, ver. 8, from the fact that the high priest entered once every year into the holy of holies, all at once inferred, that so long as there was a holy place, the holy of holies would be inaccessible? Was it not also paradoxical, when in chap. vii. 15, from the statement that the Messianic high priesthood was to be after the order of Melchisedec, he inferred that the Messiah must proceed from the tribe of Judah? He has not failed to explain the former paradox in chap. ix. ver. 9—10, and the latter in chap. vii. 16—17. He is fond of making at once a bold leap from the major proposition to the conclusion (or, as here, from the conclusion to the major proposition), and to bring in afterwards the connecting ideas. Why should he not be allowed the same privilege here? " Where a covenant is, there the covenant-maker must be dead" —certainly an enigmatical statement; but patience only for a few verses, and the author will not fail to explain it.

In Ver. 17 he again repeats the idea.. "A covenant is valid in the case of persons who are dead, as it never has force if he who makes the covenant be alive." Again very enigmatical, and again have the commentators, without delay, had recourse to the testamenti factio. A testament *may*, indeed, be overturned or revoked so long as the testator lives. But it would be too much to affirm that a testament is *never* ($μήποτε$) valid so long as the testator lives. And so, to favour the explanation " testament" the signifiation of $μήπω$ has been actually given to $μήποτε$ here for a change!

In Ver. 18. ss. the author gives the solution of all these enigmas. "The first covenant also was not consecrated without blood," ($ἐγκαινίζειν$ not "to renew," but literally, to bring a new thing into existence, into use, hence to consecrate.) Did ever any one hear of the consecration of a testament? and does not the author speak of the first $διαθήκη$ as a thing well known? But does the expression "first testament," or "testament" in general, anywhere occur in the Old Testament? Is it not rather quite evident, that in the passage Ex. xxiv. 6—8, *to which the author here refers*, it is the consecration of a בְּרִית that is spoken of? " For, after Moses had spoken every precept to all the people according to the law, he took the blood of the calves and goats, with water and scarlet wool and hyssop, and sprinkled the book of the law itself, and all the people saying: this is the blood of the *covenant* (בְּרִית) which God hath enjoined (upon me to ratify) in relation to you. Moreover, he sprinkled likewise with blood both the tabernacle and all the vessels of the ministry. And all things are by the law purged only with blood, *and without shedding of blood is no forgiveness.*"

Three things fall to be observed here. The first is of an antiquarian character, namely, that particulars are here mentioned (as the mixing of the blood with water, the scarlet wool on the stalk of hyssop) which are not to be found in Exodus, but only in Josephus. Josephus followed in this doubtless an ancient and general tradition, and our author too might, without hesitation, follow this tradition, especially as nothing depended here on archæological exactness in the statement of the event referred to, his object being only to bring that event to the minds of his readers in the way in which it was familiar to them, and to call it up vividly before them by a picturesque description of it.

Secondly, We are here perfectly satisfied that the signification "testament" for $\delta\iota\alpha\theta\acute{\eta}\kappa\eta$ will not do. In ver. 18 $\delta\iota\alpha\theta\acute{\eta}\kappa\eta$ is to be supplied at $\dot{\eta}\ \pi\rho\acute{\omega}\tau\eta$. If $\delta\iota\alpha\theta\acute{\eta}\kappa\eta$ meant "testament," then the author would have had to shew at ver. 19 ss. *that already in Moses' time also the testator, God, was dead,* or, at least, he must have regarded these burnt-offerings mentioned in ver. 19 as sacrifices which had been slain *in place of God!*

Thirdly, what seemed obscure and paradoxical in vers. 16—17 is now fully explained. "Without shedding of blood there is *no forgiveness.*" The author, therefore, has considered that covenant sacrifice described in Ex. xxiv. 6—8 to have been one of an *expiatory, atoning* kind. Some, indeed, have thought that they knew better, and have raised the objection that that sacrifice consisted of עוֹלוֹת "burnt-offerings," and that burnt-offerings had no atoning significance. But while this may be true of the burnt-offering generally, it is not true specially of the burnt-offering used in ratifying the covenant. This could not but be evident to the native Israelite who was familiar with his Old Testament. It is chiefly apparent from Gen. i. 15, where God for the first time ratifies his covenant with Abraham. Abraham there receives the command to bring sacrifices; he offers the animals in sacrifice and falls then into a deep sleep, and while he sleeps, birds of prey come down and make for consuming the sacrifice; but now fire falls from heaven and licks up the sacrifice. Upon this it is shewn to him, that as it happened to the sacrifice so will it happen to his seed; it too will be afflicted and disquieted for a time, but will then be led into glory by God himself. Thus was that burnt-offering an emblem of *Abraham himself and his seed with whom* God made the covenant. We have here, therefore, the symbolical meaning of the burnt-offering. As the sacrificer slays the substitutionary victim and commits it wholly to the flames, so ought he to give *himself* to God as one dead to his former life. Thus the עוֹלָה was, in reality, quite as expiatory as the "sin-offering" and "guilt-offering," the only difference being this, that by these latter *only certain particular sins* were atoned for, while in the former the atonement extended to the *sinner's whole person*. How much also the element of atonement belonged to the burnt-offering appears in this, that, according to Lev. xvi. 24, on the great day of atonement a burnt-offering formed the conclusion of the services "to atone for his own sins and the sins of the people." This is perfectly evident in the case of the covenant burnt-offering. The man who will enter into a covenant with God is a sinner, and as such incapable of entering into fellowship with the holy God, nay even of appearing before God's presence (Deut. v. 26.) He must die *on account of his guilt*, if a substitutionary sacrifice be not offered for him. But he must also die to his former life, in order to begin a new life in covenant with God. In short, from a simple view of the symbolical import of the covenant-burnt-offering described in vers. 18—22, the following may be stated as the result: "Where a sinful man will enter into covenant with the holy God, the man must first die—must first atone for his guilt by a death (or he must produce a substitutionary burnt-offering.") But this is precisely the idea which the author has expressed in ver. 16 s., and which there appeared so obscure and paradoxical.

It is altogether different in the case of a *testament*. There, the testator dies and gives place to the heir. Here, it is rather the *heir*, the man that is called to the possession of the heavenly good things who must die, in order to be able, as a pardoned and purified man, to enter into the new life with God. From this it is clear, that the author could only have used the comparison of a testament, if it had been his object to represent the death of Christ on the cross as the "death of God, the testator." But this would, in the first place, have been in itself absurd; secondly, there is not the slightest trace of any such reference to the death of Christ as the testator; thirdly, the author could not then have said that, already in the time of Moses, the rule expressed in ver. 16 s., had found its application.

On all sides, then, the interpretation of the word διαθήκη by *covenant* is confirmed. The only circumstance which in ver. 16 might lead the commentators astray is, that the author there lays down the principle not in the limited form ("where any one will enter into a covenant with God,") but generally ("where a covenant is"), seeing that an atoning death is necessary, not to *every* covenant, but only when a *sinner* will enter into a covenant with *God*. But this limitation, according to which it is only religio-theocratical covenants that are here spoken of, is evident enough from the context ver. 15.

Ver. 23 now forms the conclusion. That the old covenant could not be ratified without shedding of blood, without substitutionary sacrifices, was shown in vers. 18—22. That the same law is applicable also to the new covenant, is shown in ver. 23. "It was necessary, therefore, that the symbols of the heavenly things should be purged by this (by the *goats* and *calves* mentioned in ver. 19), but the heavenly things themselves by better sacrifices than these." Those sacrifices by which the old covenant was ratified, belonged to the category described in ver. 13, of those acts by which the *conscience* was not expiated and purified. The fulfilment, the new covenant as the heavenly archetype whose symbol was the Mosaic tabernacle (for, here also, as at chap. viii. 5, there is no heavenly σκηνή placed in opposition to the Mosaic σκηνή) required for its formation and consecration, *also a death*, but a *death of a different kind*. A *death*; for here as in the old covenant man comes before God as sinful, laden with guilt, and can, in that state, enter into no covenant with God; here, as in that covenant, the past guilt must be expiated by an actual death, and the sinful life must be judicially destroyed ere a new life with God can be begun, a life in which God can manifest his love positively to men, *i.e.*, as grace; here, as in that covenant, if the man does not undergo that death himself, he needs a substitutionary sacrifice. But here he needs *another sacrifice* than in that covenant, namely, that of Christ, who, as was already shown at ver. 14—and did not need to be repeated at ver. 23—has offered himself a sacrifice, not *through the flesh*, but through the *spirit*, and through the *eternal-spirit*.

At αὐτὰ δὲ τὰ ἐπουράνια κρείττοσι θυσίαις, the verb καθαρίζεσθαι is of course grammatically to be supplied; but logically this will not be suitable, because the heavenly archetype, in virtue of its being not relative, outward, imperfect, but perfect— needs no purification. With reason, therefore, have Luther, Calvin, Beza, Grotius, Clericus, Bleek, and others, supposed that καθαρίζεσθαι is used as a kind of logical *zeugma*, and that merely the idea of ἐγκαινίζεσθαι is to be taken from καθαρίζεσθαι, and supplied at the second member. For, in the new covenant, the act of redemption does not need a purification, but only the men who are to be redeemed.

Thus that second idea contained in ver. 15 : *that the new covenant could be made only by an atoning death* has, in ver. 16—23, been fully proven. Ver. 16, 17: He who will enter into a covenant with God must first atone for his sins by a death (by his own or that of a substitutionary sacrifice.) Ver. 18—22: Hence it was necessary that the covenant of Moses should be consecrated by atoning sacrifices. Ver. 23: In like manner, also, the new covenant,—only, that here a better sacrifice was necessary (the death of Christ διὰ πνεύματος.)

Ver. 24 forms *the transition to the next train of thought*. First of all ver. 24 is connected with ver. 23 by γάρ, as explanatory of the antithesis between the *symbols* and the *heavenly things themselves*. Christ has not entered into an earthly tabernacle, but into heaven (comp. on this what has been said at chap. i. 3); from this it is evident, that it was not a symbolical purging of outward figures that he had to do with, but the initiation and confirmation of a new relation between God and man. With this idea, however, the author connects a new theme by one of those easy turns which are peculiar to the Epistle to the Hebrews (comp. i. 4, ii. 5, iii. 2, &c.)

In Ver. 25—28 is shown how, from the fact that Christ offered *his own blood*, it follows that the sacrifice of Christ was made *only once*; and with this, that other sacrifices besides that of Christ are superfluous. *In this the author draws a third inference from the old principal theme at ver.* 12. He had laid down at ver. 12, as principal theme of the section, the proposition *that Christ offered his own blood.* In ver. 13, 14, he had drawn *a first inference* from this, namely, the internal and spiritual nature of Christ's sacrifice. In ver. 15—23 is a *second inference:* that through Christ's self-sacrifice, that long promised new covenant mentioned in chap. viii. 8 ss. had been founded. In ver. 25 he now brings in a *third inference,* that of the *once offering of Christ's sacrifice,* which likewise follows from the proposition, that Christ entered into the presence of the Father, not with the blood *of another,* but with *his own* blood.

"He entered, not that he might offer *frequently* as the high priest who entered yearly into the holy of holies with the *blood of another.*" The main emphasis lies evidently on the words ἐν αἵματι ἀλλοτρίῳ; hence they are placed after (just as, at chap. vii. 4, ὁ πατριάρχης is placed at the end of the sentence.) The reason why the high priest had to offer frequently was, that he offered another's blood. Thus the idea is easily extended: the reason why Christ did *not* offer *frequently* was, that he did *not* offer *another's blood.*

And it is this that is now proven in ver. 26. This verse is not intended to prove, that Christ has offered himself only once (for then it would be mere reasoning in a circle, thus: Christ has offered himself only once. For otherwise he must have offered himself repeatedly. But he has not offered himself repeatedly, ergo, &c.) In ver. 26 it is rather intended to be proven, that Christ *needed* not to offer himself repeatedly, *because* he has offered *himself.* How, from his having offered *his own* blood, the *once offering* of his sacrifice follows—it is this which is to be proven in ver. 26.—The words ἐπεὶ—κόσμου are not a parenthesis (Mill, De Wette, &c.), but belong to the substance of the reasoning; "for, otherwise (if he had not offered *his own* blood), he must often have suffered from the foundation of the world onwards." We should rather have expected: "then he must often have offered sacrifice." That the sacrificial act is here denoted by suffering is logically inaccurate, as, on the supposition that Christ had *not* offered his own blood but *another's,* his sacrifice would not then have consisted of *suffering.* The author has therefore put $\pi a\theta \epsilon \hat{\iota} \nu$ here, unconsciously, because he was *in the habit* of using $\pi a\theta \epsilon \hat{\iota} \nu$ and $\pi\rho o\sigma\phi \epsilon\rho\epsilon\iota\nu$ promiscuously of Christ. The reason why Christ, if he had offered another's blood, must have done this repeatedly—as the Levitical high priest: from of old ever and ever again—lies in what is said at ver. 13.—" But now he has appeared once in the end of the time (*i.e.* in the time of the fulfilment, the Messianic time, in opposition to the time of expectation and prophecy, comp. i. 2 and 1 Pet. i. 20), to take away sin by his own sacrifice." As the sacrifice of Christ was not a *typical* sacrifice, but the *fulfilment itself* (for the time of the Messiah *was to be* the $\sigma\upsilon\nu\tau\epsilon\lambda\epsilon\iota a$ $\tau\hat{\eta}s$ $a\iota\hat{\omega}\nu os$, the final fulfilment), it needs not to be repeated.

In Ver. 26, then, from the fact that Christ has offered his own blood, it is inferred, that he *needed* not to repeat this sacrifice; in ver. 27, 28, it is inferred from the same thing, that he *could* not repeat it. A man can offer the blood of another repeatedly, *his own blood he can offer*—in other words, *die—only once.* This is the main point in ver. 27, 28. " As it is appointed to every man once to die, so was Christ also once offered for our sins." With this principal idea, however, is entwined a subordinate idea which has no close connexion with the argument, but is added only parenthetically, namely, that, after death, the *judicari* awaits the rest of men, but the *judicare* awaits Christ.—The expression *without sin* is explained by the antithesis, *to bear the sins of many.* Irving, therefore, had no reason to infer from the *without sin* that Christ, at his first coming in humiliation, was not without sin but partook of the sinful $\epsilon\pi\iota\theta\upsilon\mu\iota a$. It is rather only the first coming *to bear the sins of others*, *i.e.* the guilt of sin, that is here opposed to the second appearing *without sin*. When he comes again *he has no more to do with sin;* he comes then not as the bearer of others' guilt, but as the holy judge of others' guilt, as a consuming fire, which stands in a hostile and negative relation to all that is called sin.

In Chap. x. 1—4 the author recurs to what is said in chap. ix. 13, 14, in order to deduce from it also, that the sacrifice of Christ was offered *only once.* Thus vers. 1—3 contains an explanation of ver. 26 of the foregoing chapter.—The subject of ver. 1 is $\acute{o}$ $\nu\acute{o}\mu os$; this subject has however the appositional clause $\sigma\kappa\iota\grave{a}\nu$

ἔχων τῶν μελλόντων ἀγαθῶν, οὐκ αὐτὴν τὴν εἰκόνα τῶν πραγμάτων. Εἰκών does not signify precisely "substance" (Luther, Peschito) much less does it denote the "mere image" in opposition to the "thing" (Oecumenius, Gregory of Nazianzum, Calvin, Tholuck), as if it were meant to be said that the law is the shadow of the gospel, the gospel itself again, however, only an image of the *good things to come;* εἰκών denotes here simply the *form* in opposition to the mere *shadow*. The genitive τῶν πραγμάτων is genitive of the substance. The form of the things themselves = the form, namely, the things themselves. The whole of this apposition is designed to show, how far it was possible and allowable to speak unfavourably of the Old Testament, and that this was done not from contempt of the Old Testament, but because, according to its divine destination, it was to be, and must be, imperfect. Comp. the remarks on chap. iv. 2, and especially the passages chap. vii. 18; viii. 7 ss.

What now is affirmed of this νόμος? It was not able, year by year, with the same sacrifices which were continually offered, to make the comers thereunto perfect. Κατ᾽ ἐνιαυτόν belongs of course to the verb. Year by year (the author here in the word θυσίαις has evidently in his mind chiefly the yearly sacrifice of atonement) the *law* remained incapable of making the comers thereunto perfect by its sacrifices, how uninterruptedly soever these also were offered. (Lachmann and Paulus join εἰς τὸ διηνεκές with τελειῶσαι; but then the remaining part of the relative clause becomes meaningless. Besides, the author says in ver. 3 also, not merely that those sacrifices were not able *permanently* to make perfect, but that they effected *no* atonement *whatever*, that they rather only pointed to the need of such an atonement.) Instead of δύναται A, C, many versions and the Peschito (here, however, giving generally a free translation) read δύνανται. Then σκιὰν γὰρ ἔχων ὁ νόμος must either be an independent clause with the partic. pro verbo finito, which, however, is altogether foreign to the style of our author. Or, we must suppose an anacolauthon; the author began the sentence with ὁ νόμος and intended originally to write δύναται; in writing, however, he inverted the idea, and made the subject of the relative clause also the subject of the principal clause. But it is far more probable that some transcriber is to be charged with this carelessness than our author, who usually writes so correctly.

In Ver. 2 the reading wavers between ἐπεὶ οὐκ ἄν and ἐπεὶ ἄν ; οὐκ is, however, already externally better attested (by A, C, D, E, Copt., Arab., Ital. Also a reading ἐπεὶ κἄν is explicable only from the matrix *ΕΠΕΙΟΥΚΑΝ*.) It is, besides, easy to see how transcribers might come to omit the οὐκ. The whole sentence (with οὐκ) has meaning only when taken as a *question* ("would they not then have ceased to be offered? as the worshippers once purged would have had no more consciousness of sin.") But if a transcriber overlooked this, and read the sentence as a thetical proposition, he must then, certainly, have held it necessary to cancel the οὐκ.—The idea is easily understood. The Old Testament sacrifices did *not* take away the *consciousness of sin*, but only *brought to remembrance* (ver. 3) year by year the *presence* of sin and guilt, and, therewith, the (continual, still unsatisfied) need of a real propitiation.

That the Old Testament sacrifices could not really atone for sin is, in ver. 2, inferred from the fact of their repetition; it would have been a meaningless ordinance if God had enjoined the repetition of a sacrifice which had already, the first time it was offered, really taken away the guilt of sin from man or from Israel. In ver. 4 the same thing, namely, the inefficacy of the Old Testament sacrifices to make real atonement is inferred from the very nature of these sacrifices. The blood of irrational animals cannot possibly take away moral guilt. (Comp. chap. ix. 14.) There is wanting in these, the two things which are necessary to a true substitution. A sacrifice which shall truly take upon itself the punishment of another's guilt must, firstly, be able to bear the *same* sufferings as ought to have been borne by the guilty person, therefore, not a *merely* bodily pain or death, but an inward suffering of the man endowed with a rational soul. A true sacrifice must, secondly, after having as a substitute endured the suffering, be able to remove again the element of substitution, *i.e.*, to place itself in a relation of internal oneness with the party represented; it is thus that the merit of Christ's suffering is appropriated by us, inasmuch as, although we stood *beside* him as other and different persons when he suffered (so that he did all that was necessary for us *without* our assistance and co-operation), we now no longer *continue* to stand *beside* him, but, by his spirit on his part, and by faith on ours, become *members* of him, to whom all now really belongs that belongs to him. For we become righteous, not as *individuals*, the descendants of the first Adam, but as those who by faith have given up themselves, who have given themselves to the death, and are now willing to have any merit before God only in so far as before *belong to Christ* and he belongs to. Both these conditions were impossible in the animal sacrifices.

Vers. 5—10. The writer in these verses shows, that *already also in the Old Testament itself*, there are intimations of the necessity of another, a better sacrifice than that of animals. In the citation from Ps. xl. 7—9 the author follows the Sept. As the Sept., however, deviates from the original, the question arises whether it has at least rendered substantially the sense of the passage.—After enumerating the wonderful and gracious acts of God, the Psalmist says: "Sacrifice and offering thou hast not desired; אָזְנַיִם כָּרִיתָ לִּי; burnt-offering and sin-offerings thou hast not required." He evidently in these words "אָזְנַיִם intends to place in opposition to the external sacrifices one of an internal and better kind, and some sacrifice or other of this kind must at least implicitly be designated by those words, "mine ears hast thou digged out." The older commentators, as also Olshausen, referred this digging of the ears in general to that *boring through the lap of the ear* of which we read in Ex. xxi. 6. When, namely, a servant had it in his power to become free, but preferred of his own accord to continue for the rest of his life in the service of the master with whom he had hitherto been, he was, in token of this, to let (רָצַע) his ear (the lap of the ear) be bored through by his master. The majority of the more recent commentators (Hengstenberg, Stier, Hitzig, Tholuck, Bleek), on the other hand, take כרה in the sense of גלה. To say that God has "digged out the ears" of a man, is equivalent to saying that he has *given* him ears, *made* ears for him." The creation or formation of an ear in the head is figuratively denoted as the digging out of an ear. And, indeed, the verb כרה (used generally of the digging of a well, a pit, and the like) would suit this representation. The meaning then would be: "Thou willest not sacrifice, but thou hast given me an ear, a capacity to hear thy commands, and thus hast pointed out what sacrifices are acceptable to thee." Meanwhile, I am doubtful after all whether the author has not had in his mind that command in Ex. xxi. 6 ; the boring through the lap of the ear might poetically be denoted as *a digging* through it, and then the sentiment: " I have let my ear be bored through by thee, *i.e.* I have freely given myself to be thy servant for the whole of my life," forms, certainly, a finer and fuller antithesis to the words: " burnt-offering, &c. thou willest not," than that somewhat vague idea: " thou hast made ears for me." But, be this as it may, one thing evidently lies in the words—the Psalmist places *obedience*, as the true sacrifice, in opposition to the animal sacrifices.

The reading in the Sept., according to Bleek's opinion, was originally ὦτα or ὤτια ; σῶμα is said to have first slipped in as a different reading, because the expression ὦτα δὲ κατηρτίσω μοι was not understood. But the oldest authorities for the reading ὦτα reach only to the time of Irenaeus, while Bleek himself must acknowledge that our author read σῶμα in his copy of the Sept. Indeed, it is much easier to understand how, if the free translation σῶμα were the original one, the reading ὦτα might arise at a later period, in the time of Origen, from aiming at conformity with the Hebrew text, than that, vice versa, from an original reading ὦτα the reading σῶμα should have arisen. We consider, therefore, the reading σῶμα δὲ κατηρτίσω μοι as the genuine reading of the Sept. The Septuagint translator might easily take the expression as it stood to be unintelligible, and substitute for it the more general idea: " thou hast prepared my body (myself) for sacrifice." The meaning remains substantially the same: "thou wilt not have animals for sacrifices, but myself." But Bleek is certainly in error when he thinks, that our author cites the entire passage on account of this word σῶμα (in the opinion that this points prophetically to the bodily death of Christ). We have seen at chap. ix. 14 that our author does *not* lay the principal emphasis on the bodily side of the sufferings of Christ; his aim is rather precisely to show, that with the blood, *qua* blood, nothing has as yet been accomplished. And indeed, at ver. 9, where he makes use of and applies the citation

Ps. xl. 7—9, he entirely drops the words σῶμα, &c. and lays all the emphasis on the words ἥκω τοῦ ποιῆσαι τὸ θέλημά σου.

The eighth verse of the psalm begins with the emphatic words אָז אָמַרְתִּי "then I spake." What follows, are the words which the Psalmist spake. "Lo, I am come" (הִנֵּה בָאתִי), not "Lo, I come" (הִנְנִי בָא); in the roll of the book it is written of me; to do thy will, my God, is my delight!" That the author omits the verb ἐβουλήθην, so that now τοῦ ποιῆσαι is dependent on ἥκω and the words ἐν κεφαλίδι &c. become parenthetical, is, as respects the sense, quite an inconsiderable deviation. More important is the question, how the words ἐν κεφαλίδι are to be explained. Hitzig, Ewald, Bleek, and others, render in the Hebrew the preposition בּ *with*, the preposition עַל *for* ("I come with the roll of the book which is written for me"). This idea would not only be unpoetical but ridiculous. The Sept. has certainly given a more correct rendering: "I come; in the roll of the book it is written of me;" although, instead of ἥκω it would be more correct to say ἐλήλυθα "I am come." The simplest explanation certainly is this, that the psalm, as the superscription says, is one of David's; only, that it was written not *after* the prophecy of Nathan pointing to the future, 2 Sam. vii., but *before* it, nay before David's ascent to the throne, but after his anointing by Samuel—during his persecution by Saul (with Ps. xl. 2—4 compare ver. 14—18). David could and must at that time have combined the old patriarchial blessing that the Prince over Israel should come out of Judah with the fact, that God had rejected Saul and chosen him; in him was the old prophecy fufilled. "Lo, I am come," he says, "in the book (Pentateuch) it is written of me" = in me is that prophecy fulfilled. And now he declares that, as opposed to *Saul*, it is *his* delight to do the will of the Lord. In this way of obedience towards God he hopes to fulfil that prophecy.

But David as an individual did not carry out the full import of this his promise; he did not wholly and purely offer his person as a sacrifice to God in unbroken obedience, but sinned grievously and in many ways. Hence the patriarchial blessing found in him only a preliminary, not a final fulfilment, as, indeed, this was afterwards (2 Sam. vii.) revealed to David himself, and was acknowledged by himself (Ps. ii. and cx.) That, however, which David did typically and imperfectly, the second David was to do perfectly. But that passage in the Psalms remained true, although it did not come to be absolute truth in the individual David. This individual spake, however, even there not from himself, not from his own sinful humanity or from chance, but from his office, and from the idea of the theocratical King, and therefore under the guidance of the Holy-Ghost. Hence it is not the individual David that is the true author of those words of the psalm, but the true heavenly Anointed made use of David as an organ, in order to express a truth which applies in its fulness not to the first but only to the second David. Hence our author has sufficient reason for saying: the Son of God, when he entered into the world to become man, spake these words. That Jesus was not the author of the 40th Psalm, the author knew as well as we. As little does he indicate that he regarded the psalm as a direct prophecy of David concerning Christ (Ps. ii. and cx. were such direct prophecies); but his meaning evidently is, that in David the Son of God spake by his Spirit. The psalm was not a direct word-prophecy pointing to Christ, but the Psalmist David was a fact-prophecy pointing to the second David, and what David promised in order to fulfil it imperfectly, that has Christ promised by David in order to keep it perfectly.

If now, according to Ps. xl., it belongs to the theocratical Anointed that he regards not animal sacrifices but the sacrifice of obedience as suitable to him, this expresses just what our author had laid down in ver. 1—4.

Ver. 8—9. The author here simply shows, that obedience was put *in the place* of the animal sacrifices, and thereby, also, declared to be *a sacrifice* and, indeed, the true sacrifice.

At περὶ ἁμαρτίας, ver. 6 and 8, θυσίαι is to be supplied. There was no Greek noun for " sin-offering ;" the idea must be rendered by the circumlocution : (θυσία) περὶ ἁμαρτίας.

Ver. 10. By the θέλημα here, as at ver. 9, we may understand either the *special* will of the Father, that Christ should suffer and make atonement for the world, or, the *general* will of God, as, for example, it is expressed in the decalogue. Either : Christ came to fulfil that special decree of redemption, and in this will (*i.e.* by the fulfilment of it on the part of Christ) we are sanctified. Or : Christ came in general to live conformably to the will and law of God, *i.e.* to live a holy life, and through this will of God (fulfilled by Christ, *i.e.* : by the fulfilment of this will on the part of Christ) we are sanctified. But, as ver. 9 belongs to the citation from the psalm, in which there was no mention of the special decree respecting the *suffering* of the Messiah, the second explanation is preferable. (That the fulfilment of the general will of God already involved the accomplishment of the special decree is, of course, self-evident. If Jesus was obedient to the Father *in general*, he was so also in that special point.)

Ἡγιασμένοι here in the widest sense " to make ἅγιοι," to take them from the profane world sunk in death, and to place them in the kingdom of God. Thus ἁγιάζειν here involves both justification and sanctification ; that the former is not excluded appears already from the additional clause διὰ τῆς προσφορᾶς, &c.

Ver. 11—18. The author here again sums up with all precision the proper quod erat demonstrandum (ver. 12—13), and, inasmuch as he represents the one sacrifice as, at the same time, the fulfilment of the promise of a new covenant (Jer. xxxi. 32 ss.) cited in chap. viii. 8 ss., he derives from this still another and concluding proof of the *once offering* of this sacrifice, and therewith of the *superfluousness and dispensableness of the Levitical ritual* beside this one sacrifice.

Ver. 11. The καί is not to be rendered "namely" (Tholuck), a signification which it never can have, and, moreover, cannot have here, as ver. 11 stands related to the foregoing not as an argument but as an inference. It means " and," " and so."— Instead of ἱερεύς A.C., Peschito, and several Fathers read ἀρχιερεύς (so also Grotius, Limborch, Lachmann, Bleek). But it is not likely that a transcriber should have changed an original ἀρχιερεύς by way of correction into ἱερεύς, on the ground that the high priest performed no daily service ; in chap. vii. 27 mention is even made of the daily sacrifice of the high priest, and yet no transcriber has thought of substituting ἱερεύς for ἀρχιερεύς there by way of correction. It is much more probable, that in order to bring our passage into conformity with that, an original ἱερεύς was changed into ἀρχιερεύς. (Especially might a *translator*, as that of the Peschito, be easily led to do so.) Internal grounds are also in favour of the reading ἱερεύς. Bleek, indeed, thinks "the treatise of the writer is entirely occupied with the comparison between the high priest of the new covenant and that of the old ;" we have seen, however, that only the third part chap. v. 7 is taken up with this. There, at chap. vii. 27, it was quite in order to speak specially of the high priest as the highest representative of the Levitical priesthood, in opposition to the Messiah, the high priest after the order of Melchisedec. Now, however, when the author has already spoken in particular of the ritual of the old covenant and of all its parts—the ministration of the priests, ix. 6, and high priests, ix. 6—the sacrifice of atonement, ix. 7, and the oblations of the holy place ix. 6—the covenant-burnt-offering, ix. 19 ss. and the various meat and sin-offerings, x. 6 and 8—it was more suitable to speak of the Levitical " priest" quite generally. Especially is the attribute πᾶς agreeable to the reading ἱερεύς. The author places the single offering of the individual Christ in opposition to all priests with all their different sacrifices.

Ver. 11. Here the idea is recapitulated which was developed in chap. ix. 13—14 and 25 ; chap. x. 1—4 ;—in ver. 12 the principal idea of chap. ix. 25—28 is recapitulated in the words μίαν ὑπὲρ, &c., and the idea of chap. ix. 24 (compare i. 3) in the words εἰς τὸ διηνεκὲς ἐκάθισεν, &c. On δεξιὰ θεοῦ compare what is said on chap. i. 3. By the mention of the second coming of Christ in judgment ver. 13 (recapitulation of chap. ix. 28), the author prepares the way for the sentiments of a hortatory kind from ver. 19 ss., to the effect that now the choice lies before them between salvation and destruction. (On ver. 13 comp. Ps. ii. and chap. ii. 8 s.)—In ver. 13 the *inferences* are recapitulated, in ver. 14 the *reason ;* in ver. 14, namely, he expresses once more the *central idea* of this whole part. Ἁγιαζόμενος is used in the same wide sense as ἡγιασμένος, ver. 10.

Ver 15—18. In these verses he infers yet again, and finally, the *once offering of the sacrifice of Christ*—laid down in ver. 14, and already proven in chap. 9—10—from the passage Jer. xxxi., and thereby brings together the ideas of the three portions, chap. viii. 8—13; chap. ix. 15—23; chap. ix. 25—28. God has promised *a new covenant,* in which he will write the law on men's hearts by the forgiveness of sins (chap. viii. 8, ss.) ; this new covenant is ratified, this forgiveness wrought out, by the sacrifice of Christ (chap. ix. 15 ss.); but where this forgiveness is, there there is no need of a repeated sacrifice (chap. ix. 25 ss.) The first of these ideas is repeated in vers. 15—17, and, with it mention is made of the second; the third is stated in ver. 18. Thus does the conclusion of this fourth principal part unite itself again with the beginning of chap. viii.

Thus has the writer reached the *innermost kernel of the Christian doctrine*. Immediately from the *consciousness of the forgiveness of sin on account of Christ's sacrifice*—the point in which the subjective consciousness harmonizes with the objective fact of the restored relation to God—he infers in ver. 18 the superfluousness of those symbolical sacrifices which had only a subjective value, and could awaken only the subjective knowledge of the *need* of an atonement (comp. ver. 3.) (This is entirely the fundamental idea of the Pauline system.) Let us now look back from this the highest point in the argumentation, to the way by which we have been conducted to it. In all the principal parts and particular sections, the author begins with the most outward and apparently accidental points of comparison and differences which offer themselves to view between the Messiah and the angels, the Messiah and Moses, the Messiah and the high priest (for example, that God calls none of the angels his son; that Moses was a servant, the Messiah the son of the house; that Melchisedec's descent is left unknown, &c.) But he everywhere shows how, in these apparently accidental things, essential relations lying deep beneath them are expressed; he follows out these relations, and reaches more universal points of comparison; it is as if one were to follow brooks which lead him to rivers, and in the end to a wide stream. The Messiah must be *the perfect messenger of God to men*, because in him the holiness of God and not merely his omnipotence are manifest, because in him the Godhead is to *become* man and humanity is to be raised to union with God. The Messiah must be *the perfect representative of men before God*, because he is to be the Son of God himself, not merely a servant, and is truly to conduct man to his true rest. The Messiah must be *a high priest, and indeed the promised, true, eternal high priest after the order of Melchisedec*, who represents man eternally and without change before God. This discovers itself *in the manner of his priestly ministration;* the sacrifice which he offered is a spiritual, moral, and therefore more than a symbolical sacrifice; it is the fulfilment of the typical things of which the tabernacle consisted, and of the typical actions of which the service of the tabernacle consisted. Thus the author comes to the *doctrine of the atonement*, and, with this, to that of the appropriation of the atonement which he handles in the concluding part.

PART FIFTH.

(Chap. x. 19—xiii. 25.)

THE LAYING HOLD ON THE NEW TESTAMENT SALVATION.

That portion of the epistle which consists of speculative reasoning has now reached its conclusion. What the author has now further to say, is intended not so much to be comprehended, as rather to be apprehended. The innermost experience of the innermost life is the *cognoscens*. To lay hold on the salvation is not an act of the head and the understanding, but the *most intensive act of the life*,—that act in which the man has the courage to declare himself bankrupt. Hence the author, from this place onwards, no longer reasons, but addresses himself to the heart and the will of his readers.

Seven lines of thought or sections can without difficulty be distinguished in this part.

1. In chap. ix. 15—25 the author lays down the proper theme of the admonition, that *to which* he admonishes.

2. In chap. ix. 26—31 he enforces this admonition by a *first* motive, namely, by calling to mind the *greatness of the danger of falling away*, and the *fearful consequences of this*.

3. In chap. x. 32, xi. 1, he adduces a *second motive*, inasmuch as he reminds the readers of *their former faith*.

4. In chap. xi. 2, xii. 3, a *third motive*, inasmuch as the author shows how all the illustrious and celebrated achievements, even under the *old covenant*, proceeded solely from this principle of *faith*.

5. In chap. xii. 4—17 a *fourth motive*, inasmuch as the writer

shows that the very thing which now terrifies his readers, *the suffering that threatens them*, brings only *blessing*.

6. In chap. xii. 18—29 a *fifth motive*. The choice between Christianity and Judaism is simply identical with that *between salvation and condemnation*.

7. Chap. xiii. forms the conclusion, containing special exhortations and references of a personal kind.

SECTION FIRST.

(Chap. x. 19—25.)

THEME OF THE EXHORTATION.

Ver. 19—25. In a long and finely constructed period, the author developes the particular points in the practical application of what has been now theoretically proven. The particle οὖν is used in the cónclusive sense. The admonition, ver. 19—25, flows as an inference from the result of the whole previous reasoning, recapitulated and concentrated in ver. 11—18. The words ἔχοντες ... πονηρᾶς form the *first member of the exhortation*. The apposition ἔχοντες παῤῥησίαν, &c., belonging to the latent subject, forms, logically considered, a kind of protasis to the verb προσερχώμεθα (as we have boldness, &c., so let us, &c.) Let us look first of all at this protasis.

Two objects depend on ἔχοντες. First, we have joyful confidence for the access into the holiest of all in the blood of Jesus. The words ἐν τῷ αἵματι Ἰησοῦ may, grammatically, be referred to the verbal idea lying in the noun εἴσοδος (Storr, Klee, Paulus, Olshausen, Bleek), according to the analogy of the passage ix. 25. Others (many of the older expositors) make ἐν τῷ αἵματι, &c., dependent on ἔχοντες; in which case, however, the determining idea expressed in ἐν τῷ αἵματι can, according to the sense and the position of the words, belong only to the first member: ἔχοντες παῤῥησίαν, and not also to the second: καὶ (ἔχοντες) ἱερέα. The meaning in both constructions remains substantially the same. Still the latter construction, as will immediately appear, yields a finer sense. Ἐν is not to be explained as a Hebraism, and taken in an instrumental sense, but in its own proper signification "in." The style of conception and expression, as a whole, is figurative, borrowed from the Old Testament ritual of the atonement festival. In that festival the high priest must have died, if he had entered into the presence of God in the holiest of all without the sacrifice of blood; only when sprinkled with the blood, and thus as it were covered with it, could he dare to enter in, and even then only with fear and trembling, and no one durst follow him. We, on the contrary, because covered with the *blood of Christ* (ἐν αἵματι therefore at ἔχοντες) have *all of us* full joyful confidence to enter into the, not figurative but, real holiest of all, *i.e.* to the opened paternal heart of God, after our high priest who has gone before us on this way, a way which is everlastingly fresh and living. Ἐγκαινίζειν, as at ix. 18 in the signification "to consecrate," "to bring into use for the first time." This *entrance which he has consecrated for us* is called a ὁδὸς πρόσφατος. This word is formed from the rad. inus. ΦΑΩ, and signifies literally "fresh slaughtered," then "new," "fresh." (So also Olshausen.) The signification "bloody" (Tholuck) belongs to it here just as little as elsewhere; nor would this signification be even suitable here, as then there would be no difference in this respect between the new covenant and the old, seeing that the Levitical high priest also might not enter into the holiest of all "without blood" (chap. ix. 7.) Πρόσφατος rather signifies "fresh," which, however, is not the same as *new*, novus, καινός, as if it were intended to designate the way opened up by Christ as a new, a later, in opposition to the Old Testament way; nor is it equivalent to *recens*, in the sense of this way being *now* as yet new, but one which would afterwards become old and obsolete; the idea is precisely the reverse, namely, that while the Old Testament atonement festivals were effectual only for a year, the entrance to God opened up by Christ is still always *new and fresh*, notwithstanding the decades that have since elapsed, consequently, that in general, it *remains everlastingly fresh*.— That way, however, is called ζῶσα in opposition to the way by which the Levitical high priest had to pass to the holiest of all, which was an earthly local way, a *place* of dead earth or stones which the feet trod, while the way to God upon which Christ has gone before us, and by which we must follow him, consists for him and for us in a *living act*; (others, as for example Olshausen, explain ζῶσα = ζωοποιοῦσα, which is contrary to the usage as well as to the context.)

Christ has gone this way before us *through the vail*,[1]—an evident allusion to the fact that, at the death of Christ, the vail was rent in twain, and the holiest of all laid open (Matth. xxvii. 51, comp. also our remarks on πεφανερῶσθαι, chap. ix. 8.) Still, it is not to be thought that Christ entered to the Father through that vail of the Old Testament sanctuary which was then rent, for the author adds the explanatory words : *that is to say his flesh.* By this is, of course, not meant that the body of Christ was that which had separated us from God (Schulz and others) ; but that the *fact* of the violent killing of the body of Christ corresponded to the *symbolical* fact of the rending of the symbolical vail. Throughout, then, we find that what corresponds to the local earthly σκηνή is not a σκηνή in heaven *in like manner local*, but that *acts* and *relations* correspond to the *localities* ; the act of the spiritual entrance to the paternal heart of God corresponds to the local entrance into the holiest of all, the internal blotting out of guilt through the atoning death of Christ corresponds to the local rending of the vail.

The second object belonging to ἔχοντες, the second thing which we possess is " a great priest over the house of God." Ἱερεὺς μέγας frequently occurs in the Sept. as synonymous with ἀρχιερεύς, and hence many (Klee, Tholuck) have here also rendered it by "high priest." But as our author elsewhere uniformly expresses this latter idea by ἀρχιερεύς, he must certainly have had a reason for using another expression here; he must have meant to say here, not that we have an high priest, but that we have " a *great* priest." And, indeed, there is nothing

---

[1] This *local* signification of διά c. gen. (comp. Luke iv. 30 ; Rom. xv. 28) should never have been doubted in our passage. Olshausen is for taking διά in an instrumental sense, and σάρξ in the sense of " suffering." But, granted that the latter were allowed, still the words διὰ τοῦ καταπετάσματος remain unexplained.

said here of the high priests as opposed to the ordinary priests, but Christ appears as the one, great, exalted priest in whom the entire idea of all ἱερατεία finds its realization, in opposition to the Levitical priests as a whole, the high as well as the ordinary priests.

In ver 23 the exhortation itself now follows: προςερχώμεθα scil. εἰς τὰ ἅγια. Does the true holiest of all stand open, it is criminal not to make use of this entrance. But how that entrance is to be made, we are told in the words *with true heart*, &c. First and above all, *a true heart* is required. This is the first condition and the ground of all faith, *that the heart be true;* that it be not biassed by self-deception regarding its wretched state by reason of sin, nor by self-deception also regarding all its endeavours, its inclinations, its plans. It is not that painful self-examination in order to search out sins which one has not that is required, as the victims of certain fanatical and morbid tendencies would demand, who make the very greatness of the corruption of which they *speak* a merit, or a ground of self-elation. No! it is enough if the man truly knows the sins which he has, and thereby comes to the knowledge that he has not merely *sins*, but *sin*, and that he is encompassed with it even in his best works. Where this knowledge takes root, it will dispel the delusive fancy that God needs no atonement, that God is only a dead idol who knows not the anger of holy love; it will dispel, too, all confidence in false self-made atonements, all merit of works, it will destroy all self-deception about an atonement through other sacrifices than the sacrifice of Christ, in like manner, also, the self-deception which leads a man to regard as meritorious, and to rest his hope on, faith itself, or an institution of faith, a church, confession, &c. A true heart is such a heart as regards itself, *the person* in its totality, in the mirror, not of a means of grace or an institution of grace, but in the mirror of *the person of Jesus Christ*, and asks itself whether it loves the Saviour above all things.

Secondly, the πληροφορία πίστεως is required, the *full undivided* faith, not a faith such as the readers of the Epistle to the Hebrews had, who to the questions: "Is Jesus the Messiah? Is he the Son of God?" &c., replied in the affirmative indeed with head and mouth, but yet were not satisfied with the sacrifice of Christ, and thought it necessary still to lean on the crutches of the Levitical sacrifices, and on these 'crutches would limp into heaven. In like manner, we will find still a *half* faith, when one belongs to the Church and attends divine service, and on a deathbed desires the word of Christ and the consolations of his grace, but yet only measures off for Christ a certain *portion* of his time and his activity, instead of having Christ at all times before his eyes and in his heart, and letting his whole being and life be penetrated by him. Christianity and the business of the present life are regarded as two things which, in respect of quantity, must be weighed against each other, lest by giving too much to the one (Christianity) the other (the earthly condition, honour, pleasure, &c.) should suffer and be prejudiced; instead of its being remembered, that what we are and do as men on the earth, we should be and do as *Christians*. But wherever there is such incompleteness of faith, such shrinking from a complete and entire devotedness to Christ, such earthly feeling and reliance upon something else, as if happiness were to come from this quarter or from that, only from some other source than from Christ, there also, the danger is great of becoming the prey of error, unbelief, and apostasy.

Thirdly, the *fruit* and *effect* of faith is required, viz. *the consciousness of sin being pardoned*: Ἐρραντισμένοι τὰς καρδίας ἀπὸ συνειδήσεως πονηρᾶς. The expression, again, is figurative, and finds its explanation partly, in chap. ix. 19 (in which is the figure of the ῥαντίζειν), partly in chap. ix. 13, x. 2 (where we find the opposition between the symbolical cleansing of the body and the real cleansing of the συνείδησις or καρδία.) Ἀπό depends on the idea of "cleansing" which is implied in the (pregnant) ῥαντίζειν. Συνείδησις πονηρά is the opposite of συνείδησις ἀγαθή, Acts xxiii. 1; 1 Pet. iii. 16 and 21; 1 Tim. i. 5 and 19. Taken exactly, however, it does not signify "evil (rebuking) conscience," but "evil consciousness," where, indeed, πονηρά is to be resolved into a genitive of the object ("consciousness of evil," consciousness of being evil.)

The words καὶ λελουμένοι . . . , κατέχωμεν, &c., form a *second member of the exhortation*. Καὶ λελουμένοι cannot, of course, be any longer dependent on προσερχώμεθα, as otherwise, an intolerable *asyndeton* at κατέχωμεν would be the result. This participle, then, rather corresponds, in the place which it occupies, to the ἔχοντες, ver. 1. ("Seeing that we have an entrance . . . . and a priest . . . . let us enter with true heart, in full faith, cleansed from the evil conscience. And if we are now washed . . . . let us hold fast," &c.) If λελουμένοι were grammatically connected with ἐρραντισμένοι (as Olshausen and others suppose), and connected, moreover, by a τοῦτ᾽ ἐστι, then might we be justified in taking λελουμένοι τὸ σῶμα ὕδατι καθαρῷ as the explanation of the figure ἐρραντισμένοι, and in understanding it in the proper sense of a *washing of the body with water, i.e.* of *baptism.* ("And as we are baptized, let us," &c.) So Bleek and others. But as λελουμένοι is quite parallel with the figurative expression ἔχοντες παρρησίαν εἰς τὴν εἴσοδον τῶν ἁγίων, and ἐρραντισμένοι also was to be taken figuratively, it is better (with Calvin, Beza, Ernesti, Limborch, &c.) to understand this λελουμένοι also figuratively (with reference to Ezek. xxxvi. 25), so that the meaning is: "And if we are now thus washed from our sins." Thus it contains that which connects it with the concluding word of the first member.

The exhortation itself is: κατέχωμεν τὴν ὁμολογίαν τῆς ἐλπίδος ἀκλινῆ, let us hold fast the profession of the hope unmoved. The profession, that in Christ, and in him alone, is forgiveness of sins to be obtained, which the readers were steadfastly to maintain before the Jews, is here called a profession of the *hope,* a designation which finds its full explanation in chap. iv. 1. It is the profession that the Christian also, nay the Christian alone, has the hope of the promised *rest;* that he, although cast out from the theocracy and the temple, persecuted, destitute of all earthly good, of all carnal hope of a Messiah, yet has the assured hope of inheriting the kingdom. To such a profession of hope belongs now, as it did then, the faith which regards an unseen and as yet unfulfilled word of God as a much surer and more certain possession (why? the parenthesis πιστός, &c., shows) than all the visible and attainable glory of the present world. But in our own day, that *profession of the hope* has again become one of the highest and most important duties, inasmuch as now οἱ κυνές (Rev. xxii. 15), both among Jews and Gentiles, as then among Jews (Phil. iii. 2) are crying out, that "man by being amused with fair promises for another world, is losing his happiness in this."

The author, in the first member of the exhortation, has said, how the Christian is to conduct himself towards God, in the second, towards the world without, and now in the *third member of the exhortation*, ver. 24, 25, he says, how he is to conduct himself towards the brethren, the Church. There is a false *considering of one another* which proceeds from selfishness and pride, and is forbidden by the apostle Paul, Gal. vi. 4. But there is also a true considering of one another, which, as it proceeds from love, has the tendency only to call forth " emulation in love and in good works," and this is recommended in the verse before us.—To this general duty, however, the special one is added, not to neglect attendance on the Christian assemblies, as many of the readers had already done through the fear of man. Ἐπισυναγωγή, formed from ἐπισυνάγειν to assemble, is distinguished from συναγωγή, inasmuch as, according to the *usus linguae*, it was not a designation for the Jewish religious assemblies which are still called " synagogues," but had always preserved the more general signification " assembly" (2 Macc. ii. 7 ; 2 Thess. ii. 1), so that it might therefore be applied to the designation of the Christian assemblies. Calvin, Hunnius, J. Capellus, Kuinoel, and others, falsely explain it of the " society of Christians," so that ἐγκαταλείπειν τὴν ἐπισυναγωγήν would be equivalent to "fall away from Christianity," "to become Jews." The great majority of commentators understand it rightly in a more special sense, namely, of becoming careless and shy in their attendance on the Christian congregational assemblies. To this remaining away from the assemblies is now opposed the παρακαλεῖν. At παρακαλοῦντες it is simplest to supply ἑαυτούς, and the object of the παρακαλεῖν may be supposed to be chiefly the attendance on the assemblies. (" But incite one another to attendance on these assemblies.") As a special motive to this, the *visible* approach of the *day* is adduced. Ἡμέρα does not denote the final judgment, but the well-known *Old Testament* idea of the יוֹם יְהוָה. The prophets (from Joel onwards) had predicted, that the Lord would, at one time, come to judge Israel and all the nations of the earth. Jesus had explained to his disciples that this *day of the Lord* divided itself into *two epochs* or acts, into a judgment upon Jerusalem, which was to be destroyed and to continue trodden down, and a judgment on the Gentiles, when their season of grace was past (Luke xxi. and Matth. xxiv.; Matthew, however, in his account of this address has regard principally to the points that relate to *Israel*, comp. my critique of the evangelical history p. 502 — 513). Here the author speaks to Israelites, and therefore of the *day of the Lord* in so far as it concerned the people Israel. That the predicted judgment upon Israel was now approaching with rapid strides, every one must in the beginning of the 60th year have "seen" ($\beta\lambda\acute{\epsilon}\pi\epsilon\iota\nu$), who was not as an obdurate Jew already stupified by the intoxicating cup which preceded the judgment. A people torn asunder by raging factions would resist the Roman power which extended over the world!

SECTION SECOND.

(Chap. x. 26—31.)

FIRST MOTIVE. DANGER AND CONSEQUENCES OF FALLING AWAY.

Vers. 26—27. The expression $\grave{\epsilon}\kappa o\upsilon\sigma\acute{\iota}\omega\varsigma\ \grave{\alpha}\mu\alpha\rho\tau\acute{\alpha}\nu\epsilon\iota\nu$ does not, according to the *context*, denote every kind of particular known sinful acts which a Christian commits even after regeneration (the 27th verse speaks definitely of *adversaries*, and in the passage from Deut. xvii. 6, cited in ver. 28, it is blasphemers of the law that are spoken of!), but neither, as regards the *meaning of the word*, does it denote the special sin of apostasy itself. The former explanation is too general, the latter too narrow. The author has rather in his mind, as regards the general character of the expression, many various *kinds* or *forms* of the $\dot{\alpha}\mu\alpha\rho\tau\acute{\alpha}\nu\epsilon\iota\nu$, as regards the context, however, only *such* kinds and forms as *lead to apostasy*, or which already involve a degree of apostasy. He, therefore, sinned $\dot{\epsilon}\kappa o\upsilon\sigma\acute{\iota}\omega\varsigma$ in the sense of ver. 26, who, from the fear of man, absented himself from the assemblies, or who, through any kind of denial of the truth, rendered it possible for him still to be allowed to take part in the worship of the temple, &c.—Now,

whoever, after having known the truth, commits such sins, therefore against better knowledge and against conscience, and thus implicitly contemns the one sacrifice of Christ, for him there exists no second atoning sacrifice, by which he can be cleansed from the guilt of this new and highly aggravated sin; but his portion is, *a*, subjectively in himself, " a fearful expectation of a judgment," *b*, on the part of God corresponding to that expectation, "the heat of a fire which is already about to consume the adversaries. (of God)." Φοβερὰ ἐκδοχὴ κρίσεως is not by *hypallage* for ἐκδοχὴ κρίσεως φοβερᾶς (J. Capellus), but is to be taken literally. He who acts thus, has before him the certainty of being judged, and this certainty is fearful, it is already in itself a punishment. As the *expectation of judgment* forms the antithesis to the existence of an atoning *sacrifice*, we shall therefore have to understand the *judgment* not of the destruction of Jerusalem, but of the *being judged* on the day of the second coming of Christ mentioned in chap. ix. 27 s. The scripture speaks of a threefold destiny after death. (Comp. our remarks on chap. xi. 39.) He who, as one born again, as a member of Christ, has fallen asleep in Jesus, comes not into judgment (John v. 24), but goes to Christ in heaven (2 Tim. iv. 18; Phil. i. 23). He who has died without being born again, but yet without positive unbelief, consequently without having had the opportunity of believing, goes into the place of the dead, into Hades; he belongs not, however, to those whose sin is forgiven neither in this life nor in the life to come (Matth. xii. 21 ss.), but is judged on the last day according to his works, and if (Rom ii. 7) he has perseveringly *striven* in well-doing after immortality, he will be reckoned among the number of those *sick* ones, for whose *healing* (θεραπεία), after the final judgment, are the leaves of the tree of life (Rev. xxii. 2). There is for him, therefore, in the interval between death and the resurrection, no fearful looking for of judgment. But he who has had the opportunity of attaining to faith, and yet with persevering obstinacy has put this opportunity away from him (Matth. xii. 21 ss.), and further, he who has attained to faith and yet has fallen away (Heb. vi. 1; x. 26—31), goes into Sheol, but with the certain consciousness that the κρίσις, judgment and condemnation, awaits him, and that that eternal fire is prepared for him which is to consume the adversaries of God (according to Is. lxvi. 24.)

Most unjustly, therefore, do Romish theologians appeal to this passage, as a proof of that purgatory which is to purge away the guilt of *all the particular sins* which are committed *by the regenerate*. Nothing is said here either of every kind of particular sins, or of people who are still in a regenerate state and have the hope of being saved, or of a purging away of those sins. On the contrary, what is not atoned for by the one sacrifice of Christ remains, according to ver. 26, still unexpiated.

That the author in ver. 26—27 was not speaking of every particular known sin committed by regenerate persons, but only of such sins as led to or involved apostasy, is confirmed chiefly by ver. 28; for in the passage here cited from Deut. xvii. 6, it is not said that every one who had transgressed any command of God is to be punished with death, but he only who was convicted by two or three witnesses of having *apostatized from God*, served false Gods and *broken the covenant*. If, then, the falling away from the old covenant was so severely punished, how much more the falling away from Christianity. This is denoted by the words καταπατεῖν τὸν υἱὸν τοῦ θεοῦ (used in Hom. Il. 4, 157, as a figure expressive of the most insolent contempt and rejection), further, as counting unholy (κοινός, as at chap. ix. 13) the blood of the covenant (chap. ix. 15—23)—for he who, not from error, but, against better knowledge, falls away from faith in the atoning death of Christ, thereby declares the death of Christ to be the just punishment of a malefactor and a blasphemer;— finally, this falling away from Christ is said to be a ὕβρις against the Holy Ghost, a wanton presumptuous casting out of this spirit, consequently an aggravated " sin against the Holy Ghost " (Matt. xii. 21 ss).

For such, God has prepared punishment, vers. 30—31. The passage Ex. xxxii. 35 is wont to be adduced as a prohibition of revenge being exercised by the injured person himself (" vengeance is mine, saith the Lord, I will repay"), but this is not its original sense. In the context it is not sins of men against men that are spoken of, but the future hardening of Israel against the saving and redeeming work of God, and thus God speaks: " *Vengeance* and *requittal* are mine (לִי נָקָם וְשִׁלֵּם) = I know to requite, I have the will and the power to do so; so that the emphasis lies not on ἐμοί but on the word ἐκδίκησις, and our author has applied the passage quite correctly. The other passage, Ps. cxxxv. 14, needs no explanation, and as little does the exclamation, ver. 31, which closes the section.

SECTION THIRD.

(Chap. x. 32—xi. 1.)

SECOND MOTIVE. CALLING TO MIND THEIR FORMER FAITH.

Ver. 32, 33. The transition is similar to that at chap. vi. 10. The readers have already at an earlier period endured manifold trials for their faith; in this lies a double motive for them not to fall away from their faith now; first, because thereby all their former sufferings would be rendered vain; and secondly, that suffering itself was an experimental testimony to the power of faith.—Φωτισθέντες denotes here, as at chap. vi. 4, the first step in conversion (see the remarks there made). Ἄθλησις a later Greek word for the classic ἆθλος. The struggles they had passed through were twofold; partly, they had already themselves become to the mass of unbelievers and enemies a spectacle (of malicious pleasure, of contempt, of delight in cruelty), inasmuch as they had endured shame and ignominy of all kinds (ὀνειδισμοί), nay, even actual afflictions (θλίψεις); partly, they had become *companions* of those who were so circumstanced (ἀναστρέφεσθαι, not pass. but mid. se gerere, versari. By this is generally understood, that the readers must have seen many *individuals* of their acquaintance enduring contempt and affliction; but the expression κοινωνοὶ γενηθέντες (not γενόμενοι) rather indicates, that they *in the act of their conversion had*, once for all, *become* members of *the society*, of which they knew that such things happen and are wont to happen to it.

Ver. 34. Instead of δεσμίοις (A.D., Peschito, Philoxen., Armen., Vulgate, Chrysostom, Theodoret, Oecumenius) many versions and the lectio recepta read δεσμοῖς μου. The latter reading, however, has less of external testimony in its favour, and, besides, might more easily take its rise out of $\delta\epsilon\sigma\mu\acute{\iota}o\iota\varsigma$ (from regard to conformity with 2 Tim. i. 16, and its being taken for granted that Paul was the author) than vice versa. Moreover, $\delta\epsilon\sigma\mu o\hat{\iota}\varsigma\ \mu o\upsilon$ is not even suitable; for granted that Paul was the author of the epistle, the Jewish Christians of Jerusalem were not, like Timothy, with the apostle in Rome, or in Caesarea, and therefore, could only very indirectly be called *companions* of his bonds; $\sigma\upsilon\mu\pi\alpha\theta\acute{\eta}\sigma\alpha\tau\epsilon$ is, however, by all means to be taken as explanatory of $\kappa o\iota\nu\omega\nu o\grave{\iota}\ \gamma\epsilon\nu\eta\theta\acute{\epsilon}\nu\tau\epsilon\varsigma$; this is evident from the $\kappa\alpha\grave{\iota}\ \gamma\acute{\alpha}\rho$. We therefore adopt the reading $\delta\epsilon\sigma\mu\acute{\iota}o\iota\varsigma$ (with Grotius, Bengel, Semler, Michaelis, Griesbach, Lachmann, Knapp, Bleek, and almost all the modern expositors.) Now, as $\kappa\alpha\grave{\iota}\ \gamma\grave{\alpha}\rho\ \ldots$ $\sigma\upsilon\mu\pi\alpha\theta\acute{\eta}\sigma\alpha\tau\epsilon$ is explanatory of $\kappa o\iota\nu\omega\nu o\grave{\iota}\ \gamma\epsilon\nu\eta\theta\acute{\epsilon}\nu\tau\epsilon\varsigma$, so is $\kappa\alpha\grave{\iota}\ \tau\grave{\eta}\nu\ \dot{\alpha}\rho\pi\alpha\gamma\grave{\eta}\nu$, &c. explanatory of $\theta\epsilon\alpha\tau\rho\iota\zeta\acute{o}\mu\epsilon\nu o\iota$. By the spoiling of their goods, we are to understand what we find still at this day taking place in the sphere of the Jewish mission; when a Jew shows himself determined to become a Christian, he is disinherited by his relations, his share in the property is withheld from him, his credit and every source of gain withdrawn; he falls into a state of complete destitution. But in our own day there is not wanting, any more than there was then, that state of mind which is expressed in the words "knowing that ye have in heaven a better property and an abiding." How do such newly converted Jews put to shame those Christians who, for example, week after week, desecrate the Lord's day by manual labour and worldly business, rather than make up their minds to suffer a trifling loss of earthly gain. There is wanting in them the faith in the divine *blessing* and in that *better wealth* !

In ver. 35 the readers are exhorted still to maintain that *joyful confidence* with which, assured of the *better wealth*, they had boldly encountered losses and sufferings; for this *confidence* will not put them to shame, the *recompense* of the hoped-for possession in heaven will assuredly be theirs. Here, of course, it is not a reward of meritorious works that is spoken of; the sole basis of that *confidence* consists in the *faith* which trusts in Christ, and only in him. He, again, who regards this *faith* and *confidence* itself as a meritorious work, only shows by this, that he has not the true *faith* and has not attained to the true *confidence*.

Ver. 36. The continuance of that joyful confidence is indispensable, because the readers are so situated as that, in order to be able to inherit the promised possession, they will still have need of great and long *patience and stedfastness in suffering*. But that patience and perseverance in suffering can grow out of no other root than out of *confidence*, is clear. He who, from the first, encounters suffering with the bold assurance that his enemies can kill only the body but not the soul, and that they can spoil him only of the worthless earthly goods but not of the *abiding property*, will from the first be prepared for a cheerful endurance of suffering, and will not fail of perseverance. But he who meets suffering without that *confidence*, full of fear and full of sorrow for the losses that threaten him, will become more comfortless and more impatient under every new trial. Thus the necessity of *patience* (the fruit) is a proof of the necessity of *confidence* (the root).—By the *will of God*, in this context, is to be understood his will that we should confess Christ's name before men. If we do this, we shall obtain as the fruit of it the fulfilment of the promise, that he also will confess us before his heavenly Father. —'Ἐπαγγελία is used here as at chap. ix. 15, xi. 13, to denote that which is promised.

In ver. 37, 38, the author shows more particularly why the readers have need of patience, because, namely, the judgment upon Jerusalem, from which only faith can save them, is now near at hand. He expresses this idea in the words in which formerly Habakkuk had spoken (ii. 30) of the then impending judgment through the Chaldeans. The passage Habakkuk ii. 3 s. is therefore by no means *cited* as a proof that now the judgment is impending[1] over Jerusalem; but the words of Habakkuk are only *applied to an analogous case* (as if, for example, a preacher in a farewell discourse to a thoroughly hardened congregation should exclaim: "How often would I have gathered you as a hen gathereth her chickens under her wings, but ye would not").— The first words ἔτι γὰρ μικρὸν ὅσον ὅσον are a free introduction of the subject by our author (perhaps a recollection of Sept. Is. xxvi. 20.) "Ὅσον, here in the adverbial signification of "only." The repetition of a word to strengthen the idea is rare in Greek.

---

[1] Falsely Theophylact: the author will prove, that if the judgment was already near in the time of Habakkuk, it must now be so much nearer (!) —This idea is indicated by nothing in the text.

—"He who comes is nigh and delays not; but the just will have life *from faith*; if, however, he *yields to fear* my soul shall have no pleasure in him." In the context of the passage in Habakkuk, people are spoken of who do not believe in the threatenings of the prophet, but carelessly pursue their course; on the contrary the term אֱמוּנָה denotes the state of mind belonging to those who believe the prophet, and expect from Jehovah alone the punishment of the ungodly, and the deliverance of the godly from the judgments. (Altogether against the context is the explanation of the words of Habakkuk: The just will remain alive because of his well doing, because of his good works.) The Sept. has therefore rightly translated באמונתו by ἐκ πίστεως.—The words ἐὰν ὑποστείληται, again, are a free translation; in the Heb. it is נַפְשׁוֹ בּוֹ הִנֵּה עֻפְּלָה לֹא יָשְׁרָה "behold, he is puffed up, his soul is not upright in him" (denoting the pride of unbelief); the Sept. has rendered it by ὑποστέλλειν; this means "to let down" (namely the sail), hence to be timorous, afraid. The Sept. has also put faint-heartedness in place of proud defiance. But, precisely in this form, the idea was doubly suitable to the object of our author, and as he does not apply the passage as an argument, but simply makes use of and applies the words in his own name, so he might, with all the less hesitation, follow the Sept. which was familiar to his readers.

In ver. 39 he expresses the idea: "We will surely not go to destruction but save our souls; consequently, we must not be afraid, but must believe," by concisely *blending the two members of the sentiment* (just as at chap. viii. 6, &c., where also he has united the two members in one sentence) thus: "We belong not to those who are afraid unto destruction, but who believe to the saving of the soul." Ψυχή is used here in the Old Testament sense for *life*. According to the context, it is the bodily preservation from the judgment impending over Jerusalem that is here spoken of.

CHAP. xi. 1. The idea ends here. Ver. 35: You must hold fast the confidence; ver. 36: for ye have need of the patience which springs from it; ver. 36—38: for the judgment upon Judea is near from which only the believing, not the fearful, are preserved; chap. xi. 1: but faith shows itself in that feeling (of confidence) which holds fast the future promised good.

Several commentators indeed (Erasmus, Böhme, Winer) would put a comma after πίστις, take ἔστι as verb. substantivum, and ὑπόστασις and ἔλεγχος as apposition to πίστις. But the sentiment: "Faith, however, really exists" would be too strange. Who had ever doubted that faith really exists in the world? And when, in support of this construction, it is affirmed that ἔστι as *copula* cannot stand at the beginning of the sentence, such passages are forgotten as Luke viii. 11 : ἔστι δὲ αὕτη ἡ παραβολή. In the preceding context of that passage it is said that the understanding of the parables is important, and then the transition is made to the explanation of the parables themselves. Just so here. In ver. 38 it was said that *faith* is *necessary ;* in chap. xi. 1 the question is answered, what then is this *faith*.

We take ἔστι, therefore, with the great majority of commentators, as copula. Ver. 1, however, does not contain a *definition* of faith (as ver. 1 does not form the superscription of a new section, but the conclusion of the foregoing), but a *description* of faith from a particular point of view given in the context (x. 34—38). It is to be shown, in how far *it is faith* which gives that *confidence* described in ver. 34. Faith is therefore viewed here not *as opposed to works*, but *as opposed to sight*, and therefore so generally as to belong not only to the *sinner* who hopes for pardon for the sake of *Christ*, but to *every one* who rests more on the unseen and the future than on the seen and present, hence also to the Old Testament believers (chap. xi. 2—xii. 1), hence also to *Christ himself* (chap. xii. 2 ss.).

Now faith is a ὑπόστασις ἐλπιζομένων. On ὑπόστασις compare what is said at chap. iii. 14. Here it is, of course, to be taken in the sense of fiducia, *firmly grounded confidence.* All faith refers to the future, and has for its basis a present *capability and necessity of further development.* The perfect man has no longer need of faith (1 Cor. xiii. 8 ss.), nor does the Son of God as eternal, or, Christ as exalted, need faith. On the other hand, as he walked in lowliness on our account, and was partaker of the yet unglorified human nature, he needed faith in the glorious issue of his work, over which a heavy cloud then hung (comp. below on chap. xii.) ; and in like manner, the Christian needs faith, as, at present, he has nothing more of the victory over sin and death than the *unseen ground of it*, namely, Christ; everything else lies as yet in the future.

As faith refers to the future, so also from its nature does it refer to the invisible, or more exactly: *to good things, which are not seen* ἔλεγχος οὐ βλεπομένων. Ἔλεγχος does not, however, (as Olshausen thinks) signify "persuasion," "the state of being persuaded," but "demonstration," "actual proof." Faith is, therefore, not merely a *subjective persuasion* that those possessions although unseen are yet present; but it is an *act* which itself gives the *knowledge and proof* of the existence of those things *not seen*. The *fact of faith* is *itself* the proof of the *reality of its object*. In faith the actual *power* of the thing believed is already manifest. Thus the author has had a reason for using in the first member, precisely the word ὑπόστασις, "grounding," "state of being grounded." He will represent faith not as a theory but as a *life-power*, which, inasmuch as it actually grasps at the future and unseen possessions, is thereby actually *assured* of them. (And so Thomas Aquinas is, although not exegetically, yet, substantially right when he explains ἐλπιζομένων ὑπόστασις from this, that faith is "the subsistence of the things hoped for themselves, the beginning of their possession already entered upon." Ὑπόστασις does not signify "subsistence," but the idea of Thomas Aquinas is quite the correct one.) For that is just the nature and characteristic quality of faith, that it begins not with theories and arguments, but with acts. Credo ut intelligam. As the new-born child does not first receive instruction on the necessity of breathing, and then resolve to breathe, but first breathes and then grows to the youth who learns to understand the process of breathing, so also must that which is born of the spirit in us first inhale in deep inspirations the heavenly breath of life, ere it can grow up to full knowledge. And as the drawing of the breath is itself the surest proof of the existence of a life-bringing atmosphere which we breathe, so is the act of that faith which *lays hold* on the future and unseen possessions, and draws *strength* from them, the most satisfactory proof of the fact that these possessions are more than mere fancies and chimeras.

SECTION FOURTH.

(Chap. xi. 2—xii. 3.)

THIRD MOTIVE. THE HISTORICALLY DEMONSTRATED POWER OF FAITH.

In Ver. 2 the theme of a new train of thought is connected by γάρ with the concluding ideas of the foregoing. Ἐν ταύτῃ γὰρ ἐμαρτυρήθησαν οἱ πρεσβύτεροι. Μαρτυρεῖσθαι occurs in an absolute sense in Acts vi. 3 and other passages, in the signification " to have for oneself a good witness," " to stand in good repute." Almost all commentators would therefore, here also, take μαρτυρεῖσθαι absolutely, and ἐν ταύτῃ as indicating the ground of it, either by making ἐν stand for διά (" on account of their faith the ancients received a good report"), or by supposing it necessary to supply an ὄντες (" as being in the faith they received a good report"). The former supposition is inadmissible as being not consistent with the good Greek style of our author; if, however, ὄντες must be supplied, it would be much better to take ἐν ταύτῃ ὄντες as expressing the import of the μαρτύριον. " They are testified of as being in the faith" = " it is testified of them that they were in the faith." And the particulars which follow would correspond much more to this idea. For, in the examples, ver. 3, ss., nowhere are eulogies mentioned which had been made upon the ancients on account of their faith, but it is merely shown how it appears from their history, that in no other state of mind can they have found the requisite strength for their achievements, but in that described in ver. 1 (and in chap. x. 35—xi. 1; enjoined on the readers).

And thus the sentiment: " in *this* state of mind 'the fathers also stood and acted " connects simply, by means of γάρ, with the exhortation x. 35—xi. 1 as a further motive.

There can also be no doubt as to what the examples ver. 3 are properly meant to show. It certainly is not meant merely to *repeat* in concrete examples the affirmation made generally in in ver. 2 *as such*, as a mere *affirmation*. Still less can it be the purpose of the author to prove some such proposition as that faith has expressed itself differently at different times, and thus to justify the *general* character of the definition in ver. 1. This is evident, already, because the first verse is neither a definition nor a superscription to the section (it rather, as we saw, forms the conclusion of the foregoing section). These examples are plainly intended *to prove* the thesis laid down in ver. 2, to demonstrate its truth. The author had said: Of the ancients also it is witnessed that they had the *faith* described in ver. 1. This is now proven, however, not directly, for the word אֱמוּנָה is, in the Old Testament, applied only in very rare cases to Old Testament persons. The author must therefore show, that the *thing* is true; that, indirectly at least, the state of mind which distinguished the ancients is described to be such as is represented in ver. 1 and denoted by the name πίστις, namely, a firm reliance on the future and the unseen. And this the author fully demonstrates.

In Ver. 3 he shows that all religion, as such, the worship of a living God, an invisible Creator, is in itself nothing else than a rising above the visible to the invisible. "By faith (not: by means of faith, not: in faith, but = by an act of that πίστις that disposition of mind described in ver. 1) we perceive that the worlds were framed by a word of God." In νοοῦμεν there lies a kind of oxymoron; νόησις generally forms the antithesis to πίστις; νόησις is perception obtained through the medium of vision. The idea therefore is, that that state of mind denoted by πίστις (the demonstration of the power of the unseen in the man) qualifies the man to *perceive* something which is properly *not perceptible*, namely, not perceptible *by the senses;* that therefore a higher sensorium above the sensual sensorium is opened up in the man. —The worlds are created by God's word, "so that that which is seen (τὸ βλεπόμενον according to A. D. E. Copt., Clem. Al. &c.) was made of that which does not appear." Beza, Bengel, Schulz, Böhme, Winer, de Sacy, Martin, Osterwald, the Portroyalists, Bleek, Olshausen, &c. refer μή as respects the position of the words, to γεγονέναι, and render: "So that that which is seen was not (again) made of that which is visible." But if this were the idea which was meant to be expressed, then the author would not have used the two words βλεπόμενον and φαινόμενα, but must necessarily have used βλέπεσθαι both times, or φαίνεσθαι both times, in order by the repetition of the same word to express what in German has to be expressed by " wieder." Besides this, the sentiment in this negative would in general be unsuitable. That the visible cannot again have proceeded from what is visible, would be no affirmation of faith but one of speculation, a philosopheme. — The translators of the Peschito and ⁹Vulgate, then Chrysostom, Theodoret, Oecumenius, Theophylact, Erasmus, Luther, Gerhard, Tholuck, and a great number of other commentators, have therefore more properly supposed a transposition (μὴ ἐκ for ἐκ μή), and with all the more reason as examples of analogous transpositions, precisely in the case of the preposition ἐκ, are not wanting. (Especially comp. the example adduced by Tholuck from Arist. Phys. (v. 1 : τὴν ἐκ μὴ ὑποκειμένου εἰς ὑποκείμενον μεταβολὴν ... ἡ γὰρ μὴ ἐξ ὑποκειμένου εἰς μὴ ὑποκείμενον οὐκ ἔστι μεταβολή.) It is wrong, however, (with Luther, J. Capellus, Calov, Bretschneider, &c.) to explain τὰ μὴ φαινόμενα by τὰ οὐκ ὄντα, " nothing," and quite as wrong to understand by it *chaos* (Limborch, &c.) The explanation of μὴ φαινόμενα which refers it to the ideas in God (in the Platonic sense) is hetereogeneous, although an approximation to the truth. The expression must rather of necessity be explained (with Tholuck) from the antithesis laid down in ver. 1. Most will depend, however, on our keeping in view the distinction between μή and οὐκ. Οὐ denies the *existence*, μή the *quality* ; οὐ says that a thing *is not* objectively, μή denies a thing as conceived or conceivable. Οὐκ ὄν denotes that which does not exist, which is not ; μὴ ὄν that whose existence, in respect of its quality, is a nonexistence, a thing unreal. In short, οὐ before adjectives is generally rendered by " not," μή before adjectives generally by " un-." Thus the οὐ βλεπόμενα are things which *are* not *at present* seen ; μὴ βλεπόμενα would be things which, under no condition, and at no time, *could* be seen. Οὐ φαινόμενα would be things which (at the time or in the circumstances spoken of in the context) do not *come* into appearance ; μὴ φαινόμενα are things which, from their nature, *cannot* come into appearance. By the plural μὴ φαινόμενα cannot however, of course, be denoted blank nothing, and just as little can chaos be denoted, which is dark and confused, indeed, but by no means lying beyond the sphere of appearance. The μὴ φαινόμενα must rather be *qualitatively-invisible* things or powers, to the νόησις of which the man raises himself in faith, from looking upon that which is *seen*. If, too, we are not at liberty to understand by this precisely the ideas in the Platonic sense, we are yet led by the expression *word of God* to think of the invisible creative powers which form as it were the import of his *word*.

In Ver. 4—7 *follow examples taken from the time before Abraham.*—Through the disposition of mind denoted by πίστις Abel offered a better sacrifice than Cain. Cain offered fruits of the field, which in themselves were not adapted for sacrifice, for the atoning עוֹלָה (comp. what is said on chap. ix. 19 ss.), and were also not so valuable as animals. Abel offered the firstlings and fattest beasts of his flock. He willingly gave up, therefore, a dear and valuable *earthly* possession for the invisible possession of the consciousness of reconciliation, and the manifestation of gratitude to God. He thus gave evidence that he had that state of mind which in ver. 1 was called *faith*. Therefore (δι' ἧς refers to πίστις, as also δι' αὐτῆς, in respect of the sense, must refer to πίστις) it was testified to him that he was righteous; for, inasmuch as God was well pleased with his offering (fire from heaven consumed it), he testified to Abel that he was justified. And therefore, also, does Abel still speak after his death. Λαλεῖ is praes. hist. referring to Gen. iv. 10 (" thy brother's blood cries to me from the ground"); as appears evident also from Heb. xii. 24. Therefore did God take it upon himself to be the avenger of the murdered one, because he had died in faith; nay on account of his faith ; for Cain had envied him just on account of God's being well pleased with him. (The reading λαλεῖται " he is still spoken of after his death" is but ill-confirmed by external proofs, and yields a most unsuitable sense ; Cain is still spoken of too ! Already the passage chap. xii. 24 proves that λαλεῖ must be the reading.)

Ver. 5—6 is a kind of sorites. *By faith* Enoch was snatched away so that he did not see death (Gen. v. 24). Wherefore by faith ? He was taken away, because he led a life well-pleasing to God ; but God can be pleased only by *faith*.—In this form, however, the reasoning is still incomplete, because built upon a

very general axiom; hence the author in the words πιστεῦσαι
γὰρ δεῖ ... ὅτι ... mentions that in the case of Enoch also, it was
that *faith* which was spoken of, and in how far it was so. Precisely
the faith that there is a God, and one who will reward those who
seek after him, found place in Enoch, and could find place in
him. Far from intending to ascribe to Enoch the *New Testament* faith, the author defines the πίστις here in its general
form as it applied to the time of Enoch. Enoch lived in that
time when the descendants of Cain were improving the earthly
life by inventions (Gen. iv. 20 ss), but amid the pleasures of the
earthly life entirely forgot God, and when, already, the Sethites
also were infected with the prevalent corruption (Gen. vi. 1 ss). In
that time Enoch led a godly life. He forgot not the invisible God
amid the things and enjoyments that were seen; he longed for
that blessedness which God is ready to give to those who seek
him.

Ver. 7. Πίστει belongs, of course, again to the principal verb
κατεσκεύασε. In how far the building of the ark was an *act. of
faith*, we are told in the apposition χρηματισθείς. Noah saw as
yet nothing of the flood, when he began to build the ark; he
acted with respect to a mere *prophecy*; but God's word was to
him more sure and certain than the supposition which had
become habitual by sight—that the course of nature would continue ever the same,—and more important, to him than all the
scorn and mockery of an unbelieving world.—Εὐλαβηθείς not
= εὐλαβὴς γενόμενος (compare Luke ii. 25; Acts ii. 5, viii. 2;
Heb. v. 7, xii. 28) but = "in wise foresight" (namely, in
that which sprung from his obedience of faith.) Prudence is
not named as the source but as the reward of his conduct. By
his believing obedience he came to be at last the one who was
truly prudent. A truth of great practical importance! He who,
like a child, blindly follows the will of God regardless of all
consequences, is the one who is truly prudent; for he builds on
the Eternal, and He will never allow his own to come to shame.
He, on the contrary, who, in the fear of man and from a wish
to please man, *reckons* when it will be profitable to follow the
Lord, he who first anxiously weighs the consequences, will with
his false wisdom assuredly come to shame. How many
Christians would there be now who, by the building of an ark

(should God command this), would take upon themselves the contempt of the whole world? We would not seek them among those who already shrink with fear from the charge of "pietism."—By his faith "Noah judged the world." Noah by his faith (*i.e.* by the building of the ark) saved himself, and thereby left the world to the destruction it deserved.

Ver. 8—19. A series of *examples* follows taken from the *lifetime of Abraham*. If Abraham, at the call of God, left his home without even knowing whither God would lead him, he rested more on things promised of God than on things present, more on the invisible faithfulness and power of the Lord than on what was visible; he showed, therefore, that he had that state of mind which the author in the foregoing section had required of his readers, and which, in respect of its main substance, he had called *faith*.—It was a demonstration of the same state of mind when Abraham, as well as Isaac and Jacob (ver. 9), went into the land which was promised to him as into a *strange land*, so that he had to dwell in tents (wander through it nomade-like), just where he found sufferance. He (as well as Isaac and Jacob) might have gone back, and dwelt in Mesopotamia as a settled home (as is shown at length ver. 15). From what other motive did the patriarchs prefer wandering in a strange land to dwelling in their native land, than that believing in the promise of God, they obeyed the command of God? Their eye was directed (ver. 10) not to the present and momentary, but to the future and heavenly, to the *blessing* which God had promised to the seed of Abraham, and through him to man, to the promised restoration of the relation of God to man which sin had disturbed. This promised blessing our author now designates as "the city having settled foundations whose builder and maker is God." The expression must, first of all, be explained from the antithesis to the *tents* in which Abraham lived. That which gave him strength to renounce a present and earthly home, and to pass his life in light unfixed tents, was the expectation of a future settled city. Many erroneously explain this city of the heavenly blessedness which Abraham (for his own person) hoped to find after his death. This is altogether unhistorical; Abraham expected after his death to be gathered to his fathers in Sheol.

Grotius, Clericus, and others somewhat better refer the πόλις to the (earthly) city of Jerusalem. This, doubtless, is the idea of ver. 10, that Abraham—on account of the *glory promised to his seed* (for ἐξεδέχετο γάρ is epexegetical of τῆς ἐπαγγελίας, ver. 9), not, however, on account of the individual blessedness subjectively hoped for by him—underwent the inconveniences of a life-long pilgrimage. But Grotius and Clericus err, when they *limit* this objective promise to the earthly building of the earthly Jerusalem. Our author, *even for the sake of his readers*, who clung with a false tenacity just to the earthly Jerusalem, would certainly not have said that the earthly Jerusalem was that, on account of which Abraham renounced a settled dwelling-place. He rather denotes by that "settled city founded by God himself," which he places in opposition to Abraham's transitory tents, the *entire and total import of the theocratical promise*, and he does this, so as that in the form of the designation, he does not confine himself to the *undeveloped* intuition which Abraham had in his lifetime of the future blessing and salvation (for Abraham had as yet, in general, heard nothing of a " city," of the earthly Jerusalem, as little as of the heavenly), but takes up at the same time the *developement* of the promise which followed from the time of Abraham to that of Christ. In David, the promise given to Abraham had found a fulfilment, preliminarily and symbolically in the founding of the kingdom and that of its principal city in splendour; but that David was not the true, last, and proper Messiah, that a second David must come, was known to the readers from 2 Sam. vii,; Ps. ii.; Ps. cx., and finally, from the history of Jesus Christ himself. Abraham was not, of course, aware of the distinction between the first and second Anointed, the first and second Jerusalem— nor does the author mean at all to say that he was; but Abraham *at all events* looked for a future settled kingdom, for a state of things in which his posterity would no longer wander in tents from place to place (Gen. xvii. 6 and 8), and on account of this hope, he bore the difficulties of a life-long state of pilgrimage. He looked therefore, in reality, for a settled city which God would found for his seed. *The Christian knows* that the future Jerusalem in the future kingdom of Christ when he has come again, will form the true, full and final fulfilment of this hope.

The words of ver. 10 are, however, not *to be interpreted* : "Abraham looked for the future Jerusalem," but the words mean only : "Abraham looked for this, that God himself would found a settled city for his seed."

Ver. 11—12. By faith Sarah received strength for the founding of a posterity : if she had not overcome that paroxysm of doubt of which we have an account in Gen. xviii. 22, (she was immediately ashamed of it, ver. 15), she would, of course, not have yielded herself to the act of generation.—Ver. 13 ss. It was also an act of faith when the patriarchs died, one after another, without having received the promise ($\dot{\epsilon}\pi\alpha\gamma\gamma\epsilon\lambda\acute{\iota}\alpha$ as below ver. 39 and chap. ix. 15, x. 36), and notwithstanding, clung to the promise, nay as it were, already *saw* from afar and *welcomed* the promised blessing. This latter they did, inasmuch as they called themselves *pilgrims* (Gen. xlvii. 9, comp. Ps. xxxix. 13). This was an expression of their longing for a country, not in any way for the earthly country which lay behind them— Mesopotamia (ver. 15) ; for had such a longing taken possession of their hearts ($\mu\nu\eta\mu o\nu\epsilon\acute{\nu}\epsilon\iota\nu$ to remember anything, here in a pregnant sense as at 2 Tim. ii. 8), they might at any moment have returned thither. That they did *not* do so, that in spite of the feeling that they were strangers they yet kept themselves from seeking again that earthly country, is to he explained simply from their believing obedience to the instructions of God, and their believing hope of the future possession of Canaan promised by God. In ver. 16 this promised future country is again called by the author a heavenly country, just as, at ver. 10, he brings *the kind of fulfilment* known to the *Christians* at the same time into the *prophetical hope*. Here, too, he will obviate the false application of the words on the part of his readers, that the earthly Canaan *as such* was the aim of the theocratical hope. That which the fathers hoped for their posterity was not the ordinary earthly possession of an earthly land or kingdom, but the *setting up of the kingdom of God upon earth*, which was to take place in Canaan. (Just as little as in ver. 10, however, is it in ver. 16 the individual blessedness after death that is spoken of.)

Ver. 17—19. *Abraham's readiness* to offer up *Isaac* is mentioned along with the rest of the acts of faith taken from the life of Abraham. Abraham, who had received the promises when God tried him, offered up his only son, him in whose person the promise rested (ver. 18, comp. Gen. xxi. 12). As Abraham cannot himself have given up hope in the promises, although he was ready to offer as a burnt-offering the son through whom, according to God's express declaration, they were to be fulfilled, nothing remains to account for this but the supposition which our author expresses, ver. 19 (and in like manner Paul, Rom. iv. 17), that God would call the dead back again to life. And, on account of this faith which held the infinite power of God to be surer than the power of death, and which, therefore, blindly surrendered itself to the incomprehensible leading of God, he received as a reward his son alive ἐν παραβολῇ. These words ἐν παραβολῇ are particularly difficult. Calvin, Castellio, Beza, Schlichting, Grotius, Limborch, Kuinoel, Bleek, &c., take παραβολή in the well-known signification *figure*, but then refer ἐν παραβολῇ to ὅθεν, and obtain the sense: " *thence* as it were, namely, as it were, ἐκ νεκρῶν, as it were from the grave, he received him back." This explanation is the harshest. For, in the first place, if παραβολή signifies " figure," it cannot then signify " as it were;" "figuratively," and " as it were " or "not properly, in a certain way," are surely very different ideas. Secondly, it is very harsh to refer back ὅθεν to ἐκ νεκρῶν instead of taking it as a causal particle " wherefore " (comp. Acts xxvi. 19), as the author assuredly intends to mention here, as at vers. 4, 7, 14, 16, the *recompense* which the believer obtained *on account of his faith*. Thirdly, however, it is besides impossible to refer ἐν παραβολῇ to this ὅθεν; the idea that Abraham received back Isaac " as it were from the dead," no one would ever express thus: " whence he as it were received him;" the pregnant idea which is intended to be in ὅθεν must have been *expressed*, at least by a καὶ ἐνταῦθεν, and the author must have said: καὶ ἐνταῦθεν, ὡς ἔπος εἰπεῖν, ἐκομίσατο αὐτόν.—Others, as Theodoret, Erasmus, Luther, Calov, Böhme, Olshausen, take παραβολή likewise in the signification " figure," but in reality give it this signification and explain : " wherefore he received him back *as a symbol* (or in symbol.) This idea is much more suitable; the author shows that that *remaining*-alive of Isaac, that deliverance from the *danger* of death, was a symbol or type of the *resurrec-*

tion of Christ the *only begotten* of God, whom God gave up as a sacrifice for the world; that resurrection through which the faith of Abraham, *that God was able to raise from the dead*, found its confirmation, and was crowned with its highest fulfilment. The only thing in this explanation at which we might stumble is, that, according to it, we should have expected rather εἰς παραβολήν; but the ἐν also yields a good sense. In a figurative act Abraham received Isaac, that is, the act of the κομίζειν was a figure and type of a later and more perfect act. The idea resulting from this explanation harmonizes with the words λογισάμενος ὅτι, &c., so admirably, and with such internal necessity, and at the same time the way is so prepared for it by the designation of Isaac as the *only begotten*, that we hold this explanation to be decidedly the true one, and therefore have no need with a *third* class of commentators (Camerarius, Ernesti, Tholuck, &c.) to take ἐν παραβολῇ = παραβόλως or "against expectation" (comp. Rom. iv. 18), παρ'- ἐλπίδα, a signification which does not belong to the noun παραβολή. Παραβολή does signify "bold venture," but the signification "in bold venture" would not at all correspond to ἐκομίσατο.

Ver. 20—22. Several examples follow in which the patriarchs, by the act of blessing their sons and descendants, declared that they participated in the hope of the future fulfilment, or, by giving commandment that their bones should be carried along with their descendants from Egypt to Canaan, proved that they expected with certainty the promised return (Gen. xv.) The first instance is that of Jacob, who blessed the sons of Joseph (Gen. xlviii. 15 ss.), by which he (ver. 21) distinctly expressed his hope of the return to Canaan. With this are connected the somewhat enigmatic words καὶ προσεκύνησαν ἐπὶ τὸ ἄκρον τῆς ῥάβδου αὐτοῦ. We have here to inquire, first of all, why these words are cited along with the rest, and then whether the Sept. has here given the right translation. Assuredly the author did not cite these words along with the rest, merely because he went on mechanically with the quotation of the passage; for the words in question do not occur at all in that passage Gen. xlviii. 15 ss., but are to be found in an earlier chapter (xlvii. 31.) The author, therefore, had certainly a definite object in view when he quoted these words. What then was this object?—In the Masoretic text, the words run thus וַיִּשְׁתַּחוּ יִשְׂרָאֵל עַל־רֹאשׁ הַמִּטָּה "and Israel leant (back again) on the head of the bed (pillow), " and this reading is not only very old (Onkelos, Jonathan, Symmachus, Aquila, Peschito), but is also plainly the more natural. The LXX read הַמַּטֶּה, and rendered just as our author cites. But it can hardly be supposed, that in the word προσεκύνησεν, which is peculiar to the LXX., there lay the idea which induced our author to cite the passage; he would hardly have cited the passage on account of the circumstance that Jacob "prayed" (as if in his habit of praying there lay a special proof of that faith described in ver. 1). I rather think that he quoted the words in order to call to the minds of his readers, who were familiar with the Pentateuch, the *context* of the passage. In the context of that passage Gen. xlvii. it is recorded how Jacob gave orders to carry his bones to Canaan; thus, then, these words lead quite naturally to the analogous command of Joseph mentioned in ver. 22.

In Ver. 23—31 follow *examples of faith from the time of Moses and Joshua.* Ver. 23. The whole existence of Moses became possible through the faith of his parents, who laid the child in the basket of reeds, confident that the infant which appeared to them as ἀστεῖον would be an object of care to the paternal eye of God which looks into the smallest things, and that God's power is superior to all, even the most evident, dangers, and is stronger than the frown of Pharoah.—Ver. 24—26. Moses himself had the choice, either to remain at the court as an Egyptian prince and to enjoy all the splendour of Egypt—but then he must renounce his faith which his mother as his nurse had implanted in his heart, and his connection with his people;— or to remain true to the God of his fathers—but then he must bid farewell to the court, and share in the difficulties of his people. His God and his theocratical hope were dearer and more precious to him than all present earthly fortune. He preferred the συγκακουχεῖσθαι to the " enjoyment of sin;" the " reproach of the Messiah" was dearer to him than all the riches of Egypt. In the expression " reproach of Christ," the author again puts into the germ the *development* known to the *Christian.* Moses had as yet received no revelation of the " Anointed;" he knew only the theocratical promise in the simple form in which it was given to the patriarchs. But the New Testament believer knows, that that simple hope was destined to find its fulfilment in the "Anointed of God." And thus the reproach which Moses endured because it was a theocratical was also a Messianic reproach —such as has received (Matt. xvii. 1), and will yet farther receive, its honourable reward through the Messiah.

Ver. 27 does not refer to Moses' wandering to Midian (Ex. ii. 15), where he indeed "feared," but to the departure from Egypt (Ex. xiv. 13.) That the two *parts* of which this departure consisted, namely, the Passover, and the passage through the Red Sea, are afterwards specially mentioned, is no reason why the event *as a whole* might not also be mentioned first. The resolution, in general, to undertake the dangerous work of delivering Israel from Egypt, was a strong act of faith (comp. Ex. iii. 11 ss.) Moses had stedfastly before his eyes God, the invisible, just as if he saw him. Τὸν ἀόρατον is here, according to the position of the words, the *object* to ἐκαρτέρησε. Καρτερεῖν as transit. " to bear anything stedfastly, or to do anything stedfastly," hence generally in reference to any person or thing to conduct oneself stedfastly. It is a pregnant idea to be explained here thus: τὸν ἀόρατον τιμῶν ἐκαρτέρησε. (So also substantially Olshausen. The construction adopted by Bleek, Tholuck, &c., is forced: ἐκαρτέρησε γὰρ, ὡς τὸν ἀόρατον ὁρῶν.)

Ver. 28 is clear. Had the Israelites not believed that God would really slay the first born,[1] or had they had no faith in the atoning power of the lambs, they would not have marked their door posts with the blood of the Passover lambs. In like manner, it was plainly a manifestation of faith (ver. 29), when they ventured into the bed of the Red Sea, between the masses of water standing wall-high on either side, which, physically considered, seemed every moment as if they must close in upon them, as they afterwards in reality did upon the Egyptians. Not less was it an act of that faith which holds the command of God to be surer than any appearance of sense, when the Israelites marched

---

[1] The simplest way of construing ver. 28 is: ἵνα μὴ ὁ ὀλοθρεύων θίγῃ τὰ πρωτότοκα αὐτῶν. Others make τὰ πρωτότοκα dependent on ὀλοθρεύων, and αὐτῶν on θίγῃ, in which, however, this αὐτῶν would be by far too vague.

round the walls of Jericho (ver. 30) with the blowing of trumpets instead of laying siege to it (Josh. vi.) And Rahab, too, was saved by her faith, she who trembled before the mighty God,— " who is a God both above in heaven, and beneath on the earth," —and saved the messengers of his people, and was therefore preserved from the destruction of the city (in the power of this faith, however, also changed her conduct, comp. Matth. i. 5.)

Ver. 32—34. The author, by means of the rhetorical formula of transition, now breaks off from adducing particular examples in detail, and passes to a summary enumeration of *names* (ver. 32) and *actions* (ver. 33.—34). The opinion of Bengel and others, that the particular acts correspond to those particular names. (so that κατηγωνίσαντο βασιλείας refers to Gideon, εἰργάσαντο δικαιοσύνην to Barak, ἔφραξαν στόματα λεόντων to Samson) is fanciful, and, in reference to ver. 35, not capable of being carried out. The relation of ver. 32 to ver. 33—34 is rather to be understood thus:— The author, *first of all*, passes from the detailed description of particular *examples* of faith to a (consecutive) enumeration of *heroes* of faith, then, however, as a longer continuation of the mere catalogue of names would have been dry, he breaks off from this also, and now (ver. 33 ss.) he groups together mere general *classes* of acts resulting from faith. Of course, the particular examples of these *genera* may be pointed out in the Old Testament history, but not so as that only one example always corresponds to each genus. Thus, the *subduing of kingdoms* was an act of which there were frequent examples. Certainly Gideon, also, subdued the power of a kingdom, that of Midian, and he did so by that faith in which, trusting more to God's promise than to horses and chariots, he dismissed the greatest part of his army (Jud. vi. 7). But Jonathan, too, when alone with his armour-bearer, he climbed up the rock Seneh, and drove the enemies' host to flight, in the strength of the faith that it is easy for the Lord to help by many or by few (1 Sam. xiv. 6 ss.),—and David, when in the power of faith he slew the giant (1 Sam. xvii. 25),—and Samson, and many others, might here be adduced as examples. *Wrought righteousness* in their official station:—this did all the judges, chiefly Samuel, in like manner the pious kings; and, in their private relations, all the righteous persons of the Old Testament; still the author must have had the first especially in view. This administration of justice was also not possible without that state of mind which, apart from all regard to earthly advantage, has respect only to the will of God, nor is it possible yet, in our own day, without this " faith," hence, neither in the private nor the public administration of justice can a people be happy, if in the one case, as in the other, it be not administered by God-fearing persons. *Obtained promises :*—chiefly of David was this true (2 Sam. vii.), then, of course, also of the entire series of the *prophets* briefly mentioned in ver. 32. ($Ἐπαγγελίαι$ denotes here not, as at ver. 13 and 39, the promised thing, *i.e.*, the fulfilment, but the prophecies themselves. The proof lies precisely in ver. 39). *Stopped the mouths of lions :*—Daniel did this (Dan. vi. 17, comp. ver. 23); less direct is the reference to Samson (Jud. xiv. 6) and David (2 Sam. xvii. 34 ss.) *Quenched the violence of fire :*— this did the friends of Daniel (Dan. iii.); they, like Daniel himself, stedfastly maintained the profession of the invisible true God, and held his almighty power to be greater than the might of the Babylonian and Median kings (Dan. iii. 17; vi. 10 and 20). *Escaped the sword :*—David did so (1 Sam. xviii. 11; xix. 10, ss. &c.), Elias (1 Kings xix. 1 and 10), and Elisha (2 Kings vi. 14 ss. and 31 ss.), but only in the case of Elisha was the escape a positive act of faith, brought about by faith, hence the reference may be properly limited to him (namely, the incident recorded in 2 Kings vi. 14, ss. where he is represented as *seeing* the *invisible* hosts of God). *Out of weakness were made strong :*— such was Hezekiah (Is. xxxviii. 3 and 5), and that in consequence of a believing prayer. Others, with less propriety, refer this to Samson (Jud. 15—16), whose strength returned to him unconsciously, and without an act of faith on his part. *Waxed valiant in fight,*—almost all the Judges were heroes in battle, then Jonathan, David, &c. $Κλίνειν\ παρεμβολὰς\ ἀλλοτρίων$ (aciem inchnare)—the reference is, here, again, to Gideon and Jonathan.

In Ver. 35 the author places over against each other two kinds of manifestations of faith—the faith of those women (1 Kings xvii. 17, ss.; 2 Kings iv. 17, ss.) whose sons were restored to *bodily* life by the prophets, and the still greater faith of the martyrs (of the time of the Maccabees), who sacrificed the bodily life in faith, and on account of faith, for the sake of the *future* resurrection to the *glorified* life. Hence he does not merely say: "Not accepting deliverance that they might obtain a better *deliverance*;" but, referring back to the first clause of the verse, he speaks of a *better resurrection.*—Τυμπανίζειν comes from τύμπανον, which signifies originally a kettle-drum, 2 Macc. vi. 19 and 28, but occurs as the designation of an instrument of torture (probably in the form of a wheel), upon which the sufferers were stretched in order then to be beaten to death. They accepted not the ἀπολύτρωσις, namely, that deliverance which they might have bought at the price of denying their faith. At ἐξ ἀναστάσεως in the beginning of the verse, ἐξ is so to be explained as that ἀνάστασις denotes the *act* of rising again. They received them from the resurrection, *i.e.* as those who had just been raised up.

Ver. 36—38. The writer returns in ver. 36 to the mention of less violent sufferings, in order, from these, to rise again a new climax, ver. 37, to the greatest tortures. Then, at the end of 37 and in ver. 38, he sets over against the cruel *death* of some martyrs, the destitute *life* of others. *Mockings*, and these of a public and most abusive kind, were endured in the Maccabaean persecutions (1 Macc. ix. 26; 2 Macc. vii. 7); *scourgings* in the same persecutions (2 Macc. vi. 30, vii. 1); *imprisonments* in the same persecutions (1 Macc. xiii. 12), and also in the Old Testament (1 Kings xxii. 27; Jerem. xxxvii. 38).—Death by *stoning*, 2 Chron. xxiv. 20, ss., comp. Matth. xxiii. 35. The torture consisting in being bound between two boards and sawn alive in two, is said, according to a tradition common to Christians and Jews, consequently an old Jewish tradition, to have been undergone by the prophet Jeremiah under Manasseh. Now follows ἐπειράσθησαν. The cursive manuscript 17 places this word before ἐπρίσθησαν; it is omitted altogether in the Peschito, Aethiop., Eusebius, and Theophylact; but these inconsiderable deviations are easily to be accounted for by the internal difficulty which lies in the word. For it is difficult to see what this jejune and general expression, "they were tempted," can have to do in this connexion,[1] and as sure as *some word* must have originally stood in this place, so sure is it that

[1] Olshausen thinks, that the temptation to apostatize from the faith is represented as the acme of all the suffering that can befall the Chris-

this cannot have been the word. Of all the conjectures which have been made, that of Sykes is the best : ἐπυρίσθησαν "they were burned" (comp. 2 Macc. vi. 11, vii. 4, s.; Dan. xi. 33). This, first of all, explains the early appearance of the reading ἐπειράσθησαν; but it accounts also for the omission of the word in in the Peschito, Aethiop., &c. For one transcriber might easily put for ἐπυρίσθησαν the synonymous word ἐπρήσθησαν, which a second might confound with ἐπρίσθησαν, or might even read it so, and therefore omit it.—*In sheepskins and goatskins*, suffering, want, affliction, and every kind of evil, lived such men as Elijah (1 Kings xix. 13 and 19; 2 Kings i. 8, ii. 8, ss.), and other prophets (Zech. xiii. 4).—"Men, of whom the world was not worthy, wandered about in deserts and in caves" (comp. 1 Kings xviii. 4 and 13, xix. 8 and 13; 1 Macc. ii. 28, ss; 2 Macc. v. 27, vi. 11). Two ideas are indicated in these words; on the one hand the greatness of the world's guilt, in rejecting men of whom they had reason to be proud; on the other, the heavenly consolation, that this world is also in reality unworthy of such souls. Let not any one who has to suffer for his faith forget this consolation, when his displeasure arises at that guilt, and his suffering appears to him as a wicked injustice on the part of the world; let him bear in mind what *honour* those are counted worthy to receive from *the Lord*, who, on the Lord's account, are reckoned unworthy by the world.

Ver. 39, 40. And yet all these (those adduced in ver. 4—38) had not (aor. for the pluperf.) obtained the promise (ἐπαγγελία, as at ix. 15, x. 36, xi. 13), and nevertheless, were so strong in faith. To the *Christian* readers who had already received so much, and for whom, therefore, the hope in reference to the future was so much easier, what a humbling motive was presented in this strength of faith shown by the *Old Testament* saints, who had to walk almost entirely in the dark, and had to look for almost everything from the future!—Μαρτυρηθέντες διὰ τῆς πίστεως—this expression has in itself (διά), and, according to the context, a different sense of course from ver. 2. In ver. 2 it was said by way of *intimation:* Already it was testified to the ancients that they were believers. Here, mention is made *retrospectively*

tian. But then ἐπειράσθησαν ought to form the conclusion, and stand at the end of ver. 38.

of "all those who through the faith (which they displayed) have gained a testimony (to their praise)."—In ver. 40 the reverse side of the motive is presented. Do those Old Testament believers present an example fitted to shame the Christian readers, inasmuch as faith was made so difficult to them and *yet* they believed, and does there already lie in this humbling example a motive for the readers to strive after that strength of faith,—so does a further motive lie in this, that the Christians have before them a glory so much the greater. In order, however, rightly to understand these words of the 40th verse:— "that God in regard to us has provided something better in order that they should not be made perfect without us,"—we must keep in view the doctrine of the Holy Scripture on the state after death (which in the evangelical system of doctrine has not been fully developed). The Scripture does not teach, that in the case of all men the last and final decision takes place immediately after death, but very plainly teaches the contrary. The consequence and punishment of sin is, according to the Holy Scripture, not eternal condemnation (this is mentioned for the first time in Is. lxvi. 24, and as the punishment of an obstinate rejection of the Messianic salvation, consequently of positive unbelief, and, in perfect consistency with this, the New Testament teaches that the punishment of the eternal second death stands connected with the positive rejection of the known and offered salvation, or the falling away from the salvation which had once been accepted. Comp. our remarks on chap. vi. 4 ss., and on chap. x. 27). The punishment of sin simply considered is death, *i.e.*, the separation of the man from God, and of nature from the man, and the body from the soul (which unhappy separation *would* indeed last for ever, and would increase, if no redemption had been offered; now, however, it lasts for ever only in the case of those who despise this offered salvation). The punishment of sin simply considered is that the soul goes into Sheol, into the kingdom of the dead, and thither go and have gone *all* who are born only of *woman*, who are only descendants of the first Adam, consequently all heathens who had not opportunity to hear of the salvation, and, in like manner, all *Israelites who lived before Christ* (with the exception of Enoch and Elijah). It is not thereby denied, that, in this Sheol, there may be a difference between the state of the penitent and pious who longed for the salvation, and that of the bold and hardened sinner. David hopes, that even in the valley of the shadow of death, God will still be with him and comfort him (Ps. xxiii. 4), and the second David has evidently taught us in the parable of the rich man and Lazarus, that there is a gulf fixed between those who suffer torment and those who are comforted with Abraham (Luke xvi. 25, 26), and, accordingly, when he himself was about to enter into Sheol, he promised to the penitent thief that to-day he would be with him " in paradise." The entrance into the heavenly holy of holies, on the other hand (Heb. x. 19 s. &c.), *i.e.*, into the sphere of *glorification* and of *glorified* nature, was first opened up by Christ's going before as the first-fruits through his resurrection and ascension, and opened for those who are, not men together with Christ, side by side with him, but, members of "the one who is in heaven" (John iii. 13)—not the posterity of the first Adam, but, by regeneration, sons of the second Adam. This the Old Testament believers were *not*. They had the subjective longing for the promised salvation, and subjective faith in it; but the real objective regeneration, the germ of new life, proceeding from the exalted Christ, which is implanted in us by baptism, and is nourished in the holy sacrament of the supper—this they had not; and we must be on our guard against losing sight of the distinction which the Holy Scripture makes in this respect between the old and new covenant. *First with us* were they to be made perfect, and were they made perfect. Christ came to them to set open for them the gates of the place of the dead (Rev. i. 18), and to lead them forth along with him (Matth. xxvii. 53; comp. John viii. 56). From that time the souls of all who die as living members of Christ go to him in heaven (Phil. i. 23; John xiv. 20), in order, at his second coming, to be united again to their bodies (Rev. xx. 4), and then to reign with Christ in glorified body over the rest of mankind, finally, however, to take not a passive (John v. 24), but an active part (1 Cor. vi. 3), in the judgment of the world. Those who are then still in Sheol are, in like manner, awaked at the judgment, and judged "according to their works," according to the rule laid down in Rom. ii. 6—8; Matth. xxv. 31 ss., *i.e.*, those who by patient continuance in well-doing have striven after an imperishable existence will now be made acquainted with the salvation in Christ (for in their case, too, the words will hold good that there is salvation in no other than in Christ), and will become whole through the leaves of the tree of life (Rev. xxii. 2), the others, however, will fall into everlasting perdition.—It is time, indeed, that this *biblical* doctrine of the state after death were again preached to *congregations;* for the common hard and truly unscriptural doctrine which knows nothing further after death than happiness or condemnation, is in its practical effects equally mischievous with the Roman Catholic doctrine of Purgatory, in which a trace of the doctrine of Sheol, but only a caricatured trace of it, is contained.

CHAP. xii. 1—3. An *exhortation* is here drawn from all that has been said in chap. xi. Τοιγαροῦν occurs seldom in the New Testament, as it expresses a fine emphasis more proper to classic Greek. Τοιγάρ serves, like the German "doch," to strengthen the οὖν. The New Testament authors, in the simplicity of their style, generally use instead of this a mere ἄρα or οὖν or διό.— Καὶ ἡμεῖς are the members of the *new* covenant in opposition to the members of the *old* covenant, mentioned in the 11th chapter. Ἡμεῖς has for its apposition the words τοσοῦτον ἔχοντες περικείμενον ἡμῖν νέφος μαρτύρων; νέφος is used also by profane writers as the poetic-figurative designation of a crowd.—The exhortation itself: *let us run with patience,* &c., is expressed in a figure taken from those prize contests which, being of Gentile origin, were transplanted among the Jews also by the Herodians, and which must have made a strong impression on the imagination of that people, as Paul too makes frequent use of them as comparisons.

In order, however, to be able to come off well in the race, one must lay aside ὄγκον πάντα, "everything that encumbers." It is insipid to explain this figure of *corpulence,* which indeed cannot be laid aside. Equally unsuitable is the interpretation by "ballast;" it is not indeed a race of ships, but a prize race of men that is here spoken of! The expression rather refers to the practice among racers of laying aside whatever they had with them or on them that was heavy, or might be a hindrance, even their very garments, in order to be able to run without impediment. If, however, it be asked what is meant by this figurative expression, the author cannot have understood by the ὄγκος *sin*, as he immediately afterwards names this as a special and principal kind of ὄγκος. Hindrances in the struggle of faith and a public profession with the fear of persecution lie not *merely* in sin, but may also lie in things which are themselves indifferent and allowed. Intercourse and friendship with old Jewish acquaintances, the relations formed by trade and merchandise, might be hindrances of this kind for the readers, and, in such a case, it was right and is still right to break entirely away from such relations, and to get rid of the fetters which they impose as soon as they threaten to become a snare, even though in themselves they should be innocent. We, too, have many and various customs of life which in themselves are quite innocent, but which through habit may become bonds that threaten to fasten themselves round the heart. It is required of us also that we be watchful and keep ourselves unencumbered, in order that in the event of the profession of our faith becoming again a thing for which we must pay dear, we may not feel fettered by trifles, but may be able freely to sacrifice all for our Lord.

Sin, however, is by all means the greatest hindrance in that contest. Every bosom sin which we cherish is a handle by which the tempter can lay hold on us, a price for which we are saleable. Hence our author gives to sin the predicate εὐπερίστατος, "encircling us, wrapping us round." (The readings of two codices: ἀπερίστατον and εὐπερίσπαστον are in a critical point of view of no significance.) The word is a ἅπαξ λεγόμενον, and has been variously explained. Some derived it from περίστημι in the signification " to draw from a purpose," and rendered : " the sin from which one can be easily converted," a sense which is here altogether unsuitable. Others, as Chrysostom, derived it from περίστημι in the signification "to encircle," but as an adj. verb. with passive sense, and rendered : " the sin which can easily be encircled," which is just as unsuitable. Kuster, Böhme, and others appealed to the signification of ἀπερίστατος, "destitute of spectators," and rendered : the sin which has many spectators and admirers. It would thus be represented as a false ornament on the racer, which attracted the admiration of the spectators, but was an encumbrance to himself in the race. But this, too, would be an artificial and far-fetched idea. Still more artificially

does Wetstein, following the same etymology, render εὐπερίστατος by "seen of many" = "which does not remain hid, but
comes at length to light." The only two suitable explanations are
—that of Salmasius and Kypke, who take it as denom. from περί-
στασις, "complication," and render "most complicated," and the
still simpler one of Oecumenius, Theodoret, Erasmus, Vatable,
Castellio, Tholuck, Bleek, &c., who derive it from the middle
περιίστασθαι, "to surround," as adj. verb. with *active* (middle)
sense, and render by insidiosus, "subtly encircling us."

Ver. 2. In that prize race we are to "look to Jesus, the leader
and perfecter of the faith." Ἀφορᾶν, like ἀποβλέπειν, denotes the
looking away from the nearest object upon which we unconsciously
look, to an object upon which the eye is consciously fastened.
Jesus is mentioned here as that object, and he is here further
called ὁ ἀρχηγὸς καὶ τελειωτὴς τῆς πίστεως. Ἀρχηγός signifies
not "beginner," does not therefore form an antithesis to τελειωτής (as if it were intended to designate Jesus as the beginning and end of faith.) He who does not, as an expositor,
practice that ἀφορᾶν in a wrong way, who does not falsely look
away from what lies nearest, the simple sense of the words, and
seek in the distance what lies quite at hand, will have little
difficulty in finding out the signification of ἀρχηγὸς καὶ τελειωτής. A long series of "witnesses" had been adduced in chap.
xi., beginning with Abel. The author and his readers along with
him look back into the past, and see, at the extremity furthest
back, Abel with his faith in the future and invisible as yet quite
undeveloped. This faith becomes ever clearer and more definite
in Abraham, Moses, and the subsequent individuals in the series;
but the foremost in the line is Jesus, the *leader* who stands at the
head, and in whom that faith appears in full and *perfected* glory.
In that he renounced all the glory which he might have had if
he had been disobedient to his Father and had followed the
seducer, and chose rather the shame of the cross—gave up the
peace and joy of life, gave up his little band of disciples to the
danger of being scattered and led astray—and, seeing before him
the apparent *destruction* of his person and cause, still remained
faithful to the wonderful will of the Father, followed his leading
in the dark, and stedfastly maintained, in spite of hell, the sure
expectation of faith that the Father would *raise him up*, and

through death destroy death—in all this, he has displayed the *perfected faith*, and leads in royal majesty the line of those *witnesses*. That which is required in chap. xi. 1, Christ has perfectly fulfilled. Nay, he not merely *had* but *was* the *substance of things hoped for !*

Instead, however, of understanding this idea of the πίστις in the general way in which it is spoken of in the context of this section, a number of commentators have known no other meaning to give to πίστις than that dogmatically defined idea of "faith in justification through Christ," an idea which has its place in the epistle to the Romans, but not here. They understand by it, therefore, that *special form and manifestation which the general state of mind denoted by* πίστις *takes in the penitent sinner, in relation to his Saviour.* According to this explanation it must appear incomprehensible how faith can be ascribed to Christ the Saviour himself, as he neither required, nor was in a condition, to believe in the forgiveness of sins for Christ's sake. In order now to escape this absurdity, some (as Schleusner, Knapp, Kuinoel) explained, that Christ is the "beginner" of faith, because, by his redemption-work, he has made faith possible for us and for him; others (as Chrysostom) that he is called ἀρχηγός, because he himself, by his spirit, works the beginnings of faith in us. In a similar way it was attempted to explain τελειωτής. (Schulz, Tholuck, and Bleek, who take ἀρχηχός = exemplar (for us) approximate to the true explanation ; Olshausen, too, who indeed allows that Christ receives those predicates in reference to his own faith, but renders ἀρχηγός by "beginner," and, instead of referring both to the series of *witnesses*, rather finds in them a reference to this,— that it was necessary even for Christ himself, to struggle on from the beginnings of faith to its completion.)

The relative sentence ὃς ἀντὶ τῆς, &c. serves most fully to confirm the explanation we have given of ἀρχηγὸς καὶ τελειωτής. As in the case of all those individual examples of faith in chap. xi. 4—31, there was always specified some visible possession which they renounced, or some earthly privation and affliction which they endured, but, on the other hand, a future reward which they saw before them — so also was it with Christ. He has endured the cross, and counted small and light the shame of this kind of death; 'for this, however, he has sat down on the right hand of God. In him the deepest ignominy was united with the highest absolute exaltation.—The only question here is, how the words ἀντὶ τῆς προκειμένης χαρᾶς are to be explained. Either (with the Peschito, Luther, Calvin, Calov, &c.) ἀντί is taken in the sense of "instead of," and by χαρά is understood the earthly joy which Christ renounced, or (with Itala, Aeth., Beza, Bengel, Hunnius, Grotius, and the most of recent commentators) ἀντί is taken in the sense of "for the sake of, for;" and by χαρά is understood the heavenly joy for the gaining of which he endured the cross. But as χαρά has the attribute προκειμένη, and this is the usual term for designating that which was "set before" the runners in a race (and such are spoken of in ver. 1—3), *i.e.* the prize set up at the goal, the second explanation is on this ground to be preferred.

In ver. 3 γάρ, because standing beside an imperative, is not argumentative, but explicative: another side of that in which the *looking to Jesus* consists is here described. Ver. 3 indeed contains also an argument, namely, the idea which forms the *connecting link* between vers. 1 and 2. "Let us run with patience—while we look to Jesus the leader of the witnesses of faith (in what respects he is so we are told in the relative sentence *who for the joy, &c.*)—remember, namely, that he had to endure *so great* a contradiction." This third idea serves to show plainly, *in how far the looking to Jesus is necessary and beneficial for them in their own race*. This was not as yet shown in ver. 2; in ver. 2 Jesus was only compared with the *witnesses*, chap. xi., and the fact that he *endured the cross and has sat down on the right hand of God* was stated only objectively, to demonstrate that Jesus has had the most perfect faith. On the other hand, it is now shown in ver. 3, how the *looking to* this *faith* (of the great leader of those witnesses, chap. xi.) stimulates us *also* to a like faith. The expression *who endured such contradiction* is no longer purely objective, but involves an implicit comparison of that which *Christ* had to suffer, with what *the readers* had to suffer. These (according to ver. 4, compared with chap. v. 33 ss.) had not yet been persecuted unto blood. They had at most endured nothing further than *contradiction;* they had been denied the right of fellowship with the Israelitish theocracy and of worshipping in the temple: they had been in various ways spoiled of their goods and insulted. By means of a litotes, the author now exhorts them to remember *that* Jesus who has endured *such* contradiction (as was described in ver. 2), a severer contradiction, therefore, than they have endured. The train of thought therefore is this: Run with stedfast patience. To the end of the course you must look to Jesus, who, in his death on the cross, has proved himself to be the absolute champion of faith. And if you are required to look to him, then you are required to consider that man who has endured *such* a contradiction—truly a greater and severer *than you* have been called to endure. Of this *looking* to Jesus and *considering* him, the consequence (and therewith also it aim) will be, that the readers do not become wearied through the flagging of their spirits. As κάμνειν is generally used absolutely, ταῖς ψυχαῖς ὑμῶν will therefore be dependent, not on κάμητε, but on ἐκλυόμενοι. Κάμνειν and ἐκλύεσθαι, however, form no tautology. Κάμνειν denotes the state of being passively wearied and *unable* to do anything more as the *effect* of the ἐκλύεσθαι; ἐκλύεσθαι denotes the being relaxed and careless as a culpable act and cause of the κάμνειν. Ἐκλύεσθαι is not passive but middle.

SECTION FIFTH.

(Chap. xii. 4—17.)

FOURTH MOTIVE. THE BLESSING OF CHASTISEMENT.

Affliction and persecution have a twofold character; on the one hand, they may be regarded as *trials of faith*, as trials showing how much of the *new man* there is in the Christian, and how strong that new man is, on the other hand, however, they are also *chastisements* and means of purification, which serve entirely to destroy the *old man*—the latter, indeed, only when the trial of faith is overcome, when there is an invigorated new man already present, who, by bearing those trials, *acquires new strength* and gains thereby new conquests over the old Adam. From this point of view, the author regards the threatening persecutions in this fifth section. He shows that that suffering has, at the same time, the quality of a means of purification and discipline, but shows also that it only then becomes a παιδεία when the Christian bears it in faith (ver. 4—11). He then (in ver. 12—17) repeats the old exhortations (chap. x. 19—25, comp. chap. xii. 1—3), so, however, as that he gives prominence to certain special points.

Ver. 4 forms the transition. The words πρὸς τὴν ἁμαρτίαν are dependent on ἀνταγωνιζόμενοι, not on ἀντικατέστητε, as the latter is already determined by the accompanying expression μέχρις αἵματος, while the former would otherwise stand quite alone, and be an aimless repetition of the idea already implied in ἀντικατέστητε. We have, therefore, to render thus: You have not yet in the struggle with sin resisted even to blood.—First of all, the question presents itself what is meant here by *sin*, whether the sin of the readers which was spoken of in ver. 1—in which case, the author in ver. 4 imputes it as a *fault* to the readers that they were remiss in the *internal* struggle for sanctification, and the expression *unto blood* must be understood *figuratively* = " you have not yet striven to the uttermost against your sins." Or, whether the objective power of sin is here meant,—sin as the enmity of the world against the gospel and its professors,—consequently, the *contradiction of sinners* mentioned in ver. 3—in which case ver. 4 contains a simple *statement of the fact*, and the expression *unto blood* can be taken in the proper sense = " you have not yet needed to resist unto blood in the contest with sinners." The words do not determine which of these interpretations is the right one. The former would certainly also be suitable to the contest. The author would, in this case, set over against the *exhortation*, given in ver. 1, to cast away all sin from them, the *statement by way of a reproof*, that the readers had as yet not rightly done this. But then, we should have expected a somewhat more detailed and pointed statement of *what* sins they were, to which especially they as yet gave place. Instead of this, the fault which he imputes to them in ver. 5, is not one having reference to particular sins (as the *hindrances* in the struggle connected with their profession), but only to their indolence in this struggle itself (consequently, to the *effect* of these hindrances), namely, the fault that they did not consider the persecutions as a blessing and a benefit. Moreover, in ver. 1 the laying aside of sin did not form the kernel of the exhortation—this lies in the words *run with patience.* On these grounds it appears to me more probable, that the *second* explanation of ver. 4 is the right one. " You have not yet needed to resist unto blood in the struggle against the power of sin, and (already) you have forgotten," &c. This, at all events, is a less violent transition. That the author says here *against sin*, and not as in ver. 3, *against sinners*, may be simply explained by this, that men collectively might as " sinners" (the *class* sinners) be placed in opposition *to Christ*, while, *vice versa*, the enemies of Christianity could not be placed as " sinners" in opposition to the readers of the epistle to the Hebrews, who were themselves sinners (ἁμαρτωλοί).

In Ver. 5—6 the author complains that his readers, although as yet by no means persecuted unto blood (comp. chap. x. 33 ss.), nevertheless already shrunk back with fear from every suffering, and must therefore have forgotten the truth (expressed in Prov. iii. 11—12) that to endure suffering and persecution is not inconsistent with standing in the relation of a child of God, and is no token of the want of fatherly love on the part of God, but on the contrary, is a proof of his fatherly love. (The trifling deviations of the LXX. from the original text make no substantial alteration in the sense.)

In Ver. 7—8 the author now expresses, first of all, the important truth, that one must *bear* the suffering *in order that* it may bring blessing, and have the quality of being a means of instruction. Εἰς παιδείαν ὑπομένετε. *Only when* it is borne in a Christian spirit as coming from the hand of God, does it produce the effect for which it is intended, *i.e.*, the destruction of the old man. " Be patient in order to your instruction."

Misunderstanding this fine sentiment, many commentators have, however, rejected the genuine and fully authenticated reading εἰς, found in the three uncial manuscripts A, D, E, which are generally collated for the Epistle to the Hebrews, in thirty other codd., in the Peschito, Vulgate, the Latin versions of the codd. D, E, the Kopt., Sahid., Aethiop., Armen, &c., and have preferred to it the entirely unauthenticated reading of some versions εἰ, which, it is held, yields a better sense. It gives a more jejune and easier sense, and this accounts for its origin. A really apposite sense, however, it does *not* give. For what sort of sense is this: " If ye patiently bear your discipline (or chastisement), then God deals with you as sons?" Surely God already *deals with them* as sons in *sending* suffering, and not first when the man *patiently ͞ bears* the suffering ; hence Grotius, Limborch, Kuinoel, Bleek, &c., have in reality felt necessitated to give ὑπομένειν here the weakened signification ".to have to suffer" ("if ye have chastisement to suffer," &c.), but this is contradicted by the context, in which ὑπομένειν and ὑπομονή is everywhere quite properly used as *terminus technicus* for the idea of patience in suffering.

And what positive reasons can be adduced against the authorized reading εἰς? Bleek asserts that discipline is not the end of patience, but the object of it. He confounds here, however, the idea of the παιδεία with that of the πειρασμός or the ͞ θλίψις. Suffering certainly becomes then, and only then, a *means of instruction and sanctification*, when the Christian receives it with patience, and submits to it without resistance. This is precisely what the author intends to say. The fact that suffering may become παιδεία to them, he mentions as a *new motive* which should stimulate the readers to exercise ὑπομονή.—It is said, further, that if the words εἰς παιδείαν ὑπομένετε are taken as an independent clause, there arises, between this and the following clause, an *asyndeton* so harsh as to be inconsistent with the usual style of our author. But what is there to necessitate our taking ὡς here as an adverb, and referring it to the noun υἱοῖς ? We take ὡς as a conjunction either in the sense of " as " (as at Luke iii. 23; Rom. i. 9; Heb. iii. 11)—" endure patiently in order to discipline, as God then treats you as sons"—or, better still, in the sense of time, "when," "so long as" (as at Luke iv. 25; Gal. vi. 10)—" endure patiently in order to discipline, when God treats you as sons."

The latter idea needs now an explanation, and this is given in the words τίς γὰρ . . . . καὶ οὐχ υἱοί. " Every son needs discipline ; he who enjoys no discipline is no genuine son."—Υἱοί, as at chap. ii. 10, is here used of *Christians* instead of the common expression τέκνα. Comp. what is said in chap. i. 5.

Ver. 9—10. The author now proceeds to consider the subject

from a new point of view. We must be patient under the divine discipline, and let it become indeed discipline to us, all the more that this discipline is for our highest good, and to train us for heaven.—Εἶτα cannot be connected with the question πολλῷ μᾶλλον ὑποταγησόμεθα, so as to make εἴχομεν καὶ ἐνετρεπόμεθα a parenthesis; this is inadmissible partly, on account of the harshness of the construction, partly, because εἶτα only occurs in questions of wonder or irony. Εἶτα must rather be taken in the signification "further," and referred to εἴχομεν. Further, we had our fleshly fathers as instructors and obeyed them; ought we not now rather to be in subjection to the Father of Spirits, and (thereby) live. In the expression καὶ ζήσομεν the writer thought in Hebrew. Σάρξ does not here, any more than elsewhere, denote the *body* (hence Creatianism appeals unjustly to this passage in support of the doctrine that the body alone is begotten by the parents, while the soul is created by God); but σάρξ denotes there, as always, the natural life produced by *creature* powers, in opposition to the life which is produced by the *saving gracious act* of God in regeneration. By the natural generation we become ἄνθρωποι σαρκικοί; it is God who, by his Holy Spirit, causes our ψυχαί to be developed into sanctified πνεύματα. (Comp. on chap. iv. 12.) True *every soul*, even that of the ungodly, develops itself into a spirit, inasmuch as it unfolds itself to a personality with a fixed character and being; but as, in our passage, it is not ungodly persons, but Christians that are spoken of, whose ψυχαί have, through the influence of God, developed themselves into πνεύματα, the author can *here*, with perfect propriety, name God as the father of the πνεύματα. At all events, the expression πατὴρ τῶν πνευμάτων here is to be explained from the antithesis οἱ πατέρες τῆς σαρκός, and is therefore not to be explained from the Old Testament expression אֱלֹהֵי הָרוּחוֹת לְכָל־בָּשָׂר (Num. xvi. 22) (Bleek), with which it has nothing at all to do. (In that expression the principal idea "Father" is wanting, and רוּחוֹת, as the additional words לְכָל בָּשָׂר show, stands in a much wider sense, and does not as here form an antithesis to בָּשָׂר.) It is, in like manner, a mistake to give to πατήρ (with Bretschneider, Kuinoel) the signification "preserver," by which the parallel with πατέρες τῆς σαρκός would be entirely destroyed.

In ver. 10 follows the idea which forms, as it were, the minor proposition between the major εἴχομεν, &c., and the conclusion πόσῳ μᾶλλον, &c., a peculiarity which we have already often had occasion to remark in the Epistle to the Hebrews (for example chap. vii. 15 ss., ix. 15—23, &c.) The *vis conclusionis* in the inference ver. 9, drawn *a minori ad majus*, lies in these two ideas, first, that earthly parents too often educate their children *according to their blind judgment*—without wisdom, from blind partiality, to gratify their vanity, for the sake of their gains— while God, who is love, has in view only the real profit of his children; and secondly, that the earthly fleshly fathers (of sanctified Christian fathers nothing is here said) bring up their children only for a *period* which is soon to pass away, *i.e.* for this earthly life, and the earthly calling, while God educates his children, for the eternal life, for " participation in his own holiness."

Ver. 11 is a precious verse to which properly *experience* alone can furnish the true commentary. All discipline seems, during the time of its continance, to be an object not of joy but of grief; afterwards, however, it yields a peaceable fruit to those who are exercised thereby, a fruit of righteousness. The gen. δικαιοσύνης does not depend directly on καρπὸν εἰρηνικόν ("peaceable fruit of righteousness"), but another καρπόν is to be supplied after ἀποδίδωσι as apposition to the first καρπόν. Thus the idea "fruit of righteousness" is epexegetical of the idea "peaceable fruit." Εἰρηνικός, however, is not to be explained from the Hebrew usage of שָׁלוֹם = "health," so that εἰρηνικός is = "wholesome" (Luther, Castellio, Michaelis, Ernesti, Bretschneider, Kuinoel), but it is to be explained (with Calvin and Tholuck) from its antithesis to the idea of the γυμνασμένον εἶναι. Exercise in hard bitter *conflict* brings *peace* as its fruit. From this, also, the idea of the δικαιοσύνη explains itself. The righteousness of which the Christian first becomes a partaker in consequence of the *finished* conflict *of purification and sanctification*, cannot be the δικαιοσύνη in the Pauline sense, the *justification before God;* this *we* have not to gain; it is already gained (comp. chap. x. 19 s.); it is not the reward of the struggle, but the coat of mail, which we must put on before the struggle, and which qualifies us for the conflict.—On the other hand, however, δικαιοσύνη does not denote merely the *perfected subjective sanctification* as such—just because our righteousness does not lie in this—but the perfect sanctification, *in so far as* it leads to the perfect undisturbed *appropriation* of justification; *i.e.* the (future) state of the new man completely purified from the old Adam, who is *therefore* free from all self-righteousness, and *therefore* rests entirely on the merits of *Christ, because* he is now entirely free from the old Adam, from sin. For it is not to be forgotten, *that it is not our holiness but our sin that makes us self-righteous.* The more disturbed the mirror is, the less do we see in it the spots which cleave to us; the purer the mirror of conscience, the clearer does the smallest stain appear in it. The man whose conscience is asleep and benumbed by sin, will rudely repel the charge that he is a poor sinner as an affront; the more earnestly and successfully a man strives against his sin, so much the more clear does his misery become to him, so much the more does pride and self-righteousness vanish, so much the more heartily does he lay hold on the merit of Christ; and when once we shall have finished the struggle, and, free from the last motion of sinful inclination, shall enter into the Holy of Holies of our Lord and Saviour, we shall then entirely acknowledge and glory in this, that we are righteous before God *only through him and through him alone; i.e.* we shall reap that "fruit of peace," that "fruit of righteousness," the now entirely appropriated *righteousness in Christ,* because we shall then stand and be willing to stand entirely in Christ and no longer out of Christ.

In Ver. 12, 13 the exhortation of ver. 2 and 3 is repeated. The readers, formerly strong in the conflict and zealous in the race, had now become feeble in the hands and slack in the knees; it was their duty to collect their strength anew. The words τροχίας ὀρθὰς ποιήσατε τοῖς ποσὶν ὑμῶν form, as is well known, a hexameter, certainly an unintentional one. The author rather intended only an imitation of the passage in Proverbs iv. 26. Τοῖς ποσίν cannot be taken as *instrumental* ("describe straight tracks with your feet"), as this figure would have no reality to rest upon, inasmuch as the feet describe no tracks, and even although τροχίαι be taken in the wider sense (= footstep), the footsteps do not properly make a line. Τοῖς ποσίν is rather the dative proper, and τροχίαι stands in the sense of "pathways." Prepare straight, *i.e. even* paths for your feet. The opposition is not between straight and roundabout, but between even and rough ways, as appears from the clause ἵνα μὴ τὸ χωλὸν, &c. which expresses the end that is sought to be gained. The readers are not themselves to throw hindrances (stones as it were) on the way, "that that which is already lame may not be quite dislocated." By the χωλόν the readers themselves, of course, are meant, in so far as they had already grown slack in the race, and were thus (speaking figuratively) lamed. They are to take care not to break entirely or to dislocate their limbs, *i.e.* to become entirely incapable of going on in the race; they are rather to strive to recover their original strength and vigour. (To render ἐκτρέπεσθαι by "turn aside from the way" would give no sense.)

Vers. 14, 15.—The exhortation in ver. 14 to strive after peace with all men, is referred by many to the relation of the readers *to the Jews*. Böhme seriously thinks that the author warns his readers against falling out with the Jews, so that they may not have to expect persecutions from them! The explanation of Grotius is more tolerable : Debetis quidem vobis, a Judaismo cavere, attamen non odisse Judaeos ; but, in this case, a more distinct and explicit warning against Judaism must have gone before in ver. 13, and even then the author could scarcely have laid down so absolutely the injunction, *follow peace with all*. It would be still better to understand διώκετε εἰρήνην as a concession ("you may indeed strive after peace with all, but only strive also, &c.) ; we should then, however, expect a μὲν . . . . δὲ . . ., and not *holiness* but faithfulness in their profession of the truth, must have been specified as the antithesis to *peace*. It is better, therefore, with Michaelis, Zachariä, Storr, Tholuck, and Bleek, to refer the whole exhortation to the relation of the readers to *their fellow Christians*, which is also spoken of in ver. 15. They are to guard against *differences among themselves*, they are not to quarrel with one another, but every one is to be earnestly intent on his own sanctification. It has appeared from the observations we have made above at ver. 11, how indispensable this sanctification is in order to attain to happiness, in order to see the Lord. In the 15th verse the two exhortations of the 14th verse are repeated, only in the inverse order. They are carefully to see (each one for himself, and also the one for the other, by means of that παράκλησις described in chap. x. 24 ss.) "that no one remain behind the grace of God" (an expression which is still to be explained from the allusion to a race towards a goal.) And they are likewise to take care "that no springing root of bitterness cause disturbance, and thereby many be defiled." For, in times when the Church is threatened and assailed *from without*, nothing is more dangerous than those internal divisions and factions, which usually arise from obstinately giving to minor differences of a merely relative value the importance of absolute differences, as, for example, is done, when in times in which the fabric of the Christian Church is everywhere in flames, and people come with the fire-engines of the home mission to set about extinguishing the fire, others appear, calling out that the Lutheran engines must not be placed among the United and Reformed engines, in order that the Lutheran jets of water may not mingle with the United and Reformed, and thus occasion a union of works. Each party is rather to work according to its own plan of operation, although these plans should even cross each other, although an incalculable amount of power and success should thereby be lost, although the house should burn down. The opposition of confessions is regarded as absolute, and treated as of greater importance than the opposition between Christ and Belial. Those Jewish Christians, also, to whom the Epistle to the Hebrews was addressed, in their relation to other Jewish Christians and to Gentile Christians, may not have been free from this disease. They, too, may have had their hearts and their heads so filled and carried away with some difference, *which reaches not into the future life*, that they had eyes only for this, and cared not for the trouble and danger which they were preparing for the Church. They considered not that it is always a subtle idolatry, which leads a man to treat a relative thing as if it were the absolute. The purity of a creed even may be made an εἴδωλον.—But wherever such perversity has found place, it becomes a *root of bitterness* ; alienation, strife, bitterness, and confusion grow out from it ; even those who stand on freer ground, and are opposed to the divisions, are yet easily offended and led to take a side and contend for it; but wo to him who *gives* the offence.

In Vers. 16, 17 the author turns back to the principal question, whether the earthly or the heavenly is most loved. Πόρνος, in this context is, of course, to be taken in that familiar symbolical sense in which it so often occurs in the Old Testament (especially Hosea i.—iii; Ez. xvi. and xxiii.), and also in the New Testament (James iv. 4), to designate those who violate the spiritual marriage-covenant with their God. Βέβηλος, as antithetical to ἅγιος, designates the same men in respect of their *profane, unspiritual* character. A warning example of this character is presented in Esau, who cared so little for the blessing of the first-born that he sold his birthright for a savoury dish, and in doing so frivolously exclaimed: "What profit then shall the blessing do to me?" (Gen. xxv. 32.) Not until God in his righteous providence brought it about, that Jacob cheated him out of the blessing, did he " cry aloud and was exceedingly grieved," and wished to have the blessing which Jacob had received. To this our 17th verse refers. Many commentators (Beza, Gerhard, Carpzov, Storr, Michaelis, Böhme, Klee, Tholuck, &c.), rightly understand, therefore, by the μετάνοια here, *the changing of Isaac's mind* (Esau found no possibility of changing Isaac's resolution). Against this it cannot (with Bleek) be objected, that Isaac did really change his mind, for, in what did this change show itself? He perceived his *error*, but he adhered to the resolution that Jacob should keep the blessing which had been given to him, and Esau could in reality move him to no change in his purpose. To this also the words τόπον μετανοίας οὐχ εὗρε are quite suitable. He found no more room (in his father's heart), where a change of mind might have taken place. Nor was there any need of a πατρός at μετανοίας, as, already at the verb ἀπεδοκιμάσθη, a ὑπὸ τοῦ πατρός must be supplied. Only according to this explanation also do the words καίπερ μετὰ δακρύων ἐκζητήσας αὐτὴν (scil. τὴν μετανοίαν obtain a meaning. These words contain a reference to Gen. xxvii. 34.—If, on the other hand, we understand by μετάνοια Esau's own inward sorrow and repentance, then the last words are meaningless and untrue; meaningless, because he who seeks repentance with tears thereby already manifests repentance; untrue, because in Gen. xxxiii. Esau shows a changed heart, emptied of revenge and reconciled. No other way remains, then, (except with Calvin, Bengel, Bleek, &c.) to take the words μετανοίας γὰρ τόπον οὐχ εὗρε as a parenthesis (but even then they give no tolerable sense), and to refer the αὐτήν which depends on ἐκζητήσας to εὐλογίαν—the most unnatural construction that can be imagined!

SECTION FIFTH.

(Chap. xii. 18—29.)

FIFTH MOTIVE. THE CHOICE BETWEEN GRACE AND LAW; A CHOICE BETWEEN SALVATION AND JUDGEMENT.

The author here, once more, states in bold poetical language the substance of that has been said, and again presents the distinction between the law as preparatory, and the fulfilment in Christ, in all its sharpness, but at the same time in all its greatness and majesty. Both are divine, but the law is terrible; does it only terrify and shake into repentance the slumbering deaf conscience,—it is intended for nothing else; it is not given to confer blessedness, it is terrible; the new covenant with its redemption is lovely and attractive. We have here quite the ground-idea of the Pauline system of doctrine, only, that Paul has developed this psychologically from the subjective experience, while our author, on the contrary, has developed it historically from the objective facts.—He shows, however (ver. 18—24), not merely how attractive and glorious the new covenant is, but also (vers. 25—29) how much more terrible it is to despise the grace of this new covenant, and how much more terrible Christ will be when he shall come again as judge, to those who have preferred the law to grace and have provoked judgment upon themselves.

Ver. 18—24 is also remarkable in respect of its form, on account of the exceedingly elegant (paratactic) structure of the period. *For ye are not come . . . but are come . . .* are the two main pillars upon which the other members of the sentiment rest. The idea expressed in προσέρχεσθε is explained, on the one hand, from Deut. iv. 11, on the other, from Heb. iv. 16 and

22. The Christians are not come to the place where a law is given, but to the city or the kingdom of reconciliation.—The description of the giving of the law from Sinai follows not the more concise account in Ex. xx., but the more detailed in Deut. iv.—v. With respect to the reading, ὄρει, ver. 18, is certainly spurious; it is wanting in A, C, in the versions 17 and 47, in Chrysostom, in the Peschito, Copt., Aethiop., Latin D and Vulgate. It is at once evident, how easily it might find its way as a conjecture into those authorities which read ὄρει; the sentiment requires a ὄρει on two grounds, partly, as antithesis to the words Σιὼν ὄρει, ver. 22, partly, as noun to ψηλαφωμένῳ, which, in respect of its signification, cannot possibly belong to πυρί. Those transcribers who have inserted ὄρει by way of correction, were thus quite right; they have just rectified an *original* mistake in the autograph. The author certainly had the word ὄρει *in his mind*, but neglected to *write it.* (For, only thus, is the omission of the word in all the old authorities to be explained.) We have thus here the rare case of a reading externally spurious, and yet internally genuine.—Ψηλαφωμένῳ, touched, *i.e.* tangible (= ψηλαφητός) designates the mount (Sinai) as an earthly mount, consisting of masses of rock, in opposition to the *heavenly Jerusalem*, ver. 22, the "mount Zion," by which is meant not the earthly geographical hill Zion, but the *Kingdom of Christ* symbolically called Zion.—Κεκαυμένῳ cannot be the attribute to πυρί; for, to designate a fire as one that is "burning" is superfluous, unless it were intended to oppose a burning fire to a painted one, which is not the case here. Κεκαυμένῳ is rather the second attribute to ὄρει, and πυρί is dependent on κεκαυμένῳ: "to the mount that could be touched and that burned with fire." Γνόφῳ, &c., depends, of course, again on προσεληλύθατε and not on κεκαυμένῳ. In addition to these sensibly terrible appearances, blackness, darkness, tempest, sound of trumpets, there was " the voice of words, which (voice) they that heard refused that any word more should be added," *i.e.* the voice of words which was so fearful in its sound and import, that the Israelites wished to hear no word further (Deut. v. 24—26.) True, the ten commandments, themselves, had not yet been spoken (comp. Deut. v. 26 ss. with Ex. xix. 17 and 20), but already the command (Ex. xix. 12, 13), that even no

beast should touch the mountain, put the people in terror. The words κἂν θήριον, &c., form the import of the διαστελλόμενον. The καὶ which follows must belong to Μωϋσῆς εἶπεν, and the words οὕτω φοβερὸν ἦν τὸ φανταζόμενον must be parenthetical; otherwise, there would be an inexplicable asyndeton between φανταζόμενον and Μωϋσῆς. The circumstance here stated, that Moses also said, " I exceedingly fear and quake," can hardly have proceeded from oral tradition. (Erasmus, Beza, &c.), but is taken from the passage Deut. ix. 19 (LXX.) True, in that place it is not the moment *before* the giving of the law that is spoken of, but a point of time *during* the giving of the law, when Moses was made aware of the golden calf (and this our author, who is so much at home in the Old Testament, must have perfectly well known); but his design, here, is not to speak particularly of what belonged to the giving of the law, but in general of the severity and fearfulness of God as he appeared on Mount Sinai. So terrible were the appearances, so fearfully did God manifest his severity, that even Moses himself—not on account of his own trespass, but on account of the sin of the people—was thrown into fear and trembling. (Knapp, Tholuck, &c.)—The Christians are not come to that *earthly* mount, where the *severity* of God was manifested, but to mount Zion symbolically so called, which is the city of the living God, the heavenly Jerusalem. The kingdom of Christ is so designated also at Gal. iv. 26. This (already present) heavenly Jerusalem is different from the new Jerusalem in the Apocalypse of John, which is not to be set up on *the earth* till after the second coming of Christ.—The words which follow are variously construed. Beza, Calov, Carpzov, Storr, &c., make ἀγγέλων dependent on μυριάσιν, and take πανηγύρει together with ἐκκλησίᾳ, so that πρωτοτόκων depends on these two substantives (" to hosts of angels, to the assembly and church of the first born.") But, in this case, it is strange that the καί which unites all the other members is wanting before πανηγύρει. Oecumenius, Theophylact, Erasmus, Luther, Calvin, Grotius, &c., likewise take ἀγγέλων as dependent on μυριάσιν, but understand πανηγύρει as apposition to μυριάσιν (" to hosts of angels, an assembly, and to the church," &c.;) but one has only to hear this rendering, in order to be convinced of what a frigid sense such an apposition would have. The only right construction is that of Wolf, Rambach, Griesbach, Knapp, Böhme, Kuinoel, Tholuck; Bengel, Lachmann, De Wette, Bleek, &c., according to which, ἀγγέλων is dependent on πανηγύρει. It is then most natural to take the two members: ἀγγέλων πανηγύρει and ἐκκλησίᾳ πρωτοτόκων as epexegetical of μυριάσιν. ("And to entire hosts: to the host of angels and to the church of the first born.") The πρωτοτόκοι are the first fruits of the regenerate, the members of the new covenant. As they are not 'described as "*being in heaven*," but "written down in heaven" (Luke x. 20; Phil. iii. 20; also Ex. xxxii. 32 s.; Dan. xii. 1; Phil. iv. 3; Rev. iii. 5, xiii. 8, xvii. 18, xxi. 27, xxii. 19), we are to understand here not those Christians alone who were already dead, but those also who were yet alive, and the μυριάδες comprehends both, the ecclesia pressa or militans, and the ecclesia triumphans. In the new covenant heaven and earth are united and reconciled (Eph. i. 10), while in the giving of the law from Sinai, a gulf was fixed between the trembling people and the terrifying *ministering spirits* (Heb. ii. 14.)

Καὶ κριτῇ θεῷ πάντων,—Primasius, Theophylact, &c., have understood these words of Christ, which is altogether inadmissible, as Christ is afterwards specially named. God the Father is certainly meant. In no case, however, can we (with Erasmus, Michaelis, Knapp, Bleek, &c.) take κριτῇ as a predicate idea ("and to the God of all *as* the Judge"), for the Christians do *not* come to God as their *Judge*, but as their reconciled Father. We must rather either (with Peschito, Vulgate, Luther, Kuinoel, De Wette, &c.) take πάντων as dependent on κριτῇ ("and to God, the Judge of all"), or connect κριτῇ as an adjectival idea with θεῷ ("and to the judging God of all"), which yields substantially the same sense. The nerve of the idea lies in this, that the believers of the new covenant may come near with boldness to the Judge of the *world*, while the Israelites could not come nigh to him, although he was *their own special lawgiver.*—The Christians can come nigh to him, for they find with him already the spirits of the just made perfect (through Christ), and the Mediator himself through whom these were made just. Τελειοῦσθαι does not denote *death*, as if in it the being made perfect consists (Calvin, Kuinoel, &c.), but is used, as at chap. vii. 11—19, x. 14, xi. 40, to denote the *accom-*

plished realized reconciliation. Perhaps the author in these "just made perfect" has had specially in his mind that host of Old Testament believers described in chap. xi.—The culminating point in the glory of the heavenly Jerusalem is *Jesus, the Mediator himself*, with his *blood of reconciliation*, which speaks better than the blood of Abel (comp. chap. xi. 4). Abel's blood cries for vengeance; Christ's blood cries for grace.

Ver. 25. With this is connected the exhortation not to refuse this Jesus who by his blood cries for grace to us. When the Israelites at Sinai (ver. 19) refused to hear God's voice and to fulfil his commands, they were punished. He, moreover, who refuses to hear the voice of grace is lost.—Εἰ γὰρ ἐκεῖνοι οὐκ ἔφυγον,—to this must be supplied τὴν τιμωρίαν; true, it is nowhere said in the Pentateuch that the Israelites had been punished because they *dared not to hear the words of God*: they are rather commended for this (Deut. v. 28, 29.) But the idea of the παραιτεῖν involves here not merely that *praiseworthy* fear, but also the subsequent *actual transgression* of the commands of God (Ex. xxxii.), which was already noticed in ver. 21. At πολλῷ μᾶλλον ἡμεῖς is to be supplied, of course, οὐ φευξόμεθα. The expression ὁ ἀπ' οὐρανῶν scil. λαλῶν finds a simple explanation in the λαλοῦντα at the beginning of our verse, and this, again, is explained from ver. 24. It is Christ, who in heaven cries for grace to us, and thus offers us grace from heaven. (Not: Christ in so far as he descended from heaven and became man, not God the Father.) As now, it is said of him (Christ) in ver. 26, that he shook the earth in the time of Moses (for οὗ can of course be referred only to τὸν ἀπ' οὐρανοῦ), we must also understand by the ἐπὶ γῆς χρηματίζων. Christ (as God the Son, God as revealing himself, comp. 1 Cor. x. 1, ss.), not Moses, nor God the Father.

Ver. 26, 27. The same Christ who has already revealed himself on Sinai as the *Lawgiver*, and who now speaks from heaven as *Mediator*, will come again as *Judge*. In proof of this the passage, Hag. ii. 6, is adduced, which, in its original import, really refers to the coming of Christ to set up his kingdom in glory. Our author plainly lays emphasis on two points in the passage, first on this, that at the second coming of the Messiah, not merely are local appearances of nature to take place on a part of the earth, but *heaven and earth*, the whole visible created world, is to be shaken and unhinged; secondly, on this, that the shaking is to take place ἔτι ἅπαξ, consequently, is to be such a shaking as makes any repetition superfluous, such therefore as is to unhinge and change everything that, generally speaking, is in its nature changeable. The ἔτι ἅπαξ is, indeed, not so explicitly expressed in the original text as in the LXX.; but it is quite clear that the prophet meant a last final shaking of the world, which was at one time to take place, so that the LXX. has substantially rendered the sense quite correctly.

Ver. 28, 29. That which cannot be shaken, which does not go down in the universal change, is the kingdom of Christ. For this is no ποιούμενον, does not belong to the creature, but is the organic assemblage of those who are born of, and filled with, the Son of God and the Spirit of God. The Kingdom of God is the body of Christ.—Παραλαμβάνειν signifies not *to take actively*, but *to receive passively*. As we have received such a kingdom, as we have become partakers of it, let us "have gratitude" (not "hold fast the grace," this must have been expressed by κατέχωμεν τὴν χάριν), and serve God acceptably with reverence and awe. (A, C, D, and versions read μετ' εὐλαβείας καὶ δέους, others μετὰ δέους καὶ εὐλαβείας. The readings μετ' αἰδοῦς καὶ εὐλαβείας and μετ' εὐλαβείας καὶ φοβοῦ have very little authority on their side.) On ver. 29 comp. chap. x. 31.

SECTION SEVENTH.

(Chap. xiii.)

CONCLUDING EXHORTATIONS.

These exhortations are not abrupt and unconnected, but are most closely related to each other, and to the import and aim of the entire epistle. They are also of such a kind, as to cause us no perplexity in the view we have taken, that the epistle is not for a church, but for a circle of catechumens ; for they all refer to the individual, not to the church life.

First, in ver. 1—6 we have exhortations respecting the individual life as such, then, in ver. 7—17, respecting the relation of the individual to the doctrine and the profession, and finally, in ver. 18—25, the conclusion of the writing.

Ver. 1—6. The first virtue which is required is brotherly love, by which is not meant the common Christian love of *man* in the relations of the natural life, at least not it alone, but chiefly, that love of the Christian to the Christian as a member with him of the body of Christ, which forms the antithesis to the *root of bitterness*, chap. xii. 15. That brotherly love which does not in the first place inquire : " Art thou a Jewish Christian ? art thou a Gentile Christian ? art thou Roman or Grecian ? United or Lutheran ? Angelican or Presbyterian ? what *doctrine* and *view* dost thou hold of the Sacrament ?"—but which first and foremost asks : " Art thou become by the *act* of the Sacrament a member of the body of Christ ? (for the church rests on the Sacrament, and not on the doctrine of the Sacrament ; on the latter rests merely the *confession*)—and dost thou stand as a member of Christ in the *life* of Christ and in his *love* ?" He who can answer this in the affirmative is a *brother*, a brother by regeneration, although I may have a purer *knowledge* on many points than he !—An essential manifestation of that philadelphian feeling is *hospitality* (ver. 2), of which we have still, in these days, the finest illustration in the practice of the Philadelphians. The motive, *for thereby*, &c., is explained from Gen. xviii.—xix., and its applicability from Matth. xxv. 44—45. If the Christian is to exercise love even towards brethren who are *strangers*, how much more towards *suffering and persecuted brethren*, ver. 3. Such exercise of brotherly love the readers required, in order most firmly to settle them in *Christianity*—more firmly than by arguments. Chiefly must they, although not yet persecuted themselves, exercise themselves and prepare for the future persecution, by actively receiving those who were already persecuted. He who was afraid of doing so showed by this act, that he would shrink with still more cowardice from his own persecution. This admonition the Christians of our own day may well lay specially to heart. For, in our day, it has become quite the fashion, even among believers, to *disown* every brother, who by taking a firm and determined stand, has brought inconveniences upon himself, and carefully to inquire whether something not quite prudent or quite justifiable may not be discovered in the way in which he has conducted himself, and then to exclaim : " Yes, but he has not done right in this and that." When the pastors of Waadt-land would not acknowledge as " bishop" a college of state councillors which tolerated and encouraged the most blasphemous abominations, there were not wanting wise people who demonstrated to a nicety, that those men had committed a mistake, that they ought to have delayed for some days. May God grant us all the grace to commit *such mistakes !*—Ver. 4 cannot be understood as a warning against an ascetical rejection of marriage (for then he must at least have said : $\tau i\mu\iota o\varsigma\ \dot{o}\ \gamma a\mu\dot{o}\varsigma,\ \dot{a}\lambda\lambda'\ \dot{a}\mu i a\nu\tau o\varsigma\ \dot{\eta}\ \kappa o i\tau\eta$), but the author exhorts that marriage be maintained in honour (and thus *honourable*), and the marriage bed undefiled. He warns against those sins which, according to John viii. 1 ss., were at that time so fearfully prevalent among the Jewish people, that all idea of punishing them had to be given up. The same corruption of the national life has spread through all Europe. The members of Christ are not to be led by such a state of things to think lightly of, and easily to excuse, such sins ; for let him who has one member belonging to hell take care lest he do not altogether belong to it. He is like a bird whose foot the fowler has bound with a thread ; he can fly about apparently free, but still he is in the fowler's power, and if he does not break the thread while it is, yet time, the fowler draws him to himself by means of it at the fitting moment, catches him and kills him. Every bosom sin is a stone which the devil has in the board[1] ; a poison which, chiefly in times of persecution, paralyses the strength of faith.— Nor is it otherwise in respect *to avarice*, ver. 5, that national sin of the Jewish people, the disposition to traffic which they have inherited from the natural life of their ancestor Jacob (comp. Gen. xxv. 31 ss.; xxx. 31—43). He whose heart cleaves to earthly possessions, will be faint-hearted in persecutions. And, in general, a family whose chief concern it is *to do the will of God*, and which commits the care for daily bread to Him who

---

[1] A German proverb meaning " to be in favour with."

will not leave nor forsake us, will lead a very different life (for example, in the sanctification of the Sabbath) from a family whose chief impelling motive is the striving after earthly possessions and wealth, and which goes along with Christianity, only in so far as it will not interfere with worldly convenience.

Ver. 7—9. According to ver. 7, ἡγούμενοι (not teachers but overseers—presbyters or apostles of the Church at Jerusalem to which the readers belonged) had already suffered martyrdom (for the readers are to consider their ἔκβασις and the *faith* thereby attested). However, during the period subsequent to the conversion of the readers no more bloody persecutions had taken place, according to chap. xii. 4. We shall therefore have to understand a reference to such men as Stephen, James the son of Zebedee, and James the younger who was stoned in a tumult in the year 62, men whose death was known to the readers, and whom they even *now* doubtless acknowledged as ἡγούμενοι. Wiesler thinks, there is a reference to the deaths of the two apostles, Paul and Peter, which followed close on each other in the year 64. These two events had certainly made a great impression on the whole society of Christians, and if Paul, although not labouring in the Church of Jerusalem, was yet reckoned among the ἡγουμένοις ὑμῶν, this is to be explained partly, from his universal *apostolical* authority, partly, from the sympathy with which the Christians of Jerusalem must have regarded his imprisonment in Jerusalem and Caesarea, partly, from his close connexion with Peter in Rome during the period immediately preceding his death.

Ver. 8 is not to be connected with ver. 7 by placing a colon after πίστιν, and supposing that ver. 8 states what is the *import* of the πίστις; for, by πίστις is meant, in the whole hortatory portion of the epistle, not faith in so far as it is an acceptance of definite doctrinal-propositions, but faith as that *disposition* of mind which holds fast on the future, and in this aspect alone can faith be spoken of in ver. 7, when it is said that the ἡγούμενοι had attested their πίστις in their death. Ver. 8 is rather to be understood as an explanation of the author's, intended as a *motive* to enforce the exhortation in ver. 7. " Imitate their faith; (for) Christ is the same yesterday, to-day, and for ever." ('Ο αὐτός is predicate.) The same Christ, trusting in whom those died, still lives to-day, and is also our consolation (Calvin.) Such explanations as the following are wrong : the Christian *religion* is everlasting, and will not be abolished in favour of the Jewish (Vatable, Michaelis, Kuinoel, &c.), or : the eternity of the λόγος as such is here spoken of (Athanasius, &c.)

To the statement that the Christ in whom those men died still lives, and that the readers are to place their entire confidence in him, corresponds the warning in ver. 9 not to let themselves be led away by various and foreign doctrines. From the clause, *for it is good*, &c., we perceive that the author must especially have had in his mind casuistic external doctrines regarding the lawfulness or unlawfulness of meats. These doctrines were ποίκιλαι ; one maintained that in the Christian freedom and deliverance from the ceremonial law they might go so far, another, somewhat farther, a third, not so far; every one drew a different line of limitation. The being occupied in general with *such* investigations, the fixing of the attention and interest on *such* questions, was, however, injurious and dangerous; for those doctrines were also " foreign," they related to a point which was irrelevant to Christianity, and led away from the main concern to things of secondary moment, which ought to be entirely beyond the care of the Christian. " For it is good, if the heart be established in *grace*, not in *meats*." Thus and only thus are the datives χάριτι and βρώμασι to be understood (this use of the dative in answer to the question *in what* or *in reference to what* an act takes place, occurs frequently, for example 1 Cor. xiv. 20 ; Rom. iv. 20 ; Acts ii. 37, &c.; comp. Winer's Gramm. § 31, 3). By taking these datives, as is generally done, in an instrumental signification (" by grace not by meats"), all logical connexion with the first member of the sentence is destroyed.

Ver. 10—14. The sentiment is expressed in a much higher form in these verses. Hitherto, it was shown, in the entire epistle, that the Levitical worship and the Levitical purity obtained by it, is *dispensable ;* that it is *no misfortune* to be without it ; and, accordingly, it had just been shown at ver. 9 that the care of the Christian is to be directed to this, that he be settled as regards grace, not as regards ordinances about meats, which *profit nothing*. The author now rises higher ; he leaps, as it were, from the defensive to the offensive; he says: it is not ill with us in this respect, but with the Jews; not we but they are the excommunicated party; we eat of the true sacrificial meat on which everything depends, and from this the *true*, the *Messianic*, our piacular meal, the Jews are excluded. This is the simple and clear statement in ver. 10. "We have an altar, of which they are not at liberty to eat, who still perform their worship in the tabernacle (the Old Testament sanctuary)." The author evidently has in his mind the holy supper, the meal of spiritual life-fellowship and union with the for us dead and now exalted Saviour. It is now shown in ver. 11—12, how that very Jesus who was rejected of the Jews, *notwithstanding* that he was rejected, nay, *because* he was rejected, is the *true* sacrifice, and in ver. 13 s., that consequently, that very company of those who believe in him which is rejected of the Jews, *notwithstanding that*, nay, *because*, it is so rejected, is the true Israel. The confirmation of this is profound, yet clear throughout. According to Lev. xvi. 27, the victim on the day of expiation, because it was (symbolically) laden with the uncleanness and guilt of the whole people, and was consequently *unclean*—not in itself, but by that transference of the guilt of others—must be *taken without the camp, and there burned.* This was done to the victim, *although* it was the same animal whose blood had atoning efficacy, and was carried into the holiest of all! Nay, still more, *because* this was done to it, *because* this animal *was regarded as unclean* on account of the guilt of others, and as unclean was cast outside the camp, *it had* atoning power. Now the same thing, only not symbolically, but really, is true also of Christ. With respect to him also, we are not at liberty to infer from his having been regarded as unclean, and cast out as a malefactor, and killed at the place of execution, that he can be no true sacrifice, and that his blood cannot be the true blood of atonement. But just as that goat, Lev. xvi., was the true symbolical atoning sacrifice, *although* it was regarded and treated as unclean, nay, *because* it was reckoned unclean on account of the guilt of others, so is Christ the true substantial atoning sacrifice, *although*, nay, *because*, he was led without the gate as a criminal, and cast out and killed by the Jews.—From this, now, it follows, ver. 13, that those who are his have not to seek the true sacrifice in the camp of the Jews, but on

Golgotha; that they are not to mourn, and be cast down with sorrow and anguish, although, like their Lord, they should be cast out and treated as unclean; their hope, ver. 14, is not directed towards an earthly citizenship in the earthly Jerusalem, but towards the heavenly citizenship in the heavenly Jerusalem, (chap. xii. 22), the everlasting city.

And accordingly it follows from this, lastly, that the Christians do not need, as the Jews, to continue to offer animal sacrifices; they are not to bring Levitical sacrifices *along with* the sacrifice of Christ, but are only *spiritually to reproduce*, in the manner described at ver. 13, the sacrifice of Christ, by which they have once for all received atonement. Hence there remains no other sacrifice for the Christian to offer, but the *sacrifice of thanksgiving and praise.*

Ver. 15—17. This idea is further developed in ver. 15, 16. The sacrifice of *praise* and of *stedfast profession* (just that reproduction of the sacrifice of Christ described in ver. 13), in addition to this, *beneficence* and communication of gifts, are the sacrifices with which God is well pleased. Κοινωνία in this usage (which first arose in the sphere of the Christian literature) occurs also at Rom. xv. 26; 2 Cor. ix. 13; Phil. i. 5.—With love to the brethren is connected by a natural association of ideas, ver. 17, obedience to the leaders of the Church. Thus the ideas from ver. 7 to ver. 17 describe in their succession a complete circle. The author at ver. 7 began with the ἡγούμενοι, and he returns to them again at ver. 17. He began with the mention of those leaders of the Church who had suffered martyrdom; he had brought them forward as an example of faith, from them he passed to *faith* itself, as opposed to foreign doctrines, then to the obligation above all to be established in grace, to the grand development of the idea that the Jew is the excommunicated party, while the Christian, precisely when he is excommunicated, then first truly enters into the true Holy of Holies, finally, to the doctrine, that the internal reproduction of the sacrifice of Christ —the bearing the reproach of Christ—together with love to the brethren, are the only sacrifices which God desires from the Christian (not as atoning sacrifices but as thank-offerings), and love to the brethren leads him back, at last, to the duty towards the ἡγούμενοι, those, namely, who are *still living.*—Directly, ver.

17 contains the truth, that the member of the church, if he has a faithful shepherd and does not follow him, is lost through his own fault. Indirectly, there lies in it also the other truth, that it is the duty of the shepherd to *watch* over the souls committed to his care, and that he must render an *account* of them all, of those also who have been lost through his fault. This is a solemn word. Let every minister of the word consider, that he has *voluntarily* undertaken this awfully responsible office. No one can excuse his indolence and negligence in this office by saying, that he has been *compelled* to undertake it. How, moreover, will the thieves (John x. 10) justify themselves before God, who have undertaken and forced themselves into the office of those who are called to administer the means of grace in Christ's stead, and have not as messengers of Christ preached His word and gospel, but their own conceits, or what might tickle the ears of the people.

Ver. 18—19 forms the transition to the conclusion. "Pray for me." This should be done at all times; the pastors should be borne upon the prayers of their people; and it is well when the people are on the Sundays reminded of this duty, as is done for example in the Liturgy of Zurich, before imparting the blessing in the words; "Pray for us, as we do also for you."—"For we think that we have a good conscience, as we endeavour to walk uprightly in all things." He who possesses a good conscience in such a manner, has a right to demand intercessions on his behalf. But the author has special occasion for desiring these intercessions, inasmuch as he is in a situation which makes it not a matter depending on his will whether he will return to his readers again. His hoping "to be restored" to the Jewish Christians in Jerusalem points to an earlier personal relation to them. We do not need to suppose, on this account, that the author must have had the official charge of a congregation in Jerusalem; it needs only to be supposed, that the author had been in Jerusalem during the first conversion of those people; so that the authorship of *Paul* would not be excluded by *this* verse.

Ver 20—21. The epistle, properly speaking, closes with the *invocation of a blessing* upon the readers. "The God of peace," he is such to the Christian, who, by faith in the sin-forgiving grace of the Saviour, has attained to peace with God. "Who has brought back from the dead the Shepherd of the sheep, the great one, in the blood of an everlasting covenant." The words ἐν αἵματι do not belong to ἀναγαγών; for the raising of Christ from the dead was not done in the blood of the everlasting covenant; nor does the position of the words suit this; the words in question rather belong plainly to τὸν μέγαν; Christ is the great, true, chief and superior shepherd, inasmuch as he has made an *everlasting* covenant by his blood (comp. chap. xi. 11 ss.). The best commentary on these words is found in John x. He is the good shepherd because he has given his life for the sheep.—Now the God who has raised up this chief shepherd, and has crowned his *faith* (chap. xii. 1—3), has also power, strength, and will to make the members of Christ's body perfect. He is to make them exercised in every good thing to the doing of his will. This, however, is not effected by God's giving us new commandments which we must now fulfil without him, but by himself fulfilling his will *in us* through Christ. Da, quod jubes, et jube, quod vis. In the new man, his own doing and the working of God are not to be separated; Christ himself living within us is identical with our sanctification. A hateful caricature of this truth is presented in Pantheism, in which the will of the natural sinful man is identified with the administration of God, and the unsanctified energy of nature is viewed as the manifestation of the absolute energy of God.

Vers. 22—25 is a postscript. It comes, at all events, from the same hand that wrote the epistle; the question, however, is, whether only from the same *hand* (so that perhaps the amanuensis to whom the epistle had been *dictated* now added the postscript in his own name, and no longer in the name of the proper author, as Tertius, Rom. xvi. 21—24), or whether from the same *subject and author*. The one as well as the other might say, ver. 22, that he had *made use of few words* in the epistle; the amanuensis might also say this, if only we suppose that the epistle was not *verbally dictated* to him, but that it was *left* to him to carry out the ideas.—On account of this brevity he hopes that the readers would take his exhortations in good part; not as if a short epistle would be more welcome on account of its *smaller quantity of matter as such*, but because in condensed diction the author is entitled to reckon on being excused for many a harshness in the exhortations, which would not so easily have been committed if he had time and leisure to be more full. But the writing is indeed concise and compressed, even in its theoretical parts. The saying truly applies to it: quot verba tot pondera. Every little sentence, nay, every member of a sentence, contains an exponent which might be developed into an entire series. Even in the choice of the themes and sections the strictest measure is observed. The author has purposely omitted much that he might have brought within the scope of his consideration. How well, for example, might he have carried out a comparison of Christ also with the Passover. But this he has only faintly indicated in chap. xiii. 10. He was evidently pressed by time and circumstances. Accordingly, he was obliged also in the hortatory pieces (chiefly in chap. vi. and x.) often to lay down solemn warnings shortly and almost unconnectedly. For this he begs to be excused in ver. 22; he could not do otherwise; he wrote *shortly* and could not but write so.

In ver. 23 he notices that Timothy has been set free. Timothy then had been imprisoned. When? on this see the appendix. When now he says, that in case (ἐὰν) Timothy shall come *soon* he will see the readers together with Timothy, this seems to imply, that *he himself* was *not* in prison, and that the hindrance to his return (ver. 19), for the removal of which he asks his readers to pray, cannot have consisted in an *imprisonment*. For had he been in prison, he must first have waited for his release, and then it had not depended on Timothy's coming soon, whether he would see his readers with Timothy or without him.—The 23d verse, therefore, leads us to the supposition that the author was free, was already about to set out on a journey, and would have taken Timothy, who had just been released from imprisonment along with him, on condition that he would come soon enough to his house, and fetch him away.

Nevertheless, a number of difficulties open themselves up here. How then could the author exhort the readers in ver. 19 to pray for him that he might be restored to them, if he was so free and ready for a journey?—Further: why in general does he write at all, if he intends to come himself to them?—I find that the commentators, hitherto, have passed too easily over this difficulty. I can see only two solutions of it. *Either* we must suppose, that the author wrote the postscript at a time somewhat later than the epistle; when he wrote the epistle he was still in prison; not till after his release did he add the postscript. But then, we should certainly have expected that, in this postscript, he would make grateful mention of his own lately and unexpectedly obtained deliverance. (Such as: But God be thanked who has done above what we ask or think, and has delivered me.) *Or* better, we suppose that the proper author of the epistle was really in prison (yet according to ver. 19 not without hope of obtaining his freedom), but that the appendix vers. 22—25 proceeds not from him, but from that *helper*, to whom he did not, perhaps dictate the epistle, but gave him only the ideas, with whom he had talked over the substance of it, leaving the conception to him. This helper had then, indeed, reason to ask excuse for himself (ver. 22) on account of certain harsh expressions. This helper relates the deliverance of Timothy. This helper is free and prepared for a journey—still, neither he nor Timothy can have gone *direct to Jerusalem*, in order to carry the epistle; otherwise, the entire postscript or (if Timothy was the bearer) at least the notice respecting him had been superfluous. But that helper hoped indeed to come soon to Jerusalem with Timothy, went, however, somewhere else before this, so that the epistle was transmitted through some other person.

From Ver. 24 it appears, that the helper was in *Italy;* for he writes salutations from the Christians of Italy. The explanation "those who have fled from Italy" (Bleek, &c.) cannot well be admitted, because then it had been strange that *only* these and not also the other Christians who lived in the place where the epistle was written, should have sent by the writer salutations to the readers. The ἀπό is easily explained; with less propriety could he have said ἐν, if he himself was in Italy; if he had said "the saints in Italy," he would thus have designated these so *objectively*, as to make it appear *that he himself was not also in Italy*. Hence he chooses the preposition ἀπό. "The saints of Italy salute you;" those who are natives of Italy, those who are there *at home*, as opposed to himself, who indeed was in Italy, but was not of Italy. Thus the Greek says (comp. Tholuck on the passage) οἱ ἀπὸ γῆς and οἱ ἀπὸ θαλάσσης, "the travellers by land, the travellers by sea," so

Polyb. 5, 86, 10, οἱ ἀπὸ τῆς Ἀλεξανδρείας βασιλεῖς, the Alexandrian kings. Comp. also Acts xvii. 3. Tholuck, indeed, has still a difficulty. Why does the author not say ἀπὸ Ῥωμῆς? First, because he would write salutations from *all* the churches of Italy; secondly, because he himself, as we will afterwards see, was not at Rome.

The concluding verses of the Epistle lead us naturally to the critical inquiry respecting its *date, aim,* and *author*, which inquiry, having now made ourselves familiar with the *contents* of the Epistle, we intend to conduct in an appendix.

APPENDIX.

ON THE DATE, DESTINATION, AND AUTHOR OF THE EPISTLE
TO THE HEBREWS.

CHAPTER FIRST.

THE CIRCLE OF READERS.

In the *want of a superscription* or address, in the *highly systematic distribution of the matter* into very distinctly defined sections, the themes of which are in every case formally intimated, as well as in the marked separation of the hortatory sections from the theoretical, finally, in the *difficulty of the diction*, the terseness of the sentiments, and that subtlety of argumentation in which much is really only indicated, and connecting links are left to be supplied by the reader's reflection (and his diligent comparison of the Old Testament with the epistle)—in all these respects the Epistle to the Hebrews is distinguished from all the other New Testament epistles, and considering all these peculiarities we may well say (what Berger[1] has said with substantial truth, although in a wrong way), *that the Epistle to the Hebrews is no epistle in the true and proper sense, or at least is no epistle in the ordinary sense.* The author on his part has not surrendered himself to the free and unrestrained effusion of his thoughts, cares, wishes and feelings in this writing (as Paul does even in the most systematic of his epistles, that to the Romans), but he has worked out and

[1] Göttinger Theol. Bibl. part iii. p. 449 ss.

elaborated it according to a well-considered plan, so that he evidently subordinates the subjective flow of his thoughts and feelings to this objective plan. The strict order of his argumentation is never broken in upon by overflowing emotions (as is done for example in Rom. i. 22 ss.; ii. 1 and 3 ss, and 24; iii. 5 and 9; vii. 24; xi. 33, &c.). The readers on their part could not possibly have understood the Epistle to the Hebrews if, like the rest of the New Testament epistles, it had been read a single time before an assembly of the Church; the Epistle to the Hebrews, in order to be understood, must be gone through section by section, slowly, carefully, and repeatedly, with continual comparison of the Old Testament passages cited in it and their connexion. Upon this the author has evidently reckoned.

It was then no ordinary epistle; it was more than an epistle, *it had in reality something of the nature of a theological treatise*, and in so far Berger is certainly right. But he evidently went too far when he thought that the Epistle to the Hebrews was a *mere treatise* written not at all for a *definite* circle of readers, but for the entire Christian, or at least Jewish Christian public (something in the same way as the Gospel of Matthew). He found himself in this case driven to the unnatural supposition, that the appendix chap. xiii. 22—25 was first added supplementarily by one who was sending the treatise on to some other churches. But by this nothing is gained. For not merely in the appendix, but also in the epistle itself (chap. xiii. 19) *personal* relations of the author to the readers are presupposed, and moreover, the style of the exhortation points to a quite definite class of readers. Not only is it a very special error or spiritual malady that is counteracted throughout the entire epistle, not only must an exact acquaintance with the spiritual state of the readers be presupposed in the hortatory parts, but in the passage chap. v. 12 it is even indicated that the readers collectively had passed over to Christianity together at one and the same time, and in chap. vi. 10 and chap. x. 32, ss., reference is made to their former conduct, their former fortitude in the faith as contrasted with their present faintheartedness,—limitations of so definite a kind that we cannot suppose *a whole church* to be addressed, but only a very narrow and definite *circle of individuals*.

The Epistle to the Hebrews, then, deviates from the nature of an epistle, in so far as relates to the *manner in which its contents are represented*; but it is an epistle in so far as relates to *the destination for a definite circle of readers.*

That we are to seek for this circle of readers among the Jewish Christians is, in the main, self-evident from the contents of the epistle; nay more, we are at liberty to seek these Jewish Christians only in Jerusalem. The import of the epistle as a whole, and in its particular parts, has indeed the one practical aim of convincing the readers that it was no misfortune, and in no way dangerous as regards the salvation of their soul, *to be excluded from the temple and the temple worship*, and to make it clear to them that the central point for the Israelite who believes in the Messiah does not lie in Israelitism or-Leviticism, but in Messiaism. The readers, therefore, did not only participate with many Jewish Christians living out of Jerusalem in the common erroneous notion that the Jewish theocracy with its ritual was the main concern, and that the Messiah was sent only on account of it, and therefore for those who have part in it, not indeed as a secondary thing, but still only, so to speak, as a reward and a gift testifying complacency with this theocracy. Not only had they not yet comprehended that the Jewish theocracy was rather established on account of the Messiah, and the Messiah sent on account of the whole world. But to this theoretically erroneous view there was added, in their case, the practical danger of being really and truly shut out from the temple-worship; nay, it was this danger, evidently, that first awakened and called out the theoretical error. For the whole polemical aim of the epistle is directed not against conscious heretics and blameable heresy (as, for example, that of the Epistle to the Galatians), but against an aberration which had its root in ἀσθένεια.—The readers were too weak, too undeveloped in faith and knowledge to be able to bear and to overcome the *terrible feeling of being shut out from the old theocratical sanctuary*. Hence the theoretical statements of the epistle have an altogether unpolemical thetical form, they are milk for the weak (chap. v. 12); what of polemical is in it is directed solely against the sin of faintheartedness, never against intentional error.—But that *practical* danger could exist in this form only with such Jewish Christians as lived *in Jerusalem itself.* Elsewhere in Palestine and among the dispersion errors might arise similar to that in the Galatian Church, but never could those circumstances exist out of which such an *involuntary fear of exclusion* might spring. For where no temple was, there the fear of exclusion from the temple could not practically be felt. To be excluded from a local synagogue could in itself be regarded as no misfortune, as the constitution of synagogues was entirely a matter of freedom (they arose in Jerusalem between 460 and 480), and the Jewish Christians very soon everywhere separated themselves from the synagogal communion; besides, nothing is said in the Epistle to the Hebrews of an excommunication from Jewish synagogues, but of exclusion from the temple and altar and the Israelitish theocratic church as a whole. Such could be practically felt only in Jerusalem itself. (Comp. Bleek i. p. 29.)

True, in one respect the excommunication from the temple might affect Jewish Christians *out of* Jerusalem, namely, when they came to Jerusalem to any of the three great festivals and then found the temple closed against them. But if the author had had such Christians in view, he would certainly have given more prominence in the epistle to the feast of the Passover, of Pentecost, and of Tabernacles, and have shown that these were dispensable, while he rather puts the ritual of those feasts quite in the background, and places in the foreground only the sacrifice of atonement. The readers, then, are certainly to be sought for in Jerusalem.

But again, it cannot have been the entire church in Jerusalem for which the epistle was intended. Already do the passages chap. vi. 10 and chap. x. 32 ss. forbid this; for it is scarcely conceivable that a church, the number of whose members extended at all events to thousands, should formerly have been together as one man bold and true to their profession, and should afterwards have collectively as one man become weak and fainthearted. Besides, the passage chap. ii. 3 leads us to think only of such readers as had been converted subsequent to the time of Christ's ascension, who, in general, lived at a later period, and who therefore had not themselves been witnesses of the public labours of Jesus. Moreover, the passage chap. v. 12, in particular, forbids our supposing that the epistle was addressed to that entire church which was the mother church of all, which numbered among its members at all events many who had grown grey in Christianity, many who had been the personal disciples of Jesus, and again many who had been added at a later period from year to year. How could it be said to such a church : " According to the time ye ought already to be teachers, but yourselves need again to be instructed?" As regards the time, the members of this church were not like each other in respect to the time of their conversion, but different to the extent of perhaps thirty years; then it could not be presupposed of several thousands that they ought to be teachers; still less would this be said of a church in whose bosom there existed in reality many teachers ; least of all can it be supposed, that such a church should as a body have so retrograded that it again needed milk. All these circumstances, taken together with the whole style of representation which characterises the epistle, must induce us to understand the words chap. v. 12, *ye have need that one teach you,* as implying that the readers *were in reality again taken under instruction,*[1] *i.e.* that the epistle *was intended for a limited circle of neophytes in Jerusalem, who had become timorous lest they should be excluded from the temple worship, threatened to withdraw themselves from Christianity* (chap. x. 25), *therefore were taken anew under instruction, and for whose instruction the Epistle to the Hebrews was to form a sort of guide.*

CHAPTER SECOND.

TIME OF COMPOSITION.

When this epistle was written can be determined only indirectly and by approximation, and this too only by the most careful consideration both of the import of the epistle as a whole, and of its particular intimations. The import of the epistle as a whole leads, as has been already shewn, to the conclusion, that

[1] This *teaching* cannot be referred to the doctrines contained *in the Epistle to the Hebrews itself.* For it has for its object the στοιχεῖα, which are *not* taught in the Epistle to the Hebrews.

access to the temple and temple worship was either rendered difficult or altogether forbidden to the readers. This circumstance, however, yields a pretty certain *terminus a quo*, a point of time *before* which the epistle can certainly not have been written. We learn from Acts xxi. 28—29 that in May 58, when Paul came to Jerusalem from his third mission tour, the Jews charged him with having taken into the temple along with him a *Greek*, an uncircumcised person, namely, the *Gentile Christian* Trophimus, and thereby having profaned the holy place. Now, whether this was an intentional pretext, or, as appears, from ver. 29 ($\dot{\epsilon}\nu\acute{o}\mu\iota\zeta o\nu$), a mere mistake, so much, at all events, may be inferred from the nature of the accusation, as also chiefly from ver. 24, that at that time *Jewish Christians*, as circumcised and as native Israelites, were not prohibited from going into the temple. *The Epistle to the Hebrews must therefore have been written after the year* 58, but it cannot have been written very soon after the event recorded in Acts xxi. There must have been an interval during which the hatred of the Jews against Christianity rose to a degree considerably higher.

As the extreme *terminus ad quem*, the year 66 offers itself, which was the first year of the Jewish war. That the Epistle to the Hebrews was written before the destruction of Jerusalem appears not only from those particular passages in which the Levitical ritual is spoken of as still subsisting (chap. ix. 8, x. 1), but, even if we had not those passages, might be inferred, with undoubted certainty, from the import and the practical aim of the epistle. We must evidently come down a series of years from that extreme *terminus ad quem*; it is not probable that the epistle was written immediately before the beginning of the war, when the external fermentation and decomposition of the Israelitish national life had already come to a height. The circumstances presupposed in the epistle resemble much more the first beginning of that fermentation than its completion.

Certain $\dot{\eta}\gamma o\acute{v}\mu\epsilon\nu o\iota$ had already, we know, suffered martyrdom (chap. xiii. 7); the readers themselves, also, had already suffered loss in their earthly possessions (chap. x. 34), and many of their fellow-believers had been imprisoned; they themselves, however, had not yet needed to strive even unto blood (chap. xii. 4, comp. our remarks on the passage). On the other hand, it is taken for granted everywhere in the hortatory portions, that severer persecutions may come, nay, will come ; the readers are systematically prepared for these, and exhorted to submit to the sufferings that were before them as a discipline from God (xii. 5 ss.), not to become fainthearted (x. 38 s.), to persevere in patience (x. 36), to imitate the faith of the martyrs (xiii. 7), and, like Christ and all the Old Testament saints, to keep fixedly and alone before their eye the future goal, the entrance into the holiest of all (chap. xi. and chap. xii. 1—3). Do we find, now, traces of the condition of the Jewish Christians in Jerusalem growing worse after the year 58 ? First of all, the *persecution under Nero in July* 64 may be mentioned, which, although it did not extend over the orbis terrarum, must yet have reacted also on Palestine. Were the Jews already full of bitterness against the Christians, and was their fury restrained from arbitrary outbreaks only by the power of the Romans, then the Neronic persecution would certainly be a signal for them which would not require to be given a second time. To persecute these Christians who were now held to be criminals against Cæsar, was no longer wrong, and would bring with it no danger. These Christians, whose leaders, Peter and Paul, had been murdered so shortly after each other as criminals and rebels, had no claim to, and no hope of, protection on the part of the Romans. Certainly, then, there began in the summer or harvest of the year 64 a season of aggravated persecution for the Christians of Jerusalem.

But this aggravation was not the first since the year 58. Already, under the procuratorship of Porcius Festus (60—62), according to the accounts of that period which Josephus has left behind him, the unbridled spirit of the Jews rose to a height hitherto unknown. Already in the year 57 (comp. Wiesler's Chron. d. Apgsch., p. 79) a first attempt at insurrection on a large scale was made, that of the Sicarii, but was put down (Acts xxi. 38 ; Jos. Antiq., xx. 8, 5 s.; bell. jud. ii. 13, 3 s.) ; under Festus, again, arose the multitude of Goetes and false Messiahs ; the fever of false Maccabeism raged widely, and ate into the vitals of a people become inwardly corrupt and morally dissolute. The Roman scourge came down ever more heavily on the subdued rebels (Jos. Antiq. xxiv. 5 ; xxv. 8). We can easily see now, how the Christians as "adherents of a Messiah" must have been exposed to the suspicion of the Gentile magistrates, who it can hardly be supposed would investigate with any great care into the nature and character of each particular Messiah, but in whose eyes all hope of a Messiah and all speaking of a Messiah must soon have been stamped as unlawful, and scouted as a Jewish association for treasonable purposes, after some dozen of Messiahs had, one after another, put themselves forth as agitators and rebels. How easy in these circumstances must it have become for the Jews to blacken the Christians in the eyes of the Romans, or to obtain a bill of indemnity for any arbitrary persecutions of the Jews! It is certain, then, that the year 60 or 61 formed an epoch of increased trouble to the Christians, and Josephus expressly relates (Antiq. xx., ix. 1) that after the departure of Festus, and before the arrival of his successor Albinus, the Apostle James, the son of Alphaeus, was stoned at the instigation of the high priest, Annas the younger. This murder was certainly the signal for something further.

Accordingly in the year 62, the difficulties of the Christians in Jerusalem began to increase, and in the harvest of 64 there was a second and still greater aggravation of them. We can suppose, therefore, that the epistle to the Hebrews was written *either* late in the summer of 64—in which case the passage chap. xiii. 7 will refer to the death of the Apostles Peter and Paul, which, as we have seen, is not absolutely impossible—or it might have been written in the year 62 or 63, after the death of James the son of Alphaeus—in which case the passage chap. xiii. 7 would have to be referred chiefly to James the son of Alphaeus, whose mere name must of itself, however, have reminded the readers of the earlier death of James the son of Zebedee. We may, in the meantime, choose either of these two dates, although the passage chap. xiii. 7 is certainly capable of a simpler explanation according to the *latter* supposition, for then the author would allude to the martyrdom of men who had actually suffered death *before the eyes* of the readers, and were therefore *patterns* to them of faith in the proper sense of the term, and who also in the strictest sense had been $\dot{\eta}\gamma o\acute{u}\mu\epsilon\nu o\iota$ in the church at Jerusalem. (The readers might thus have witnessed the death even of James *the son of Zebedee*, although they were still at that time Jews.

And he, too, might be reckoned among the ἡγούμενοι ὑμῶν because he had laboured in the church with which the readers had since become connected, and as one of the Apostles whose divine calling they acknowledged since their conversion.)

Let us see, now, whether the passage chap. xiii. 23 gives any more definite information as to the time when the epistle to the Hebrews was written. Timothy had been in prison, and had just recovered his freedom when the epistle was written, or at least when it was sent off. At the same time, we have gathered from the passage chap. xiii. 23—24 that the person who *wrote* or *worked out* the epistle was free, was in Italy, in a different place, however, from Timothy (if Timothy, who has just been set free, comes to him soon he will set out with him to the east), that, on the other hand, the proper *author* of the epistle from whom the *material* (but not the diction, comp. chap. xiii. 22) emanates, and in whose name the epistle on to chap. xiii. 21 is written, was by no means so independent as to be able to set out as soon as he might please to Jerusalem, but was so restrained by the circumstances of some kind or other in which he was involuntarily placed, that he exhorted his readers (chap. xiii. 19) to pray God that he might be again restored to them.

Now, when could Timothy have been in prison in Italy?—During the imprisonment of the Apostle Paul at Rome, several of his helpers were involved in the judicial procedure against him and detained for a while in custody ; so Aristarchus (Col. iv. 10) and Epaphras (Philem. xxiii.) It is not impossible that Timothy, also, might have been kept in confinement at that time. When the Apostle Paul wrote the epistles to the Colossians and Philippians Timothy was actually with him (Col. i. 1 ; Phil. i. 1.; ii. 19). True, the Apostle does not precisely *designate* him as his fellow-prisoner, and makes no precise mention of an imprisonment of Timothy ; but even the circumstance that the epistle to the Philippians was written precisely in the name of Paul and *Timothy* (i. 1), and that Timothy, thereby, joins in the thanksgiving for the *gift* which was sent εἰς χρείαν—this circumstance almost warrants the reference, that Timothy was *imprisoned* together with Paul. Just because the Apostle throughout the whole epistle speaks in *his own* person, addresses his exhortations in his own name, speaks chap. iii. 4 ss. of his own — exclusively of his own—former circumstances, because, in a word Timothy has no part in the *contents* of the writing,—that superscription *Paul and Timothy servants of Jesus Christ* would properly have had no meaning if it did not point to this, that the *occasion* of the epistle—the gift which had been received—equally concerned Timothy and Paul,[1] and this, indeed, is only conceivable on the supposition that Timothy shared in the fate of Paul as a prisoner. The analogous passage Col. i. 1 would then have a similar explanation. This supposition is confirmed, however, by the passage Phil. ii. 19. Paul *hopes* that he will be able soon to send Timothy into the East. Why is this an object of *hope* to him? If Timothy was free, then he might simply have *determined* to send him thither. He *hopes* to send him, so soon as he knows how it may go with his own case (ver. 23), and, in the same way, he *hopes* or "trusts" (ver. 24) that the Lord will soon procure freedom for himself "also." These words, *that I also myself shall come shortly*, are so parallel with the words *I hope to send Timothy shortly unto you*, that it is not too bold to suppose, that Timothy also, who "as a son with the father hath served with me" (ver. 22), and who alone of all has not sought his own (ver. 20, 21), was involved in the procedure against Paul and imprisoned. If Timothy had been free, why did not Paul send him at once with Epaphroditus, or rather why did he not send him *instead* of Epaphroditus, who (ver. 27) had just recovered from a deadly disease?

It is not to be supposed that we adduce these passages as affording a *conclusive* proof that Timothy was at that time in prison with Paul, but we think we have only shown from them the possibility that he *may* have been at that time in prison. The Epistle to the Philippians was written in the year 62, at all events before the third year of Paul's imprisonment at Rome, where his situation became worse. Now, if the setting at liberty of Timothy recorded in Heb. xiii. 23 is identical with that which Paul *hopes* for in Phil. ii. 19, then the Epistle to the Hebrews was written somewhere towards the end of the year 62, therefore just after the death of James the son of Alphaeus.

---

[1] The circumstance that Timothy may, perhaps, have written the epistle to the Philippians as ταχύγραφος does not suffice to explain the superscription Phil. i. 1. The tachygraphist never wrote his name in the *superscription* along with that of Paul.

If this were the only time when an imprisonment of Timothy in Italy is conceivable, then would the choice which was left open above, between the year 62 and the year 64, be thereby already determined. But Timothy, after having been actually sent by Paul into the East, was urgently entreated by Paul (2 Tim. iv. 21), whose case in the meanwhile (during the first half of the year 63) had taken a very serious turn, to come back to him before the harvest of 63. We may be sure that he complied with this request of his "father." Then, however, it is possible that he himself was involved in the procedure against Paul,— possible also, that after Paul's death he was taken prisoner in the persecution under Nero (July 64.) *In short, an imprisonment of Timothy in Italy may likewise be conceived of as possible in the year* 64; only, that his being again set at liberty is less probable on this occasion than in the year 62.

We have therefore not yet got beyond the alternative between the harvest of 62 and late in the summer of 64. The Epistle to the Hebrews might have been written at either of these two points of time. The inquiry as to the author will, perhaps, be the first thing to throw a clearer light on the question.

CHAPTER THIRD.

WHETHER WRITTEN ORIGINALLY IN GREEK.

Before we can proceed to the inquiry respecting the author of the Epistle to the Hebrews there is still a preliminary question which must be settled, namely, whether this epistle was really *written originally in Greek*, or whether it is not merely a translation or a reproduction of an *Aramaic original*. There is nothing in the epistle itself that could lead to the raising of such a question; but a series of Church Fathers speak of an original Aramaic writing, and therefore we are not at liberty entirely to evade the question.

The most ancient of these Fathers is Clemens of Alexandria, of whom Eusebius relates (vi. 14), that in his Hypotyposes he has undertaken ἐπιτετμημένας διηγήσεις (investigations) respecting all the books of the Holy Scripture, and in regard to the Epistle to the Hebrews has come to the conclusion : Παύλου μὲν εἶναι, γεγράφθαι δὲ Ἑβραίοις Ἑβραϊκῇ φωνῇ, Λουκᾶν δὲ φιλοτίμως αὐτὴ μεθερμηνεύσαντα ἐκδοῦναι τοῖς Ἕλλησιν· ὅθεν τὸν αὐτὸν χρῶτα εὑρίσκεσθαι κατὰ τὴν ἑρμηνείαν ταύτης τε τῆς ἐπιστολῆς καὶ τῶν πράξεων. But the last words of this citation show clearly enough how Clement arrived at this view. It is not a *tradition* which he follows, but a scientific conjecture which he raises. The dissimilarity in style between this epistle and the epistles of Paul, and its similarity to the writings of Luke, struck him (justly); he perceived that the epistle cannot have come from Paul in this form; but as the general tradition of the East (as we shall see in the following chapter) named Paul as the author, Clement was led to ask: May not the epistle in its present form in reality, perhaps, have proceeded from another—from Luke? Wherefore not, he thought; how very possible is it that Paul wrote[1] to those Aramaic speaking Jewish Christians in their own language, and that a disciple of Paul (for example Luke himself, whose style so much resembles that of the Epistle to the Hebrews) afterwards worked out the epistle for a wider circle of readers.—But that Clement here in reality gives only a subjective conjecture, and not an ecclesiastical tradition, appears most clearly from this, that his disciple Origen departs from the supposition of an originally Aramaic writing, although he retains the substance of Clement's view. He, too, notices (in Euseb. vi. 25) the difference in style between the Epistle to the Hebrews and the Pauline epistles; he, too, does not venture to carry back that epistle in its present form directly to Paul; but he can explain this phenomenon by a *simpler* (and indeed a far more probable) conjecture, namely, by the supposition that Paul *did not verbally dictate this epistle*, but only delivered in free oral discourse the thoughts and the development of the thoughts, the composition and elaboration of which he left over to one of his disciples (τὰ μὲν νοήματα τοῦ ἀποστόλου ἐστίν· ἡ δὲ φράσις καὶ ἡ σύνθεσις ἀπομνημονεύσαντός τινος τὰ ἀποστολικὰ καὶ ὡσπερεὶ σχολιογ-

---

[1] Ἑβραϊκὴ φωνὴ denotes here of course not the ancient Hebrew, which indeed was intelligible only to the learned Jews, but the Aramaic. Comp. Acts xxii. 2.

ραφήσαντος τὰ εἰρημένα ὑπὸ τοῦ διδασκάλου.) Origen would certainly not have fallen upon this method of solving the question, if there had been in existence a *tradition* in any degree to be depended on in favour of an originally Aramaic writing; for then he would not have at all needed this new conjecture. That he thought it necessary to modify the opinion of Clement can be explained only on the ground that this was only an opinion, only a subjective supposition. We certainly meet this supposition also in later Church Fathers. Eusebius himself also repeats it (iii. 38); he speaks, however, so entirely in the same way as Clement—in like manner adducing the internal grounds which are in its favour—that it is apparent he is there only stating the conjectures of others. (Ἑβραίοις γὰρ διὰ τῆς πατρίου γλώττης ἐγγράφως ὡμιληκότος τοῦ Παύλου, οἱ μὲν τὸν εὐαγγελιστὴν Λουκᾶν, οἱ δὲ τὸν Κλήμεντα—Clement of Rome—ἑρμηνεῦσαι λέγουσι τὴν γραφήν· ὃ καὶ μᾶλλον εἴη ἂν ἀληθὲς τῷ τὸν ὅμοιον τῆς φράσεως χαρακτῆρα τήν τε τοῦ Κλήμεντος ἐπιστολὴν καὶ τὴν πρὸς Ἑβραίους ἀποσώζειν κ.τ.α.) That this conjecture was one which he had adopted from others and not the one which was familiar to Eusebius, Bleek has already justly inferred from the fact that Eusebius elsewhere speaks as if the *Greek* Epistle to the Hebrews comes from Paul. (In his Comm. on Psalm ii. 7 he says that Paul, in the Epistle to the Hebrews, has made use of the LXX., with which as a νομομαθής he was well acquainted.)

Jerome, too, (Script. Eccl. 5) says: scripserat Paulus, ut Hebraeus Hebraeis, Hebraice, ut ea quae eloquenter scripta fuerant in Hebraeo, eloquentius verterentur in Graecum; but Jerome also adds: et hanc causam esse, quod a ceteris Pauli epistolis discrepare videatur. (Later, also, we meet the same view in Oecumenius, Theophylact, and Johannes Damascenus.) But it is always evidently the *old conjecture of Clement* which in every case recommended itself on the simple ground, that every one noticed the dissimilarity in style between the Epistle to the Hebrews and the Pauline epistles.

The Church Fathers inform us respecting another book of the New Testament that it was written originally in Aramaic, namely, the Gospel of Matthew. But we must beware of placing these two accounts parallel with each other. In the case of Matthew the tradition respecting its Aramaic origin begins with the Presbyter John (comp. my Kritik. der evang. Geschichte p. 767 ss.), and continues through the whole series of the Church Fathers without being encumbered by the faintest trace of an opposite tradition; nay, it is confirmed by the abundant traces of the existence of a " Gospel to the Hebrews" distinct from the Greek one of Matthew, which was still used without hesitation in the first centuries even by the Catholic Church, and only gradually came to be the sole possession of the Nazarites and Ebionites, and in their hands was greatly vitiated; finally, even the Greek Gospel of Matthew bears, throughout, an Aramaic colouring, and has quite the nature of a reproduction of an Aramaic original (although not of a verbal translation). Thus for example it has only one *paranomasia* (Matt. vi. 16), and this, too, of such a kind as that it may have arisen unconsciously (comp. my Kritik. der evang. Geschichte p. 764—766).

It is altogether different with the Epistle to the Hebrews. The scanty series of notices respecting its Aramaic original begins, as we have seen, very late, and begins with an *evident conjecture*, which was afterwards readily adopted by others on *internal grounds*. There is nowhere the faintest trace of an Aramaic original of the Epistle to the Hebrews, and our *Greek* Epistle to the Hebrews is, in fine, so original throughout, so evidently *thought in Greek*, both in form and import, that the supposition of its having arisen from an Aramaic original becomes at once an impossibility.

To begin with what is most external, we would refer to *the multitude of Greek paranomasias and plays upon words*, of which only *some* (for example ὑποτάξαι and ἀνυπότακτον, ii. 8; ἀπάτωρ, ἀμήτωρ, vii. 3; ἐγγίζομεν, ἔγγυος, vii. 19 and 22; παραμένειν, μένειν, vii. 23—24; ἡγησάμενος, ἡγιάσθη, x. 29, &c.) could have arisen unconsciously in the hands of a translator, while the *most* are certainly intended (for example πολυμερῶς καὶ πολυτρόπως, i. 1; ἔμαθεν ἀφ' ὧν ἔπαθεν, v. 8; καλοῦ τε καὶ κακοῦ, v. 14; βρώμασι καὶ πόμασι, ix. 10; ἀόρατον, ὁρῶν, xi. 27; μένουσαν, μέλλουσαν xiii. 14, &c.). All that can be directly inferred, indeed, from this mass of paranomasias is, that our epistle cannot be the *literal* *anslation* of an Aramaic original; that it may have been a nree *reproduction* of such an original is not thereby set aside.

This reproduction, however, must have been executed in so free manner that, in the form and *structure of the periods*, as well as in the *transference of the ideas*, the writer has not bound himself down to the original; for the construction of the periods is so genuinely Greek, so rich, so fine, the language is so select and expresses modifications of ideas so delicate (for example μετριοπαθεῖν, εὐπερίστατος, μισθαποδοσία, &c.), that there are no Aramaic ideas and words whatever to which these Greek ones would correspond. The writer must, therefore, have *entirely recast* his original—and that not merely as regards the form, but also the matter. All the argumentations are so fine, so closely knit and interwoven with the grammatical form of the finely constructed period, that if this form was not possible in the Aramaic original, then must also the entire development of the thought have been different. Compare for example Heb. chap. i. 1—3; chap. ii. 2—4 and 9, 10, and 14, 15; chap. iii. 1, 2 ss; chap. iv. 9 and 6, 7; chap. v. 7—10; chap. vii. 5—12, and ss. Let any one only try to render back these passages into the poor Aramaic language, and he will be convinced that more than the half of the sentiments, but chiefly and entirely their fine connexion, would be lost.

To this is to be added, finally, the use which is made of the LXX. We have seen in the particular passages that the argumentations based on Old Testament citations are *substantially* correct, and really founded on the sense which those citations have in the original. But we have in like manner seen, that those argumentations, *in respect of form*, correspond to the words and expressions used in the LXX, even in those instances in which the Septuagint, although rightly rendering the sentiment as a whole, yet does not correspond to the most direct *grammatical* sense of the Hebrew original. Thus, for example in chap. vii. 8, the argumentation is based on the word ὑποτάσσειν, which does *not* occur at all in the Hebrew original of the psalm. In like manner chap. iv. 5 s.; chap. x. 5—7, &c. These argumentations also the writer must have entirely recast.

In short, the entire Epistle to the Hebrews is in form and matter thought out in Greek. Granted that it really had an Aramaic writing for its basis, our Greek Epistle to the Hebrews would still not be a reproduction of this original writing, but an *entirely new and original writing*, to which the Aramaic writing bore the relation of a mere preparatory work, and we should not be at liberty to say: " The Epistle to the Hebrews was originally written in Aramaic," but more correctly would have to say: " The writer of the Epistle to the Hebrews made use of another writing of *similar* import, which happened to be written in Aramaic, as a preparatory work." But herewith the whole conjecture vanishes. For there are no positive grounds for this conjecture, and, thus modified, it would not even serve the end which it was intended to serve by Clement of Alexandria. If Paul had intended to deliver in writing to *the author of the Epistle to the Hebrews* a scheme of contents for the epistle which was to be written, in order that this author might *carry it out*, he would at least not have written this scheme in the Aramaic language. If, however, Paul or any one else had written and sent an Aramaic epistle to the Jewish Christians in Jerusalem, and some other (Luke or any one else) had set himself to translate it into Greek for the more general use of all Christians, he would have really *translated* it, and not have made something quite different out of it.

The conjecture of Clement, therefore, is mere conjecture, and indeed it is *not even fitted* to explain the coincidence of the un-Pauline style and the oriental tradition of the Pauline authorship. In no danger of being misled by this conjecture, we can now pass to the inquiry respecting the author of the Epistle to the Hebrews.

CHAPTER FOURTH.

THE WRITER. A) EXTERNAL TESTIMONIES.

On directing our view, first of all, to the external testimonies respecting the Epistle to the Hebrews, we encounter the striking phenomenon, that the entire Eastern Church decidedly and from the very first holds the epistle to be *Pauline*, while the *Western* either makes no use of it until the time of the Arian controversy, or, if it uses it, does not reckon it among the Pauline epistles, or, finally, declares it to be decidedly un-Pauline. *The Eastern Church had no other opinion than that Paul was the author of the Epistle to the Hebrews.* As the first witness Clemens Romanus (A.D. 96) is wont to be adduced, who has certainly a greater number of allusions to the Epistle to the Hebrews than to any other epistle of the New Testament. (In the 36th chapter of his Epistle to the Corinthians he gives pretty large and *literal* extracts from Heb. i. 4, ss.; more than once he repeats the words Heb. iii. 2, &c. &c. See the passages in Kirchhofer's "Quellensammlung zur Geschichte der neutestamentlichen Kanons," p. 233—238.) But nowhere does Clement *name* the Epistle to the Hebrews, nowhere does he *name* Paul as its author. Now, as there is no necessity for supposing that his partiality for this epistle was occasioned by his partiality for *the person of its author*, seeing that the contents of the epistle might quite as well account for this partiality—further, as the person of the author might have been especially dear to Clement even although he had not been Paul himself, but one of those *fellow-labourers* mentioned in Phil. iv. 3, it follows that no *certain* conclusion can be drawn from Clement's partiality for the Epistle to the Hebrews, that he recognised this epistle as Pauline. Still less, indeed, can any inference be drawn against its having been written by Paul from the fact that Clement does not name the title and author. For, in his allusions to the Epistles to the Thessalonians (Clem. 1 Cor. xxxviii.), Galatians (1 Cor. xlix.), Romans (chap. xxxiii.—xxxv.—xxxviii.—xlvi.), Colossians (chap. xxi.), Ephesians (chap. xlvi.), Timothy (chap. xxix.), &c., he also names not the title and author; only (in chap. xlvii.) when he cites the first of Paul's epistles to the Corinthians does he remind the Corinthians—having special occasion to do so—of that which Paul had already written to them.

The series of properly Oriental witnesses for the Pauline authorship of the Epistle to the Hebrews begins with Pantaenus. Clement of Alexandria appeals to him, the μακάριος πρεσβύτερος, for the information that Paul had put no inscription to the

Epistle to the Hebrews, because he did not wish to urge his apostolical authority on the Jewish Christians. (Ἤδη δὲ ὡς ὁ μακάριος ἔλεγε πρεσβύτερος, ἐπεὶ ὁ κύριος ἀπόστολος ὢν τοῦ παντοκράτορος, ἀπεστάλη πρὸς Ἑβραίους, διὰ μετριότητα ὁ Παῦλος, ὡς ἂν εἰς τὰ ἔθνη ἀπεσταλμένος, οὐκ ἐγγραφει ἑαυτὸν Ἑβραίων ἀπόστολον, διά τε τὴν πρὸς.τὸν κύριον τιμὴν, διά τε τὸν ἐκ περιουσίας καὶ τοῖς Ἑβραίοις ἐπιστέλλειν ἐθνῶν κήρυκα ὄντα καὶ ἀπόστολον.) In like manner Dionysius of Alexandria (in Euseb. vi. 41: Ἐξέκλινον δὲ καὶ ὑπανεχώρουν οἱ ἀδελφοί· καὶ τὴν ἁρπαγὴν τῶν ὑπαρχόντων, ὁμοίως ἐκείνοις οἷς καὶ Παῦλος ἐμαρτύρησε, μετὰ χαρᾶς προσεδέξαντο, comp. Heb. x. 34.) In like manner, Alexander of Alexandria (in Socr. i. 3, Theodoret. h. e. i. 4.) Methodius of Lycia (A.D. 290) conviv. decem virginum, oratio 10, pag. 96 and 116, cites the passages Heb. x. 1 and xii. 1 with the words κατὰ τὸν ἀπόστολον and κατὰ τὸν διδάσκαλον Παῦλον. A Synod held in Antioch about the year 264 against Paul of Samosata, cites in its Synodal writing (in Mansi coll. conc. tom. i. pag. 1036) the passage Heb. xi. 26 as the words of Paul. That Clement of Alexandria held Paul to be at least the *original author* of the Epistle to the Hebrews, nay, that it was just the tradition respecting the Pauline authorship that induced him to devise that conjecture about an originally Aramaic writing in order to explain the difference in style, we have seen from the passage already adduced (in Euseb. vi. 14), in which, indeed, he appeals also to Pantaenus in support of its having been written by Paul. In another passage, also (Strom. vi. p. 645), he cites the Epistle to the Hebrews as Pauline (Ἐπεὶ καὶ Παῦλος ἐν ταῖς ἐπιστολαῖς οὐ φιλοσοφίαν διαβάλλων φαίνεται. . . . . . . .Ἡ πάλιν, φησὶ, χρείαν ἔχετε τοῦ διδάσκειν ὑμᾶς, τίνα τὰ στοιχεῖα, &c. Heb. v. 12 —ὡσαύτως καὶ τοῖς ἐξ Ἑλλήνων ἐπιστρέφουσι Κολοσσαεῦσι· βλέπετε &c.—Col. iv. 8.)—Origen likewise cites the epistle as Pauline (comm. in Joh. opp. iv. p. 60: καὶ ἐν τῇ πρὸς Ἑβραίους ὁ αὐτὸς Παῦλος φησιν—then follows Heb. i. 1—2;—in like manner in his comm. in ep. ad Roman. opp. iv. p. 579 and 659.) Origen too was driven only by this general tradition, of the Pauline authorship to that conjecture which has been formerly mentioned, and which (in Euseb. vi. 25) he expresses in the following words: Ὁ χαρακτὴρ τῆς λέξεως τῆς πρὸς Ἑβραίους ἐπιγεγραμμένης ἐπισ-

APPENDIX. 397

τολῆς οὐκ ἔχει τὸ ἐν λόγῳ, ἰδιωτικὸν τοῦ ἀποστόλου, ὁμολογήσαντος αὐτὸν ἰδιώτην εἶναι τῷ λόγῳ, τουτέστι τῇ φράσει· ἀλλά ἐστιν ἡ ἐπιστολὴ συνθέσει τῆς λέξεως ἑλληνικωτέρα, πᾶς ὁ ἐπιστάμενος κρίνειν φράσεων διαφορὰς ὁμολογήσαι ἄν. Πάλιν δὲ αὖ, ὅτι τὰ νοήματα τῆς ἐπιστολῆς θαυμάσιά ἐστι, καὶ οὐ δεύτερα τῶν ἀποστολικῶν ὁμολογουμένων γραμμάτων, καὶ τοῦτο ἂν συμφήσαι εἶναι ἀληθὲς πᾶς ὁ προσέχων τῇ ἀναγνώσει τῇ ἀποστολικῇ.—'Εγὼ δὲ ἀποφαινόμενος ἔποιμ' ἄν, ὅτι τὰ μὲν νοήματα τοῦ ἀποστόλου ἐστὶν ἡ δὲ φράσις καὶ ἡ σύνθεσις ἀπομνημονεύσαντός τινος τὰ ἀποστολικὰ, καὶ ὡσπερεὶ σχολιογραφήσαντός τὰ εἰρημένα ὑπὸ τοῦ διδασκάλου. Εἴ τις οὖν ἐκκλησία ἔχει ταύτην τὴν ἐπιστολὴν ὡς Παύλου, αὕτη εὐδοκιμείτω καὶ ἐπὶ τούτῳ· οὐ γὰρ εἰκῆ οἱ ἀρχαῖοι ἄνδρες ὡς Παύλου αὐτὴν παραδεδώκασι. All the following Greek Church Fathers name the epistle as Paul's: Eusebius places it in his canon among the Pauline epistles (Euseb. iii. 25, see farther on this below), in like manner Antonius, Athanasius, Didymus, Theophilus of Alexandria, the two Gregories, Basilius, Epiphanius, James of Nisibis (in Galland. bibl. patr. tom. 5. p. 16 and 53), Ephraim of Syria, the two Cyrils, Chryrostom, &c.

Nevertheless, some have ventured to call in question the antiquity and unanimity of this oriental tradition. Bleek (i. p. 108) thinks that by the ἀρχαῖοι ἄνδρες to whom Origen refers might also be meant merely, Pantaenus and Clement of Alexandria; not only, however, is it improbable that Origen should have designated these his immediate predecessors and teachers by so vague an expression, but the *usus linguae* is directly against this. (For example, Eusebius ii. 1, where he narrates the death of the *Apostles*, says: καὶ ταῦτα μὲν ὡς ἐξ ἀρχαίων ἱστορίας εἰρήσθω; in iii. 24, he says, the Gospel of John has had the fourth place assigned to it rightly by the ἀρχαῖοι.) Chiefly, however, is the context conclusive against that interpretation. For Clement of Alexandria had *not unconditionally* held that Paul was the *immediate* author of the Epistle to the Hebrews; how then can this Clement be brought forward among those to whom those churches might appeal which held the epistle to be *directly Pauline*? The sense of the passage is plainly this: The Alexandrians cannot, indeed, believe that this epistle, with this style, was thus composed by Paul himself; but whosoever will yet hold Paul to be the immediate and proper author (therefore in *opposition* to Clement!) we can do nothing against him, since even the ancients have handed down the epistle to us as one of Paul's."

And, accordingly, a second objection also is herewith refuted (Bleek p. 107). In the words εἴ τις οὖν ἐκκλησία ἔχει ταύτην τὴν ἐπιστολὴν ὡς Παύλου there evidently lies the presupposition, that only *a few churches* at that time held the epistle to the Hebrews to be a work of Paul. But the question treated of in the context of this passage is, not at all, whether the epistle was written by Paul or came into existence *without Paul having anything to do with it*. That the ancient tradition imputed it to Paul was a settled point, and only the certainty of this tradition could induce Clement and Origen to form those two conjectures, by which the un-Pauline style *at variance with* the tradition might be explained.[1]—The question with Origen is rather, whether the epistle, *precisely as we have it in Greek*, can have come directly from Paul. The old tradition called it Pauline; the un-Pauline style had, however, justly struck the Alexandrians; it had become the settled opinion among them that the epistle in its present form could not be directly from Paul; either it is a translation of an Aramaic original (as Clement wrongly supposed), or, according to the preferable conjecture of Origen, Paul did not dictate the words of it but gave only the νοήματα for it. These views, under the influence of the catechist school in Alexandria and the neighbourhood, may have been generally spread; hence Origen carelessly mentions them; but then it may have struck him, that this hypothesis might give offence, that there might possibly be churches which would zealously maintain the *immediately* Pauline origin; against these, he says, we cannot take any steps as the ancient tradition names the epistle simply as one of Paul's. That the words ἔχει αὐτὴν ὡς Παύλου, according to the context, form the antithesis, only to the view of Origen, and not to an opinion according to which the authorship of Paul would be absolutely denied, is indeed clear as the sun.

[1] How altogether untenable is the opinion of Bertholdt (Einleit. iv. 2914 ss.), that the Alexandrines—those who observed and always so strongly urged the *un-Pauline* character of the style—were the first who raised the *conjecture* of a Pauline authorship and that "on exegetical grounds."

Origen, certainly, also presupposes an *absolute denial* of the Pauline authorship as possible, but only as *possible*, when (in Matth. xxiii. 27) he says : Sed *pone, aliquem* abdicare epistolam ad Hebraeos, quasi non Pauli ... sed quid faciat in sermones Stephani, &c. ? The learned Father may have heard something of the Western views concerning the epistle to the Hebrews ; at all events, he would not have spoken thus (*pone, aliquem*) if (as Bleek will have it) there had been around him entire churches and countries which held the Epistle to the Hebrews to be un-Pauline! He there also as well as in ad Afric. chap. ix., distinctly takes it for granted that some might feel themselves compelled to doubt the authority of the Epistle to the Hebrews *on internal grounds*, namely, on account of the passage Heb. xi. 37 (where prophets are spoken of who were *sawn asunder*, while no such case is recorded in the canonical books of the Old Testament).

Again, reference has been made to the fact that Eusebius reckons the Epistle to the Hebrews among the *antilegomena*, inasmuch as he relates of Clement of Alexandria that in his Strom. he made use of proofs also ἀπὸ τῶν ἀντιλεγομένων γραφῶν, namely, from the Wisdom of Solomon, Sirach, *the Epistle to the Hebrews*, and the epistle of Clemens Rom., Barnabas and Judas. But that the epistle to the Hebrews is here reckoned among the *antilegomena* is very simply explained from this, that Eusebius himself (vi. 25) knew and mentions that some held Luke, others Clement of Rome, to be the *proper and immediate* author of it, and that (Euseb. iii. 3 ; vi. 20) the whole western church *entirely* denied it to be Paul's. In *this* sense he might call it an ἀντιλεγόμενον. But how firmly settled that tradition of the *Pauline authorship in general* was in the east is evident from this, that Eusebius in his *principal passage on the Canon* (iii. 25) *does not adduce* the Epistle to the Hebrews among the antilegomena, and was therefore conscious of having already included it among the " ἐπιστολαῖς Παύλου ;" accordingly, the same Eusebius cites it as *Pauline* in not less than twenty-seven passages. (Comp. Bleek, p. 149—150, Anm. 173.)

Finally, the learned and extensively read Jerome, who made use of the library of Caesarea, and therewith of the entire Christian literature of the first centuries, says, that the Epistle to the Hebrews was ascribed to the Apostle Paul *non solum ab ecclesiis orientis, sed ab omnibus retro ecclesiasticis graeci sermonis scriptoribus* (ep. ad Dard. p. 608).

Thus, then, the thesis is fully confirmed—*that the primitive and general tradition of the East is in favour of the Pauline authorship.* It is also confirmed by the remarkable circumstance, that the Epistle to the Hebrews, as is still evident from the numbering of the Kephalaia in the cod. B, originally stood between the Epistle to the Galatians and that to the Ephesians, and was not till a later period in the fourth century placed after the Epistle to the Thessalonians (as in cod. A and C), and still later, after the Pastoral Epistles.

It was altogether different in the *West*. That bishop of Lyons, Irenaeus, who was among the first to follow the practice of citing the New Testament writings by their titles and authors, has, as is commonly supposed, *not at all* cited the Epistle to the Hebrews, at least not by its title and author; nay, there is a notice, certainly a very late one, to the effect that Irenaeus held the Epistle to the Hebrews to be un-Pauline. Meanwhile, these points would need a special examination. Only the *second*, viz., that Irenaeus never names the Apostle Paul as the author of the Epistle to the Hebrews, is beyond all question true. There are serious doubts, on the other hand, against the *first*, that Irenaeus was not at all acquainted with the epistle, and did not make use of it. Eusebius (v. 26) notices a writing (now lost) of that Church Father with the express remark, that in it Irenaeus "mentions also the Epistle to the Hebrews." Ἀλλὰ γὰρ πρὸς τοῖς ἀποδοθεῖσιν Εἰρηναίου συγγράμμασι καὶ ταῖς ἐπιστολαῖς φέρεται καὶ βιβλίον τι διαλέξεων διαφόρων, ἐν ᾧ τῆς πρὸς Ἑβραίους ἐπιστολῆς καὶ τῆς λεγομένης σοφίας Σολομῶντος μνημονεύει, ῥητά τινα ἐξ αὐτῶν παραθέμενος. These words may have a twofold sense. Either the apposition παραθέμενος serves to state more precisely *how* and *in how far* he mentions the Epistle to the Hebrews ("he mentions it by adducing passages from it")—and then Irenaeus may not, perhaps, have so much as named the title "ἐπιστολὴ πρὸς Ἑβραίους, but only have cited particular passages of the epistle—or παραθέμενος serves to specify the occasion on which he has really "mentioned" the Epistle to the Hebrews *as such*, *i.e.*, has named it ("he mentions it on the occasions on which he adduces passages from it")—and in this case Irenaeus must in those citations have actually called the epistle by its name "Epistle to the Hebrews." In favour of the latter interpretation is the circumstance, that a *mere making use* of ῥητά from the Epistle to the Hebrews, *without naming* this epistle, occurs also in the writing adv. haer., and could not be adduced as an exclusive peculiarity of the writing " διαλέξεις;" meanwhile, those mere allusions are so few in number, and, besides, so doubtful, that they may easily have escaped the notice of Eusebius. However this may be, little, on the whole, depends on which of those two interpretations is held to be the correct one. *According to each of the two, Irenaeus at least knew the Epistle to the Hebrews;* but from neither can it be inferred that he must have held it to be Pauline. That he *knew* the epistle, is certainly confirmed in some measure by those allusions in the writing adv. haereses. True, indeed, when he describes God as faciens omnia, et visibilia et invisibilia, et sensibilia et insensata, et coelestia et terrena, *per verbum virtutis suae,* there might be in this latter designation (certainly a very unusual one) an *accidental* coincidence with the ῥῆμα τῆς δυνάμεως αὐτοῦ, Heb. i. 3. As little can it be with any certainty inferred from the words: ὅπου γε Ἐνὼχ εὐαρεστήσας τῷ θεῷ ἐν σώματι μετετέθη, τὴν μετάθεσιν τῶν δικαίων προμηνύων (v. 5, 1) that the Bishop of Lyons was acquainted with Heb. xi. 5, as these words might quite as well be explained from our acquaintance with Gen. v. 24 (LXX). On the other hand, in a third passage (iv. 11, 4): Quae (munditiae exteriores) in *figuram futurorum* traditae erant, velut *umbrae cujusdam descriptionem faciente lege,* atque delineante de temporalibus aeterna, *terrenis coelestia,* it would be difficult not to see a recollection of passages in the Epistle to the Hebrews (x. 1, σκιὰν γὰρ ἔχων ὁ νόμος τῶν μελλόντων ἀγαθῶν; comp. viii. 5, σκιᾷ τῶν ἐπουρανίων; ix. 23, τὰ ὑποδείγματα τῶν ἐν τοῖς οὐρανοῖς).

The supposition that the Epistle to the Hebrews was entirely unknown to Irenaeus is therefore quite untenable. On the other hand, *there is not the slightest trace of his having ever declared it to be Pauline.* On the contrary, it is thought that there is *a trace of his having held it to be un-Pauline.* Stephanus Gobarus (living in the sixth century) records (in Photii bibl. cod. 232, ed. Bekk.

p. 291) that Irenaeus and Hippolytus held the Epistle to the Hebrews to be un-Pauline. Hippolytus has manifestly (Phot. cod. 121) denied the Pauline origin of the epistle; but whether this saying of Stephanus *in reference also to Irenaeus* is founded on definite positive statements, may be very much doubted. For had such statements been to be found in the writings of Irenaeus, then Eusebius would assuredly have adduced the substance of these statements, in the passage (v. 8) in which he brings together all that Irenaeus had expressed respecting the biblical books. It is therefore far more probable that Stephanus *presumed*, from the rare and scanty use which Irenaeus makes of the Epistle to the Hebrews, from his silence respecting the author, and, finally, from the view entertained by his disciple Hippolytus, that his teacher also, Irenaeus, must have held the Epistle to the Hebrews to be un-Pauline. Was this conjecture right? I believe we shall have to decide this question by a docta ignorantia. It is certainly not impossible that Irenaeus held our epistle to be un-Pauline; but it is quite as possible that he had brought with him from Asia Minor to Lyons the tradition respecting the Pauline origin, *but that he was unwilling to urge this on the Western Church*. He may, therefore, have cautiously avoided citing the Epistle to the Hebrews as Pauline in contradiction to the universal opinion and tradition of the East; for an ecclesiastical tradition so general demanded respect and forbearance, according to Irenaeus' own principles (comp. his second fragment on the Passover controversy in Eusebius v. 24.) As he was, nevertheless, unwilling to deny the tradition which he had brought with him from Asia Minor, he therefore in general avoided making any particularly frequent use of the Epistle to the Hebrews, and he might do so all the more easily as the point of this epistle was directed against Judaism, whereas the point of his own polemics was directed against Gnosticism, so that the Epistle to the Hebrews was in reality for him not so indispensable.

But that in the West this epistle, at the time when tradition, even that respecting the canon (*i.e.* respecting the books to be read in the churches), was fixed, *i.e.* shortly after 100, was as yet by no means generally known and spread, is apparent from numerous facts. In the Novatian controversy (from 251 onwards) Novatian could have found in the whole of the New Testament no more convenient proof of his principle, that Christians who in persecution had denied the faith ought not again to be received into the fellowship of the Church, than the passage Heb. vi. 4 ss. As Novatian, notwithstanding, makes no use of this passage in his writings (see these in Galland. bibl. patr. iii. 287 ss.), he must, therefore, either have not at all known the Epistle to the Hebrews or have held it to be no authority. Victorinus (A.D. 303), the Muratorian Canon, and the presbyter Gajus (about 190), count only 13 Pauline epistles. (On Gajus comp. Euseb. 6, 20 s.) Cyprian says in two passages (adv. Jud. i. 20 and de exhort. mart. 11) that Paul wrote to seven churches; besides Rome, Corinth, Ephesus, Colosse, Philippi, Thessalonica, and Galatia, there remains here no place for the "Hebrews." And no weight is to be given to the consideration, that Cyprian may not have counted the Epistle to the Hebrews because its readers (as we saw) formed no *church*; he reckons the *province* of Galatia as a *church!* Tertullian, in a passage (de pudic. 20) where everything depended on his being able to confirm the authority of the Epistle to the Hebrews, with great decision and candour names *Barnabas* as its author. *From the second to the fourth century, then, in Italy as in Africa, the Epistle to the Hebrews was held to be un-Pauline.* As yet at the time of Eusebius, at least in Rome, the doubt as to the Pauline authorship had not entirely disappeared, as Eusebius (iii. 3) records ("Ὅτι γε μήν τινες ἠθετήκασι τὴν πρὸς Ἑβραίους, πρὸς τῆς Ῥωμαίων ἐκκλησίας ὡς μὴ Παύλου οὖσαν αὐτὴν ἀντιλέγεσθαι φήσαντες, οὐ δίκαιον ἀγνοεῖν. Comp. Euseb. vi. 20: ἐπεὶ καὶ εἰς δεῦρο παρὰ Ῥωμαίων τισὶν οὐ νομίζεται τοῦ ἀποστόλου εἶναι.) For, of *earlier* opponents of the Pauline origin of the epistle (ἠθετήκασι) he says, that they had appealed to "the Roman Church;" of his own time he says, that *some* in Rome held the epistle to be un-Pauline.

First in the time of the Arian controversy, then, there took place a revolution of opinion on this question in the West, and *a complete victory over the Western tradition by the Eastern* brought about, doubtless, through the influence of the oriental Nicenes, who now indeed found their most faithful allies and fellow-sufferers in the Western Church, and came into the most active contact with it. Hilary of Poictiers (A.D. 368), Lucifer of

Cagliari, Ambrose (398), Philastrius, Gaudentius, Jerome, &c., consider the Epistle to the Hebrews as a work of the apostle Paul.

Now, just as the attempt has been made to overthrow the fact that the primitive tradition of the East declared the epistle to be Pauline, so, on the other hand, it has also been attempted to do away with the equally certain fact, that the West, in the fourth century, held the epistle to be un-Pauline. Stuart has conjectured that the West was originally at one with the East on this question, and that Marcion, who came to Rome in the time of the presbyter Gajus, first infected the West with his doubts as to the Pauline authorship—a conjecture which needs no refutation. Tertullian, the energetic opponent of Marcion, who in his opposition to the Gnostics, never fails to impute to Marcion as a crime his every doubt respecting the authenticity of a biblical book, does not in a single syllable charge him with holding the Epistle to the Hebrews to be un-Pauline (adv. Marc v. 20), and he himself declares the epistle to be a work of Barnabas! Assuredly he would not have adopted this view from Marcion!—Hug likewise thinks that the Western Church originally possessed the Epistle to the Hebrews, but when the Montanists appealed to Heb. vi. 4 ss. (Hieron. adv. Jovin. ii. 3), from opposition to them, it was first ignored (as was done by Irenaeus), and then declared to be spurious. But Tertullian also, who was himself a Montanist, or had been, had no other opinion than that the epistle proceeded from Barnabas! And how, in general, would the whole immense church of the West have declared an epistle to be spurious, which according to tradition was apostolical, merely in order to be able to get rid of a single argument of a sect! It might, on the same principle, have declared the entire New Testament to be spurious, on account of the Gnostics and Ebionites!

These two theses then may be considered as thoroughly confirmed, *that the tradition of the East held the epistle to be Pauline, that, on the other hand, the West came to know it in general at a later period, and then very decidedly held it to be un-Pauline.* The question now arises, what *critical inferences* are to be drawn from this phenomenon? Not a few draw from it the simple result, that "the external testimonies contradict each other, and consequently, that the internal reasons alone must decide." Such a procedure, however, deserves to be characterized as hasty and groundless. The eastern and the western traditions are not two equal, but opposite, mathematical quantities which cancel each other and reduce each other to nothing, but they are facts which are to be *weighed*, nay more, which are to be *explained*.

In weighing the two traditions against each other, that of the East is the heavier in the scale. First of all, it is reasonable to expect a surer and more general knowledge concerning the author of an epistle in the district *to which* that epistle was written, than in that *from which* it was written. In Jerusalem, whither the epistle had been sent, it *must* have been known and learned who the author was; for, although he does not name himself in the inscription, the bearer of the epistle would certainly not deliver it with the words: " Here I bring you an epistle out of Italy from *somebody*; who that somebody is however you must not know"—for then had the authority of the epistle been but ill cared for! but the bearer must, in all probability, have brought to the teacher of that circle of readers an additional private writing, and to the circle of readers themselves have mentioned and certified the name of the author. From thence, along with the epistle (which soon indeed came to have a high significance for the whole of oriental Christendom, being, as it were, a divinely authenticated document for the loosing of the band between Christianity and Judaism), the knowledge of its author, too, must have spread—first, and most surely, to Lesser Asia, Syria, Egypt! What we learn there respecting the Epistle to the Hebrews we shall have to consider as the surest information.

It was altogether different in Italy, where the author wrote. True, he writes salutations from the Italian Christians, but this surely does not necessitate the supposition that he first sent round everywhere to the Christian churches of Italy, announced his intention to write to some Jewish Christians in Jerusalem, and obtained authority from them to send their salutations. The salutation, chap. xiii. 24, is in so vague and general a form as to lead to the supposition, that the author ventured to write it at his own hand. Let it be granted, however, that in the author's immediate neighbourhood the notice would be spread that he was writing to Christians in Jerusalem, this notice would be forgotten in the next months, years, decades. The Western Church did not happen at first to see the epistle itself. Very natural! The epistle, in respect of its import, had an interest only where there were Jewish Christians who still from piety observed the Levitical law; such there were in Palestine, Syria, Alexandria, doubtless also in Lesser Asia. In Italy the Jewish Christians were small in point of numbers, and gradually decreasing; there they were from the commencement more mixed with Gentile Christians. The Epistle to the Hebrews came also into the Western Church, but late and slowly; it was not, so to speak, waited for and read with avidity as a practically important writing. It came thither slowly, by means of copies. No Paul had named himself in the inscription; it was therefore not at all imagined that the epistle was Pauline. In the beginning of the second century it was not yet received into the ecclesiastical collection of books prescribed to be read (the canon) of the Western Church; now as from the beginning of the second century, from the death of the last apostle, the Church clung with tenacity to all old tradition, the Western Church also made no change in its canon; the Epistle to the Hebrews indeed gradually spread, but *the old tradition of the West had not reckoned it among the canonical epistles;* consequently it was allowed to stand outside the canon, and, least of all, was there any inclination to acknowledge it as Pauline. Now, that in the fourth century the Western Church followed the oriental tradition so soon as that Church came into more lively contact with it, can only be explained from the fact, that the Eastern Church must have had *weighty positive reasons in support of it.* In general, the Eastern differs from the Western tradition as regards the Epistle to the Hebrews in this, that the former bears a *positive,* the latter a *negative* character. The former went out from the knowledge that the epistle was Pauline, and only afterwards were doubts awakened (in the Alexandrians) on account of the style, which, however, could not overthrow that tradition, but only led to attempts to reconcile them with it. Nor was there any doubt in Alexandria as to who was the first and proper author, but only as to who was the translator, or who had worked it out, whether Clement of

Rome or Luke. It was a settled point, that Paul was the proper author. The tradition of the Western Church, on the contrary, went out from an ignorance of the epistle, an ignorance of the author, and we meet nowhere any positive statement respecting the person of this author, with the single exception of that of Tertullian. True, when he names Barnabas, Tertullian seems to express not a *subjective conjecture* but a *tradition;* at all events, however, this tradition was only a *local* one, and in all probability rested, in its *first* origin, only on a conjecture. Origen, (in Euseb. vii. 25), when he brings together all the opinions respecting the Epistle to the Hebrews, *knows nothing* of that of Tertullian ; Jerome (cat. 5) adduces it as "juxta Tertullianum," and has therefore regarded it as entirely a subjective view of this Church Father.

These considerations will suffice to convince us, that the critic—let him, if he will, form an opinion respecting the author of the Epistle to the Hebrews only on internal grounds—is, at all events, not at liberty to set up any hypothesis which leaves it unaccountable, *how the Eastern Church came to the consciousness of having got this epistle as one sent by Paul.*

And now if, in the second chapter, it was left an open question whether the Epistle to the Hebrews was written in the year 62 *before*—or in the year 64 *after* the death of Paul, the decision already inclines to the *first* of these dates. For, let it also be granted, that the Eastern Church had actually erred in considering the apostle Paul as the author, even this error would cease to be explicable, if the Epistle to the Hebrews generally speaking came first into the east after the death of the apostle. Think only of Heb. xiii. 19.

CHAPTER FIFTH.

CONTINUATION. B) INTERNAL REASONS.

Let us now look at *the epistle itself;* let us inquire whether it contains any *special intimations* respecting the person of its author; let us consider its *doctrinal import, its diction and style*, that we may see whether the epistle can be Pauline.

A) PARTICULAR INTIMATIONS.

Against the possibility of the Pauline authorship of the Epistle to the Hebrews is generally adduced the passage chap. ii. 3, where the author *distinguishes himself from the Apostles*, while Paul is elsewhere wont studiously to lay stress on his apostolical authority (Gal. i.; 2 Cor. xi.—xii.)—But unjustly. The author, in that passage, does not distinguish himself from the apostles as one who is not an apostle, but, as one who was not an eye-witness he distinguishes himself from the eye-witnesses of the life and labours of that Son of God who brought the salvation. The author is not addressing those who cast doubts on his authority, and the question in the Epistle to the Hebrews is not whether Paul derives his office as immediately as the twelve from Christ, or whether he has it from men; but the antithesis in that passage is between the word of *the law*, which was spoken by *angels* on Sinai, and the word of the New Testament *salvation*, which has been made known "to us" first by *the Lord himself* and then by *ear-witnesses* (therefore is perfectly sure— comp. ἐβεβαιώθη.) Paul himself could not have written otherwise here; he too could and must include himself, along with his readers, among those who had not themselves been witnesses of the life of Jesus. Accordingly, on the supposition of the Pauline authorship, the ἡμεῖς explains itself admirably even when taken as the 1 plur. *communicative* which is *not even necessary.* For ἡμεῖς is said in opposition to the cotemporaries of Moses, and only denotes generally the Christians; and if the author, in the course of the period v. 3, continues in the 1 plural with which he had begun, he had in view there certainly, as appears from the context, not so much himself as his readers. "How can we escape," &c. is only a milder form of: "How can *ye* escape?" and the 1 plur. is not so much communicative as *insinuatory.* This passage, then, nowise presents any hindrance to the supposition of the Pauline authorship. Quite as little does the passage chap. xiii. ver. 19; comp. our remarks on that passage.

On the other hand, again, no inference can be drawn that the Apostle Paul was the writer, from the circumstance that in chap. xiii. 23 the author speaks of his "brother Timothy." Paul certainly gives him the same designation in Col. i. 1. But why may not another helper of Paul, for example a Luke, a Mark, have given to Timothy as his fellow-helper the name " brother ?" Only so much can be inferred from the postscript chap. xiii. 20 ss., that the author must have been a man *who belonged to the specially-Pauline circle*, and was in Rome either in the year 62 or in the year 64.

B) THE DOCTRINAL IMPORT.

The argument which some have founded on the doctrinal contents of the epistle against the authorship of Paul will not stand the test. It is maintained that *there is no trace of such an allegorical interpretation of the Old Testament in the Pauline epistles.* There is already a mistake here, however, in speaking of an " allegorical " interpretation. That interpretation is called allegorical in which a symbolical sense is *arbitrarily* sought in a passage which is to be understood in the simple natural sense. When, in the account which is given of the feeding of the five thousand men, the twelve baskets full of the remaining fragments are explained of the twelve apostles whom Christ left over, or left behind to the world, as the twelve bearers of that bread of life which he himself had not yet distributed—this is an allegorical interpretation. Such interpretations are certainly not found in the Pauline epistles, but as little are they to be found in the Epistle to the Hebrews. We have to distinguish the objective *type* from the subjective arbitrary allegorical interpretation. Types must arise from this, that preliminary and imperfect fulfilments, precede the final perfect fulfilment of the promises of salvation. The deliverance from Egypt was *really* a fulfilment of the promise given in Gen. xv., but it was not yet the true fulfilment; the promise that all nations should be blessed in the seed of Abraham was not yet fulfilled. The kingdom of David was really a higher and more perfect step in the possession of Canaan than the conquests of Joshua, but still not yet the last. Here, then, the preliminary fulfilment is *really* in itself, and objectively, a type of the perfect, *just because both refer to one promise, and correspond to one promise*. Thus, the intercourse between God revealing his presence in the Holiest of all, and the people represented by the Levitical priests and sacrifices, was *really* a type of the perfect reconciliation of God with the New Testament Israel, that divine community into which all nations of the earth were to be received, in order to be blessed in it; but the one was a type of the other, just because, in the former, there was only an imperfect fulfilment of what was perfectly fulfilled in the latter. The supposed "allegorical interpretation" of the Old Testament in the Epistle to the Hebrews, or, more correctly, the *typology* in this Epistle, consists simply in the author's showing, *that the types were only types, i.e.,* in other words, that no prophecy found a *perfect* fulfilment in the old covenant, that all fulfilments rather pointed always again to a further future. It was, for example, no arbitrary allegorizing, but pure objective truth to say, that the state of separation between God and the people under the old covenant, the existence of two compartments in the tabernacle, a Holy of Holies and a $\pi\rho\omega\tau\eta\ \sigma\kappa\eta\nu\eta$, the necessity of ever-repeated sacrifices, pointed to a relation of man to God which was not yet established. *This* typology, however, we find also in Paul's writings. When Paul, Gal iv., sees in the two wives of Abraham and their sons—of whom the one was by nature the elder, and yet was rejected, while the other, as the possessor of the promise of grace, was the heir—a typical foreshadowing of the relation between the natural posterity of Abraham, the legally righteous, natural Israel, and the New Testament Israel holding fast the promise, this is just such a typology as we find in the Epistle to the Hebrews, nay, a bolder instance of it. But the fact that such typologies occur seldom, and by the by, in Paul's writings, while in the Epistle to the Hebrews they form the substance of the writing, is naturally accounted for by the *aim* and *object* of the Epistle to the Hebrews, which is, to consider the Old Testament institutions with the intent to discover whether, and in how far, they point forwards to something more perfect. But a difference which can be explained by considering the *object* of a writing, ought not logically to be made a ground from which to infer a different author.

Nor is it otherwise with reference to a second consideration, viz., *that the doctrine of the resurrection, which plays so important a part in Paul's writings, is not treated of in the Epistle to the Hebrews.* It was necessary that Paul should develope this doctrine in detail when writing to the Corinthians, because they disputed it, in like manner to the Thessalonians, because they had false apprehensions of it. But in what part of the Epistle to the Galatians, for example, has Paul even made mention of the resurrection? The objection would only have any force if, in the Epistle to the Hebrews, there was some indication of the non-existence of the resurrection being presupposed. But, indeed, the antithesis between the humiliation and exaltation of Christ, the suffering and glorification of believers, forms rather the *ground tone* upon which the whole symphony of ideas in the Epistle to the Hebrews is built! Comp. Heb. i. 3, ii. 5—9, and 10—15, x. 19, ss., xi. 5, xii. 1—3, and 18—24, and 26—29, xiii. 14.

A third objection is founded on the circumstance of the Pauline doctrine, *that the Gentiles also are called to the gospel,* not being found in the Epistle to the Hebrews. Very naturally! This question had been settled in the year 51 in Jerusalem (Acts xv.); and in the year 55, in opposition to the Galatian false teachers. From the fact that this question is not again touched in the Epistle to the Hebrews, the only reasonable inference that can be drawn is, that the readers of the Epistle to the Hebrews did not doubt the lawfulness of the baptism of uncircumcised persons; only the emancipation of *native Israelites*—of the circumcised, the Jewish Christians—from the ritual of the temple, was not yet clear to them. But that the author, on his part, must have been convinced of the right of the uncircumcised to be received into the Church, follows, as the most necessary consequence, from the whole doctrinal position of this epistle! If even the *Jewish Christians* are to *go out* from the $\pi\alpha\rho\epsilon\mu\beta o\lambda\eta$ (xiii. 13), how much less could he expect the *Gentile Christians* to *enter into* this $\pi\alpha\rho\epsilon\mu\beta o\lambda\eta$?—But why does he, in chap. ii. 16, place the "seed of Abraham" in opposition to the angels, and not humanity as a whole? Just because the "seed of Abraham" forms here the antithesis to the *angels*, and not to the *Gentiles*, it follows, that this expression (which is therefore used there in reality not in the empirico-historical sense, but with evident reference to Gen. xxii. 18, consequently, in the prophetico-ideal sense) must embrace the entire *Messianic Church*, the *spiritual* seed of Abraham,[1] and *is used therefore quite in the Pauline sense* (Rom. iv. 16).

A fourth objection, *that the opposition between* ἔργα *and* πίστις *is not developed*, has more apparent reason. But neither, for example, is this opposition developed, nay it is not even touched, in the Epistle to the Thessalonians. Tholuck, indeed, thinks that we were entitled to expect that antithesis precisely in the Epistle to the Hebrews, as the error of the Hebrews consisted in an unintelligent cleaving to the *works of the law*. But this may be very much doubted. The Levitical ritual *acts* might certainly be designated as *works of the law*; but this could be done properly only in so far as any one considered these to be *meritorious services* on his part. This the Galatian false teachers did. They were proud of their extraordinary perfect fulfilment of the ritual and ceremonial ordinances, and thought that they could thereby acquire righteousness before God, and deserve heaven. The readers to whom this epistle was addressed appear in a quite different position. Their malady was not pride and self-righteousness, but fear and scruples of conscience. They thought not that they *did* and *deserved* something great when they kept the law, but they believed that they *needed* the Old Testament means of atonement in order to be free from guilt. They were not *work-righteous*, on the contrary they were *earnestly desiring atonement* (nowhere does the author find it necessary to prove to them that an atonement is necessary), but they could not yet believe that the *one* sacrifice of Christ was sufficient. Thus, in their case, the opposition could not be that between ἔργα νόμου

---

[1] Those are certainly wrong, who think that the idea of a *spiritual* seed of Abraham is there expressed *explicite*; but it would, in like manner, be wrong to understand the word in the *empirical* sense (=people of the *Jews*). The idea is evidently this: God has not given such promises as Gen. xii. 15, 22, &c. to the *angels*, but to the *seed of Abraham*, therefore to *men*.

and πίστις, but only that between the σκιὰ νόμου and the τελείωσις. In dealing with such readers Paul also could certainly not write otherwise than is written in the Epistle to the Hebrews. For no one will fail to perceive, that the difference between the doctrinal system of the Epistle to the Hebrews and that of the Epistle to the Romans is only a formal one. The Epistle to the Hebrews represents precisely the same thing in its objective-historical aspect as is treated in the Epistle to the Romans in its subjective-psychological aspect. *Moreover, the latter is not altogether wanting even in the Epistle to the Hebrews.* We refer to chap iv. " the word which did not mingle itself in faith with those who heard it," and the " living word with which we have to do" (ver. 2 and ver. 12—13). Further, comp. our concluding remark at Heb. x. 15—18, and our introductory remark to the section Heb. xii. 18—29.

The last objection rests on this, that Paul always represents Christ only as the *sacrifice*, not as the *priest*, while it is precisely the reverse in the Epistle to the Hebrews. But, here also, there is no material difference. For if Paul in Eph. v. 2 teaches that Christ *gave himself* an offering and sacrifice (in like manner Gal. ii. 20), and if the Epistle to the Hebrews speaks of a priest who *offered himself* (vii. 27, &c.), then Paul certainly considers Christ not merely as the offered but also as the offerer, and the Epistle to the Hebrews considers him not merely as the offerer but also as the offered. One might really suppose that the two propositions: Christus *sacerdos* immolavit *se ipsum*, and : *Hostiam* immolavit, Christus sese *ipse*, come pretty much to the same thing! There remains, therefore, at most only the question why Paul does not elsewhere also *designate* Christ as the true " priest," why he has not applied the word ἱερεύς to him, if (as Tholuck says) "he had become conscious of the idea of the Messiah's priesthood in the lofty form in which it appears in our epistle."—But whether or not Paul might use the word ἱερεύς, he at all events opened up the view and the representation of a priesthood of Christ when in Eph. v. 2 ; Gal. ii. 20 he wrote : Christ offered himself as a sacrifice. Here certainly he did not think of Christ as a *lay* person, who offered *himself* to *another* priest instead of an animal ! And in Rom. viii. 34 he ascribes also the priestly work of *intercession* to Christ.—But that *the word* ἱερεύς is used precisely in the Epistle to the Hebrews finds its natural explanation in this, that the point from which the author of the Epistle to the Hebrews *started* in his argumentation was the priestly institution, and he proved that *this* institution of the Old Testament also is fulfilled in Christ. In Eph. v. and Gal. ii. on the contrary he starts from the *work of Christ*, and touches only slightly and casually on the analogy between it and the Old Testament sacrificial ritual—just as much so as, for example in 1 Cor. v. 7, he touches on the analogy between Christ and the Old Testament passover lamb.

There is, therefore, *in the doctrinal system of the Epistle to the Hebrews* no peculiarity which forbids us from ascribing its authorship to the Apostle Paul.

On the contrary, there are in the Epistle to the Hebrews a multitude of most peculiarly Pauline ideas. The designation of God as the one by whom and for whom are all things, is Pauline (with Heb. ii. 10, ss.; comp. xi. 36; 1 Cor. viii. 6); the idea of the Son as the *exact image* of the Father (with Heb. i. 1, ss.; comp. 2 Cor. iv. 4; Col. i. 15, s.); the exaltation of Christ above the angels (with Heb. ii. 9; comp. Phil. ii. 9, ss.) into heaven (Heb. iv. 14, vii. 26, and Eph. iv. 10), besides, the remarkable and *quite special* idea that God the Father alone is excepted in the subjection of *all things* to Christ (Heb. ii. 8, 9; 1 Cor. xv. 27); that the exalted Christ intercedes with the Father for his own (Heb. vii. 25; Rom. viii. 34); that he has destroyed death and its power (Heb. ii. 14; 1 Cor. xv. 54, s.; 2 Tim. i. 10); again the *remarkably special* combination of ideas, that Christ, having died once, cannot die again (Heb. ix. 26, ss., x. 12; Rom. vi. 9, s.); farther, that Christ died for every creature (Heb. ii. 9; Eph. i. 10; Rom. viii. 22); that when he comes again, he will come not as a Saviour but as a Judge (Heb. ix. 27, s.; Tit. ii. 13; 2 Tim. iv. 1 and 8; Rom. viii. 24, xiii. 11); that, till then, he rules and reigns at the right hand of God (Heb. i. 3, x. 12, 13; 1 Cor. xv. 25).—In like manner, that the law cannot save, and is destined to be abrogated (with Heb. iv. 2, vii. 16—19, ix. 9—13, viii. 7, x. 14, xvi. 20, comp. Rom. ii. 29; 2 Cor. iii. 6, s.; Gal. iii. 3, iv. 3 and 9). The designation of the law as a *shadow* (Heb. viii. 5, x. 1; Col. ii. 17). The putting together of the ἐλπίς with the πίστις and with the ἀγάπη (Heb. vi. 10 s., x. 22, ss.; comp. 1 Thess. v. 8 and 1 Cor. xiii. 13). The request to be interceded for (Heb. xiii. 18, s.; Phil. ii. 14, i. 25; Philem. xxii.), and the antithesis between τέλειος and νήπιος (Heb. v. 13, 14; 1 Cor. iii. 1, xiii. 11; Rom. ii. 20; Eph. iv. 14).

Especially remarkable, however, is the agreement of the Epistle to the Hebrews with Paul in the reference to the second psalm (Heb. i. 5, ss.; comp. Acts xiii. 33, ss.), and in the inference, drawn from Abraham's readiness to offer up Isaac, that Abraham believed in the possibility of a resurrection of Isaac.

This Pauline complexion of the doctrinal system does not, indeed, necessitate our coming to the conclusion that Paul was the author of the epistle, but still leaves room for the possibility of another author; this other, however, must at all events be sought for among the disciples and helpers of the Apostle Paul; our epistle must have emanated from this circle; only thus can the recurrence of Pauline ideas and combinations of ideas—even in the minutest particulars—be accounted for.

C) WORDS AND PHRASES.

Many *dogmatical expressions* peculiarly Pauline are also found in our epistle. The doctrine that Christ intercedes for us with the Father (Heb. vii. 25; Rom. viii. 34) is expressed by the same word ἐντυγχάνειν, that of his having destroyed death by the same verb καταργεῖν (Heb. ii. 14; 2 Tim. i. 10). Further, the phrase ὁ θεὸς ζῶν (Heb. x. 31, used elsewhere only by Paul), the expression δίκαιος κατὰ πίστιν (Heb. vii. 25), the use of καυχᾶσθαι (Heb. iii. 6; otherwise, for example, Jam. iv. 16). Further, comp. Heb. ii. 4 with 1 Cor. xii. 4—Heb. xiii. 20 with Rom. xv. 33, xvi. 20; 2 Cor. xiii. 11; Phil. iv. 9; 1 Thess. v. 23—Heb. xii. 1 with 1 Tim. vi. 12; 2 Tim iv. 7.—Finally, the genuine Pauline expression περισσοτέρως; Heb. xii. 19, and πέποιθα, Heb. xiii. 18.

There are again indeed dogmatical expressions which do not recur in other Pauline epistles. The frequent use of τελειοῦν can scarcely be adduced as belonging to this class, as the word is also found in Phil. iii. 12; the frequency of its occurrence in the

Epistle to the Hebrews is to be explained from the object of the writing, namely, to shew the fulfilment of all the Old Testament types, and does not therefore point to a different writer. In like manner, the designation of Christ as the ἀπόστολος θεοῦ to men (iii. 1) is explained from the context, as we have seen in the interpretation of the passage, and Paul himself would have been able to find no other word to express the appellative idea of יהוה מלאך without, at the same time, expressing the Gentile idea "angel."—On the other hand, reference may justly be made to the use of ὁμολογία (iii. 1, iv. 14, x. 23), ἐγγίζειν τῷ θεῷ (Heb. vii. 19) and the allusion to John x. 1 (Heb. xiii. 20). These, however, are still no conclusive proofs against the Pauline authorship. Particular expressions not occurring elsewhere are found in *every* epistle of Paul, and it must have been a strange and not very accountable solicitude on the part of the apostle, if, in any epistle, he had set himself to avoid all such expressions as he had not already used in former epistles.

If, now, we look at the remaining phrases, in a dogmatical point of view indifferent, we are at once struck with a great dissimilarity from the Pauline style consisting in this, that far fewer and weaker *Hebraisms* occur in the Epistle to the Hebrews than elsewhere in the Pauline epistles. Hebraisms are, indeed, not altogether wanting also in our epistle; but they are found, partly, only in those passages in which reference is directly made to Old Testament declarations and expressions[1] (for example κοπή, vii. 1, peculiar to the usage of the LXX.; ἐν τῇ ὀσφυΐ εἶναι, vii. 10), or they are phrases which were entirely naturalised in the speech of the Christians, and whose foreign origin was no longer felt by any one (γεύεσθαι θανάτου, ἰδεῖν θάνατον, οὐχ εὑρίσκετο, λαλεῖν = דָּבָר, ῥῆμα = prophecy.) Or finally, but only seldom, there are loose connexions of sentences which are indeed *conceived in Hebrew*, but are, at the same time, also tolerable for the Grecian ear, and cannot be said to be not Greek, as for example chap. xii. 9, καὶ ζήσομεν for ἵνα ζῶμεν. There occur also the expressions Ἀαρών, Χερουβίμ, Ἱεριχώ used indeclinably; finally, also, genitives of quality, for which the classical Greek would rather have

---

[1] Hebraisms in the *citations* properly so called from the LXX. (for example chap. vi. 14) are, of course, not at all taken into view.

used adjectives. All these single instances, however, are very far from giving to the writing as a whole that *Hebrew colouring* which belongs to the Pauline epistles; in it all is thought in *Greek*, in the writings of Paul the *Semitic connexion of the thoughts* is everywhere apparent. Now this can scarcely indeed be explained by the circumstance, that Paul has, in this writing, carefully elaborated a treatise, and not surrendered himself as elsewhere to the impulse of his feelings. It would be wrong to deny that a man of the mind of Paul, if he had *made it his aim* to write good Greek, such Greek as that of the Epistle to the Hebrews, might have accomplished it. But it will be all the more difficult to perceive, why he should have studied to attain so fine a Greek style in writing precisely to the *Hebrews*.

D) THE STYLE.

This leads us now to the style as a whole. No small portion of the peculiarities which are commonly adduced as arguments against the Pauline authorship may, more correctly considered, be reduced to this, that the Epistle to the Hebrews is written in a *more select style* than the Pauline epistles. To this belongs the use of sonorous compounds as μισθαποδοσία, ὁρκωμοσία, then such turns as ὅσον—τοσούτῳ, κοινωνεῖν with the genitive of the thing (while in Rom. v. 17; 1 Tim. v. 22 it is used with the dative), σκότος as masculine (while with Paul it is always neuter), farther, the frequent use of the elegantly connecting adverb ὅθεν (for which Paul uses διό, διὰ τοῦτο), ἐάνπερ (for which Paul uses εἴγε and εἴπερ), εἰς τὸ διηνεκὲς, διὰ παντός (for which, except in Rom. xi. 10, Paul always uses the more homely πάντοτε, while this occurs only once in the Epistle to the Hebrews, chap. vii. 25.) Now, this more select style affords certainly an indirect argument against the Pauline authorship; for, although the circumstance that the Epistle to the Hebrews has the nature of a treatise and was worked out with more scientific composure and care, may *in some measure* account for the author's having paid more attention to the *diction* than he did in other epistles properly so called, it still remains unaccountable, as has been already observed, that Paul should have aimed in so high a degree at a fine style when writing *precisely to the Jewish Christians in Jerusalem*, while he gives himself free scope in writing to the Ephesians, Corinthians, Romans, &c. That so elegant a structure of period as we find, for example, in chap. i. 1—3; chap. x. 19—25; xi. 32—38; xii. 18—24—that so elegant an arrangement of the words as we find, for example, in Heb. vii. 4 (θεωρεῖτε δὲ, πήλικος οὗτος, ᾧ καὶ δεκάτην Ἀβραὰμ ἔδωκεν ἐκ τῶν ἀκροθινίων, ὁ πατριάρχης) was not *natural* to the apostle Paul, is but too apparent from the Pauline epistles! In such passages he must not merely have written more composedly and carefully, but must have made the style precisely the subject of artistical study, and that he should have done so is in the least degree credible in the case of a missive intended for the Jewish Christians in Palestine.

In addition to this, there are certain expressions of a more trifling kind, which are all the more important precisely because they cannot be reduced under the general head of style, but have their origin, doubtless, in unconscious habit. The author of the Epistle to the Hebrews uses in comparisons παρά with the accusative (four times), which never occurs in Paul's writings; he uses the word μακροθυμία (vi. 12 and 15) to designate an idea for which Paul always employs the proper favourite expression ὑπομονή; he uses καθίζειν intransitively, which Paul, with the exception of the single passage 2 Thess. ii. 4, always applies intransitively in the sense of "set;" he says in seven passages Ἰησοῦς (especially remarkable in chap. xiii. 20), and Ἰησοῦς Χριστός only in two passages (xiii. 8 and 21), while Paul never says Ἰησοῦς alone, but (according to Stuart's enumeration) Ἰησοῦς Χριστός 68 times, and Χριστός 198 times, and ὁ κύριος 147 times; finally, he cites Old Testament passages with the words πνεῦμα λέγει, or, merely λέγει, while Paul usually introduces citations by γέγραπται (only in 1 Tim. i. 4, and Gal. iii. 16 by πνεῦμα λέγει). The Rabbinical controversial formulas, too, so common in Paul's writings (for example when an objection is introduced with the words ἀλλ' ἐρεῖ τις) are entirely wanting in the Epistle to the Hebrews.

That the Epistle to the Hebrews always strictly follows the Sept. in the citations, while Paul often cites freely, is a circumstance to which, considered in itself, no weight can be attached.

APPENDIX.

To account for this it has only to be remembered, that the author of this epistle wrote *with the Sept. in his hand*, and with the intention that his writing should be *formally studied* by his readers and *compared* with the Sept. It is a circumstance of more importance that the citations of our epistle follow the recension which is contained in the cod. Alex., while those of Paul, when he follows the Sept., for the most part agree with the cod. Vatic. (Bleek p. 369 ss.)

But what *seems* more significant than all this is the *manner in which the thoughts themselves are arranged, and the proofs adduced.* The method of passing, immediately at the conclusion of a section, to the theme of a new section, and in this way intimating that theme, is nowhere to be found in Paul's writings. (With the transitions Heb. i. 4 ; ii. 5 ; iii. 2 ; iv. 1 and 14 ; v. 10, &c., comp. the abrupt transitions Rom. iii. 1; v. 1; vi. 1 ; vii. 1; viii. 1 and 12 ; ix. 1 ; xii. 1; 1 Cor. v. 1 ; vi. 1; vii. 1 ; viii. 1; ix. 1; xii. 1; xv. 1, &c.) Paul generally adduces his proofs immediately, by appealing to the inner experience (for example Rom. vii.), or when he actually deduces propositions from propositions, he simply makes one proposition follow another with a "because;" and carries forward the chain of ideas without logical arrangement, now looking backwards now forwards (comp. for example, Rom. i. 19, 20 ; ii. 14—16 ; iii. 4—8), and often interrupts himself by accessory ideas (for example, Rom. v. 13—17.) In the Epistle to the Hebrews we find everywhere a strictly syllogistical arrangement of the members composing the proof, and that generally in such a form as that the conclusion is forthwith inferred from one of the two premises, while the other connecting premiss is brought in afterwards (comp. our remarks on Heb. xii. 10.)

All these considerations are so forcible and conclusive that we can say nothing else than this : *By how much the spirit and doctrine of the epistle is Pauline, by so little can it be supposed that this diction should have come from the hand of the Apostle.*

CHAPTER SIXTH.

CONCLUSION. THE PARTICULAR HYPOTHESES.

After having without prejudice ascertained the particular phenomena external and internal, which fall to be considered in the question respecting the author of the Epistle to the Hebrews, and after having carefully examined every one of them, it will now be an easy matter to test the different opinions which have been put forth concerning the person of its author. We may divide these opinions into *three classes*. First, that of those who hold the apostle Paul to have been the immediate and proper author of the epistle (as Gelpke, Hug, Klee, Paulus, Stein); a second class embraces the views of those who exclude the apostle Paul from all share in the production of the Epistle to the Hebrews; a third class is formed by the conjectures of those who, as already *Origen*, hold that the epistle was written in the name of and by commission from the Apostle Paul, under his authority, nay under his special influence, but not written with his own hand nor verbally dictated by him.

The view which belongs to the *first class* has commonly been too roughly handled, and set aside as insipid. That no argument against it can be drawn from the external testimonies, we have already seen at the end of the fourth chapter of this inquiry, and have come to the conclusion, that precisely in the supposition of a Pauline authorship does the *positive* tradition of the East, in like manner as the *negative* tradition of the West, find its explanation. The inference also which is wont to be drawn from Heb. ii. 3 against the Pauline authorship, has already (chap. v. at the beginning) appeared to us to be of no weight. One argument only remains in full force against that view—viz. the peculiarities of style. Only by a forced process may these peculiarities be broken down, and in this state, one by one, weakened of their effect; in fact, it cannot be proven with mathematical certainty that it was absolutely impossible for the Apostle Paul to throw himself, for once, into a different kind of style; but no positive reason can be discovered, by which the Apostle Paul should have been induced to write in a style so different from that to which he was accustomed, and a sound critical mind will be ever and again forced into the conviction, that in the Epistle to the Hebrews another hand than that of Paul held the pen.

Nor is it otherwise with the *second class* of hypotheses, how great soever the number of those whose views are to be ranked under it. Already must reasonable doubts be awakened by the single circumstance, that criticism has arrived at no judgment in any measure certain as to *who* the author can have been if it was not Paul. Criticism has split itself into many hypotheses on this point, against every one of which there are substantial doubts. The most untenable of these is the conjecture which makes *Clement of Rome* the author; it remains untenable even when separated from the auxiliary conjecture with which it appears in ancient times to have been connected (in Euseb. iii. 38), namely that Clement only translated the epistle from an Aramaic original (it is so separated by Eusebius and Calvin, who, besides, expresses himself hesitatingly). This conjecture as a whole evidently rests on the circumstance that many ideas of the Epistle to the Hebrews recur in the Epistle to the Corinthians of Clement. But we have already seen (chap. iv.) that the relation between these two epistles does not resemble that between Paul's Epistle to the Romans and his Epistle to the Galatians, or that between the Epistles to the Ephesians and the Colossians—in other words, that it is not one spirit and one doctrinal system from which the two epistles, our Epistle to the Hebrews and the Epistle of Clement, have proceeded with equal originality—but rather that Clement, in *particular passages* of his epistle, *alludes to particular passages* of the Epistle to the Hebrews, *cites* them, and thus places himself in a relation of *dependence* on the Epistle to the Hebrews, just as he places himself in dependence on the particular Epistles of Paul. The *spirit* of Clement's epistle—in so far as Clement does not give citations but writes independently—is altogether different from the spirit of the Epistle to the Hebrews. His relation to it was evidently the relation in which one stands to the writing of another.

In like manner untenable is the opinion that *Mark* was the

author of the Epistle to the Hebrews; not because Mark, as belonging to Jerusalem (Acts xii. 13), must have been better acquainted with the temple than our author, from a false exegesis of chap. ix., is made out to have been, but because Mark did not belong to the *Pauline* circle[1] either in the course of his outer life (comp. Acts xv. 37—40; 1 Pet. v. 13), or in his inner character,—because he did not stand in the near relation to Timothy described in Heb. xiii. 23, and, moreover, as regards his style, deviates still more than Paul from the Epistle to the Hebrews.

Nor can *Aquila* be thought of as the author, inasmuch as he was not living in Italy in the years 62 ss. but in Ephesus (2 Tim. iv. 19), while the Epistle to the Hebrews was written in Italy (comp. our explanation of xiii. 24).

With greater confidence have J. E. Chr. Schmidt, Twesten, Ullmann, and recently Thiersch declared *Barnabas* to have been the author. But, as we have already seen (chap. iv.), appeal can be made in support of this hypothesis to anything but ancient ecclesiastical tradition, with the exception of Tertullian. On the other hand, it is not to be objected to this hypothesis, that such a *supposed* want of acquaintance with the temple as is found in the Epistle to the Hebrews would not be conceivable in the case of a Levite (Acts iv. 36). Nor can any argument against it be drawn from the so-called "epistle of Barnabas," which is altogether unlike the Epistle to the Hebrews, as this epistle, although written by a man of the name of Barnabas, can hardly have been written by that Barnabas who is mentioned in the New Testament. With more reason is reference made against this hypothesis to the circumstance, that Barnabas (according to Acts xiv. 12), was inferior even to Paul in the gift of eloquence, while the author of the Epistle to the Hebrews far surpassed Paul in skill in the use of language. To this is to be added, that Barnabas, from the time spoken of in Acts xiv., completely retires from notice, and disappears from history. In the Pauline epistles written from Rome mention is nowhere made of him.

Titus also was at that time in Dalmatia (2 Tim. iv. 10). Even on this account, we are not at liberty to suppose that he can have been the author, nor has any one in reality suggested him.

[1] He was, however, for a while in Rome at the same time with Paul, according to Col. iv. 10; Philem. 24.

On the other hand, Luther, Clericus, Semler, Dindorf, Zeigler, De Wette, Tholuck, Olshausen, and Bleek have conjectured that *Apollos* was the author. He was, indeed, an eloquent man and mighty in the Scriptures (Acts xviii. 24; comp. 1 Cor. i. 4), who from the very first was wont to dispute with the Jews (Acts xviii. 28). And as exceedingly little is known of him, a number of conjectures are possible in regard to him; he *may* have laboured in Palestine, he *may* have acquired great influence there; he *may* have had in view in the expression *my brother Timothy*, Heb. xiii. 23, merely the general brotherly relation of the Christian to the Christian; *for*, he cannot have stood in a special relation to Timothy before the year 64, which is the latest date that can be supposed for the composition of the Epistle to the Hebrews; nor can he have been in Italy at the time of Paul's imprisonment, as Paul never mentions him. And there are certainly no inconsiderable difficulties which stand in the way of this hypothesis, and which can be obviated only by a very unnatural explanation of the passage Heb. xiii. 24. Besides, it is not very probable that Apollos can have coincided so thoroughly with the Pauline system of doctrine, from the intimations which we find in the Acts of the Apostles and in the Epistle to the Corinthians.

With much more reason may it be supposed that *Silas* or *Luke* was the author. The former view has been defended, although but weakly, by Böhme and Mynster, the latter by Grotius. Against Luke, something has been made of the circumstance that he was a Gentile Christian (Col. iv. 14, comp. with ver. 10, s.), while the Epistle to the Hebrews must of necessity have been written by a Jewish Christian. This latter is inferred from the fact that the author in chap. i. 1, speaks of the "fathers," where it is evidently the people of Israel that are meant, and that in chap. xi. 2 he calls the believers of the old covenant οἱ πρεσβύτεροι. Had he spoken of "our fathers," then there would be some ground for the inference; but it is difficult to see why an author, writing to Jewish Christians, should not have been able so far to forget himself or his readers as to say: "Beforetime God has spoken to the fathers by the prophets." Surely the Gentile Christians, too, had with Jesus the Messiah, received also the word of prophecy; surely they, too, had entered into the right and relation of children among the people of God! And *that same Luke* speaks of the events which happened to Jesus among the Jewish people as περὶ τῶν πραγμάτων ἐν ἡμῖν πεπληροφορημένων. Such passages, therefore, as Heb. i. 1; xi. 2, cannot be made to bear against the authorship of Luke. On the other hand, the circumstance speaks for Luke, that from the year 62 onwards he was with Paul in Italy, and a fellow helper with Timothy (Philem. i. and 24); Silas stood in the same relation to Timothy (comp. 1 Thess. i. 1); true, in the year 62, Silas was not in Italy, but he was certainly there with Peter " ἐν βαβυλῶνι" in the year 64, immediately after the death of Paul (comp. 1 Pet. v. 12). Now, as the Epistle to the Hebrews must have been written either in the year 62 or in the year 64 (see above chap. ii.), in the former case Luke might be held to be the author, in the latter case Silas.

This hypothesis would certainly, so far as we have gone, be the *most tolerable;* but there is one reason also for rejecting it, the same by which *this entire second class* of hypothesis is overthrown. *The firmness and unanimity of the oriental tradition remains altogether inexplicable, if it be not supposed that the Epistle to the Hebrews came to Jerusalem, under the name and the authority of Paul.* (See above chap. iv. at the end.) And thus, indeed, there is not wanting the "occasion" demanded by Bleek (p. 393) for supposing, that "precisely Paul" was, at least, the indirect author of the epistle.

This brings us to the *third class* of conjectures, which, however, has received but small accessions since the time of Origen, so that we are spared the trouble of enumerating various particular hypotheses, and instead of this, can immediately pass to a positive construction of the right view.

The data at which we have arrived in chap. iv.—v. form the starting point:

(1.) The tradition of the East is capable of explanation only on the supposition, that the epistle was handed to the readers under the name of Paul.

(2). That the Western Church was at first unacquainted with the epistle, is fully accounted for by the circumstance of its having been designed for the Jewish Christians of Palestine, and the ignorance of that Church, at a later period, respecting its author, is explained by the want of an inscription, and the un-Pauline style.

(3). The author stood in a near personal relation to Timothy.
(4). The doctrine is Pauline, the diction un-Pauline.

Let us now call to mind a very remarkable circumstance already hinted at in the explanation of chap. xiii. 19 and 22, ss., but which has as yet been entirely unobserved, viz., that chap. xiii. 22—25, cannot have been written *in the name* of the person who wrote chap. i. 1—chap. xiii. 21, nevertheless, that it must have been written *by the same hand*. The postscript is not in the name of him in whose name the epistle was written; for the person in whose name ver. 19 is written was, against his will, so situated as to be prevented from setting out on a journey to the readers. This did not depend on his own will; nor did he by any means hope to be shortly set free, but he admonished the readers to pray that he might be restored to them; he therefore took it for granted that he would be still in confinement when the readers should have received the epistle into their hands. On the other hand, the person in whose name ver. 22—25 is written is already about to set out on a journey, and it depends only on the speedier or later coming of Timothy, who had just been set free, whether he will set out towards the East along with him or alone.

And yet, the postscript is written and composed *by the same hand* that wrote and composed the epistle. For, in ver. 22, the author of the postscript apologizes for several harshnesses in his admonitions, and asks the readers to excuse these on account of the short and compressed character of the writing. The postscript, therefore, does not proceed from an *amanuensis* to whom the epistle had been *verbally dictated*, but from one to whom the *material had been given while the diction was left to himself.*

Who then was the author? who the composer? The composer was a friend or fellow-helper of Timothy (xiii. 23), but was not, precisely at that time, in the same place (xiii. 23, ἐὰν . . . ἔρχηται) in which Timothy had, up till about that time, been imprisoned. Now, we found (see above, chap. ii.) *in the Epistle to the Philippians*, the clearest traces of an imprisonment of Timothy. Paul would like to send Timothy into the East, but *cannot* yet do so; he *hopes*, however, to be able shortly to send him thither. *When Paul wrote the Epistle to the Philippians, in the year 62, Timothy was accordingly in prison, but with the hope of being soon released. At that time Luke was not precisely in Rome itself;* for Paul sends no salutations from him to the Philippians, who were so well known to him. Shortly afterwards, we suppose the Epistle to the Hebrews to have been finished, certainly a few days after the departure of Epaphroditus, (Phil. ii. 25). Paul we suppose, intended to have fully talked over the subject with Luke, perhaps to have given him a scheme or preparatory work in writing; he himself was deprived of the leisure necessary for the composition by the legal procedure against him, which precisely at that time (Phil. ii. 23) had passed into a new stage. Luke worked out the epistle for Paul, and as in his name, not however in Rome, where perhaps he himself might have been involved in the procedure against Paul, but in another place in Italy, somewhere in the neighbourhood of Theophilus. When the work was finished, the news reached him that Timothy had been set free in Rome. He himself purposed to set out for the East, though not directly to Palestine (for, in xiii. 23, he takes it for granted that the Epistle to the Hebrews would be in the hands of the readers before he should see them personally); Timothy, too, in company with whom he wishes and hopes to make the journey (ver. 23) was (according to Phil. ii. 23) shortly to direct his course to Lesser Asia. How exactly do the most particular, the most trifling notices harmonize here!

I think I am even warranted in saying that this hypothesis leaves nothing unexplained. First of all, it completely explains the *internal phenomena* of the epistle. Commissioned by the apostle Paul to work out the writing, Luke wrote *in the name* of Paul (xiii. 19), only, however, in that part where he added the personal concluding requests (which had possibly been given to him in writing by Paul); nowhere did he *affect* to speak in the name of Paul or to allude to events in the life of Paul; nowhere, indeed, with the exception of chap. xiii. 19, does a first person singular occur, while the omission of an inscription becomes also perfectly intelligible. On the other hand, it becomes also perfectly intelligible how Luke, writing in virtue of a commission from Paul, might speak of the members of the Old Testament covenant simply as "the fathers," the "elders." This hypothesis

---
[1]

explains the combination of thoroughly Pauline ideas and doctrinal forms of expression with the un-Pauline diction ; it explains, also, the circumstance that of all the New Testament writings, precisely those of Luke have most similarity in point of style with the Epistle to the Hebrews (in so far, namely, as Luke has not interwoven notices prepared by others into his Gospel and Acts of the Apostles). How similar in style are the two introductions, Luke i. 1—4 and Heb. i. 1—3 !

Secondly, the origin of the *ecclesiastical tradition* becomes intelligible on this hypothesis. The bearer of the epistle, who is unknown to us, delivered it to the readers as an "epistle which Paul sends to them," and thereby as a Pauline epistle. Assuredly he did not fail to communicate to them what was necessary respecting the peculiar manner in which it had been prepared, to tell them that the epistle was written by the hand of Luke, and at the same time not verbally dictated to Luke. *Without such a notification none of the readers could have understood the postscript, especially ver. 22 and ver. 23.* But, in a way which is easily conceivable, the notification was soon lost.

What the readers found in the epistle was kept and considered, with reason, as the *teaching and the admonitions of the apostle.* And thus the epistle was regarded as one of Paul's ; it was written auctoritate Pauli, and, in reality also, Paulo autore,—wheresoever the epistle spread, it carried with it the information that Paul was its author. And how highly important did this epistle, designed at first only for a very limited circle of readers, become, even in the course of the next ten years, for the whole of Palestine, Syria, Egypt, for Asia Minor, too, in short, for all quarters where were parties of Jewish Christians who had not yet raised themselves to the Pauline stand-point. This epistle was, indeed, a document which contained a divine warrant for the complete severance of Christendom from the mother's lap of the bodily Israel ! For the Western Church, which from the first was entirely under Pauline influence, the epistle for the same reason did not possess this practical importance ; it had long before been rendered superfluous here by the Epistle to the Romans ; the state of things as a whole which occasioned the necessity for an Epistle to the Hebrews in the East, had been obviated long before in Italy by the Epistle to the Romans. What wonder, then, that the Epistle to the Hebrews should have spread there late and slowly; and if it did not spread there until after the Church of the West had closed its canon (in the beginning of the second century), if it did not spread until the period when every Church carefully adhered to ancient tradition, it is then easy to comprehend, how hesitation should have been shown in opening up again the closed door of the canon for the Epistle to the Hebrews, till then unknown; it is perfectly conceivable how this epistle, which had no inscription and was un-Pauline in its style, should not have been acknowledged as Pauline; and if, now, there had actually been preserved, say in Rome, from the time of Clement onwards, a notice of the existence of this epistle, but at the same time also a notice that Paul had not composed it *himself*—does not the opposition of the Western Church to the Pauline authorship become doubly intelligible?

In the third place, the conclusion to which we have come respecting the *circle of readers* for whom this epistle was intended, beautifully harmonises with our hypothesis, that Paul was, at least indirectly, the author of it. The question indeed has been asked, why precisely the apostle of the Gentiles should have come to write to Jewish Christians in Palestine. We know, however, that the epistle was not written to churches, not even to a church, not to the Church of Jerusalem, but to a *limited circle of individual Jewish Christians in Jerusalem, whose conversion had taken place not very long before*. May it not have been such Jewish Christians as had been converted just about the time when Paul was taken prisoner in Jerusalem (Acts xxi. ss.), who perhaps were first awakened by Paul himself, during those seven days when as yet he went out and in in freedom (Acts xxi. 27), and were brought to embrace Christianity by his powerful address (Acts xxii.)? What a great and profound crisis arose in those days among the Jews themselves, is evident from Acts xxiii. 9; even in the company of Paul's bitterest enemies there were those who sought to frustrate the plot which was formed to murder him, by betraying it to the nephew of Paul (Acts xxiii. 16). But, be this as it may, Paul was from that period so firmly rooted in his love for the Church in Jerusalem (Acts xxi. 17), and he so identifies his cause with that of this Church, that this of itself already suffices to explain, how he may have addressed a writing to *individuals* among the Jewish Christians of Jerusalem. For, let it be granted also, that these individuals were not gained over to Christianity precisely through Paul's personal influence, still *Luke* remained those two years in Jerusalem (Acts xxi. 15, ss.; xxvii. 1, ss.; comp. Luke i. 3, παρηκολουθηκότι πᾶσιν ἀκριβῶς), and thus the readers were certainly well enough acquainted at least with him, so that at his suggestion, and through him, Paul might address a writing to them. The notice, too, respecting the former zeal of these readers (Heb. vi. 10; x. 32, ss.) thus obtains a sufficient explanation.

Finally, this hypothesis throws light on the passages which refer to an impending persecution, as well as the reference to the martyrdom of the ἡγούμενοι (xiii. 7.) The Epistle to the Philippians had been written in the year 62, and the Epistle to the Hebrews sent soon afterwards to the East. Just at that time the apostle James, son of Alpheus, had been stoned; the news of his death would just have reached Italy when Luke was writing the epistle.—Shortly afterwards, Luke, as well as Timothy, set out on a journey eastward, first to Asia-Minor, but Luke (Heb. xiii. 23), certainly, also to Palestine. Luke returned back to Paul earlier than Timothy (2 Tim. iv. 11), standing faithfully by his spiritual father even to his death. Timothy also received a pressing charge to return (2 Tim. iv. 21), and would doubtless comply with it. Paul suffered martyrdom in the beginning of 64. Among the revelations of the Holy Spirit, whose instrument he was, and which he has left behind him as an everlasting legacy, the Epistle to the Hebrews occupies a very important place. It is the knife which completely severed and delivered the new-born church of the New Testament Israel from the maternal womb of the Old Testament theocracy. And therefore, it not merely *had* a significance for the Christian Church at the time when the Lord visited with judgment the unbelieving seed of Abraham, but it has a *permanent* significance, as a writing which will be lighted up anew in flaming characters every time the attempt is made again to drive back the Church, which has been perfected for ever by one sacrifice, within the limits of a Levitical sacrificial service and a slavish hierarchy, and again to hide behind a veil the access to the sacrifice of Christ, which stands freely and directly open to every individual.

LITERATURE.

In the *Patristic period* we find, in Origen, only fragmentary explanations. The commentary of Theodoret is well known, and in many respects justly celebrated; but Chrysostom, in his 34 homilies, penetrates still deeper into the spirit of the Epistle to the Hebrews.

In the *Reformation period* Erasmus has furnished, in his Annotations (1516) and his Paraphrasis (1522), an excellent preparatory work for the grammatical interpretation of the epistle; Zuingle, Calvin, Beza, Piscator, have, each in his own way, handled the Epistle to the Hebrews along with the rest of the New Testament writings; there are special commentaries by Oecolompadius (explan. ad Epist. ad Ebr. 1734) and Breuz (1751.) After that, it was especially *Reformed* theologians who applied their exegetical labours to the Epistle to the Hebrews. Chiefly to be named are Hyperius (Zurich 1587), Junius (1590), Drusius, Ludwig de Dieu, Jac. Capellus the elder, Ludwig Capellus, Cameron (Adnot. in Ep. ad Hebr. 1628, op. posth.), Heinsius, then Cocceius (Leyden 1659), together with a whole series of Federalists, in England Hammond and Whitby, the Armenians Limborch (Rotterd. 1711), Clericus, Wetstein, and Grotius. Of the *Lutheran* theologians only Hunnius (Frankf. 1589), Joh. Gerhard (Jena 1641), Seb. Schmidt (Strasb. 1680), Sigm. Jac. Baumgarten (Halle 1763), and Calov (in the Bibl. illustr.), are to be noticed in connection with the Epistle to the Hebrews.

In the *Rationalistic period*: Morus (Leipzig 1776), J. D. Michaelis (Frankf. and Leipz. 1780)), Zachariä (Gött. 1793), Heinrichs (Gött. 1792), Hezel (Leipz. 1795), Ernesti (Lect. Academ. ed. Dindorf, Leipz. 1795.)

Belonging to our own century, are Storr (1809), Böhme (Lepz. 1825), Kuinoel (Leipz. 1831), Klee (Mainz. 1833), Paulus (1833), Menken (special commentaries and homilies on Heb. ix.—x., and Heb. xi., 1821 and 1831), Tholuck (Hamb. 1836), especially, however, the profound and copious commentary by Bleek (Berlin 1828—1840).

www.ingramcontent.com/pod-product-compliance
Lightning Source LLC
Chambersburg PA
CBHW070057020526
44112CB00034B/1424